INDONESIA
TODAY

INDONESIA TODAY

CHALLENGES OF HISTORY

EDITED BY
GRAYSON LLOYD
SHANNON SMITH

ROWMAN & LITTLEFIELD PUBLISHERS, INC.
Lanham • Boulder • New York

First published in Singapore in 2001 by
Institute of Southeast Asian Studies
30 Heng Mui Keng Terrace
Pasir Panjang
Singapore 119614
http://www.iseas.edu.sg/pub.html
ISBN 981-230-138-0 (soft cover)
ISBN 981-230-139-9 (hard cover)

This book is part of the Indonesia Assessment Series, Research School of Pacific and Asian Studies, The Australian National University.

First published in the United States of America in 2001 by
Rowman & Littlefield Publishers, Inc.
4720 Boston Way
Lanham, Maryland 20706
http://www.rowmanlittlefield.com
for exclusive distribution in North America and Europe.
ISBN 0-7425-1762-4   (soft cover)
ISBN 0-7425-1761-6   (hard cover)

The responsibility for facts and opinions in this publication rests exclusively with the editors and contributors and their interpretations do not necessarily reflect the views or the policy of the publishers or their supporters.

ISEAS Library Cataloguing-in-Publication Data

Indonesia today: challenges of history / edited by Grayson J. Lloyd and Shannon L. Smith.
   1.   Indonesia—Politics and government—1998–
   2.   Indonesia—Economic conditions—1945–
   3.   Indonesia—Social conditions.
   I.   Lloyd, Grayson J.
   II.   Smith, Shannon L.
DS644.5 I412   2001   sls2001012803

Copy-edited and typeset by Japan Online, Pershore
Indexed by Jean Kennedy, Canberra

Printed in Singapore by Prime Packaging Industries Pte Ltd.

CONTENTS

TABLES

FIGURES

CONTRIBUTORS

Greg Barton
Senior Lecturer, School of Social Inquiry, Deakin University

Kelly Bird
Partnership for Economic Growth Adviser, Bappenas; Research Associate,
Indonesia Project, Australian National University

Susan Blackburn
Senior Lecturer, School of Political and Social Inquiry, Monash University

David Bourchier
Lecturer, Department of Asian Studies, University of Western Australia

Richard Chauvel
Head, Department of Asian and International Studies, Victoria University of
Technology

Robert Cribb
Reader, Department of History, University of Queensland

Howard Dick
Associate Professor, Australian Centre for International Business, University
of Melbourne

R.E. Elson
Professor, School of Asian and International Studies, Griffith University;
Director, Griffith Asia Pacific Council

Greg Fealy
Research Fellow, Research School of Pacific and Asian Studies, Australian
National University

Philip Kitley
Senior Lecturer, Department of Humanities and International Studies,
Faculty of Arts, University of Southern Queensland

John Legge
Emeritus Professor, History Department, Monash University

Timothy Lindsey
Associate Professor, Faculty of Law; Director, Asian Law Centre,
University of Melbourne

Grayson J. Lloyd
PhD Candidate, Research School of Pacific and Asian Studies, Australian
National University

Angus McIntyre
Senior Lecturer, Department of Politics, La Trobe University

Marcus Mietzner
PhD Candidate, Research School of Pacific and Asian Studies, Australian
National University

Goenawan Mohamad
Senior Editor, *Tempo*

M.C. Ricklefs
Professor of Asian Studies and Director, Melbourne Institute of Asian
Languages and Societies, University of Melbourne

Shannon L. Smith
Observer, Indonesian Political and Economic Affairs, Canberra

Atmadji Sumarkidjo
Editor, *Suara Pembaruan*

Adrian Vickers
Associate Professor, Centre for Asia Pacific Social Transformation Studies,
University of Wollongong

Thee Kian Wie
Economic Historian, Centre for Economic and Development Studies,
Indonesian Institute of Sciences (PEP-LIPI)

Pierre van der Eng
Senior Lecturer, School of Economics, Faculty of Economics and
Commerce, Australian National University

Wihana Kirana Jaya
Lecturer, Faculty of Economics, Gadjah Mada University

ACKNOWLEDGEMENTS

This book is based on the proceedings of the 2000 Indonesia Update Conference, held at the Australian National University (ANU), Canberra, on 6–7 October 2000. The conference, and this volume, received generous financial and logistical support from a wide range of organisations, including the Australian Agency for International Development (AusAID) and the Research School of Pacific and Asian Studies (RSPAS) at the ANU. The conference attracted speakers and representatives from numerous universities and research centres in Australia and overseas.

We would like to thank a number of people for their contributions. The conference was organised by Bob Lowry of the Australian Defence Force Academy, who brought together a diverse and eminent group of scholars. Valuable support was provided by Karen Nulty, Liz Drysdale, Trish van der Hoek and Lynn Moir of the Indonesia Project in the Division of Economics, RSPAS, as well as by a small group of Indonesian and Australian students. Particular thanks are due to Dr Chris Manning, Head of the Indonesian Project, and the session coordinators, Bob Elson, Robert Cribb and Howard Dick.

This volume is published by the Institute of Southeast Asian Studies (ISEAS), Singapore, in what is now a traditional arrangement. We greatly appreciate the involvement of ISEAS, especially its Managing Editor, Triena Ong, in the publication of the book. The manuscript was deftly and expertly prepared by Beth Thomson, and the index was compiled by Jean Kennedy.

Finally, we appreciate the efforts of all contributors who drafted and revised their papers in order to meet a very demanding publishing deadline. In particular, we are grateful for the contribution of Emeritus Professor John Legge. He has written widely on Indonesian history and his thoughts presented here in this volume set the scene for the thoughtful perspectives on Indonesian political, economic and social history that follow.

Grayson J. Lloyd and Shannon L. Smith
Canberra, February 2001

GLOSSARY

abangan	a 'nominal' Muslim
ABRI	Angkatan Bersenjata Republik Indonesia (Armed Forces of the Rebublic of Indonesia), now the TNI
adat	tradition, custom
adat istiadat	customary law
aliran	ideological streams, an anthropological term used to differentiate major ideological and cultural groupings in Indonesian society
angket	investigation
APRA	Angkatan Perang Ratu Adil (Army of the Just Prince)
azas tunggal	sole philosophical principle
BAIS	Badan Intelijen Strategis (Strategic Intelligence Body)
Bakin	Badan Koordinasi Intelijens Negara (State Intelligence Coordinating Agency)
Bakorstanas	Badan Koordinasi Bantuan Pemantapan Stabilitas Nasional, (Coordinating Agency for the Maintenance of National Stability)
Bapedal	Badan Pengendalian Dampak Lingkungan (Environmental Impact Management Agency)
Bappeda	Badan Perencanaan Pembangunan Daerah (Regional Development Planning Board)
Bappenas	Badan Perencanaan Pembangunan Nasional (National Development Planning Board)
bekking/dekking	literally 'backing', the mechanism by which state officials protected street-level *preman*
Bhinneka Tunggal Ika	Unity in Diversity (or, We Are Many but We Are One), the national motto
Binnenlands Bestuur	Department of the Interior, now Departemen Dalam Negeri
BPK	Badan Pemeriksaan Keuangan (National Auditing Board)

BPS	Badan Pusat Statistik (Central Statistics Agency)
Bulog	Badan Urusan Logistik (national food logistics agency)
bupati	regent, head of a *kabupaten* (regency or district)
CEDAW	Convention for the Elimination of All Forms of Discrimination against Women
CSIS	Centre for Strategic and International Studies
daerah	region, territory
Daerah Istimewa	Special Region
Daerah Tingkat I	highest level of local government, comprising the provinces
Daerah Tingkat II	level of local government comprising the *kabupaten* and *kotamadya*
dalang	shadow puppeteer
Darul Islam	House of Islam (rebellious Islamic movement in Indonesia, 1948–62)
desa	village
Dewan Dakwah Islamiyah Indonesia	Indonesian Islamic Preaching Council
Dewan Nasional	National Council
DOM	Daerah Operasi Militer (Military Operations Area)
DPR	Dewan Perwakilan Rakyat (People's Representative Council), Indonesia's Parliament
DPRD	Dewan Perwakilan Rakyat Daerah (Regional People's Representative Council), a sub-provincial parliament
dwifungsi	literally, 'dual function'; the military's doctrine stipulating a dual socio-political and security function
EPZ	export-processing zone
fatwa	ruling
FDI	foreign direct investment
Fraksi Reformasi	Reform Faction
Front Hizbullah	Army of God Front
Front Pembela Islam	Defenders of Islam Front
FSPC	Financial Sector Policy Committee
FUII	Front Umat Islam Indonesia (Indonesian Muslim Community Front)
G30S	30th of September Movement
gali	*gabungan anak liar* (wild gang)

GAM	Gerakan Aceh Merdeka (Independent Aceh Movement)
GBHN	Garis-garis Besar Haluan Negara (Broad Guidelines of State Policy
GDI	gross domestic investment
GDP	gross domestic product
GEM	gender empowerment measure
Gerwani	Gerakan Wanita Indonesia (Indonesian Women's Movement), a women's organisation affiliated in its later years with the PKI
GKI	Gereja Kristen Injil di Tanah Papua (the principal Protestant church in Papua)
GNP	gross national product
Golkar	Golongan Karya (Functional Groups), state political party under the New Order
GPP	gross provincial product
Guided Democracy	regime of President Sukarno, 1957–65
haj	pilgrimage to Mecca
Haji	someone who has made the pilgrimage to Mecca
halal	things that are unreservedly deemed permissible for a Muslim to consume, use or do (usually used of food)
Hankam	Departemen Pertahanan dan Keamanan (Department of Defence and Security)
HDI	human development index
HMI	Himpunan Mahasiswa Indonesia, a modernist Islamic student organisation
HPAE	high-performing Asian economy
IAIN	Institut Agama Islam Negeri (State Institute for Islamic Studies)
IBRA	Indonesian Banking Restructuring Agency
ICMI	Ikatan Cendekiawan Muslim Indonesia (Indonesian Muslim Intellectuals' Association).
ILO	International Labour Organisation
IMF	International Monetary Fund
IMR	infant mortality rate
Inpres	Instruksi Presiden (Presidential Instruction), a program of special grants from the central government
Intel	intelligence agent/service
IPKI	Ikatan Pendukung Kemerdekaan Indonesia (League of Supporters of Indonesian Independence)

japrem	*jatah preman* (illegal rents)
jawara	(see *preman*)
kabupaten	regency or district
Kasad	Kepala Staf Angkatan Darat (Army Chief-of-Staff)
kecamatan	subdistrict
kekeluargaan	family principles
kelompencapir	discussion groups
kiai	an Islamic scholar, teacher and leader
KISDI	Komite Indonesia untuk Solidaritas Dunia Islam (Indonesian Committee for World Islamic Solidarity)
KKN	*korupsi, kolusi, nepotisme* (corruption, collusion, nepotism)
KNIL	Koninklijke Nederlandsche Indische Leger (Royal Netherlands Indies Army)
Kodam	Komando Daerah Militer (Regional Military Command)
Komnas HAM	Komisi Nasional Hak Asasi Manusia (National Commission on Human Rights)
komunistofobia	fear of communism; term established by President Sukarno
Kongres Alim Ulama	Congress of Islamic Scholars
Kopassus	Komando Pasukan Khusus (Special Forces Command), Red Berets
Kopkamtib	Komando Operasi Pemulihan Keamanan dan Keterbitan (Operations Command to Restore Order and Security)
Kostrad	Komando Cadangan Strategis Angkatan Darat (Army Strategic Reserve Command), Green Berets
kota/kotamadya	municipality
krismon	monetary crisis
laskar/laskyar	militia or irregular forces
Mahdi	messiah in Islam
Masyumi	Majelis Syuro Muslimin Indonesia (Consultative Council of Indonesia Muslims), major modernist Islamic political party in the 1950s
Men/Pangad	Menteri/Panglima Angkatan Darat (Minister/Commander-in-Chief of the Army)
Menhankam/Pangab	Menteri Pertahanan dan Keamanan/Panglima Angkatan Bersenjata (Minister of Defence and

	Security/Commander-in-Chief of the Armed Forces)
MOU	memorandum of understanding
MPR	Majelis Permusyawaratan Rakyat (People's Consultative Assembly), Indonesia's supreme sovereign body
Muhammadiyah	Indonesia's largest modernist Islamic organisation
MUI	Majelis Ulama Indonesia (Indonesian Council of Islamic Scholars)
Muslimat NU	the women's wing of NU
NASAKOM	an acronym coined by Sukarno to promote cooperation between Nationalist (*Nasionalis*), Religious (*Agama*) and Communist (*Komunis*) groupings in Indonesia
negara	state
New Order	regime of President Soeharto, 1966–98
NGO	non-government organisation
NIE	newly industrialising economy
NPL	non-performing loan
NU	Nahdlatul Ulama (Revival of the Religious Scholars), Indonesia's largest traditionalist Islamic organisation
OECD	Organisation for Economic Cooperation and Development
OPM	Organisasi Papua Merdeka (Organisation for a Free Papua)
P3M	Pusat Pengembangan Pesantren dan Masyarakat (Centre for the Development of Islamic Boarding Schools and Society)
P4	program of Pancasila indoctrination
pamong praja	the postwar term for the territorial civil service
PAN	Partai Amanat Nasional (National Mandate Party)
Pancasila	the five guiding principles of the Indonesian state
Pangab	Panglima Angkatan Bersenjata (Commander-in-Chief of the Armed Forces)
pangreh praja	the indigenous colonial administrative corps
Parindra	Partai Indonesia Raja (Greater Indonesia Party)
PBB	Partai Bulan Bintang (Crescent Moon and Star Party)
PDI	Partai Demokrasi Indonesia (Indonesian Democratic Party)

PDI-P	Partai Demokrasi Indonesia-Perjuangan (Indonesian Democratic Party of Struggle), party led by Megawati Sukarnoputri that effectively replaced PDI in the post-Soeharto era
pembangunan	development, building
Permesta	Piagam Perjuangan Semesta Alam (Universal Struggle Charter)
persatuan dan kesatuan	union and unity
pesantren	traditional Islamic boarding school
PIR	Partai Persatuan Indonesia Raja (Greater Indonesia Unity Party)
PK	Partai Keadilan (Justice Party)
PKB	Partai Kebangkitan Bangsa (National Awakening Party)
PKI	Partai Komunis Indonesia (Indonesian Communist Party)
PKK	Pembinaan Kesejahteraan Keluarga (Family Welfare Program)
PKP	Partai Keadilan dan Persatuan (Justice and Unity Party)
PNI	Partai Nasional Indonesia (Indonesian National Party)
PNU	Partai Nahdlatul Ummah (Muslim Community Awakening Party)
Poros Tengah	Central Axis (loose coalition of Islamic parties)
PP	Peraturan Pemerintah (Government Decree or Regulation)
PPP	Partai Persatuan Pembangunan (United Development Party)
PRD	Partai Rakyat Demokratik (Democratic People's Party)
preman	bandit, gangster/gangs, standover man, thug, criminal
premanisme	criminal state/criminal politics
priyayi	aristocratic or official member of the governing elite of Java
Prokasih	Clean Rivers (project)
proyek	project
PRRI	Pemerintah Revolusioner Republik Indonesia (Revolutionary Government of the Republic of Indonesia)

PSI	Partai Sosialis Indonesia (Indonesian Socialist Party)
PWI	Persatuan Wartawan Indonesia (Indonesian Journalists' Association)
rakyat	people
Ratu Adil	the 'Just King' of Javanese messianic tradition
RCTI	Rajawali Citra Televisi Indonesia (free-to-air commercial television station)
reformasi	reformation – with particular reference to political and social reform
RMS	Republik Maluku Selatan (Republic of the South Moluccas)
RPKAD	Resimen Para Komando Angkatan Darat (Army Paracommando Regiment)
RRI	Radio Republik Indonesia (state radio broadcaster)
Sakernas	Survei Angkatan Kerja Nasional (National Labour Force Survey)
santri	a devout or conscientious Muslim
Sarekat Islam	Islamic Association (anti-colonial political movement, established in 1912)
Satgas Papua	pro-independence militia in Papua
satgas	*satuan tugas* (security forces)
SBI	Sertifikat Bank Indonesia (Bank Indonesia Certificates), bonds issued by Bank Indonesia
SCTV	Surya Citra Televisi (free-to-air commercial television station)
Sekretariat Negara	State Secretariat
Seskoad	Sekolah Staf Komando Angkatan (Army Staff Command College)
Shafi'i	one of the four Orthodox Schools of Law in Islam
shari'ah	Islamic law
Shi'ite	an adherent of Shi'ism, a minority school of Islam sometimes regarded with suspicion by Indonesia's Sunni or Orthodox Moslems
Siskamling	Sistem Keamanan Lingkungan (Local Security System), also known as *sistem swakarsa*
SME	small to medium-scale enterprise
SOE	state-owned enterprise
Staatside	supreme constitutional principle
Sufi	Islamic mystic

Supersemar	Surat Perintah Sebelas Maret (Letter of Instruction of the Eleventh of March), the document Sukarno signed giving power to Soeharto
Susenas	Survei Sosio-Ekonomi Nasional (National Socioeconomic Survey)
Taman Siswa	Garden of Students (educational movement founded by Ki Hadjar Dewantara)
TNI	Tentara Nasional Indonesia (Indonesian National Army), the collective term for the infantry, navy and airforce
tuanku	Minangkabau title of respect for a religious leader
tunggal	unity
TVRI	Televisi Republik Indonesia (state television broadcaster)
ulama	Islamic religious scholar
uleëbalang	Acehenese aristocrat
umat	the Muslim community
UN	United Nations
UNDP	United Nations Development Program
VOC	Vereenigde Oost-Indische Compagnie (Dutch United East India Company)
Volksraad	People's Council – colonial era parliament
wali	apostle of Islam; high civil servant
walikota	mayor

1

THOUGHTS ON INDONESIAN HISTORY

Grayson J. Lloyd and Shannon L. Smith

It is indeed timely, given the wide-ranging changes and pressures in Indonesia in the last few years and the transition to a new century, that illumination is cast not merely on recent events but on seminal issues and episodes in Indonesia's social, political and economic history. The task of this volume is therefore doubly difficult: charged with surveying the past, it must also provide an 'update' of recent events in the conventional sense. What it offers, then, is a study of selected aspects of the past. This incorporates analysis of political parties and parliament, the role of ideology, the Leftist movement, political leadership and women's status in Indonesian society, as well as trends in poverty, economic directions, visions of the future, survival of the empire, rebellions against and aspects of central control and definitions of the state and influences on its development. It is not a history of Indonesia, because such a task would require more scholars and more space than the confines of this volume permit, and because Indonesia is replete with much history awaiting 'discovery' and recording in areas that have so far eluded the gaze of scholars.

The events of the last three or four years in Indonesia have sparked critical assessment and rethinking in all sectors by foreign and indigenous observers alike. The Philippines-style people's power movement that helped throw Soeharto from office in May 1998 has since broken up into disparate and often disorganised social and political movements and factions. The widespread expectation of the emergence of a new system of political stability accompanied by a vibrant civil society has been hamstrung by a plethora of factors. The June 1999 general election was Indonesia's first democratic parliamentary election since 1955 and provided a tremendous fillip to the aspirations of millions of disenfranchised citizens who wished to play a part in their nation's destiny. However, the difficulties of implementing a democratic structure and adhering to a democratic ethos after a sustained and pervasive period of authoritarianism have been reinforced overwhelmingly under the faltering administration of Abdurrahman Wahid (known affectionately as Gus Dur). Allegations of corruption and financial and legal impropriety have been levelled at this administration as the once ubiquitous 'collusion, corruption and nepotism' (KKN) chant has again infiltrated the political scene and exacerbated the machinations and personality politics of Indonesia's divided political elite.

More fundamentally, there remain the problems of reforming the banking and legal systems, refining the operation of political parties, attracting foreign investment and maintaining national unity. The implementation of the decentralisation laws 22 and 25 promulgated in 1999 is a huge administrative and political responsibility. But problems persist on a number of fronts, including the task of dealing with the communal unrest in Maluku province, the escalating presence of radical Islam, the need to formulate effective human rights legislation and deal with abuses of the past, and the manner of handling the increasingly vociferous calls for independence in Papua and Aceh. While Aceh and Papua are distinct case studies, they are to some extent united in spirit by East Timor's independence and by a history of brutal repression and exclusion, particularly under the New Order. The increased, indeed proactive, role of the People's Representative Council (DPR) in the era after Soeharto has also contributed to the sustained scrutiny of the government and the executive. This is a positive move, because too often in the past the converse applied and the result was a 'floating mass' form of political participation where people only participated when they were told to do so. But it should not be forgotten that in this transitional phase, one of Indonesia's greatest challenges is to attain effective leadership however unrealistic (or deterministic) this may be. This leadership must be capable of engendering the confidence and the patience of a real constituency demanding overnight *reformasi*; and capable, too, of maintaining national unity for the term of its natural life against xenophobic nationalism and exponents of destabilisation.

In its tumultuous journey in the post-Soeharto era, Indonesia has therefore been confronted with a pot-holed road of problems and issues often requiring immediate or, more challengingly, definitive resolution. However, to surmise that the vast array of problems placed before the Habibie reform cabinet and its successor, the cabinet of national unity of Abdurrahman Wahid, are amenable to easy resolution is grossly to misunderstand the nature of Indonesia and the complexity, paradox, infinite variety and capacity for ideological and intellectual contortion of its history. As the chapters in this volume indicate, there is little that Indonesia and the Indonesian people have not experienced in the past and, at the same time, there is much to confront that is new (in whatever context), or different, or simply a solution to problems and issues borne of the past.

The purpose of each of the chapters in this volume, although distinct in style and methodology, is manifest. Each has attempted to resurrect particular aspects of the past – certain events, images, protests, beliefs, correlations and practices all of which impact on perceptions of the present and expectations for the future. This volume therefore houses a myriad of themes. If there is a *benang merah,* one underlying current, then it is Indonesia's struggle with the concept of being a truly inclusive nation, and its inability to invest real meaning in the slogan 'Unity in Diversity' (*Bhinneka Tunggal Ika*). But this underlying current has a number of corollaries. The closest is Indonesia's inability to fashion an acceptable sense of national identity that is consistent with principles which have emerged from its history of struggle. But other corollaries are easily distinguishable. These relate to the struggle for equality faced by women, minority ethnic groups and the economically disadvantaged, the distrust of plurality, the wholesomeness of community, the apparently paradoxical acceptance and rejection of change, and the propensity for political conservatism to emerge after periods of great social or political change and violence. Coterminous with these is the subjugation of class (the money and power accumulation of the ruling class excepted), the condemnation and adoration of ideological and cultural deviation, and a seemingly boundless capacity for renewal and revival. The Indonesian nation and people constitute such a large and inaccessible canvas that 'Western'-imposed constructs such as *santri, priyayi, abangan* or *aliran*, and others such as Feith's 'administrators' and 'solidarity-makers', while useful tools, are rarely capable of revealing the whole story.

This book is unique in the Indonesia Assessment series in that it is dedicated to studies of Indonesian history and thus presents a distinct blend of writing on contemporary events and historical issues. It also sets a precedent with the inclusion of a short concluding chapter. The chapters contained in this volume, apart from the economic and political updates of recent events in Part I, address various periods in Indonesia's history, many offering a comparison between different eras and current events. The seven chapters in Part II address a compelling range of issues seminal to political history. The contributions in Part III provide a survey of key issues in Indonesia's economic history. Those in Part IV address a diverse range of issues germane to social history. The political, economic and social history sections are each introduced by 'Brief Reflections' – written by Bob Elson, Howard Dick and Robert Cribb respectively – which have been included in the numbering of the chapters and highlight significant events, challenges, and key periods and issues in the respective fields. Part V, 'Indonesia's History Unfolding', offers a brief reflection on the status and nature of Indonesian history and the historical process.

After delivering the historian's caveat that 'history will tell us that the future is likely to be unexpected', John Legge proffers in Chapter 2 a nuanced study of key themes, periods and scholars in Indonesian history. He highlights the speed of change in events in Indonesia during the revolutionary period and the several decades that followed, the emergence of the landmark scholarship published by Kahin, Feith and others, and the mood shift from optimism to pessimism after the turbulence of the 1950s. He notes the sometimes ambiguous influence of Western terminology on the Indonesian political and cultural landscape and the obfuscation resulting from the meshing of indigenous and externally imposed constructs. He closes with a reflection on the ongoing tensions of the motto 'Unity in Diversity' emerging from Indonesia's awkward transition to an artificial nationhood. Drawing attention to the continuation of patrimonial forms in the 'modern' Soeharto state, he also questions the subdued focus on violence in writing on Indonesian history against a more pervasive focus on (internationally acceptable) ideals of harmony and syncretism.

RECENT DEVELOPMENTS

In Chapter 3 Marcus Mietzner analyses a series of key issues troubling Indonesia under the administration of President Abdurrahman Wahid. His chapter focuses on institutional reform, separatism and local autonomy, the position of the military, legal reform, political parties and the political economy. He argues that the ability to deal with the complexity of these issues is contingent upon the strengthening of the country's political framework. One of the problems is what he terms the 'collectively cultivated constituency cronyism' manifested in the fight for control over economic assets between the Nahdlatul Ulama (NU), the Indonesian Democratic Party of Struggle (PDI-P) and the National Mandate Party (PAN). The rampant political conflict among the elite has resulted in the neglect of crucial institutional, legal and military reform and the subordination of fundamental issues of constitutional reform, thus exacerbating institutionalised political instability. It is precisely this problem of institutionalised political disorder, he argues, which obstructs the process of economic recovery and threatens the possibilities of continued democratisation.

Kelly Bird presents an economic overview of Indonesia's prospects in Chapter 4. His title notwithstanding, his prognosis on the whole appears rather optimistic. He points to the buoyancy given to the economic recovery of the last 12 months or so by the recovery in consumer spending and export growth, particularly the rise in non-oil manufacturing exports. But Bird also points to one problem Indonesia has experienced, at least since the events of May 1998: the need to restart investment to sustain medium-term economic recovery. The nexus between political and economic problems is clear when one views not only the incomplete corporate debt restructuring process and the fragility of the banking sector, but also the uncertainty of the application of the rule of law and the tenuous political environment.

POLITICAL HISTORY

Bob Elson's introduction to the political history section encapsulates some of the challenges for historians writing on Indonesia's political history. There is a significant need, he says, for historians to research Indonesian politics in all of its depth and infinite variety and with a seriousness of purpose so far lacking in the discipline. This disinterested application to the task of serious historians can produce fertile results and assist greatly in providing answers to a myriad of unanswered yet seminal questions in Indonesian history.

Adrian Vickers argues in Chapter 6 that those who write about Indonesia's history need to come to terms with the realities of Indonesia's past in their representations of the present. He is interested in the varying and often contradictory ways in which the New Order has been portrayed. The New Order was a government of appearances, but was it 'the state' dominating over society or was it Soeharto? The New Order state, he posits, was many things at the same time – it was a rentier or plunderer state; an *asal bapak senang* (ABS) state; a criminal state; a capitalist state; a military–bureaucratic state; and it was, in a sense, a reincarnation of the Dutch colonial state. In short, it was an aberration perpetuated by the Cold War, and it was surprising that it lasted as long as it did. Furthermore, 'due to the longevity of its appearance of order and control under one man', it stood out in the region against all comparisons, Myanmar excepted. And finally, he argues, it attempted to uniformalise Indonesia's historical diversity, deny its heterogeneity and internal contradictions or unsavoury aspects, and present a sanitised version for international (and domestic) consumption.

Angus McIntyre follows in Chapter 7 with an analysis of the middle way leadership concept. Indonesia's survival as a 'voluntary association', he posits, is contingent upon the type of leadership it receives. Strong leadership, characterised by moralism, divisiveness and political division, thrives in an authoritarian system. But in the post-Soeharto era the Indonesian people have endorsed a nascent democratic system for which adherence to middle way leadership, and its affinity with civic nationalism and inclusive politics, is required. The dangers for Indonesia's future are evident in the events of the past. As McIntyre asserts, when the middle way partnership of Sukarno and Mohammad Hatta collapsed in 1956, Sukarno became more associated with certain ethnic and political groups within the nation rather than identifying with the nation itself. In terms of learning from the middle way precedent, Abdurrahman Wahid's beginning was not auspicious. One can simply hope that the lessons of Abdurrahman's grab for political power can be absorbed and that his reputation for tolerance is rekindled in a structure of middle way leadership needed at this time of great national fragility.

In his chapter surveying the function of parties and parliament in historical perspective, Greg Fealy draws several interesting conclusions. He argues that individual leaders, because of their almost cult status, dominate modern parties to a much greater extent today than was the case four decades ago. Ideological and policy disputes are less a part of party activities in the post-Soeharto era, whereas money in party politics and physical intimidation are much more a part. Moreover, the linkage between parties and a nation's intellectual life was much stronger in the 1950s than today. The changes with respect to parliament are no less considerable, he asserts. This is because of at least three factors: the increased role of the DPR in relation to the executive in the post-Soeharto era; the greater involvement of the DPR in presidential appointments; and the parliament's reassertion of its rights of interpellation of the executive. But, he suggests, some key questions remain, notably pertaining to legislative initiative and the representational capacity of MPs. Together with other factors, these are of prime concern to an electorate vastly more interested and involved in the political process since the downfall of Soeharto.

In Chapter 9, the first of two papers in the volume dealing with aspects of political ideology, David Bourchier traces the evolution of political conservatism through phases of romantic traditionalism, corporatist anti-partyism and the New Order's 'integralist developmentalism'. He addresses the issue of whether political conservatism may be about to enter a fourth phase, because so many figures who were products of the New Order political environment remain in place and are obstructing the process of reform. Such a phase would be likely to have much in common with those that have gone before it, with an emphasis on elite dominance militating against mass participation in politics, and an appeal to unity based on an idealisation of the communalistic and harmonistic elements of traditional Indonesian culture. Whether, or to what extent, this so-termed fourth phase is manifested will depend greatly on the ability of the Abdurrahman administration to free itself of New Order ideology and construct a more inclusive and heterogeneous concept of nationhood.

The ethos of Goenawan Mohamad's chapter, 'Remembering the Left', is encapsulated in his opening vignette focusing on a courageous meeting in June 1996 of the Democratic People's Party (PRD) where, under the threat of arrest, young PRD activists upheld their right to oppose the injustices of the Soeharto regime. In this chapter Goenawan explores the meaning and role of the Left in Indonesian political culture and society, particularly in the relative freedom afforded in the post-Soeharto era. He notes how the Left became a statement of opposition for many who grew up during the New Order, often expressed in art and culture. He also indicates that the new Left, in many respects detached from the Left of the past, is a disillusioned ideological force and politically impotent. But the legacy of the massacres of communist supporters in 1965–66 still haunts Indonesian society, to such a degree that Abdurrahman Wahid's suggestion to revoke the 1966 decision by the People's Consultative Assembly (MPR) outlawing the Indonesian Communist Party (PKI) and the dissemination of Marxist–Leninist ideology was met with much rancorous opposition. However, the president's efforts at political reconciliation reverberate with meaning beyond politics – they are representative of efforts to come to terms with Indonesia's sometimes bloody and unjust past. As Goenawan asserts, part of the problem with such a task is to develop a way of achieving reconciliation that is as inclusive of as many elements of society as possible. This will require moral leadership within the elite together with a willingness to distribute justice free from the exigencies of the present and the prejudices of the past.

In Chapter 11, Atmadji Sumarkidjo addresses the relevance of the Indonesian military (TNI) at this important crossroads of *reformasi* and change. His study examines the machinations within the military leadership (*pimpinan TNI*) during the New Order period, and President Soeharto's checkerboard-like manipulation of one individual and organisation against another in order to preserve his power. He argues that Soeharto became increasingly authoritarian during his time in power, ultimately interfering in TNI personnel issues and appointments to such an extent that the TNI was completely subordinated to his wishes and excluded from the reins of political power by the time he fell from office. In the post-Soeharto era, Atmadji argues, the TNI has struggled to play an effective role in Indonesian society and politics amidst increasing and widespread calls for reform and change, notably from within its own ranks. He concludes by touching on the need for the provision of an adequate budget for the TNI to help cut back on the historical military/business linkage, the importance of thorough-going doctrinal revision within the TNI, and the necessity for greater investment in high-calibre training for the new generation of officers.

Richard Chauvel's chapter on the changing dynamics of regional resistance argues, in part, that the Indonesian nation has struggled to retain its diversity and as a consequence its unity has suffered. He highlights General Nasution's efforts in the 1950s and early 1960s to establish unity and security throughout Indonesia against the background of widespread regionalist and secessionist campaigns, and focuses on the dynamics of the rebellions in Aceh and Ambon in the 1950s. During the New Order the struggle for unity and security took on a more brutal aspect as the people of Aceh and Papua in particular became estranged from the Indonesian 'family'. Underlying his argument is the assertion that while history, religion and ethnicity have been used by regional protagonists to enunciate their causes, changing cultural, economic and political norms also mould the form of resistance to the authority of Jakarta. The loss of East Timor has, he says, underlined the challenge for the administration of Abdurrahman Wahid: to fuse the democratic and nationalistic imperatives in order to maintain the integrity of Indonesia.

ECONOMIC HISTORY

In introducing the section, Howard Dick reflects on how the study of Indonesian economic history is finally coming of age. He argues that the New Order focused its attention on economic development for the future, to the detriment of learning from the economic failures of the Sukarno and Dutch colonial eras. As one of the keys to understanding the Indonesia of today is to consider history, Dick suggests that the economic policy-makers of today pay heed to the past.

Thee Kian Wie in Chapter 14 examines the political economy cycle of the New Order, from the economic crisis of the mid-1960s through to the 'miracle economy' characterised by high economic growth and targeted restructuring of the mid-1980s and 1990s – an episode much lauded by the international community – and the eventual slide into a 'melt-down economy', leading to the political and social unrest that caused the downfall of President Soeharto. Thee highlights the New Order's positive economic achievements – rapid economic growth led to structural changes in terms of a shift of production from agriculture to manufacturing and services, and greater importance was placed on foreign trade – as well as the corresponding social benefits arising from higher standards of living. He also dwells on the negative aspects of economic development – including unequal income distribution, urban–rural and regional disparities, and the degradation and depletion of environmental resources. Thee argues that the New Order's political legitimacy was based on its economic performance and ability to deliver rising standards of living for the people. But at the same time, the New Order was marked by restricted competition, monopolies, favoured treatment and KKN practices. It was these abuses, then, that undermined the New Order's political legitimacy, leading to economic downturn and Soeharto's eventual fall from power.

Pierre van der Eng looks at the Indonesian economy from a long-term perspective in Chapter 15. He challenges the usual assumption that Indonesia was until recently a development failure by showing that its long-term growth performance has in fact been impressive, if uneven. By Western standards, and in the context of 20th century Asia, Indonesian economic growth has been high. Van der Eng demonstrates that this economic growth was accompanied by significant improvements in standards of living, through all strata of Indonesian society.

Howard Dick takes as his starting point the current interest in institutional development and the suggestion that economic development cannot be sustained by fragile political, economic and social institutions and systems. Dick outlines Indonesian economic and political development during the 20th century and attempts to provide an understanding of their patterns of interaction. He argues that one of the lessons of the Asian crisis is that economic development needs to be supported by institutional development; the question for Indonesia is whether its politicians have the political will and skill to foster that development.

In Chapter 17, Wihana Kirana Jaya and Howard Dick offer a study of institutional reform in centre–region relations, of particular relevance given the moves towards decentralisation of central government functions since 1999. They assert that Indonesia has followed a zigzag pattern between decentralisation and centralisation since the colonial government's Decentralisation Law in 1903. The sudden reversal of half a century of centralisation has witnessed a diminution in powers for the provinces and a restoration of certain powers and revenues to the local government level. Theoretically, the proposed political, administrative and fiscal decentralisation will bring government closer to the people. In practice, however, the new arrangements are likely to emphasise administrative rather than political reform, with the central government retaining ultimate decision-making power in national budget policy. Moreover, implementation of the process will be complicated by money politics, absence of the rule of law, the need for effective guidance by civil society and the other wide-ranging problems currently faced by Indonesia.

SOCIAL HISTORY

Robert Cribb's 'Brief Reflections on Indonesian Social History' identifies three key axes germane to tracking the evolution of social history and changes in Indonesia. These are the axes of mobility and immobility, social rigidity and social flux, and isolation and cosmopolitanism. In the post-Soeharto era, he argues, the challenge for social historians is to understand how change is occurring and where it is leading Indonesia, and to deal with this change and associated factors within a more intellectually rigorous framework.

Underlying M.C. Ricklefs' novel topic, 'Indonesian Visions of the Future', is a complex historical survey. In brief, Ricklefs posits in Chapter 19 that 'volatility is a legacy of Indonesian searches for a better future'. Such searches have been underpinned by a series of recurrent themes. These are, notably, the beliefs that the past was better than the present and that a better future will revive the benefits of an idealised past; that ways of realising a better future have provoked dispute, sometimes violent in nature; and that various leadership groups and individuals have consistently failed to deliver the promised better future. From such a legacy Indonesians have been imbued with a distrust of institutions and political leadership, and a willingness to experiment with vastly different forms of ideology and leadership. Furthermore, Indonesia's history has been one of constant flux, with certain ideas and concepts – such as federalism, party politics, the Islamic state, the Leftist movement or the ideology of Pancasila – rising and falling and perhaps in some cases rising again according to their currency in the political and social milieu. Ricklefs concludes with the hope that the failures of Indonesia's past do not discredit the notion of Indonesia.

In Chapter 20, Greg Barton presents a timely analysis of the role of Islam, both politically and socially, in Abdurrahman Wahid's Indonesia. He argues that three things suggest at face value that Islam is operating as an anti-modern force stymieing the move to liberal democracy. The first is the 'santrification' of Indonesian society, evident for some years. The second is the relevance of Islam in Indonesia's political life as a force, or phalanx of forces, criticising the Gus Dur administration. The third is the extent of communal unrest and violence, which is a reminder of the significance of Islam. Barton points to the involvement of extremist 'religious' groups in what are as much political as religious or communal events in Maluku as indications of a worrying trend. He argues, however, that the Islamisation process need not challenge Indonesia's moderatism and pluralism, and that *santri*fication, for instance, has contributed not only to greater piety but also to greater tolerance. The progressive liberal ideas and emphasis on education of massive Islamic organisations such as the NU, previously headed by Abdurrahman Wahid, have reinforced this process. Radical Islamists, or those who would vote in a general election for an exclusively Islamic agenda, are overwhelmingly in the minority. Their threat is nonetheless real because, as Barton argues, their policies and the publicity they receive can be manipulated by competing factions within the Indonesian elite. The future is bright given the standing of National Awakening Party (PKB) traditionalists and liberal modernist *santri*, but violence can always emerge from narrow sectarianism.

Philip Kitley argues in Chapter 21 that the development of the media in Indonesia has been marred by bans and repression. The New Order government tried to enforce control over the media through restrictive legislation and the corporatisation of professional journalists, as well as threats and acts of retribution against certain individuals or organisations who challenged the maintenance of national law and order, cultural values and (the New Order-created) identity. In the mid-1980s, he says, the focus of the government's use of the media switched from motivating the people for development to an emphasis on the Pancasila media project with its focus on indigenous values. The government sought to erase the boundaries between itself and the people by speaking of the nation as a family and portraying those who espoused alternative discourses as challenging the idea of an inclusive Indonesian family to which all speakers belonged. Predictably, the ideological gap between media producers and the idealised role constructed for them by the state resulted in the failure of the government's program. Professional media exponents reserved the right to write against the dominant paradigm and were exposed through their work to alternative views and concepts. This exposure, and these ideas, gradually filtered through to the population at large. In conclusion, Kitley argues that freedom of the press needs to be understood as a right to be informed, to ask questions and to deal with difficult issues. Those in the media, and the public they serve, have the right to make their own choices and form their own opinions free from government manipulation.

In Chapter 22 Susan Blackburn notes that aspects of gender inequality in Indonesia have most often been identified by organised, mostly urban-based, women whose actions have been determined by their degree of support and the tolerance of the state. Notably, however, women lacked meaningful parliamentary representation, and were not given leading positions in business and the bureaucracy. Traditionally women pointed to unequal status in education and marriage, and sometimes redress (or partial redress) was forthcoming. But as the 20th century progressed, new organisations led by younger women urged the redress of issues such as violence against women – in the home and elsewhere – as well as discrimination and inequality at work and in political representation. Blackburn also highlights the diversity of views among Indonesian women, particularly apparent in the growing reluctance of women outside Jakarta to allow those in Jakarta to represent their needs. She argues, in part, that the emphasis in Indonesia on unity and social harmony, particularly but not exclusively in the New Order period, has conditioned the way in which women express their needs. Because women have been socialised to care for others, she suggests, they have not readily identified their own rights. But the gaps in gender equality are manifest, and the hope in the era of *reformasi*, to the extent that it permeates socially and culturally and into relations between men and women, is that the needs of all women will be clearly recognised.

In his chapter on the Indonesian 'criminal' state, Tim Lindsey argues that the origins of *premanisme* reside in the 1945 Constitution and the integralist state envisioned by its authors. He highlights the state-sponsored nature of the criminal elements operating under the authoritarian New Order and surveys the transition of these elements upon the collapse of the New Order structure. The administration of Abdurrahman Wahid, Lindsey posits, is challenged by the legacy from the New Order of exponents of state *premanisme* in the bureaucracy, military and other sectors. These same criminal elements, no longer backed by the state, have been forced to 'go private' in the post-Soeharto era. Abdurrahman has attempted to act against some of the *preman* but these efforts have so far proved inadequate. The *preman* are, however, increasingly susceptible to societal backlashes against criminality as they no longer enjoy state support. The basic question relates to control of the state apparatus, and whether a strengthened and functioning legal system – capable of preventing or punishing violence and corruption – can overcome *premanisme*, or whether society will deal with the *preman* on equal but extra-judicial terms.

In Chapter 24, Robert Cribb canvasses the prospect of Indonesia shedding the burden of empire and discusses the resistance to this concept in elite circles where the emotional power of the 'idea of Indonesia' is prevalent. The Indonesian experiment, he asserts, is contingent upon three factors: the potency of centrifugal forces in the outlying regions; the ability of the centre to accentuate the positive features of Indonesian unity; and the desire of the island of Java to remain a part of Indonesia. Pointing to the experience of empires in history, he notes that the more successful the process of the imposition of a broad imperial identity is, the less appealing the whole structure may become to the 'dominant' group – the Javanese in the Indonesian context. He dismisses the view that Java needs to remain a part of a united Indonesia for economic reasons or because it would disintegrate under the weight of ethnic divisions were it to separate from Indonesia. He concludes by pointing to the absence of Javanese restiveness and political assertiveness, and of the direct discrimination against other indigenous ethnic groups that was a marker of the collapse of the Ottoman, Mongol and many Western colonial empires. Given the current parlous economic and political climate, the failure of the decentralisation and democratisation processes could lead to a less powerful attachment to the idea of Indonesia, and the exploration of more radical solutions.

The historical experience of the Indonesian nation has been rich, varied and frequently elusive of definitive explanation. But from all of this what lessons can be learned? At least two principles of immediate relevance may be distilled. The first is that the present climate, teeming with uncertainty and intrigue, is merely another challenge in a long series faced by the Indonesian nation and people. Second, time spent remembering and reflecting on history is indicative of a progressive society. It is unlikely such an exercise will provide an epiphany for Indonesia's leaders and intellectuals – scholars and thinkers have grappled, and are still grappling, with the sense and meaning of modern Indonesia – but it can highlight salient factors for consideration. Only those nations whose inhabitants have an awareness of what has gone before and are reconciled with its positive and negative aspects – the extraordinary and the eminently forgettable – will be able to deal effectively with the demands of the present and some of the challenges likely to be faced in the future. Misrepresentation of this past – whether wilful, misguided or through ignorance – will almost certainly have a deleterious impact.

2

THE CONTINGENT AND THE UNFORESEEN

John Legge

My brief for this chapter is more than a little daunting, as I have been asked to consider what 100 years of Indonesian history might tell us about the future. No less! Both parts of that assignment pose problems. First of all, does history tell us anything about the future? Are there any lessons to be drawn? Marx, in the opening sentence of *The Eighteenth Brumaire of Louis Bonaparte* (1926, p. 23), refers to Hegel's view that history repeats itself – that 'all great events and personalities in world history reappear in one fashion or another' – and he tacks on his own rider: 'the first time as tragedy, the second as farce'. For my part I'm not sure that history can tell us anything about the future except that it is likely to be unexpected. Perhaps H.A.L. Fisher was right when he said, in the Preface to his *History of Europe*, that there was only one safe rule for historians – that they should recognise in the development of human destinies 'the play of the contingent and the unforeseen'. When I was a student of history at the University of Melbourne we were taught to regard Fisher with a certain degree of contempt, as a historian who could not see patterns, regularities or process in the events of the past, only one event following another 'as wave follows upon wave'. Sixty years later, and with an eye to Indonesian history, I am inclined to believe that Fisher may have had a point.

Second, I am not at all certain what '100 years of Indonesian history' is intended to convey. Is it the things that have happened in that 100 years? Or the things that have been said – and are still being said – about the things that have happened? The events of the past or the writings about the events of the past? Perhaps both. In the following pages, however, I will be trying to address the second of these rather than 'history itself'.

At a quick glance, writings about Indonesian history and the shape of events themselves display a sharp break around the middle of the 20th century. Before World War II most historical work, predominantly Dutch, was concerned either with early history, and with the construction from fragmentary archaeological, epigraphical and literary sources of a chronology of events, or with the presence of European powers from the 16th century, with the commercial activities of the Dutch United East India Company (VOC) and with the high imperialism of the late 19th century. The overall picture was of a past shaped mainly by external forces: India – the perception of the Indies as part of 'greater India' as Georges Coedès (1948) saw it in his study of what he called the 'Hinduised States' of Indochina and Indonesia – Islam and, of course, Europe.

There were challenges to that view. J.C. van Leur in the 1930s rejected the idea that Indian influence came by way of colonisation and conquest and questioned the theory that it was the product of trading contacts. He described the early commerce of the archipelago as a peddling trade, not a capitalist trade, and argued that, as such, it could not have been the bearer of high culture. Indian and later Islamic influence he saw not as a matter of external imposition but of local initiative selectively borrowing external forms in support of local polities and constituting what he called, in a famous phrase, 'a thin and flaking glaze' leaving the main body of local cultures essentially intact. The so-called Hindu–Javanese period of Indonesian history, for example, he saw as a case of Indonesian polities absorbing those aspects of Indian culture which would help to sustain the emergence of centralised hierarchical authority. It was a court matter – a selecting of ideas, ritual and organisation, not a matter of general cultural diffusion.[1] This was a very different emphasis from that of Coedès.[2]

Similar judgments were made about the penetration of Islam from the 12th century onwards, and about the initial impact of Portuguese and Dutch commerce from the beginning of the 16th century. The VOC, in establishing trading stations, was seen as fitting in with existing patterns of local trade and as making merely a peripheral impact on the archipelago. Though its range and strength made it gradually the paramount power in the region, its relations with local rulers were seen as more like a system of international relations than a system of colonial overlordship, at least until the territorial expansion of the Dutch empire in the 19th and 20th centuries brought the diverse societies of the archipelago for the first time into an administrative unity.

By the early 20th century the Indies had become clearly a Dutch possession and the focus of scholars was directed mainly to the character of Dutch rule and the changing emphases of Dutch policy, from the economic expansion of the Liberal phase to the self-conscious benevolence of the Ethical Policy. Such studies as J.S. Furnivall's *Netherlands India* were in no doubt that local initiative had been subordinated to foreign power.

World War II, it could be said, broke the continuity of events and also of the way in which events were perceived. The Japanese sweep through Southeast Asia and the occupation of the colonial dependencies of Britain, France, the Netherlands and the United States destroyed the apparatus of colonial rule and rendered impossible its simple restoration when the war was over. While the imperial powers in different ways attempted to reassert control over their former dependencies, they did so within the dynamics of a changed global situation. Emerging nationalisms, the formation of new states – India, Pakistan, the Philippines, Indonesia, Malaya and Singapore – the drawn-out agony of the Vietnam war and the changing balances of power after the victory of the Communist Party in China in 1949 affected not merely the study of these events as they evolved but also the way in which the earlier history of the region was examined. For Indonesia, for example, the significant developments of the first half of the 20th century – the development of new political and cultural movements such as Sarekat Islam, Pujangga Baru and Taman Siswa, the rise of the Communist Party (PKI) and the revolts of 1926–27, the formation of the Indonesian Nationalist Party (PNI) – assumed a new shape in the light of the outcome of the struggle for independence.

The postwar period in fact saw a vast expansion of Southeast Asian studies in the West, as well as in the institutions of the new nations themselves. To a great extent this was policy-driven. The politics of Indonesia's struggle for independence had profound implications for the future political stability of the region and, with the establishment of the Cold War setting, it was a matter of urgency for outside players to understand the nature of the changes taking place in the societies and polities of the area as a whole. Hence there evolved a focus on new political forces and on questions of modernisation and development, and these needed to be observed against the background of a longer past. And new nations, too, required new histories to sustain the assertion of new identities and the sublimation of old legacies.

One characteristic of the development of Western studies in the 1950s and 1960s was the confidence of scholars as they approached the problems of the new Southeast Asia, seeing it as an exciting new field of study to be opened up. Some difficulties were recognised – problems of sources for early history, questions of bias in the highly charged atmosphere of the day, dangers of Eurocentricity in the treatment of other societies and cultures. (Van Leur again, and his remark that 'with the arrival of ships from western Europe, the point of view is turned a hundred and eighty degrees and from then on the Indies are observed from the deck of the ship, the ramparts of the fortress and the high gallery of the trading house'.)

Nevertheless, while these problems were given a passing nod, there was a belief that, with care, the job could be done. A series of seminars mounted by D.G.E. Hall at the University of London in 1956–58 was a case in point. The scholars gathered there surveyed the problems of writing Southeast Asian history but, though cautious in the light of the difficulties, in the end they had no fundamental doubts about their craft (Hall 1961). And a few years later, in

1961, John Smail, in a famous paper, addressed the problem of Eurocentricity and the natural tendency to interpret developments in terms of local response to the external challenge. He introduced the idea of the autonomy of Southeast Asian history and argued that, notwithstanding the undoubted impact of full Dutch empire, local cultures remained resilient. Even such developments as the emergence of a new Western-educated elite could be seen as part of a local evolution that could be studied successfully by foreign observers (Smail 1961). Along with the confidence went a sense of optimism about the future. It was a new world. The days of colonialism were over and liberal scholarship had high expectations that the new nations would provide stability and development in the future.

For Indonesia one may take George McT. Kahin's (1952) study of the revolution, one of the first wave of postwar scholarly works, as reflecting these characteristics. Kahin carried out fieldwork in Indonesia in 1948 and 1949 and was thus a close observer of the later stages of the struggle. He forged close links with some of the leading figures of the republic and clearly sympathised with their aims. His general interpretation was straightforward. He set the struggle against the background of colonial rule. The general picture was of the pre-war emergence of nationalism as a natural product of the high imperialism of the late 19th and early 20th centuries, shaped by changing emphases of Dutch policies and especially by the educational policies of the 20th century, which assisted the growth of a new Indonesian elite, educated but underemployed and ready to take advantage of the Japanese defeat of the Dutch. (Nationalism, in effect, is seen, before Ben Anderson had coined the term, as the imagining of a new community.) The end of the war thus found a nationalist leadership in place and ready to maintain a four-year-long resistance to the return of Dutch power. Enlightened, democratic in temper, its members gave ground for hopes for the future of the new republic. For Kahin the story had a tentatively happy ending. His closing sentence catches the mood: 'Whatever the case, if in attempting to solve their great post-revolutionary problems the Indonesian people were able to demonstrate the same qualities they had shown in their struggle for political independence their chances of success appeared strong' (Kahin 1952, p. 480).

Herbert Feith's *Decline of Constitutional Democracy in Indonesia* did for the 1950s what Kahin's *Nationalism and Revolution* had done for the late 1940s. Both remain the standard works covering two of the commonly perceived divisions of the history of the republic: the revolution, the period of constitutional democracy, Guided Democracy, the change of regime (1965–68) and the Soeharto presidency, leading to the next change of regime (Habibie to Gus Dur). But by 1962, the publication date of Feith's study, the optimism reflected in Kahin's work had dimmed.

As the century unrolled there were shifts in modes of interpretation of these successive stages, and of the years leading up to them: changes in style, changing perceptions of what seemed an appropriate subject matter for study, changes in fashion about what would constitute a satisfactory explanation of events. The differences were in part due to changing angles of vision – later observers knew what had happened in the intervening years – in part to the preferences (values) of historians and in part to actual changes in the Indonesian situation (noting that, as the actual changes are seen and described by observers, there may be a difficulty in distinguishing between perception and reality). Kahin's work and others that followed in the 1950s were largely political analyses, concerned with the identification of political forces, primarily within an Indonesian elite: political parties, the emergence of the army as an extra-parliamentary force, the growth of the PKI, the dissidence of elements in Sumatra and Sulawesi. The changing balance of such forces over the 1950s had made the provisional constitution no longer in line with political realities. The return to the Constitution of 1945 and the introduction of the forms of Guided Democracy were explained in these terms.

Historians, in approaching these events and while focusing primarily on what might be called the political level, were increasingly influenced by the methods and findings of the neighbouring social sciences. W.F. Wertheim (1965) and Harry Benda (1962) both argued that historians had to be social scientists themselves, and many historians found that conceptual formulations by political scientists, anthropologists, sociologists and others were useful in illuminating events at the political level in Indonesia. Feith's characterisation of the Indonesian elite as divided between administrators and solidarity-makers and Sartono's attempt to establish a taxonomy of movements of peasant unrest in Java were examples (Feith 1962; Sartono 1973).

But of particular importance in reshaping perceptions of Indonesia's social and political landscape were Clifford Geertz's series of conceptual analyses: agricultural involution and the idea of 'shared poverty' in a wet rice society, the cultural variants of *priyayi*, *santri* and *abangan* in Java, the idea of the 'theatre State', compounded of Islamic and Hindu–Buddhist elements, to characterise the cosmologically based, hierarchical order of Java and Bali, and the more general notion of *aliran* or cultural streams running vertically through the diverse societies of the archipelago (see, for example, Geertz 1960, 1963, 1965, 1968, 1980). Whether Geertz discovered these categories or invented them remains a matter of debate. Were they there to be observed or did he impose them on the Indonesian scene? Did the analysis depend on evidence or did it merely offer one way among others of looking at a complex society? The *aliran* concept is obviously far from precise but it seemed to make sense of the election results of 1955: Masyumi strength outside Java and in West Java, NU's base in the *santri* of East and Central Java, and the appeal of the PNI and the PKI to the *abangan* of Java. But this was a very rough set of correspondences, and how far they sprang from *aliran* attachments and how far they were a reflection of other causes it is perhaps impossible to say. The same may be true of Feith's identification of two broad political subcultures in Indonesia, described as Javanese–aristocratic and Islamic–entrepreneurial. In this way he attempted to bring together a diversity of geographical, ethnic and social divisions and to relate them to themes in Indonesian history: the contribution of Hindu–Buddhist civilisation in Java, the commercial experience of the archipelago over the centuries, the uneven penetration of Islam and differences within the Islamic community.

Through concepts of this kind foreigners and Indonesians alike have struggled to make sense of the complexities and ambiguities of Indonesian political behaviour in the post-independence era and to find explanations not only for party allegiances but for such developments as the growth of separatist movements in the Outer Islands in the 1950s or the sharpening of political divisions in the 1960s. What is worth noticing in these analyses is that they reflect a shift in the categories of explanation. Whereas the initial concern of Western scholars, at least in the early years of the republic, was with political forces, intra-elite conflicts and changes in the domestic balances of power, there later appeared a tendency to seek explanations in aspects of Indonesia's traditional social order.

One of the elements of traditional order, at least as it was perceived by historians and others in the 1960s and 1970s, was the residue of Indian influence in Java and Bali as expressed in views about the nature of political authority. Drawing in part on an influential article by Robert Heine-Geldern in 1942, observers pointed to the hierarchical and centralised character of earlier Javanese kingdoms, embodying ideas of a divine kingship and of a parallelism of the universe and the terrestrial order, with the capital of the ruler seen as the magical centre of the realm and the ruler – the descendant or incarnation of a god – maintaining the unity and harmony of the kingdom, mirroring that of the cosmic order. The reality was never like that. The history of Javanese kingdoms was very much a matter of fairly continuous conflict. Pigeaud, in introducing his translation of the 14th century epic, the *Nagarakertagama* of the Kingdom of Majapahit, stressed the precarious nature of royal power and saw the 'perennial division and reunion of the realm' as an inherent part of the system (Pigeaud 1960, p. 122). And the theoretical emphasis on harmony, centrality of authority and the indivisibility of the kingdom may well be seen as a response to that turbulent reality.

Attention to this kind of cosmology is reflected not only in the work of historians engaged in the study of earlier kingdoms – Soemarsaid Moertono's (1963) examination of Mataram from the 16th to the 19th century, for example, which discerns a blending of Islamic and earlier elements, or M.C. Ricklefs' (1974) examination of the rule of Sultan Mangkubumi in Yogyakarta in the latter part of the 18th century and of the inherent difficulty of conceiving of a continuing division of the realm – but also in that of observers of the 20th century scene both before and after the formation of the republic. Heather Sutherland (1979), in exploring the formation of the modern bureaucratic elite, pointed to the way in which traditional elements survived, first in the development of a colonial bureaucracy and then in the greatly altered circumstances of the post-revolutionary scene. The colonial service, the *pangreh praja*, she argued, should be seen simultaneously 'as heirs to the local rulers of pre-colonial days and also as agents of the Netherlands government; they were neither exclusively the one nor the other, but both' (p. 2). The roots of the service 'reached back far into Java's history, into the political and social patterns of early indigenous states' (p. 3). And even as the social origins of its membership changed and as a 'new *priyayi*' emerged in the 20th century, there were still continuities of values and practice to be observed, continuities even as the *pamong praja* (the postwar term for the territorial service) came increasingly to be staffed by military officers and to be subordinated to effective military rule (p. 159).

Similarly, others have turned to traditional order to explain developments of the present and the recent past. Bernhard Dahm (1969) portrayed Sukarno as reflecting many of the traits of a traditional ruler. In his illuminating essay, 'The Idea of Power in Javanese Culture', Ben Anderson (1972a), while recognising the conceptual difficulty of discussing the implied political theory of another culture using such terms as 'power' and 'authority' drawn from a Western analytical framework, proceeded to a systematic account of traditional Javanese political assumptions and noticed their continuing impact in modern Indonesia. He commented in particular on the tension between centre and periphery, and the president's claim to embody the unity of society. Nationalism itself was seen not as a political credo but as expressing a fundamental drive for solidarity and unity in the face of the disintegrating forces of colonial capitalism – 'an attempt to reconquer a primordial one-ness' (Anderson 1972a, pp. 22–4). Ruth McVey (1965) found signs of the PKI's ability, during the early 1960s, to attract members of the Javanese peasantry through its manipulation of traditional perceptions. And Soedjatmoko (1967, p. 275) pointed to the cultural roots of modern political parties, which he saw not as associations formed to advance alternative programs but as 'the political representatives of cultural solidarity groups which are tied together by primordial loyalties of great intensity'.

As a broad generalisation, then, it might be said that between the late 1960s and early 1970s the focus of historians and political scientists was less on the rapidly changing balances of political pressure groups and more on what seemed to be the more permanent underpinnings of political action –

those traditional features of Indonesian society that were stable and persistent. (Though it did not seem to be noticed at the time, it could be said that the new focus implied something of a retreat from the hitherto fashionable assertions of van Leur. If the traditional features of Indonesian society illuminated features of modern political behaviour, the external influences over the centuries must have been more than a thin and flaking glaze. And since the perceived tradition was to a considerable degree seen as stemming from the early kingdoms, it might appear that Coedès had after all had the better of the argument!)

This shift may in part be a reflection of changing events in Indonesia. A focus on parties, pressure groups and political forces might have been appropriate enough for the events of the constitutional period of the 1950s, and a focus on traditional forms may have reflected the political style of Guided Democracy and the subsequent New Order, placing its emphasis on the nature of leadership and on the bases of authoritarian rule. Be that as it may, the shift had its own difficulties.

The antithetical terms 'tradition' and 'modernity' are often used as though their meaning is clear. But 'tradition' implies a judgment made now about what was the case in the past, and in making such a judgment much depends on the perceptions of the modern observer. For Indonesia, Indian and Islamic influences are normally seen as absorbed into an older indigenous tradition. But what about the changes taking place after the establishment of a European presence? Has the emergence of the late 19th and early 20th century elite also been absorbed? In practice traditional and modern elements, however defined, are so intermixed that to oppose the two may be misleading. One may accept that the traditional/modern antithesis may sometimes serve a useful analytical purpose, but only for particular purposes and within the framework of a particular enquiry.

And, of course, assertions about tradition and change are never neutral. They are loaded with values. These may be displayed in various ways. If aspects of the major developments of the 20th century can be seen as rooted in the past, the colonial era itself appears as merely an interlude like the other external pressures that went before, and the essential autonomy of Indonesian history is preserved. Again, to appeal to tradition as an explanation of much that is observed in the present, and to stress the inertia of tradition, may have the conservative effect of drawing the attention of observers away from elements of change. To focus, for example, on Geertz's three variants in Javanese social order, or on ethnic divisions across the archipelago, may play down conflicts between emerging classes and in this way serve the interests of existing elites. Finally, was Soeharto to be seen during his long presidency as performing a modernising role or might he be seen instead as calling on traditional motifs to sustain his authority? Perceptions of continuities or of discontinuities are alike constructions of the observer and may have different purposes to serve.

Recognition of the values embedded in alternative approaches may have helped to undermine the confidence of the early postwar analysts. What is seen from a privileged vantage point in the present, what is taken for granted and what is selected for comment is necessarily shaped by interest, purpose and culture, and reflects fundamental assumptions about how the world is constituted. Is there any avenue of escape? Soedjatmoko, in 1965, spoke of the 'polyinterpretability' of historical reality, and discussed this from the angle of Indonesian historians considering Indonesia's own history. Their interest in the past was expected to serve the needs of the present by sustaining a sense of national identity. Did that mean that their work would necessarily display a conflict between their patriotism and their professional obligations? Soedjatmoko's answer was that the apparent conflict could be overcome. Indonesian historians could not escape their participation in the society about them but must still be constrained by their professional discipline. For the outside observer, too, that is perhaps the best that could be expected, though so-called scientific historians may also unconsciously shape a picture of the past to serve the values of the present.

Another approach to these uncertainties was that which was stimulated by developments in literary theory – by post-modernist and post-structuralist discourse. Much earlier, of course, C.C. Berg had criticised N.J. Krom's use of classical texts to establish a history of Javanese kingdoms, arguing that Krom's sources were not historical in character (see, for example, Berg 1961). They had a different, magical, function to perform – the creation of an alternative reality, to provide a legitimate ancestry for a usurper, perhaps, or to sustain a subsequent world view. The later development of critical theory went far beyond that, concentrating not on supposed matters of fact but on the inner relationships of texts, on codes and symbols which could give insights not into events but only into the cultural conventions of the societies that produced the texts. The language was the language of image and myth, discourse, signs and symbols.

This kind of analysis applied not only to texts in the literal sense – inscriptions, chronicles and so forth – but to texts by analogy – cultural traits, patterns of behaviour, actions that reflected the sign system of those who performed them. One may think of James Siegel's examination of Acehenese historical thinking or Anthony Day's exploration of Javanese concepts of time, prophecy and change or Jane Drakard's study of royal authority in Minangkabau.

The post-structuralist approach landed some scholars in the ultimate scepticism of a Derrida, arguing that texts, whether written or acted, were self-regarding, referring only to themselves and not to a reality outside themselves, that they had meaning only in their relationship with a reader and that there could therefore be no valid reading, only a continuing deconstruction of deconstructions and a constant deferring of judgment. The almost paralysing uncertainty inherent in this approach stood in sharp contrast to the confidence that had marked the earlier postwar onslaught on Southeast Asia. Indeed it tended to suggest that historical study was not, in the end, about an external world about which accurate statements might be made, but only about the perceptions of historians themselves.

Others, however, have drawn on critical theory not to reject the validity of the historical enterprise but to strengthen it by stressing the attentiveness and sensitivity required in the examination of the sign systems of other cultures or by using alternative readings to revise earlier fashions of interpretation. Oliver Wolters (1982/1999) is one who has shifted the framework of historical inquiry by opening up reflexive, ethnographic approaches to the exploration of other societies and other times. In so doing he challenged the confidence of earlier scholars while adding new dimensions to the way the past may be studied. A different kind of example is provided by John Pemberton's (1994) study of the public ceremonies and domestic rituals of Java, which led him to a reversal of the fashion of appealing to tradition to explain current trends. In place of the idea of an underlying cultural order that might be invoked to explain the present, he suggested that perceptions of culture and tradition were, on the contrary, shaped by the needs of the present. The idea of 'Java', he argued, if not an invention, was at least a deliberate revival of traditional perceptions in the interests of a repressive regime.

PROSPECTS

After this scamper through some of the changing fashions of interpretation, and subject to the uncertainties that I have raised, can one hope with any confidence to characterise the shape of Indonesia's history over the century that is coming to an end, and from there to detect trends that extend into the future? Almost certainly not. However, I suppose I am committed to having a go. There seem to be some turning points and some natural divisions in the course of events, as I have already indicated. These might include, for example, the extending power and authority of colonial rule, accompanied by the emergence and development of a nationalist movement, albeit with a variety of elements, the cultural ferment of the 1930s, the Second World War and the Japanese occupation, the revolution, constitutional democracy, Guided Democracy, the fall of the first president and the bloody transition to the New Order – and the next regime change, beginning with Habibie and still unfolding under his successor. But can we see where these stages are heading? The trouble about stages and turning points is that they are not objectively 'there' in the texture of events. They are there because we put them there. And we only perceive them as such long after, when we know what happened subsequently.

Having said all that, I wouldn't want to depart from the conventional perceptions of the pre-war development of Netherlands India, and one cannot escape the idea of the Japanese defeat of the Dutch, the occupation and the subsequent struggle for independence as constituting a cataclysmic division. But what of the subsequent history of the republic? Are there continuing themes – issues which remain, possibly in different forms, through the perceived stages of that history?

One may, perhaps, point first of all to the tension expressed in the motto of the republic itself – usually translated as 'Unity in Diversity'. On the one hand we have the emergence in the first part of the century of a nationalist movement seeking to unite the archipelago and presented by Sukarno as overarching and disciplining other ideologies. On the other hand is the fact that the Dutch dependency of Netherlands India was a recent creation, and did not remove the continuing differences between, and within, regions – ethnic, linguistic, religious, cultural and economic differences. This tension was acute in the early years of the republic and in different forms remains evident today. One component in that tension is the varying position and differing varieties of Islam within the archipelago, again a product of its longer history.

Secondly, one can point to continuities in the way alternative political forms have presented themselves and how they have been debated. In the 1950s the forms of parliamentary democracy were simultaneously criticised and defended until the return to the 1945 Constitution and the transition to Guided Democracy in 1959, a move that was justified in part as representing a return to traditional forms and processes of Indonesian society. What happened between 1957 and 1959 was a political change of some magnitude, though probably less than a regime change. That term would appear more applicable to what happened between 1965 and 1968, though this still occurred within the framework of the 1945 Constitution. One can detect shifts in the course of the Soeharto period, as the earlier concern with reversing the excesses of the Sukarno period and the emphasis on economic development gave way to a streamlined authoritarianism, military dominance and the prevalence of corruption in various forms. The aggravated authoritarianism and conspicuous nepotism in turn evoked ideological reactions, the call for *reformasi* and democracy, reminiscent of earlier debates.

Thirdly, one may notice the survival of patrimonial forms in the supposedly modern Soeharto state. (Whether this reflected underlying cultural patterns or, as Pemberton suggests, it was a deliberate appeal to a traditional order, does not matter at this point.) The territorial bureaucracy was hijacked by the army as army officers came to occupy many of the levels of the territorial service from province to subdistrict. This control was further underpinned by the army's own provincial and subprovincial commands, paralleling the administrative structure of the state.

The fall of Soeharto and accession of Habibie, for all its major policy shifts (including the opening of the door to a possible withdrawal from East Timor), might be seen as another transitional period leading to the elections and the 1999 session of the People's Consultative Assembly (MPR), events which at this distance might have a claim to be represented as a change of regime corresponding in magnitude to that of 1965–67. Is this a case of history repeating itself? And if the appalling events of 1966 make that regime change appear as tragedy, Gus Dur sometimes seems to be playing to the idea of repetition as farce.

That irreverence aside, how far do these continuing themes persist in the new situation, perhaps in new forms?

Clearly Indonesia's regional tensions continue, reflecting the artificiality of the political unit created by the Dutch. In the 1950s the proposed solution to the problem of regional dissidence was the delegation of an increased degree of autonomy to descending levels of local government: province, *kabupaten* and 'level 3' (the village or groupings of villages). The problem, however, was that the powers that the centre was prepared to concede were insufficient to meet regional demands. The powers demanded were what might be called powers of national policy, which the centre had to retain if Indonesia was to stay a united state. Currency control was one area where exporting regions saw themselves as subsidising the island of Java but where power could not be shared. The question of regional autonomy has re-emerged with a vengeance, but again autonomy legislation, though promising to delegate significant powers, appears to take it all back by reserving the areas of national policy. In the 1950s federalism was a dirty word in the backlash against Dutch efforts to retain influence by creating a United States of Indonesia, a solution that was decisively rejected after the transfer of sovereignty. At century's end one may wonder whether a federal type of solution might not be the only way of satisfying some regional demands. Aceh and West Papua would be the test cases.

Whether this would enable the archipelago to hold together goes along with the question of whether, within the framework of the 1945 Constitution, a revived democratic practice can satisfy other domestic demands, or whether the available machinery of central administration, backed in some way by military power, within a captive Gus Dur or successor administration, will again reinforce the authoritarian tradition that has marked the trends of the past 40 years.

Finally there is a further theme which must be mentioned. One cannot avoid noticing the presence from time to time of extraordinary violence in Indonesian affairs, a violence that appears to go beyond the requirements of the issues being fought over at any time: the 'social revolution' in east Sumatra in 1946, the killings of 1965–66, the violence attendant on the withdrawal from East Timor, both before and after the ballot, the present violence between Muslim and Christian in Ambon. Have observers of Indonesian history tended to play down these recurring episodes, choosing rather to emphasise ideas of harmony or of syncretism as the essential features of Indonesian society and outlook?

I leave these and other questions for other writers.

NOTES

1   See van Leur (1955). Van Leur's analysis of early trading patterns received support later from O.W. Wolters, whose definitive study saw the expansion of commerce as an indigenous and not an Indian achievement (Wolters 1967, p. 247).

2   For a sorting out of the issues involved in the Indianisation debate, see Mabbett (1977).

PART I

RECENT DEVELOPMENTS

3

ABDURRAHMAN'S INDONESIA: POLITICAL CONFLICT AND INSTITUTIONAL CRISIS

*Marcus Mietzner**

When Abdurrahman Wahid took office as Indonesia's fourth president in October 1999, many hoped that the country's first democratically elected leader would show the way to long overdue institutional reform of the political system. Abdurrahman won the presidential race as a compromise candidate, with representatives from most political forces joining what soon was to be called the 'cabinet of national unity'. The international community, after initial irritation caused by Megawati Sukarnoputri's failure to gain the presidency, pledged support for the new administration, hoping that Indonesia would return to political normality and ultimately achieve economic consolidation. Those observers who had closely followed events leading to Abdurrahman's election were more pessimistic, however. Abdurrahman's obsession with becoming Habibie's successor forced him to alienate former allies and make false promises to previous enemies, and was a shaky platform from which the country had to embark on its historic journey of political reform. The highly heterogeneous composition of the cabinet and the unpredictability of its leader were unlikely to guarantee the political stability Indonesia needed to restructure its political framework. The facade of political harmony in late October 1999 disintegrated within a month. By then, the first minister had been sacked, with six more to follow before the formation of a new cabinet in August 2000.

The challenges that the Abdurrahman administration faced were enormous. The project of fundamentally reforming the country's political structure covered six main areas. First, the institutional framework of the political system had to be redefined and modernised. Since the 1950s, the state institutions had been manipulated by a succession of authoritarian regimes, using the ambiguity of the 1945 Constitution to legalise their grip on power. As a result, the institutional relations between the presidency, parliament (the People's Representative Council, or DPR) and the People's Consultative Assembly

(MPR) were shrouded in legal uncertainty, leaving constitutional experts wondering if Indonesia adhered to a presidential or a parliamentary system, or a chaotic mixture of both. If Indonesia wanted to institutionalise its democratisation process, the constitutional framework had to be reformed by a coordinated effort to draft a blueprint for the relations between the state institutions, and an action plan to implement it by changing the constitution as well as related laws and government regulations.

A second issue related to the codification of relations between the centre and the regions, incorporating detailed arrangements for financial and political autonomy regulated by government decrees. Local governments all over the archipelago expected clarification about how the new autonomy laws would affect their home regions.

Third, the Indonesian National Army (TNI) had to be contained by a strong institutional control mechanism, reducing its influence on politics and convincing it to concentrate on defence matters rather than internal security. At the same time, however, its institutional unity and instrumental efficiency had to be guarded, as the fragmentation of the TNI would pose a greater danger to further democratisation than its push for continued political power.

The fourth point was that Indonesia's notoriously corrupt legal system had to be cleaned up. The corruption of New Order judges still posed a serious threat to the restoration of international confidence in Indonesia's economic and political stability.

A fifth area of concern was the development of political parties as the foundation for the future democratic system. The Guided Democracy and New Order regimes had emasculated Indonesia's political parties since the late 1950s, making it difficult for the post-Soeharto administration to rely on a strong network of political parties.

Finally, the new administration shouldered huge expectations from the Indonesian people to facilitate the recovery of the economy. With Indonesia experiencing its third year of continued economic crisis, many observers predicted things would get better as soon as a democratically elected government was put in charge.

After one year in office, little progress has been made in the six sectors mentioned above. The reasons for this are manifold. The first is that the decades-long political stagnation under the New Order permeated the post-Soeharto political elite more than initially hoped. Corruption, misuse of political office for personal interests, neglect of public accountability – all these features of the New Order administration have become part of a political culture resistant to structural change. Second, the deep divisions within the political elite have led to the subordination of the reform project to the personal interests of the political protagonists. Abdurrahman is preoccupied with political survival in a hostile environment, and his main rival, Amien Rais, is focused on bringing down his administration. Third, traditional divisions within Indonesian society have re-emerged in the form of openly practised constituency cronyism. Abdurrahman's granting of privileged economic access to Nahdlatul Ulama (NU) leaders is one such example. In this chapter, I will examine political developments under the administration of Abdurrahman Wahid in the six areas outlined above. Unless the institutional weakness of the country's political framework is addressed seriously, no significant change can be expected in any of the sectors for the remainder of the president's term in office.

STATE INSTITUTIONS REVISITED: A REFORM ABORTED

Abdurrahman Wahid's appointment as president, while widely acknowledged as the most democratic election of a head of state in Indonesia's history, pointed to the institutional weakness of the country's democratic system. Abdurrahman, who had run as the semi-official presidential candidate of the National Awakening Party (PKB) in the general elections of June 1999, controlled only around 8% of the seats in the 695-strong MPR. Through a series of brilliant political manoeuvres, Abdurrahman was able to defeat his longtime friend Megawati, convince his former enemies in the modernist Islamic parties and Habibie-loyal faction within Golkar to support him, and secure the military's cooperation by generous offers of cabinet representation. While his success constituted a tremendous personal victory for a veteran political player – and a considerable comeback for a man many believed was out of the race after two strokes and because of various other physical handicaps – in constitutional terms it carried considerable long-term risks. Unlike presidential systems where the head of state can govern with the authority of a mandate for a fixed term in office, the Indonesian system gave both the DPR and the MPR unspecified – and unpractised – powers to demand the president's accountability and remove him if he was deemed guilty of violations of the constitution, the law or the state policy guidelines. This complex institutional relationship between the president, the parliament and the assembly meant that Abdurrahman would have to maintain the composition of his alliance for a five-year term in order to secure a majority in both the DPR and the MPR.

Abdurrahman was well aware of the institutional conflicts ahead of him, and he was one of the first to propose structural reform of the constitutional framework. He believed that the solution to the constitutional conflict was direct presidential elections which, he confidently predicted, he would win by a large margin. When faced with the threat of impeachment by the 2000 annual session of the MPR, he told his inner circle that he was considering calling direct presidential elections as soon as the MPR session was over and the necessary amendments to the constitution had been made (interview with Djohan Effendi, State Secretary, 18 June 2000). Abdurrahman instructed PKB leaders to fight for the amendments in the MPR (interview with Effendi Choirie, 10 May 2000). The Working Body of the MPR, which had established an ad hoc committee in November 1999, had already prepared drafts for constitutional amendments that, if accepted, would have fundamentally restructured the political landscape of Indonesia. At the end of July 2000, a detailed review of the constitution was completed. The report showed that there were significant differences between the political parties on reform issues, but most of the 11 factions had indicated that they favoured direct presidential elections, the adoption of which would have facilitated wide-ranging structural change.

The reality, however, was different. In the run-up to the annual session in August, all major political parties were preoccupied with political manoeuvring. Abdurrahman isolated himself politically by firing seven ministers and presidential secretaries, and through various corruption scandals and allegations of nepotism, financial and legal irregularities, and controversial dismissals and appointments. While the presidential palace was busy devising strategies of how to survive the annual session, the president's adversaries were equally engaged in organising counter-strategies to control or replace him.[1] Short-term politicking pushed the important constitutional debate into the background. At the end of the session, none of the fundamental questions had even been touched on during 21 hours of deliberations (NDIIA 2000, p. 4). Instead, the MPR passed minor revisions that strengthened the legislature in relation to the executive, further empowering a parliament that had already established itself as a powerful organ in controlling the president. These changes are likely to increase political conflict rather than lessen it.

The failure to address constitutional change was the result, in part, of nostalgic conservatism exhibited by the nationalist parties in the MPR. The Indonesian Democratic Party of Struggle (PDI-P), after supporting reform during the deliberations in the ad hoc committee, had to give in to pressure from Megawati Sukarnoputri, who was opposed to both direct presidential elections and the abolition of the MPR. Her reasons for blocking the reform measures remain unclear. In her opposition, Megawati was joined by the military and police as well as smaller nationalist factions in the MPR. This nationalist bloc saw the 1945 Constitution as the basis of the state, the reform of which would immediately impact on the solidity of the nation. This sentiment was fed by the Islamist parties in the assembly, especially the United Development Party (PPP) and the Crescent Moon and Star Party (PBB), which demanded the reinstitution of the Jakarta Charter by changing Article 29 of the constitution (*Panji Masyarakat*, 30 August 2000). Faced by demands to revise the Pancasila state, the nationalists opted to reject the reform project as a whole.

THE FRAGMENTATION OF CENTRAL AUTHORITY: SEPARATISM AND LOCAL AUTONOMY

The central government has seen a rapid fragmentation of its political and military authority since Abdurrahman took office in October 1999. While this loss of central authority is partly due to the decentralisation process initiated by the Habibie government, it has been aggravated by the failure of the central administration to channel this process through coherent and precise government regulations. The inability of the Abdurrahman administration to issue urgently needed technical guidelines forced the MPR to set a deadline of December 2000, by which time all regulations had to be available to the various regions. Although the government speeded up its efforts after the August 2000 MPR session, by October many regions were still waiting for detailed tax regulations. Confusion about the application of local autonomy has led to early warnings that around 80% of the regency governments will not be ready for the planned hand-over of authority scheduled for 1 January 2001, and will therefore ask the provincial governments to take over. It has also produced new political tension in traditionally anti-centralist areas like oil-rich Riau and gas-producing East Kalimantan.

In Aceh and Papua, the absence of a consistent strategy towards the demands of the troubled provinces has led to a deterioration in the political and security situation in the two areas. Since taking office, Abdurrahman has claimed on several occasions that a solution to the problems in Aceh is near. In reality, he has relied heavily on the mobilisation of international opposition to Acehenese demands for independence, believing that this would be sufficient to demoralise the movement. Besides confronting Aceh with potential international isolation, the president continued to believe that his status as an Islamic leader made him the natural mediator for the conflict. In May, the government signed a truce with the Independent Aceh Movement, GAM, which came into force in June and was extended in September. GAM representatives signed the treaty as a first step towards international recognition, while Abdurrahman Wahid thought that the GAM had finally been forced into compromise. Confident that Acehenese independence was now off the table, the central administration took its time to draft special legislation with offers of Acehenese autonomy. At the annual session of the MPR in August 2000, 10 months after Abdurrahman's election, the special legislation had still not been completed, leading the MPR to set the administration yet another deadline of 1 May 2001 to deliver the draft.

In the meantime, the armed conflict in Aceh continued, with more than 120 people killed during the truce period between June and September, and large parts of the countryside effectively under GAM administration (*Far Eastern Economic Review*, 5 October 2000). Indications that the GAM itself was split in various factions gave Abdurrahman hope that he might be able to strike a deal with its moderate wing, but violent clashes between rival GAM elements complicated an already difficult situation given the feeling of exasperation among the local population at the unfulfilled promises of the central administration. One of the main reasons for continued distrust of the centre has been the perceived inconsistency of its political elite (*Gatra*, 29 January 2000).

While Aceh has seen a continuation of its crisis inherited from the Soeharto and Habibie governments, the situation in Papua has undergone dramatic change since the Abdurrahman administration came to power. Since its integration into Indonesia in 1969, Papua has been viewed by Jakarta as an area too backward, ethnically heterogeneous and politically fragmented to produce an efficient independence movement. While human rights violations by the military and the massive outflow of mining revenues to Jakarta have fuelled demands for independence throughout the New Order period, Indonesia's historical claim on the territory and the inefficiency of the Papuan dissidents led most Indonesians to believe that Papuan independence was a non-issue. However, the separation of East Timor had a tremendous impact on the spirit of the Papuan independence movement. While the Habibie government's attempts to separate Papua into three provinces were interpreted by Papuans as an attempt to divide their nationalist caucus, Abdurrahman was acknowledged as being sympathetic to their cause, but was unable to convince them to remain within the unitary state.

The president, for his part, applied the same double strategy as in the Aceh case: while mobilising international support for Indonesia's national integrity, he lobbied Papuan leaders to assure them of his sympathy. Believing that his popularity would facilitate smooth negotiations to solve the problem, Abdurrahman even funded a Papuan congress in May that ended with a declaration of Papuan independence – a demand he was not prepared to fulfil (*Tempo*, 27 August 2000). Significantly, long-term residents of the territory reported that the first half of 2000 brought more political change than three decades of Indonesian integration; however, the central administration still saw no necessity to speed up the drafting of a coherent autonomy package. Papuans formed militias that took over security tasks, and the Papuan flag was now flying freely. In desperation the president said that the Papuan flag could be flown until the annual session, explaining neither the rationale behind this deadline nor the action to be taken after that date. In early October, the police started to take the flags down, leading to a bloody incident in Wamena and increased political tension in the province.

THE INDONESIAN MILITARY: WEAKENED, BUT NOT CONTROLLED

The decline in central authority over the regions has been severely aggravated by the fragmentation of the military's command structure. The loss of central control over the TNI's territorial system has not only contributed to the deterioration of the security situation in Aceh and Papua, but has also worsened communal conflicts in Maluku and the crisis in West Timor. Several factors have catalysed this rapid degeneration of the military's central command.

First, it has been Abdurrahman's strategy to weaken the TNI's power centre in order to prevent the rise of a strong military leader with political ambitions. The traumatic experience with Wiranto convinced the president that weak military commanders in the centre would guarantee presidential supremacy over the military and lead to the TNI's departure from the political stage (*Far Eastern Economic Review*, 3 February 2000). While this strategy brought TNI Headquarters and the Ministry of Defence under Abdurrahman's control, it has led to the loss of authority of the military's power centre over its branches in the regions.

The appointment of Admiral Widodo as commander in chief in November 1999, the first head of the TNI with a navy background, alienated army commanders in both the centre and the regional commands, with many of them privately ridiculing their superior. Wiranto's dismissal as Coordinating Minister for Political and Security Affairs in February 2000 in the wake of the East Timor investigations has contributed to the process of increasing autonomy for individual officers and their units in the regions. The appointment of Mohamad Mahfud as Minister of Defence in August, which one high-ranking general described as 'laughable', has done little to stop this process (*Tajuk*, 31 August 2000).

Besides Abdurrahman's attempts to subordinate the military leadership under his control, a series of uncoordinated reforms of the political system has contributed to the weakening of the military's position in Indonesian politics.[2] The revision of the political laws and the new autonomy regulations have reduced the TNI's representation in the central and local parliaments, with most military governors and regents losing their offices until 2003 and a total abolition of TNI representation in the DPR scheduled for 2004. The establishment of press freedom has ensured continual debates about the TNI's human rights violations and warnings of the dangers of a military comeback. Equally, the introduction of human rights legislation has led to widespread reluctance among military commanders to get involved in politically sensitive cases and intercommunal clashes.

Furthermore, state institutions, most notably the DPR and the National Auditing Board (BPK), have exerted pressure on the TNI to increase public accountability, particularly in the light of international scrutiny. Finally, the changed political environment has led to the loss of institutional orientation among the commanders, with TNI officers increasingly defining their own strategic and institutional agendas. The uncoordinated and improvised manner in which the reforms were conducted have left the military weakened, but without an institutional mechanism to control its actions. This has created a situation in which fragments of the frustrated officer corps act independently from the line of command, with conflicts in Ambon, North Maluku and West Timor prolonged by individual military involvement.

The delay in drafting a blueprint and action plan for military reform has been caused by three factors. The first is the divisions in the political elite; the second is the lack of civilian expertise in military and defence issues; and the third is the reluctance among the top brass to accept the reduction of its political significance. Seeking political support from the TNI, Amien Rais, for long the most vocal proponent of the military's exclusion from both the DPR and the MPR, suddenly stated in June that the TNI/Polri faction should be maintained in the MPR to advise civilians on security issues. Abdurrahman, with only his PKB faction undoubtedly loyal to him, needed to strengthen his meagre power base in the assembly. The 38 military and police representatives provided a welcome target for lobbying efforts. The PDI-P, in turn, saw the military as a genuine nationalist partner against Islamic demands for the reinstitution of the Jakarta charter and radical constitutional reform. In the end, only the PPP and PBB pushed in the MPR commissions for the abolition of TNI/Polri's representation in the MPR by 2004, but they lost out against a broad coalition of parties which finally decided to allow the military and police to remain in the assembly until 2009.

Another obstacle to institutionalising effective control mechanisms over the military has been the paucity of civilian expertise in military and defence issues. While civilian government circles and parliamentary factions had the legal authority to set guidelines for the military, the task was surrendered to TNI elements within the Ministry of Defence. The revision of Law No. 20/1982, which will define the TNI's role in state defence and revoke its socio-political function, was sent to academics and observers in June only after its completion. The draft pointed to a third difficulty in establishing civilian control over the military: it underlined that the military is prepared to use civilian weaknesses, or inattentiveness, to defend as much as possible of its political influence. In the draft, 'national defence' was defined as 'the effort to neutralise every threat, both from abroad and within, in any form and shape whatsoever, be it defensive or active'.[3] As in the case of the TNI's continued representation in the MPR, which openly contradicted the military's rhetorical commitment to a withdrawal from politics, the new definition of national defence jeopardised its self-proclaimed concentration on defence matters and the hand-over of domestic security to the police.[4]

The reluctance of military officers to contribute to the creation of a strong institutional framework for the TNI's future role reflected not only the resistance of vested interests and political conservatism, but also substantial conflict within the ranks of the TNI. The dynamics of the power struggle within the TNI had serious consequences for the coordination of the internal reform process. The five TNI institutions involved in drafting the military's reform proposals (TNI Headquarters, Army Headquarters, the Ministry of Defence, the TNI Staff and Command School and the National Resilience Institute) have all produced separate concepts for reform, with competition among the institutions depending on the extent of rivalry between the individual officers holding key positions in them. The problem of the TNI will stay on the political agenda for as long as the civilian elite proves incapable of drafting an effective blueprint for the role of the military in a modern and democratic state.

ABDURRAHMAN'S *IGNORANTIA IURIS*: THE LONG WAY TO LEGAL REFORM

The establishment of the rule of law was one of Abdurrahman Wahid's main projects when taking office. The country's notoriously corrupt judicial system needed fundamental reform if Indonesia was to restore the confidence of the international business community. Equally important was to rebuild the confidence of the domestic audience, which sometimes resorted to horrific measures to settle legal matters it believed the police and the legal apparatus were either uninterested in or incapable of handling.

Abdurrahman, convinced that any reform had to begin at the top, identified the Supreme Court as the source of the malpractices and promised to replace its personnel. As the replacement of Supreme Court judges had to be approved by parliament, the process of appointing 17 new judges took almost a year (*Tempo*, 26 March 2000). The replacement of New Order judges by more honourable figures, many of them without background in the judicial administration, was an important initial step in the reform of the legal system. But without structural change in the institutions, clarification of the separation between the executive and the judicature, and professionalisation of the educational system for judges and attorneys, the exchange of personnel will have a limited impact. The provisional nature of the current approach was demonstrated by the fact that the Ministry of Justice sent Jakarta-based judges of dubious reputation into remote areas, exporting corruption into the regions without explaining why the outer provinces deserved more corrupt judges than the capital (*Forum Keadilan*, 23 April 2000).

The president, despite his rhetoric repudiating New Order practices, continued to intervene heavily in the legal apparatus to pursue political aims. No example is more telling than the fate of the governor of Bank Indonesia, Syahril Sabirin. Abdurrahman, angry that Syahril had been involved in the closure of two of his banks in March 1999, wanted to replace him immediately after taking office. In December 1999 he called Syahril and told him he would be replaced.[5] Informed that the law stipulated that the governor could only be dismissed by the parliament, Abdurrahman insisted on changing the regulations. Reminded again that the president had no authority to change a law, Abdurrahman ordered Attorney General Marzuki Darusman to lead negotiations with Syahril, confronting him with the choice of either accepting an ambassadorship or facing investigations over his role in the Bank Bali scandal. Syahril refused to strike a deal and was arrested in June, being one of the few suspects in the case taken into detention, while the main actors were either never charged or acquitted.[6]

In a similar demonstration of what one sharp observer called Abdurrahman's *ignorantia iuris*, the president recommended halting investigations into the business irregularities of his conglomerate friend Marimutu Sinivasan (*Forum Keadilan*, 28 May 2000). Furthermore, he saw no legal problem in receiving US$2 million from the Sultan of Brunei. Nor did he have a problem in asking the deputy chair of the Logistics Agency, Bulog, to provide him with considerable funds while refusing to issue a presidential decree, and then watching the latter go to gaol for transferring parts of the requested funds to the president's masseur (*Forum Keadilan*, 11 June 2000). This relaxed attitude towards the law was further underlined when he told the police to question alleged political troublemakers in July[7] and ordered the arrest of Hutomo Mandala Putra after the fatal bomb explosion at the Jakarta Stock Exchange in September. In both cases the police refused to follow the orders as evidence was unavailable, leading to the dismissal of Police Chief Rusdihardjo immediately after the bomb affair. The dismissal itself constituted an open breach of the MPR decree that allowed the replacement of the police chief only after consultation with the parliament.

With the president using his executive powers to influence the legal apparatus, and openly violating guidelines set to ensure public accountability, the government has lost some of its credibility in implementing legal reform (*Tajuk*, 31 August 2000). Much of the lower-level corruption during the New Order was rationalised by references to the corruption of the presidential family. The unlawful practices of the Abdurrahman administration therefore have a negative effect on reform-minded judges and attorneys whose support is important for the legal restructuring process.

CENTRALISATION AND FRAGMENTATION: THE PARADOX OF POLITICAL PARTIES IN THE POST-SOEHARTO ERA

The establishment of an institutional decision-making process in modern democracies requires functioning political parties. In Indonesia, political parties had been systematically weakened since the experiment with parliamentary democracy ended in the late 1950s. After Soeharto's downfall, the redevelopment of institutionally strong and democratically organised political parties was one of the main preconditions for progress towards democratisation. While 48 parties contested the June 1999 general elections, only six qualified for the next elections by meeting the 2% threshold.

The process of consolidation in the larger parties during the election campaign, and their uniting behind the common cause, ended abruptly once the votes had been counted. Disputes about the internal distribution of seats, differing views about coalition alternatives on both the national and local levels and personal rivalries between party functionaries became common features within most of the organisations. Internal splits within parties allowed some New Order officials to retain their positions by bribing dissident faction members, who opted for a neutral candidate and financial reward rather than hand victory to an internal party opponent (*Gatra*, 25 March 2000). The inclination of regional politicians to vote against the official party line has severely limited the influence central party boards can exert over their branches, obstructing the establishment of political parties as crucial elements in the institutional process.

Paradoxically, the fragmentation of the political parties in the regions was accompanied by the centralisation of authority in the hands of charismatic party leaders at the national level. Thus, while factions in local party branches often staged brutal campaigns against each other when the other side was suspected of violating the principles of democracy and transparency, at the national level authority was surrendered to the undisputed chairperson.

The party most confronted with regional fragmentation is the one that gained most votes in the general elections, Megawati's PDI-P. Equipped with comfortable majorities in many regency parliaments in Central and East Java, the party was suddenly forced to provide candidates for the administrative jobs available after the term of the New Order-appointed local governments had run out. The shortage of educated and skilled party officials to fill the position of regent or other senior posts in the administration opened the gate for external candidates with sufficient financial resources to secure support from segments of the local party branches. The power of these local dynamics overrode the influence of the central board to have its candidate elected. However, at the first PDI-P congress in Semarang in March 2000, fragmentation was pushed aside and loyalty shown to the party's chair, Megawati

Sukarnoputri, who was re-elected by acclamation and allowed to choose the composition of the central board. Party members who had argued that Megawati should concentrate on her duties as vice-president, or at least allow an open election with several candidates, were viewed as traitors (*Tempo*, 18 June 2000). Indeed the two main obstacles to the establishment of an institutional decision-making process within the PDI-P – the concentration of central authority in Megawati's hands and the fragmentation of the regional branches – were consolidated rather than solved by the congress.

Within Abdurrahman Wahid's party, the PKB, while the extent of centralisation of authority in the hands of its charismatic leader is similar to that experienced by the PDI-P, regional fragmentation is much less of a problem. Until the party congress in Surabaya in July 2000, the leadership of Matori Abdul Djalil had been challenged by local party leaders, as Abdurrahman had sent no convincing signals that he wanted Matori to serve another term as chair (*Tajuk*, 15 March 2000). East Java chair Choirul Anam ignored instructions from the central board regarding coalition arrangements for regency elections in East Java, leading to unexpected defeats such as the one in Jember (interview with Matori Abdul Djalil, 28 February 2000). Only after a series of disappointing election outcomes, for which Choirul had to take responsibility, did the central board prevail over the authority of the regional chairman. After the July 2000 election of Abdurrahman as supreme chair of the party, and the confirmation of Matori, the problems of further fragmentation seemed to cease. The problems for the PKB's institutional development resided in the overwhelming dependence on its leader. Using his cultural, historical and spiritual status as the patriarch of an NU dynasty, Abdurrahman not only ignored his party's decision to nominate Megawati for the presidency, but brushed aside statutes issued by the Surabaya congress to claim single authority to appoint the party's central board. Now holding a position similar to that once held by Soeharto within Golkar, Abdurrahman has expressed his determination to develop the PKB as his electoral machine to contest the upcoming general elections.

The party founded by Amien Rais, the National Mandate Party (PAN), has also experienced regional fragmentation and concentration of central authority since its establishment in August 1998. Splits within the party have led to prolonged crises in several branches. In the centre, Amien Rais had to balance pluralist and Islamist party elements, with the February 2000 congress in Yogyakarta avoiding open conflict only through Amien's determined intervention (*Forum Keadilan*, 13 February 2000). Amien has allowed open challenges to his bid for the chair and has ensured that the party's institutions become part of the decision-making process. His commitment to party reform has been overshadowed, however, by his uncontrolled political ambition and his reputation as a political opportunist (*Forum Keadilan*, 23 January 2000).

Golkar, for its part, has recovered from deep fragmentation after Habibie's defeat in the presidential elections. After threats by Habibie supporters to seek revenge, party chairman Akbar Tanjung was able to consolidate the Habibie-loyal eastern Indonesia chapters after a series of tactical successes. Lacking the cultural charisma of his three colleagues in the PDI-P, PKB and PAN, Akbar's authority within Golkar rests on his popularity as chair of the DPR and his political skills in managing the party.

Political parties in post-Soeharto Indonesia still function within the paradigm of personality-oriented politics, thus leaving open the possibility of disintegration should their various charismatic leaders leave the stage. They have neglected the development of institutional mechanisms to produce policy-oriented programs and have not provided a structural and organisational basis for the future leadership. At the same time, the lack of authority of the central boards over the regions obstructs the development of the political parties as national bodies socialising the policies of the centre and accommodating the aspirations of the regions. The paradox of charismatic power and structural weakness will continue to dominate Indonesian party politics at least until the current veteran leadership steps aside.

THE POLITICAL ECONOMY: THE FIGHT FOR RECOVERY AND ASSETS

The slow pace of constitutional and legal reform has contributed to the continued political instability that in turn constitutes the biggest obstacle to economic recovery. While the rise in exports generated moderate economic growth, no significant capital inflow occurred in the first year of the Abdurrahman presidency. Besides the institutional insecurity, it has been the fierce battle for economic assets between the political powers that has scared investors away. When the first Abdurrahman cabinet was formed in October 1999, all major political forces were given access to the economic assets controlled by the central government. The PDI-P gained control over economic policy and the state enterprises, the PAN was handed the Ministry of Finance with its authority over state banks, Golkar was granted the Ministry of Industry and Trade, the military maintained control over the mining sector, the PPP was given responsibility for social security policy, small enterprises and cooperatives, and the president claimed over-all authority over economic direction.

As these areas of responsibility occasionally overlapped, ministers of the rival political parties clashed over fundamental government policies, but in general there was a common understanding that every party had received a reasonable share of the economic cake. In November 1999, however, the president started to dismantle the joint agreement for equal economic distribution.

Hamzah Haz was the first minister to be dismissed; Laksamana Sukardi and Yusuf Kalla followed in April 2000 (*Tempo*, 28 May 2000). Kwik Kian Gie was put under the humiliating control of his own assistant, Dipo Alam (*Forum Keadilan*, 28 May 2000). The president placed loyalists in key economic positions, with his long-time political operator Rozy Munir taking control over state enterprises, and Luhut Panjahitan, once his favourite for the position of commander-in-chief, made Minister for Industry and Trade. Most delicately, his flamboyant younger brother Hashim Wahid took up an unspecified position at the banking restructuring agency IBRA (*Tempo*, 14 May 2000).

These controversial appointments raised concerns about the way Abdurrahman mobilised funds for his political machine. In the wake of the Bulog scandal and the affair of the 'private' donation from the Sultan of Brunei, the public was amazed to learn that large parts of the Brunei funds had ended up with the chairman of the PKB branch in Aceh, and that non-government organisations who had allegedly benefited from the funds had never actually received any money (*Tajuk*, 22 June 2000). Further insight into presidential financial practices was provided by reports in August that Abdurrahman's staff had handed a dubious British public relations adviser US$300,000 in cash. Presidential advisors were quick to assure the public that no state funds had been used, unaware that this statement provoked more questions than it answered (*Tempo*, 13 August 2000). With presidential intervention into the economic process mounting, the political parties saw their own access increasingly limited. They began to mobilise political opposition against the president in the form of calls to explain the dismissal of Laksamana and Kalla to the parliament, and constant threats to impeach the president at the annual MPR session in August 2000.

The president reacted nervously to the threats, with announcements of the imminent arrest of political troublemakers sending the exchange rate through the Rp 9,000 to the US dollar mark by early July. Attempting to ease tensions, Abdurrahman apologised to parliament for the problems created by Laksamana's and Kalla's dismissal, and promised in front of the MPR on 9 August to hand over daily administration of the government to Megawati. This masterful political manoeuvre pre-empted all attempts to unseat him, but only the most optimistic observers believed that it solved the long-term political problems.[8] In fact, the negotiations for the subsequent cabinet reshuffle – more a presidential monologue than political bargaining – proved that Abdurrahman was about to gain exclusive access to the economic assets of the country. When he told Amien that he would dismiss Bambang Sudibyo from the Finance Ministry, it was clear to the MPR chair that the president aimed at a cabinet of loyalists, with key economic ministries in the hands of personal friends. When Abdurrahman announced the new cabinet line-up on 23 August 2000, with the widely criticised Priyadi Praptosuhardjo as Minister of Finance and the equally problematic Rizal Ramli as Coordinating Minister for the Economy, the rupiah dropped by 400 points within hours (*Gatra*, 9 September 2000).

The background of this intense battle for control over economic assets is a collectively cultivated constituency cronyism in which political parties fight to satisfy their respective communities by granting them access to the distribution of material gains. Abdurrahman, for 15 years head of the NU, is under pressure from his constituency to use his powers to deliver the economic assets from which NU leaders felt excluded during the New Order period. Similar expectations towards their respective leaderships came from the nationalist lower-class constituency of the PDI-P and the modernist middle-class community voting for the PAN. The PDI-P-sponsored security forces in Central Javanese cities, consisting of the unskilled and underemployed male youth that gave the party victory in the elections, have engaged actively in protecting the businesses of their patrons. This battle for dominance over the economic infrastructure, combined with a lack of public accountability, constitutional control mechanisms and legal institutions, is likely to obstruct structural reform and thereby delay the country's economic recovery.

CONCLUSION: POLITICAL CONFLICT AND INSTITUTIONAL CRISIS

During a state visit to Chile in early October 2000, Abdurrahman claimed that Indonesia had succeeded in overcoming two fundamental problems. He said that the danger of separatism had been contained. He then pointed out that economic recovery had been achieved, boasting that the real problem was the inability of the existing infrastructure to accommodate the extraordinary extent of economic progress made since his coming to power (*Suara Merdeka*, 2 October 2000). The analysis of political developments during the first year of Abdurrahman's administration suggests that such a view is overly optimistic. The high level of political conflict among the elite has prevented significant progress in the major sectors of institutional, legal and military reform, with New Order-inherited problems of regional discontent remaining unresolved. The commitment to address fundamental issues of constitutional change has been subordinated to the main focus of the intra-elite power struggle – the political survival of the president. Without the reform of the constitutional system and a clear order regarding the relations between the state institutions, political instability will remain an institutionalised phenomenon. This institutionalised political disorder in turn constitutes the biggest obstacle to economic recovery and overshadows prospects for further democratisation in Indonesia.

NOTES

* I am grateful to Greg Fealy for helpful comments and detailed editing work. This is a condensed version of the original paper. Parts will appear in an extended form in a forthcoming Monash Asia Institute publication.

1 Among the scenarios debated was a Megawati presidency with Akbar Tanjung as her deputy. As early as January 2000 representatives of the Islamic parties had agreed that bringing Abdurrahman to power had been a huge miscalculation, and were ready to give Megawati a chance (*Tempo*, 23 April 2000).

2 Abdurrahman's government contributed only minor structural reforms to the process, with most of the measures initiated by the Habibie administration. Under Abdurrahman the dissolution of the traditionally military-dominated office of the Director-General for social–political affairs at the Ministry of the Interior in February 2000, and the abolition of the security board Bakorstanas in March, added to the decline in military authority in local politics (*Tajuk*, 15 March 2000).

3 See *Rancangan Undang-Undang Republik Indonesia Nomor () Tahun () Tentang Pertahanan Nasional*, Draft Juni 2000, Bab I: Ketentuan Umum, Pasal 1, Paragraf 1.

4 The 'new paradigm' for the military's position in Indonesian politics, presented by Wiranto in September 1998, was actually a recycled version of a concept developed in early 1997. Only after society's cool response to the concept did the TNI proceed a step further, in April 2000, by declaring that its socio-political function had ended and by endorsing civilian supremacy over the military (see ICG 2000a, p. 14).

5 The description of events is based on notes made by Syahril and published shortly before he was arrested. Neither Abdurrahman nor Marzuki have denied the accuracy of the account, but insisted that their actions had been 'misinterpreted' (*Tajuk*, 8 June 2000).

6 While both Abdurrahman and Marzuki denied that they used threats of legal consequences to force Syahril to resign, the tapes of telephone conversations of Syahril and Marzuki between March and May 2000 provide sufficient evidence that Marzuki traded the law against political interests (*Forum Keadilan*, 27 August 2000).

7 The two main targets of Abdurrahman's request were Ginandjar Kartasasmita and Fuad Bawazier. While both New Order ministers had been involved in a number of cases worthy of investigation, Abdurrahman pushed for legal steps only after they had been rumoured to be behind political manoeuvres aimed at the president's removal from office (*Forum Keadilan*, 27 August 2000).

8 How serious Abdurrahman was about sharing power with Megawati was underlined by his determined rejection of an MPR decree formalising the arrangement. At one point, he even threatened to allow the military to take over government if the MPR proceeded with its demand (*Forum Keadilan*, 20 August 2000).

4

THE ECONOMY IN 2000:
STILL FLAT ON ITS BACK?

Kelly Bird*

Indonesia's GDP grew moderately well in 2000, confirming that the country's economic recovery is gaining momentum. As a consequence, the government raised its official forecast of economic growth for the whole of 2000 from 3–4% to 4–5%. Although its recovery has been slower than that of other countries affected by the Asian crisis, Indonesia's most recent growth rates are similar to those reported for Thailand. Economic recovery in 2000 was led by a rebound in consumer spending and export growth. Retail, auto and motorcycle sales all grew at double-digit rates. Non-oil exports reached record levels and were more than 26% higher than in 1999. In fact, manufacturing exports grew faster in Indonesia than in most other Asian countries in 2000. New investments, however, remained low, and the restarting of foreign and domestic investment will be critical for sustaining economic recovery over the medium term and creating jobs for Indonesians. Indonesia's sluggish investment rates are probably due mainly to delays in restructuring corporate debt and the fragile banking sector. Continuing concerns about poor security, the uncertain political situation and the rule of law may also be factors deterring new investment.

REAL SECTOR RECOVERY

After the massive decline in real GDP – which the Central Statistics Agency (BPS) estimated to be 13.7% lower in 1998 than in 1997 – positive economic growth has been sustained since the fourth quarter of 1999. The economy grew by 5.1% in the third quarter of 2000, up from 4.5% in the second quarter and 4.0% in the first quarter. Based on these trends, growth for the entire year should be about 5.0%.[1] A notable characteristic of the recovery is that those sectors with large tradable components – for example manufacturing –

did not contract as much as non-tradable sectors and have more or less recovered to their pre-crisis levels (Table 4.1). For instance, levels of agricultural and mining output were close to pre-crisis levels and the manufacturing sector stood at 96.2% of its 1997 level. On the other hand, levels of output of the construction and commerce sectors in the first three quarters of 2000 were about 67% and 87% respectively of 1997 levels, although the pace of recovery in these sectors was increasing. This asymmetric response is to be expected given the substantial real depreciation of the rupiah, which by the end of November 2000 was 50% lower than in June 1997. The steep depreciation in the rupiah has made it more profitable to produce tradable than non-tradable goods.

Figure 4.1 documents Indonesia's progress relative to the three other countries most seriously affected by the currency crisis. Indonesia had by far the largest fall in GDP in 1998 and was the slowest to recover in 1999. However, its recent economic growth rates are similar to those reported for Thailand, which appear to have settled at around the 5% rate. In contrast, Korea and Malaysia have made rapid recoveries and their real GDP rates surpassed pre-crisis levels well before the first quarter of 2000.

FIGURE 4.1 Regional Economic Growth Rates, 1997(Q1)–2000(Q3) (year-on-year, %)

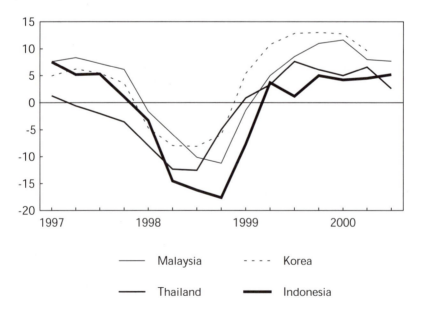

Source: National Income Accounts.

TABLE 4.1 GDP Relative to Pre-crisis Levels

Sector	1st Three Quarters 1998 Relative to 1st Three Quarters 1997	1st Three Quarters 1999 Relative to 1st Three Quarters 1997	1st Three Quarters 2000 Relative to 1st Three Quarters 1997
Production			
Agriculture	96.8	99.5	98.4
Mining	95.8	96.2	98.9
Manufacturing	90.3	91.1	96.2
Oil	101.9	109.2	112.7
Non-oil	89.0	89.1	94.4
Agro-processing	105.3	110.0	109.6
Textiles, footwear & leather products	85.3	83.9	90.4
Wood products	77.0	61.8	90.5
Paper & printing	94.1	96.4	101.7
Fertilisers, chemicals	79.3	88.5	97.8
Non-metallic products	67.7	69.3	76.6
Iron & steel	76.2	69.2	73.9
Machinery	49.8	36.1	88.9
Electricity & utilities	102.6	111.4	119.1
Construction	60.3	60.6	66.9
Commerce	85.7	82.2	86.7
Transport & communications	83.8	83.8	92.3
Finance & business	96.8	73.6	77.8
Expenditure			
Consumption			
Household	95.9	98.9	101.5
Government	86.3	87.9	93.2
Investment	70.1	51.8	58.7
Exports	132.6	79.8	93.8
Imports	111.9	60.2	64.5
Total GDP	88.3	87.5	91.5

Source: BPS.

Like the rest of Asia, Indonesia's economic recovery in 2000 has been driven by consumer spending and export growth. Table 4.1 illustrates that household consumption did not fall as sharply as investment and exports; it has grown since the second quarter of 1999 and by the third quarter of 2000 was 1.5% above pre-crisis levels. According to the BPS national income accounts, exports and fixed investment continued to fall until the middle of 1999 but began to grow rapidly in the first semester of 2000. By the third quarter of 2000, total exports were almost back to their 1997 level, but investment was still only 59% of the pre-crisis level. However, the export figures in the national income accounts appear to overstate the fall in exports in 1999, and a recent study by Rosner (2000) shows that real exports (export volumes) actually expanded by 20% between June 1997 and December 1999.

Consistent with the official national income accounts, other more specific indicators show that economic recovery in 2000 has been led by consumer spending and export growth. Indeed, real sector indicators suggest that the economy may be growing faster than has been generally thought. Some of these indicators are reviewed below.

ECONOMIC INDICATORS

Industrial Production

Electricity consumption by industry is a good indirect indicator of industrial production (Figure 4.2). Consistent with the contraction in industrial output, electricity sales to industry fell in 1998. Consumption began to grow from the second quarter of 1999 and continued to grow rapidly in 2000; electricity sales to industry grew by 10% in the first 11 months of 2000 over the same period in 1999, indicating a pick-up in economic activity during this period. The growth in consumption slowed in the second quarter of 2000, but this was primarily due to an April increase in electricity tariffs of some 60%.

Consumer Spending

Indicators show that consumer spending continued to grow rapidly in 2000. Indexes of consumer spending on both food and non-food items have almost recovered to their pre-crisis levels (Figure 4.3). This recovery began in the last quarter of 1999 and accelerated in 2000.[2] These indexes are consistent with other data on retail sales. For example, the Indonesian Retailers Association reports that retail sales by the modern markets (adjusted for inflation) were up 20% in 2000. In its interim financial report, PT Matahari, a large department store chain, reported a rise in sales of 26% in the first half of 2000. Interest-

FIGURE 4.2 Electricity Consumption by Industry and Business, January
1996 – November 2000 (kWh billion)

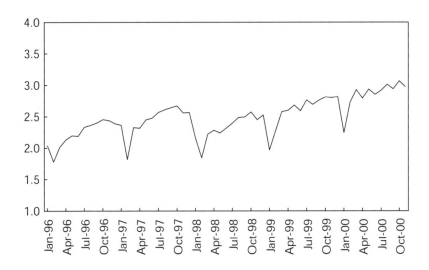

Source: PLN.

ingly, sales were up 9% in Jakarta, but 22% in comparable stores outside
Jakarta. Other corroborating evidence of renewed business confidence in the
consumer market segment was the recovery in advertising expenditures.
Recent data show that advertising expenditure in the first semester of 2000,
also adjusted for inflation, was about 45% above expenditure in the same
period in 1999 (ACNielsen).

Contrary to the popular view that most of the increase in consumer spending was on necessities like food and clothing, automobile sales grew rapidly
in 2000; by June they had recovered to their 1996 levels (Figure 4.4). Part of
the rebound in auto sales was probably due to purchases deferred in 1998.
Sales are therefore expected to level off over the next year, as they appear to
have done in Thailand and Malaysia. Automobiles are typically purchased by
higher-income families and by businesses, so auto sales may not be indicative
of the spending power of lower-income groups. However, sales of motorcycles – which are predominantly purchased by the lower and middle-income
groups – also picked up in 2000 (Figure 4.4). The sales figures for 2000
shown in Figure 4.4 do not include imports of motorbikes from China, which
are estimated to be around 125,000 (or about 11% of total domestic sales).
This surge in consumer spending occurred despite tensions among the politi-

FIGURE 4.3 Indexes of Consumer Spending, 1997(Q2)–2000(Q2)
(1997(Q2) – 100)

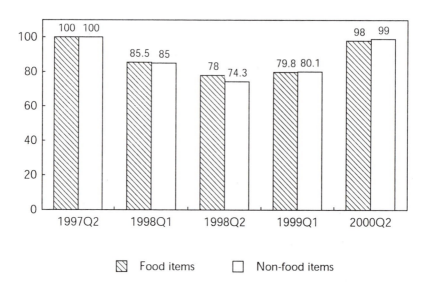

Source: ACNielsen-Indonesia.

cal elite, especially leading up to the annual session of the People's Consultative Assembly (MPR) in August 2000. This is consistent with the view
expressed by some economists that consumers and businesses are becoming
more resilient with regard to the political situation in Indonesia.

Non-oil Exports

Indonesia's non-oil export performance in 2000 was the best ever recorded.
Not only were Indonesia's exports 16% higher in value (in US dollars) than
in the first semester of 1997, they were also growing much faster than non-oil
exports in neighbouring countries (Figures 4.5 and 4.6). Exports of manufactured goods fared even better and are now 31% higher than in 1997. A significant proportion of recent growth in Indonesia has been in the electronics
sector, where monthly exports have more than doubled since February 2000
and total exports for the first seven months of the year were 88% above their
level in the same period of 1997. The recent export boom in electronic goods
appears to be due to expansions undertaken by both Korean and Japanese producers to take advantage of Indonesia's improved comparative advantage in

FIGURE 4.4 Domestic Auto and Motorcycle Sales, January 1996 –
November 2000 (thousand units)

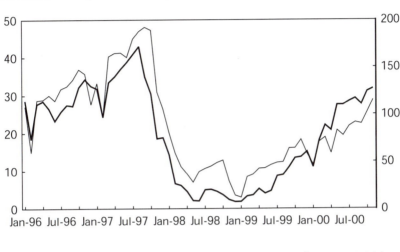

━━━━ Autos (left-hand side)   ━━━━ Motorcycles (right-hand side)

Sources: Association of Automotive Assemblers and Manufacturers; Association of Motorcycle
Assemblers and Manufacturers.

this sector. Exports of other manufactured goods also performed well. Chemicals and machinery both experienced very high growth in the first semester of 2000 relative to the first semester of 1997. Traditional exports such as textiles and garments held up well.

The sudden surge in exports in 2000 indicated that the benefits of a highly depreciated real rupiah exchange rate, relative macroeconomic stabilisation and an easing of political tensions were beginning to show. However, this export boom partly reflected a 'catch-up' based on Indonesia's improved competitiveness due to the real exchange rate depreciation. Thus, the extremely high growth rates in the first part of 2000 are not likely to be sustained over the medium term, and we would expect rates of export growth to converge back towards their historical levels. The success of the export sector also reflected the dynamic benefits of trade liberalisation and industry deregulation, which began in the mid-1980s. These reforms greatly improved competitiveness and helped create a private sector that could respond to adverse economic conditions.

Indonesia's export incentive – as measured by its real exchange rate – is far more favourable to producers than is the case with its major regional com-

FIGURE 4.5 Regional Growth in Non-oil Exports, 1999–2000 (%)[a]

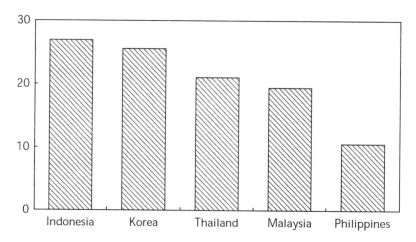

a Measured in US dollars. Exports for Indonesia and Korea refer to the first semester of 2000
   compared with the same period in 1999; exports for Thailand refer to January–May 2000 compared with the same period in 1999; exports for the Philippines refer to January–April 2000
   compared with the same period in 1999.

FIGURE 4.6 Regional Growth in Non-oil Exports, 1997–2000 (%)[a]

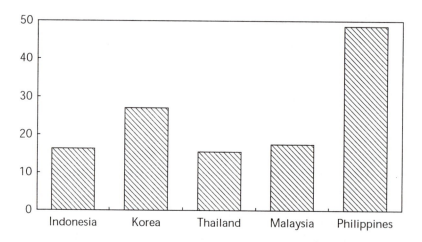

a Measured in US dollars. Exports for Indonesia and Korea refer to the first semester of 2000
   compared with the same period in 1997; exports for Thailand refer to January–May 2000 compared with the same period in 1997; exports for the Philippines refer to January–April 2000
   compared with the same period in 1997.

petitors. As of November 2000, the rupiah had fallen about 14% more than the Thai baht, the Philippine peso and the Malaysian ringgit, and was over 25% lower than the Korean won.

Investment

Investment was hard hit by the economic contraction of 1998 and has been slow to recover (Table 4.1). Indicators of investment activity in Indonesia suggest that little investment has occurred, and that little is planned in the near term. Approvals, both foreign and domestic, remain at historically low levels. Imports of capital goods are showing signs of a turnaround in the fourth quarter of 2000, but remain well below pre-crisis levels (Figure 4.7). The import data do not, however, include imports of goods to firms in the export-processing zones (EPZs), which Bank Indonesia estimated were growing rapidly. According to Bank Indonesia estimates, imports to EPZs rose from US$6.9 billion in 1998 to US$8.9 in 1999, a 25% increase. Imports for the first quarter of 2000 stood at US$3 billion – suggesting a figure of US$12 billion for the year – some proportion of which would have been capital goods. Imports of capital goods by firms producing for the domestic market were nevertheless low.[3] One bright spot on the investment front has been the recovery of

FIGURE 4.7 Imports of Capital Goods (US$ million)

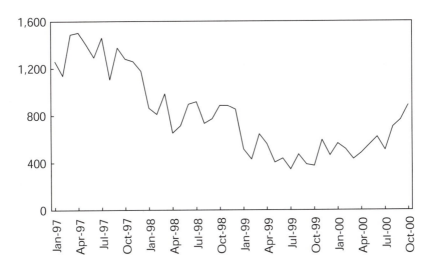

Source: Trade statistics.

FIGURE 4.8 Cement Sales to the Domestic Market, January 1996 – November 2000 (million tons)

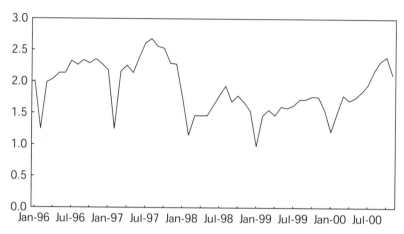

Source: Indonesian Cement Producers Association.

cement sales to the domestic market, indicating higher levels of construction activity. Cement consumption grew by 20% in the first 11 months of 2000 compared with the same period in 1999 (Figure 4.8). Evidently part of this growth in cement demand was driven by the retail sector, through an increase in new housing starts and home renovations as well as government spending on infrastructure.

The low investment rate is not surprising given that there is excess production capacity – investment activity is typically the last to pick up during a recovery. At current rates of growth in consumer spending and exports, some industries should soon be approaching full capacity; renewed investment activity will be crucial in sustaining this growth over the medium term. So far, bank credit expansion has been negligible[4] – as has also been the case in Thailand, Malaysia and Korea – in part because of the weakness of the banking system, but also because thousands of corporations still have unrestructured loans with the Indonesian Banking Restructuring Agency (IBRA). This has created much uncertainty for creditors and investors. Continuing concerns about political and social instability have also deterred businesses from undertaking major new investments.

There are two pertinent questions about the pattern of economic recovery in 2000. First, how could domestic consumer spending suddenly surge when the economy was in deep recession throughout 1998 and most of 1999? Second, how could firms finance their activities when the domestic banking system remained stagnant?

The answer to the first question lies partly in the normal business cycle. When economic fundamentals worsen, there is often a drastic initial effect, followed by a partial recovery. This is called the 'accelerator principle', and explains why even the worst slumps are normally followed by a spontaneous partial rebound. The recent surge in exports should also raise consumer spending further through the 'multiplier effect'.[5] But there are several other factors that have contributed to the recent recovery.

First, part of the rise in consumer demand in 1999 and 2000 is probably attributable to deferred spending from 1998. Consumer expectations were extremely low in 1998 and early 1999; Indonesians were uncertain about their future income prospects and concerned about the political environment. High interest rates also dampened consumer spending. As interest rates fell and confidence began to edge higher, consumers began to save less and spend more.

Second, in early 1998 many companies (including some exporters) lost their lines of credit from domestic banks. This meant that they were short of cash to support their operations, and for some it meant reducing production even further. Over time, however, firm owners found ways to overcome this problem. They borrowed from family and friends, used accumulated savings to finance core activities, and ploughed back a larger proportion of retained earnings in their companies.

This provides a partial answer to our second question as well, of how firms were able to finance their activities at a time when the domestic banking system remained stagnant – the non-performing loans of domestic banks were persistently high at around 34% of total loans, and there was little credit expansion in the first semester of 2000. But the explanation also lies in the pattern of economic recovery. The Indonesian data are consistent with a recovery in the tradable goods sector (especially exports of manufactured goods) and a sluggish recovery in the non-tradable goods sector (the commerce and construction sectors). There is anecdotal evidence that major exporters are financing expansion through both retained earnings and (in some cases) access to international capital. Certainly, given export performance over the past year, trade finance does not appear to be a major constraint facing established major exporters. A few 'quality borrowers' producing for the domestic market are tapping the domestic bond market. Large consumer goods producers – *kretek* producer Sampoerna and noodle producer Indofood among others – have successfully raised funds this year by selling rupiah-denominated bonds. In contrast, most firms producing for the domestic market, especially those producing in the non-tradable sector, appear to have relied on retained earnings and savings to fund their activities. This phenomenon has also been reported for other countries that have experienced banking crises, most notably Mexico (Krueger and Tornell 1999).

SUSTAINING THE ECONOMIC RECOVERY

Indonesia has made a partial recovery from the economic crisis, as predicted in a Bappenas White Paper in mid-1999 (Bappenas 1999). However, it needs sustained economic growth to create jobs for those made redundant by the crisis and for the growing pool of new entrants in the labour market (estimated at 2–3 million per year). Higher economic growth over the medium term depends crucially on stimulating investment. In this regard the major policy challenges to any sustainable economic recovery will include achieving fiscal sustainability, maintaining price stability and resolving the corporate debt overhang.

Fiscal Sustainability

A major challenge facing the Indonesian government over the medium term is fiscal sustainability, defined here as a reduction in the debt burden (debt as a ratio of GDP). Total government debt rose from 23% of GDP in March 1997 to 90% of GDP in 2000. However, contrary to the common perception, foreign debt increased only modestly, from US$51 billion in 1997 to US$66 billion in 2000 (Figure 4.9). The present ratio of external debt to GDP is comparable to the 1990 level in Indonesia, and to that of the Philippines and Malaysia at the end of the 1980s. The bulk of the increase in total government debt stems from the government's bank restructuring program, estimated at US$81 billion (Rp 650 trillion at US$1 = Rp 8,000) in rupiah-denominated bonds issued to recapitalise banks and compensate Bank Indonesia for liquidity credits (Figure 4.9).

Public debt imposes a heavy burden on government finances – total debt servicing obligations were estimated to be close to US$10 billion in 2000 (about 44% of total budget revenues), of which about US$6 billion was the interest cost on domestic bonds alone (World Bank 2000a). This has severely constrained both public expenditure on infrastructure, education and health as well as the flexibility of fiscal policy. While the government's debt level is large, it is manageable – Malaysia, Mexico and the Philippines, with similar government debt levels at the end of the 1980s, succeeded in reducing them to sustainable levels. However, the fiscal budget, and therefore government debt, is extremely vulnerable to changes in the macroeconomic environment, whether these be increases in interest rates, a sharp depreciation of the rupiah or a slowdown in economic growth.[6]

FIGURE 4.9 Central Government Debt, 1996/97–2000 (US$ billion)

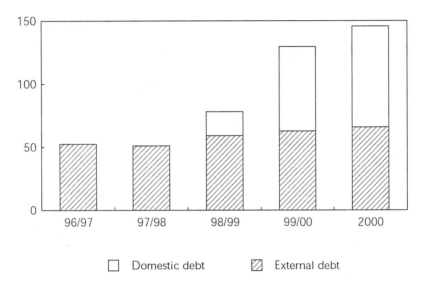

□ Domestic debt   ▨ External debt

Source: World Bank (2000a).

The government is of course well aware of its tenuous fiscal position and ran a conservative fiscal budget in 2000.[7] Indeed, the overall fiscal deficit is expected to be well below the 5% projected in the 2000 draft budget, which assumed a primary fiscal surplus of 1.5% of GDP and interest costs on government debt of 6.5% of GDP (Fane 2000). The expected improvement in the primary fiscal surplus is mainly due to high oil prices, which have averaged around $28 per barrel this year compared to the 2000 draft budget assumption of $20, but also due to lower than expected current expenditures (*Jakarta Post*, 6 September 2000).

The 2001 draft budget, announced on 2 October 2000, projects a budget deficit of 3.7%. Important features of the budget included an increase in fuel prices by an average of 12% in October 2000 with plans for a further increase in April 2001. Financing of the deficit would come from three main sources: privatisation of state enterprises (Rp 5 trillion), asset sales under the IBRA (Rp 27 trillion) and donor country funding.

While the IBRA achieved its Rp 18 trillion target for the 2000 financial year, its progress on asset sales to date has been disappointing. The government postponed a number of planned sales, including those of Bank Central Asia and Bank Niaga. The slow pace of sales is partly due to the government's reluctance to dispose of assets at so-called 'fire sale' prices. The IBRA's view is that the value of assets will rise with economic recovery and thus that it will be able to achieve better prices by postponing sales to a later date. International experience suggests that this is not the case – the longer a government-run asset management unit (AMU) such as the IBRA holds onto assets, the greater their depreciation in value and the larger the opportunity cost to the government in the future (Stone 1998). This is because the owners (or AMU-appointed managers) do not have the right profit incentives to maintain asset values for a government-run AMU. Moreover, investors and creditors are reluctant to provide financing or equity when there is uncertainty over the ownership of assets. Consequently, the asset values depreciate even when the economy is growing and the value of comparable assets in the private sector is rising.

Perhaps an even more difficult task facing the Indonesian government is the privatisation of state-owned enterprises. Initially it announced that 10 state enterprises would be privatised between April and December 2000, including two mining companies, two pharmaceutical companies, a plantation and a trading company. Nine other companies (including blocks of shares in Telkom and Sarinah department store) were put on a standby list for sale in case the first 10 did not sell. However, none of the 10 companies nor any of the reserve companies were privatised in 2000. Senior government finance officials explained to parliament that economic and security problems had hampered privatisation efforts and that the government did not want to receive a 'fire sale' price (*Jakarta Post*, 6 September 2000). Nonetheless, privatisation is politically unpopular, in part because many Indonesians feel that state enterprises are national assets that should not be sold to private enterprises, but also because full privatisation puts an end to hidden cross-subsidies to employees, favoured customers and suppliers.

Apart from their key role in financing the budget deficit, the privatisation of state enterprises and the sale of assets under the IBRA will be important in ensuring that any economic recovery is sustainable. Accelerating privatisation and IBRA asset sales would be a major factor in changing investor perceptions about both the Indonesian government's commitment to its economic recovery strategy and the country's medium-term economic prospects. The asset sales would attract net capital inflows, and this in turn would strengthen the rupiah. Large discounts on initial IBRA asset sales would be expected (as has been the case in most other countries with a similar experience), but these would diminish once investor interest increased and the sale process was seen to be transparent and credible.

Another important feature of the 2001 draft budget is the transfer of 25% of total budget revenues to local municipalities and city councils under the decentralisation laws due to be implemented in 2001. This is an area of great uncertainty. While the revenue transfers have been provided for in the budget, it is still unclear how the expenditure functions will be transferred to the regions. The central government needs to ensure that the transfer of expenditure responsibilities is carried out with minimal disruption to the provision of public services in the regions.

The bank recapitalisation program is nearing completion (Table 4.2). The government has announced that it intends to finalise the recapitalisation of the last state-owned banks – Bank Nasional Indonesia, Bank Rakyat Indonesia and Bank Tabungan Indonesia – as well as the bank merger between the nationalised Bank Danamon and several other smaller banks taken over by the

TABLE 4.2 Progress on Bank Restructuring as of December 2000

Initiative	Outcome
Bank restructuring program	
Bank closures/takeovers	69 of 237 banks
Bank mergers	4 of 7 state banks
Nationalisations	13 banks
Bank recapitalisation program	Banks recapitalised through issue of government bonds
Estimated cost of entire program	Rp 650 trillion
Asset resolution strategy under AMI[a]	
Assets transferred to AMI	Rp 120.5 trillion[b]
Restructuring of NPLs under AMC[a]	
Number of debtors	1,689
Book value of loans transferred to AMC	Rp 256 trillion
Loan recoveries	Rp 15.4 trillion
Restructured loans	Rp 13.0 trillion
Proportion of total NPLs at IBRA	8%

a The IBRA comprises two major divisions, asset management investment (AMI) and asset management credit (AMC). AMI is responsible for asset recoveries; AMC is responsible for the sale and restructuring of non-performing loans (NPLs).
b Includes assets pledged by banks taken over by the IBRA as a guarantee for Bank Indonesia liquidity credits in 1998 (Rp 112 trillion) and Rp 8 trillion in non-core bank assets. Loans transferred from banks to the IBRA amount to Rp 256 trillion. Thus the total book value of assets/loans transferred to the IBRA amounts to about Rp 376 trillion. This figure does not include the IBRA's bonds in recapitalised banks.

Source: IBRA monthly reports.

FIGURE 4.10 Growth in Base Money (annualised, %) and Monthly
Inflation (%), June 1998 – November 2000

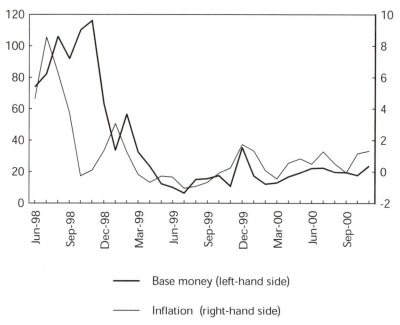

Source: Bank Indonesia, *Financial Statistics*.

government in 1998. It has also agreed to recapitalise Bank Bali following
agreement by the former owner, Rudy Ramli, to drop legal action against the
government. With these banks recapitalised, the total cost of bonds issued
under the program is expected to reach Rp 650 trillion (US$81 million at an
exchange rate of US$1 = Rp 8,000).

Price and Exchange Rate Stability

Inflation rose to 9.3% in 2000, causing some concern that inflationary pressures are accelerating. McLeod (2000a) points out that the recent increase in
underlying inflationary pressures is partly due to the acceleration in the
growth of money supply in recent months.

Figure 4.10 presents annualised money supply growth rates and monthly
inflation rates since June 1998.[8] It shows that the downward trend in money
supply growth was lost at the end of the third quarter of 1999. The annualised
growth rate increased from a low of 6.5% in July 1999 to 22% in July 2000.

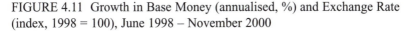

FIGURE 4.11 Growth in Base Money (annualised, %) and Exchange Rate (index, 1998 = 100), June 1998 – November 2000

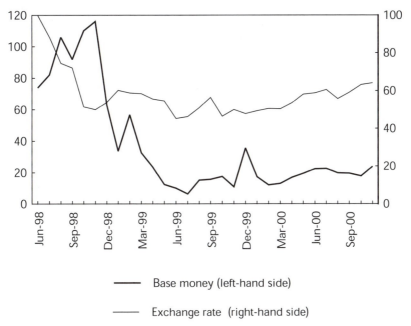

————— Base money (left-hand side)

————— Exchange rate (right-hand side)

Source: Bank Indonesia, *Financial Statistics*.

Not surprisingly, the recent acceleration in money supply growth corresponds closely with rising retail price inflation. World Bank country director Mark Baird is reported as saying that Bank Indonesia would need to manage monetary policy better in order to keep inflation under control (*Observer*, 12 September 2000).

Figure 4.11 shows that the strong recovery in the rupiah exchange rate in the latter part of 1998 and in 1999 was not sustained in 2000. By the end of the year, the rupiah had depreciated by about 33% from its January 2000 level – far more than other major currencies in the region. The impact of this depreciation has been multifaceted. Whereas it has made tradable goods more profitable to produce and thus encouraged exports, it has also raised the rupiah cost of servicing external debt for corporations, thus reducing the profitability of non-exporting firms and delaying progress on corporate debt restructuring.

Recent volatility in the rupiah is partly due to political factors. Growing investor concerns over political and social stability leading up to the MPR session in August 2000 increased the risk premium of holding rupiah, thus contributing to the currency's sharp fall. The equally sharp recovery – from a low of Rp 9,500 to the US dollar just before the MPR session to Rp 8,200 after it became apparent that the president would not be impeached – confirms that some of the recent volatility has been due to political uncertainty. While political and security factors may help explain sharp, temporary jumps in the rupiah exchange rate, they do not explain the systematic weakening of the rupiah since October 1999. As McLeod (2000a, p. 19) correctly points out, the weakening of the rupiah throughout 2000 corresponds closely to the slackening of monetary control during this period. This positive correlation between money supply growth and rupiah depreciation is clearly depicted in Figure 4.11.

Where excessive money supply expansion is the major cause of currency depreciation and inflation, the appropriate response by monetary authorities is to reduce growth in money supply and, thus, allow interest rates to rise. Interest rates on Bank Indonesia bonds (SBIs) did increase in 2000, from under 11% in February to 14.9% by December. But, as McLeod (2000a) points out, Bank Indonesia appears to be reluctant to raise SBI rates sufficiently high, for fear of the impact this would have both on its own interest costs – Bank Indonesia issues debt in the form of SBIs – and on the cost to the government of servicing the enormous volume of bonds it has issued to recapitalise the banking system.

Corporate Debt Restructuring

The issue of restructuring corporate debt, both foreign and domestic, is central to Indonesia's recovery, and was at the heart of disagreements with the International Monetary Fund (IMF) in 2000. The corporate sector remains highly leveraged, with a relatively high external debt of around US$64 billion (World Bank 2000a). A large proportion of this debt remains in default. The recent rebound in the real sector has improved the cash flow of many companies, and this should allow some of them to work their way out of debt. But for many other firms, some form of corporate restructuring will be needed to improve their balance sheets.

Indonesia's private debt resolution framework comprises the IBRA, which has the task of assisting the Indonesian government in its banking sector restructuring and recapitalisation program, and the Jakarta Initiative, a private agency that mediates between debtors and creditors to negotiate solutions outside the court system. While the IBRA is primarily concerned with implementing the government's bank restructuring program, it has also become a major player in corporate debt restructuring by virtue of the fact that as much as Rp 256 trillion in non-performing loans has been transferred to it from domestic banks (Table 4.2).

While the number of deals reached on corporate debt has risen in recent months, progress has been painfully slow relative to other crisis-hit countries, most notably Korea and Thailand. Recent estimates indicate that as of December 2000, only about 17–21% of Indonesia's external debt was at any stage of restructuring, and probably less than half of this had actually been restructured in the sense that debtors had completed implementing the terms of their debt deals (Bird 2000). About US\$9.4 billion of this debt was subject to some form of restructuring under the Jakarta Initiative and possibly another \$3–4 billion had been restructured outside the resolution framework (Table 4.3). According to the IBRA, as of December 2000 about 74% of the total book value of loans of the 21 largest debtors (Rp 88 trillion) was covered by memorandums of understanding (MOUs), although only about 15% of this amount had actually been restructured (Table 4.2). This compares unfavourably with surrounding countries, where success in restructuring debt has reduced uncertainty, restarted capital flows and underpinned recovery. In addition, the

TABLE 4.3 Progress on Restructuring of Corporate External Debt as of December 2000

Settlement	Value/Proportion
Out of court settlements	
Under Jakarta Initiative	
Implemented or agreed debt restructuring	US\$9.4 billion
Proportion of total external debt	15%
Outside Jakarta Initiative	
Implemented or agreed debt restructuring	US\$3–4 billion[a]
Proportion of total private external debt	5–6%
Court settlements	
Restructured debt/liquidations	37 cases[b]
All settlements	
Proportion of total private debt restructured or under restructuring agreement	17–21%

a Author's estimates, based on media reports, securities firms' reports and industry interviews.
b Includes enterprises holding domestic debt.

Source: Adapted from Bird (2000), based on data from the Jakarta Initiative, World Bank and author's survey.

World Bank (2000b) recently questioned the quality of some of the MOUs signed between the IBRA and large debtors on the grounds that they do not reflect commercially viable debt-restructuring plans. Many of the deals primarily involve the rescheduling of repayments of principal rather than actual restructuring, and are unlikely to return the companies to a manageable debt level. The risk is that many of these loans may again become non-performing a few years down the track. A wider range of debt restructuring is required to minimise this risk, including debt–equity swaps and the sale of assets.

In response to slow progress in debt restructuring as well as pressure from the IMF, the Indonesian government introduced several new policy initiatives in early 2000. It established the Financial Sector Policy Committee (FSPC) as an interministerial committee to oversee the work of the IBRA and the Jakarta Initiative. One of the first rulings of the FSPC was to permit the IBRA to engage in a full range of debt-restructuring methods, including debt for equity conversions and debt forgiveness. The FSPC also strengthened the Jakarta Initiative's mediation procedures, introducing several 'sticks' to induce recalcitrant debtors to negotiate with creditors in good faith.[9] For example, debtors who refuse to negotiate in good faith under the Jakarta Initiative can now be referred to the Attorney General for the initiation of bankruptcy proceedings. The FSPC has also introduced a 'one-stop' service to remove any regulatory and taxation obstacles to debt-restructuring deals concluded between creditors and debtors.

While these changes have helped to strengthen and accelerate the restructuring process, they are unlikely to bring recalcitrant debtors and creditors to the negotiating table. The main problem is a legal/political one: very few debtors have been successfully liquidated through the courts. By mid-2000, only about 37 firms had been restructured or made bankrupt through the commercial courts (Table 4.3). Most of the bankrupt firms were relatively small, and no large debtors have been restructured by the courts. In almost all the instances where the IBRA was the plaintiff applying to a commercial court for the liquidation of a non-cooperative debtor, the court ruled in favour of the debtor. Clearly the bankruptcy court has been ineffective in liquidating non-cooperative debtors or acting as a credible threat to delinquent debtors. In part this has been due to a lack of expertise by the courts in handling bankruptcy cases, but endemic corruption in the legal system has played a bigger part.

A number of minor changes have been made to the court system to improve transparency, but these do not appear to be working effectively. One recent change was to replace most judges in Jakarta with those from outside Jakarta, presumably because they were thought to be less corrupt. A second change was the appointment of ad hoc judges to the commercial courts, although initially they were not permitted to participate in bankruptcy proceedings as a result of a dispute with the Supreme Court, which refused to publish dissenting judges' legal opinions.

CONCLUSION

Indicators of economic activity suggest that the Indonesian economy grew more strongly in 2000 than has generally been appreciated. Growth was driven by record exports and a strong rebound in consumer spending on non-durable and durable goods. Maintaining the momentum of recovery in 2001 and beyond will depend on an improved environment for domestic and foreign investors. One problem that has inhibited a recovery in investment is the large stock of unrestructured corporate debt. Resolution of this problem will be critical for achieving high, sustainable growth over the medium term. There are other significant risks to recovery, including inflationary pressures, an uncertain political situation and external factors. Any further slowdown in the US economy will almost certainly affect Indonesian exports, especially of electronics, and thereby dampen economic growth in 2001.

NOTES

* The opinions and views expressed in this paper are the author's alone and should not be attributed to any of his affiliated institutions. The author is, of course, solely responsible for any errors.

1 The economic growth rates for the first two quarters of 2000 have been revised upwards since their first publication by BPS. First quarter economic growth was revised up from 3.2% to 4.0%, and second quarter growth rate from 4.2% to 4.5%.

2 The source of these data is ACNielsen, which surveys sales of more than 1,200 small and large retail outlets in the 12 major urban centres every quarter.

3 There is anecdotal evidence of efficient import substitution arising from the more favourable rupiah exchange rate. For example, domestic demand for automobile spare parts appears to have shifted from imported to locally produced parts.

4 Bank Indonesia's June 2000 lending survey of 15 banks representing 75% of total bank deposits found that Rp 15.8 trillion of new loans had been extended since the beginning of 2000 – a modest increase of 5% for the first half of the year. As this figure included both loan renewals and restructured loans, genuinely new lending was likely to have been less than reported (World Bank 2000b, p. 10).

5 An increase in exports raises incomes, which in turn increases consumer spending.

6 A recent World Bank (2000a) study on government debt in Indonesian estimated that a one percentage point increase in the SBI rate would increase the cost of servicing domestic debt by Rp 4 trillion annually, or 0.3% of GDP. The same study highlighted the need to achieve rapid economic growth. It showed that to reduce

government debt from 90% to 67% of GDP in five years would require economic growth of 6% per year; the government would need to run primary fiscal surpluses of 2% of GDP per year and reach its revenue targets for the sale of IBRA assets and the privatisation of state-owned enterprises. Economic growth of 3% per year, a primary fiscal surplus of 1% of GDP and recovery of only half of the targeted revenues, on the other hand, would not be sufficient to reduce the debt burden below 90% of GDP.

7   See Wallace (1999) for an analysis of the government's fiscal response to the crisis.
8   Money supply is measured by base money, which is the sum of currency in circu-lation, cash held by banks in Bank Indonesia's vault and demand deposits in the banking system.
9   In addition: (1) non-IBRA-led cases can be transferred to the Jakarta Initiative for restructuring; (2) the Jakarta Initiative has introduced time-bound mediation pro-cedures for debtors and creditors; and (3) the Jakarta Initiative can refer non-coop-erative debtors to the FSPC for review.

PART II

POLITICAL HISTORY

5

BRIEF REFLECTIONS ON INDONESIAN POLITICAL HISTORY

R.E. Elson

Indonesian politics has been poorly served by historians. Most of the seminal books were contemporary of their time – one thinks of Anderson's *Java in a Time of Revolution*, Feith's *Decline of Constitutional Democracy*, Crouch's *Army and Politics in Indonesia* or even Robison's *Indonesia: The Rise of Capital* – and written by scholars whose primary intellectual affiliation was not the study of history. One struggles to think of more than a handful of major works on the history of Indonesian politics.

There are numerous reasons why this is so. The practice of the discipline of history is generally very weak in Indonesia,[1] which means that there has been – apart from odd sensationalist newspaper and magazine exchanges about such things as who really found the generals' bodies at Lubang Buaya or the whereabouts of the missing Supersemar letter – little sign of intellectual excitement or historical debate about the country's politics. More importantly, perhaps, Indonesia has never been a place that made historical research on modern themes easy, especially for foreigners. With a few exceptions, government archives on the post-1945 period remain closed to domestic and foreign researchers; continuous runs of Indonesian newspapers are difficult to find; and obtaining interviews requires stamina, patience and even courage, as well as well-placed local go-betweens – and that before the interview has even begun. There is, finally, the supreme difficulty of the subject matter itself; the political history of modern Indonesia is a cascade of related and unrelated themes and plots, a whirling kaleidoscope of people, emotion, interests, skulduggery, nobility and violence not lending itself readily to interpretation.

This, then, is precisely why the application of the specific skills of the historian is so vital today. While Indonesians are not professionally adept at history, they are deeply historically minded, by which I mean that a large portion of the identity they create for themselves depends on some deeply held sense of the past and its meaning. The problem, for the most part, has been that historians' (both Indonesian and foreign) deprecation of the modern in Indonesian history has allowed sparse, distorted, simplistic and misleading understandings to emerge and dominate consciousness, discourse and even policy making.

There are familiar and obvious examples of this phenomenon, such as the myth that Indonesia always existed ('waking up' only in 1908), that the Indonesian National Army was the defender of the nation in the period of the revolution (the TNI was, in fact, a hopeless shambles; what saved the republic were its *pejuang*, or fighters, not the TNI), that Sukarno was a great leader, that 1950s democracy was bound to fail because of its inappropriate application to Indonesia's 'culture' and historical circumstances, and, more recently, that Soeharto was no more than a corrupt thug. Such myths contain wisps of truth, but parading them as though they encompass more than that does everyone a disservice, especially Indonesians themselves.

Indonesian politics requires the disinterested yet passionate work of serious historians. They have two major tasks. The first is to begin the process of deep research. Apart from a few notable examples – in particular the revolutionary and early independence periods, where scholars like Benedict Anderson, Anthony Reid, Robert Cribb, Anton Lucas, and George and Audrey Kahin have dug deeply, with fertile results – much of the modern period remains seriously understudied. The outstanding work of Herbert Feith and Daniel Lev on the 1950s and early 1960s excepted, few have bothered to dip into the exceptional riches of the newspapers of the 1950s or to test the memories of those few participants of the period who still survive.

Similarly, much of the work of the New Order period has centred on the army; it is work of a high standard, but mostly written by political scientists who have little detailed knowledge of the earlier phases of the army's development. Beyond that, the New Order has been the terrain of political scientists or journalists who have taught us much, but focused on a particular political or journalistic slant. The first task of historians of modern Indonesia is to take their sources – in all their variety – seriously, and to explore them seriously.

The second, and more difficult, task is to make sense of it all. Notwithstanding the high-quality labours of numerous scholars, we have no clear sense of the meaning – or meanings – of modern Indonesia. There are a vast number of different versions of Indonesia's political past (and indeed present) to be taken into account and longer-range questions that need inquiry and analysis in order to begin the process of approaching those meanings. How important, for instance, are political institutions? What roles have political parties, parliament and for that matter the army played in Indonesian democracy, and have these roles changed, particularly in relation to the executive?

Can we speak of political ideology in Indonesia? What is the status and legacy of the Pancasila, what is the nature of political conservatism, and why has the Left (and its ideas) fared so badly in modern Indonesia? Furthermore, what is the basis for political leadership in Indonesia and what are the prospects for effective presidential guidance? More generally, why has Indonesia's recent past been so replete with recurring tragedy? What has 'region' meant in modern Indonesia? And, more theoretically, how do we untangle the continuities from the discontinuities of this past, so better to appreciate future trajectories and anticipate opportunities as well as dead ends?

These questions, and others like them, are as important as they are fascinating. They require the attention of serious historians of Indonesia, because no one else has the means to answer them with the seriousness of method and insight that they demand.

NOTE

1   I remember how astounded I was during extended archival research visits in 1976 and 1984 that, in so heavily populated a nation as Indonesia, I rarely saw an Indonesian researcher appear in the archive building.

6

THE NEW ORDER: KEEPING UP APPEARANCES

Adrian Vickers

This whole continent [Asia] is like ... Disneyland without the safety precautions. (Neal Stephenson 1999, p. 349)

Our study of Indonesia – 'our' being Australian, but also other non-Indonesian, scholars of Indonesia – is tied up with a series of presuppositions about the New Order. Journalism and 'pop' academia latches too easily onto complex and sometimes problematic theories and produces simplistic understandings of politics. I argue that the New Order was an ostensibly capitalist but in fact Stalinist state, although it did not fit the latter bill well either. It was a product of Cold War anti-communist hysteria, which was why it was defended beyond its use-by date by everyone from Ronald Reagan to Paul Keating. A lack of historical understanding about the aberrant nature of the New Order has produced a nostalgia for authoritarianism that has gripped critics of the Wahid regime, both within and outside Indonesia. Abdurrahman Wahid, the fourth president, is seen not only as too casual in style for the men in suits from the IMF, but as 'feeble'.[1] This chapter seeks to disrupt the view that 'the state' is the problem in Indonesia, and in so doing challenge more general views about the New Order.

WHAT WAS THE NEW ORDER AND WHAT DID IT DO?

What was the 'New Order', the government headed by General Haji Muhammad Soeharto between Sukarno's surrender of power – Supersemar – in 1966 and Soeharto's resignation in 1998? Most media and many academic commentators have written of this period as a monolithic one (Pemberton 1994). Some of the early descriptions of the New Order suggest that it had similarities with the New Order in 1998. Most notably, an essay by Lance Castles

(1974) describes the corruption, conspicuous consumption and arbitrary use of power of the regime in the early 1970s. The many commentators who kept telling us that the fundamentals of the Indonesian economy were sound up to May 1998, and that Soeharto started off well but went wrong in his later years, would do well to read his observations, coming as they did before the Pertamina scandal. Nevertheless, the continuities in the regime should not blind us to the massive shifts that occurred between 1966 and 1998. The New Order period is best seen as consisting of at least three related stages.

The first was the 'honeymoon' period, as Umar Kayam has called it, of 1967–74. This was a period of relative openness, in that there was freedom of the press, and the military did not dominate all aspects of government but was part of an anti-communist alliance with students, Islamic groups and a range of political leaders from the Sukarno period. Soeharto ruled as part of a triumvirate with the left-wing (Tan Malaka-ist) Adam Malik and Hamengkubuwono IX, a Sukarnoist liberal. This period ended with the Malari events, which not only signalled the suppression of the students but served to cover Soeharto's suppression of potential rivals in the military. Through the triumph of Ali Moertopo and those around him in the aftermath of Malari, a stream of political developments led from there to the invasion of East Timor.[2]

The second, 'Stalinist', period from 1974 to 1988/89 was one in which the totalitarian aspirations of the New Order came to the fore. Campuses were 'normalised'; military and bureaucratic structures were tightened so that Soeharto's challengers were marginalised; and the ideological campaigns more usual in socialist states, notably P4/Pancasila indoctrination, were inaugurated. David Bourchier (1996a and in this volume) has produced the best descriptions of the ideology of this period.

At the end of the 1980s international pressures led to deregulation and the pretence of 'openness', which made some of the contradictions of the regime more apparent. This third period might be considered as the long goodbye of a leader surrounded by yes-men, living out fantasies of consumption coupled with immoral displays of power. This was not so much a 'liberal' period of deregulation as a period of unrestrained plundering of the economy.

The New Order has been analysed in two contradictory ways: by focusing either solely on 'the state' (a triumph of 'state' over 'society') or entirely on Soeharto. In the post-1998 literature it has been convenient to blame everything on this one man, the supreme *dalang* (shadow puppeteer). For those who were part of the New Order – or almost anyone who lived in or visited the country – such a focus means we do not have to analyse responsibility for the many sins committed between 1965 and 1998 any further. Such an analysis fits into the cult-of-personality aspect of the Stalinist period, and often limits political analysis of Indonesia to describing the comings and goings of a few key leaders or potential leaders – what historians call the 'great man' view of history.

Rather than this authoritarian image of the God-like *dalang*, I prefer the metonymy used by M. Dwi Marianto (1994) to explain the surreal nature of life under the New Order. Dwi refers to the political culture of the regime as a *helm* ('helmet') culture. What he alludes to is the way in which everybody in Indonesia used to wear helmets when riding motorbikes. It was important to wear a helmet, not because you were worried about injury, nor because you were a good citizen and believed in the law and the government, but because the police would 'fine' you if you were not so attired. Everybody knew that the 'fines' went straight into the pockets of the policemen involved. The helmets people wore were not motorcycle helmets in the strict sense, but rather construction helmets, or anything else that looked like a helmet. These would not have provided much in the way of protection but that was not the point. Nowadays you see a lot of people riding without helmets, another sign of change.

The *helm* image works quite well in explaining the New Order as a government of appearances. The government worked hard to create an appearance of economic prosperity, an appearance of rice exports, an appearance of no corruption, no famines or unrest, no ethnic or religious conflict – even an appearance of capitalism. Such appearances did not protect many heads during the economic collapse of 1997 and its aftermath. Although the New Order appeared to be a departure from the past in Indonesian history, it should not be seen as more successful, stronger or more orderly than the current regime. I will explain aspects of this government of appearances by detailing some of the historiographic and analytical problems we have all encountered in describing the New Order.

THE NEW ORDER: STATE VERSUS SOCIETY?

The New Order's appearance as a strong, stable and centralised state, indeed a police state or military dictatorship, was part of its set of appearances. That is what the rest of the world – particularly Britain, the United States and Australia – liked about it, the idea that it provided 'security'. That is why we do not like the 'archipelago of instability' of which Indonesia is now part. Australian reporting on Indonesia is filled with endless cliched rehashings of 'The Year of Living Dangerously'; Indonesia looks worse post-Soeharto than it did during the reign of the dictator. Reports on the 'feeble' and disorganised Gus Dur in the *Sydney Morning Herald* and other newspapers suggest nostalgia for the good old days of 'strong' government.

What is at issue is how analysts more precisely define 'the Indonesian state' and, having defined it, decide whether it is 'weak' or 'strong'. 'Strength' here seems to rely on the notion that the state as an entity is greater, more powerful, than the sum of powers held by its personnel. The personnel of the state did indeed have power. Members of the Soeharto extended family cum inner circle and members of the military/intelligence apparatus could make people do things against their will. They were above and beyond any form of law, and could appropriate money, sex and people's lives at will. If you accept that Soeharto, his family, his cronies and other top military people were the state from 1967 to 1998, then read no further. However, if you want to find a state of which they were both inside and outside, then more description is needed.

Anderson's article 'Old State, New Society' (1990, originally published 1983) provides one of the most influential discussions of the New Order state. It argued that one of the New Order's key features was concentration on the '*state qua state*'. This in turn has helped to fuel an anti-state view among Indonesian intellectuals that has not been very helpful in the post-Soeharto period. As well as feeding into neoliberal views, making it difficult to restore functionality to processes of government, anti-statism has given rise to vigilante attacks and the proliferation of militias formed by political parties. But was the New Order about 'the state'? Anderson (1990, p. 95) provides a basic definition of the state as 'an institution' that is more than 'either a legal fiction or a collectivity of persons (the bureaucracy)'. Anderson's argument includes a distinction between state and 'extra-state' organisations (such as voluntary/mass-based organisations), the latter achieving power in revolutionary situations when the state is 'disintegrating'. He sees the New Order as a triumph of the state over society and the nation.

Such a view makes most sense when contrasting the New Order with the Old Order, and works best for the Stalinist years of the regime when it was written. Anderson argues that the state was 'weak' during the early years of independence, and that the army 'strengthened', indeed 'resurrected', the state, partly motivated by Soeharto's experiences of state fragility between the 1940s and 1960s (Anderson 1990, pp. 108–11). Given the problems of Indonesia after Soeharto, Anderson's analysis also explains the undermining of national sentiment by the New Order. The ideals Sukarno mobilised in nation building in the 1940s and 1950s are very weak at the beginning of the 21st century.

If the state is a matrix of institutions, what are they? The first and most obvious is the complex of intelligence organisations, the security state. Tanter (1990b) has elaborated the security state in a highly nuanced fashion – a picture that remained largely accurate up to 1998. Tanter noted the problems that this complex had of coordination, and of surveillance of such a large population, concluding that:

its ambitions are undoubtedly totalitarian: in the sense of acquiring comprehensive information about any and all potential sources of social and political disruption to the state-ordained process of capitalist growth. The machinery of surveillance undoubtedly does not live up to the claims of its planners, but equally, it is clear that it is able to achieve a remarkable degree of penetration of a large number of target groups (Tanter 1990, p. 269).

He indicates that when specific individuals or groups were targeted, as in East Timor or, we might add, Aceh, the surveillance state worked well. It was less efficient in terms of its operation on the population at large, but managed to spread enough terror for people to be too scared to do anything that would threaten it.

Tanter, like Anderson, is partly correct in his assessment of the security state, but tends to assume a single aim or purpose of surveillance. The various apparatuses of security did not need to know what whole populations were doing, but only what specific activists, dissidents and resistance groups were planning. Until the archives are opened up we will not know what they did with the information they collected, but I doubt that it all circulated in a massive cross-indexed database.

The identity of Intel agents in Bali was not secret – anyone could point them out. They wanted people to see that they had power, and this was more important to them than taking notes on subversive conversations. Indeed they were more concerned with running the local drug scene and finding ways to extract money from the general population than serving a larger institutional set of aims.[3]

In East Timor, the chief concern of the military was to monitor resistance. While the consistent use of torture and murder may have worked well to terrorise the Timorese, it was hardly an efficient instrument of state institution building because it made the population hate the Indonesian state. Acts of murder and torture created solidarity among members of the Indonesian military – a kind of male bonding through the committing of atrocities.[4] But at the same time the military was careful to keep up appearances, and rather than display the corpses, simply buried them under the roads and public buildings that symbolised *pembangunan (*literally 'building'), the New Order's version of development (see also Tsing 1993, pp. 90–91).

The brutal solidarity forged in the army was helpful in maintaining the military's various business ventures. Each district command operated a variety of (loosely 'legal') businesses that generated thousands of dollars a month, as well as offering free 'services'. Added to these were the proceeds from bribes and lucrative illegal businesses. In Bali the military and intelligence people ran the hawking of watches on Kuta Beach and the local prostitution business, as well as making money from land deals and, of course, drugs. What is surprising in studies of the military in Indonesia – in contrast with those on Thailand, for example – is the lack of examination of the business roles of the military, including its legitimate business interests.

What is also inconsistent in terms of the security state as an institution of a strong New Order state was its need to draw on extra-state elements. These elements were initially known as Ali Moertopo's 'zoo', and then more generally as part of *politik premanisme* ('thug' politics). Their income was linked to that of the military. Besides being paid directly for 'rent-a-riot' services, such groups as Pemuda Pancasila extracted money from all levels of business, thus forcing costs up, although they made up for this by keeping labour costs down.[5] If the security state worked so well as an institution, why did it need to outsource to a motley collection of gangsters? Most Indonesians understood who these gangsters represented, their basic mode of operation and that they occupied a realm somewhere between order and disorder. Siegel's (1998) analysis of the public discourses of criminality demonstrates that the excesses of murder blurred the distinctions between 'criminal' and 'state' entities in Indonesia to the point where 'law' and 'legality' lost all content (see further Lindsey in this volume). The undermining of all legitimacy for the institutions of 'law' (principally the security apparatus, the police and the judiciary) meant that the New Order security state could more accurately be termed a criminal state.

The bureaucracy had similar problems to the security apparatus as far as institution building was concerned. It suffered from a surplus of departments filled with underpaid and underemployed staff, charged with carrying out overlapping and uncoordinated regulations.[6] For example, in Bali, when a consultant on a conservation project enquired about the policing of pollution in the mangrove swamps around Denpasar, three or four government institutions claimed to have jurisdiction. Each had regulations that existed completely independently of each other, as well as its own set of fines varying from Rp 5,000 (A$1 at that time) to Rp 5,000,000. Despite this, none had ever actually fined anyone for polluting the waterways.[7]

Such tales of overlapping and ineffectual bureaucracy also abound in transport, planning and the arts, areas with which I am familiar. The workings of the bureaucracy, identified as the agency by which the state penetrated to the foundations of village society, are nowhere better typified than in the collection of statistics. I was discussing the use of statistics in a funding proposal with a group of young NGO workers when the father of one cut in, 'Oh yes, they're all just made up (*dibikin-bikin*)'. His opinion had some weight, since he worked in the provincial office of the Department of Statistics. When asked further about this, he said that he had tried to maintain some professional pride by keeping the statistics within about 10% of what he thought they might be. The appearance of accurate measurement, of modern surveillance, was important as a *raison d'être* of the bureaucracy. So statistics were published, down to village monographs produced by each *desa* (village) numbering every pig and coconut tree.[8]

Anna Tsing (1993, pp. 107–8) gives a nice vignette of the state's penetration of the *desa*, or more accurately the *daerah terpencil/terasing/tertinggal* ('isolated'/'alienated' areas, or areas 'left behind'). In her account of the marginal people of the Meratus mountains in Kalimantan, she describes how a villager was set a target of getting 40 women involved in family planning – the price of being allowed to hold village elections. The women were not interested in signing up, and the men were put off when the resident American anthropologist told them that this was a program to limit the number of children. But all that was needed was a list of names, so the leader persuaded 40 of his co-villagers to put down their wives' names, which were duly reported. A shipment of contraceptives was then sent out, never to be used for the purpose of inhibiting conception. This would have gone down in central government statistics as the successful introduction of a family planning program.

The New Order's strong bureaucratic state is perhaps better termed the *asal bapak senang* (ABS) state – meaning to 'keep the boss' (or whoever is higher up the bureaucratic or corporate ladder) 'happy'. One example of ABS culture in the bureaucracy involves the large strands of previously untouched rainforest in Kalimantan and Sumatra. These forests were stripped by national and international consortiums under Bob Hasan, with the collaboration of Kopassus, which was supposedly responsible for 'protecting' the national park areas.[9] According to forestry regulations, the firms responsible for denuding Kalimantan were supposed to undertake reafforestation projects, and were reported in government departments as having done so despite the fact that the trees had not been planted. Under ABS culture Indonesians were told that Soeharto was popular and in control, that there was no corruption, that the country enjoyed ethnic and religious harmony, that rice production increased every year, that the five-star hotels in Bali enjoyed full occupancy,[10] that the majority voted willingly for Golkar in elections, that unemployment rates were lower than those in Australia and that workers were paid at the proper rate. Instead of calling the New Order state a 'military–bureaucratic state', we might better term it a 'criminal–ABS state'.

Related to the appearance of order and functionality in the bureaucracy was the appearance of capitalism. The campaigns of national indoctrination, the imprisonment of political dissidents and propaganda about the Great Bapak (always depicted as *senang*, or happy), along with the reign of terror and the domination of one ethnic group (the Javanese) over others, were not so different from events in the USSR, North Korea or China. However, Indonesia was counted as being part of the 'Free World' because it was officially a capitalist state.

H.W. Arndt, weighing up the 'credits' and 'debits' of the early New Order in 1971, was critical of its problems of unemployment, lack of improvement in the standard of living for the majority of the population, and dependence on foreign aid. At the same time he praised the economic management of the technocrats, who had inflation under control and the basis of reform under way. He noted particularly that there had been a ruthless suppression of the Indonesian Communist Party (PKI), but that 'in power General Soeharto has been very much less ruthless than a Communist leadership would have been ... and in many respects less autocratic, and much less erratic than his predecessor, Sukarno' (Arndt 1971, p. 78).[11]

This 'better than the communists' view helped sustain Indonesia in international eyes through the Pertamina crisis and through a downturn in the 1980s related to world oil prices. The view meant that billions in loans, particularly from sources such as the World Bank, were continually channelled into Indonesia, making it one of the most indebted countries in the world. The same group of technocrats who were seen as the agents of Indonesia's economic recovery in the first period of the New Order were also viewed as the good guys trying to get Indonesia back on track in the late 1980s. It must have come as a relief to Cold War supporters of Indonesia when the statistics finally showed annual growth rates of around 7% in the 1990s. Schwarz (1999, Ch. 3) portrays the technocrats as fighting the good fight of liberalisation against the patrimonial and nationalist streams in government.

Various analysts who attempted to describe the relationship between the state and capitalism in Indonesia had to come to terms with the continuation of state monopolies. These monopolies began with Sukarno's nationalisation of foreign companies in the late 1950s, when the army was able to legitimate its economic activities (hitherto described as 'smuggling'). These monopolies were tolerated by international bodies such as the IMF and World Bank and by various multinationals for as long as the technocrats were there to give the appearance that free markets would be coming. The deregulation of the late 1980s did not reduce the number of state monopolies; if anything it gave rise to more and more extravagant schemes, such as the Timor car (described by one foreign journalist as a name akin to Mercedes Benz calling a car the 'Auschwitz'). Deregulation enabled more access to funding through the diversification of banking and opening up of the stock exchange.

Before 1988 various monopolies, World Bank projects and other government projects (*proyek*) were the main sources of revenue for those in power. All those who could skimmed a percentage off these *proyek*. Indonesian capitalist ventures were inhibited from getting too big, because as soon as they reached a certain size they would have to 'sell' a large share of the company to a member of the Soeharto–military group (with no money actually being received). Bigger schemes were formulated, with foreign investors induced to invest as much money as possible, which would also be siphoned off. The Busang gold mine was a triumph of the culture of appearances: the world's largest discovery of gold, with foreign investors throwing money at the ruling clique to get access to it. What did it matter that there was no actual gold?[12] Laws and regulations concerning transparency were introduced, and audits carried out on businesses. Nobody policed these regulations, but because the changes had the appearance of the right type of capitalism they were approved by the World Bank (Schwarz 1999, p. 314).

Törnquist (1990) and Tanter (1990a) have both labelled the Indonesian state's economic role as that of a 'rentier'. Tanter uses the term 'rentier–militarist' to describe it in terms of a state where 'capital accumulation comes not from productive investment ... but from unproductive appropriation of a portion of the economic surplus by a group of rentiers' (p. 57). Writing before the period of 'deregulation', Törnquist saw the monopolies as particularly detrimental to the advancement of social welfare, but argued (p. 44) that: 'we are not talking about plundering the state. Our rentiers, and especially the financiers, must see to it that their clients are doing reasonably well so that they can pay and not turn to other patrons'. Törnquist is correct to avoid the neoclassical fallacy of identifying liberalisation and democratisation, and his emphasis on seeing the rentiers as a class is important. It is apparent that class analysis has disappeared from much of the discussion of Indonesia, whether by the media or by academics, where the vague term 'elites' is bandied about. Does this term refer just to members of the government and rich business people, to all those otherwise included in the middle class, or to the ruling class?

However Törnquist's analysis does not work for the final period of the New Order, because by the middle of the 1990s the rentiers were devouring the state. The difference between 'surplus' (profits) and the economic 'base' (conditions of reproduction) was no longer clear, and the plundering of resources was making almost all projects economically non-viable, as well as seriously eroding the national resource base and causing significant problems of pollution. However, it needs to be remembered that this was not a *degeneration* of the system; the Pertamina scandal had demonstrated that in 1974 equally destructive plundering was going on.[13]

In summary, the New Order state was a 'rentier' or plunder state, a criminal state and an ABS state, with all the appearances of a capitalist, military–bureaucratic state. That is, there is no one correct way to sum up 'the state'. It had a variety of contending and contradictory elements and was dominated by a ruthless class that saw it as an instrument to accumulate money and power. This class undermined the legal bases of state institutions. In the post-Soeharto period it has played a major role in the destruction of areas of Indonesia, such as Maluku, which would indicate that the building of a state institutional basis that would outlive a particular group of personnel was not achieved, and was probably never intended. The inability of Soeharto to step down before 1998, despite ill health, reinforces this argument.

Most analyses of the state come from the centre, that is, they are based on a view that assumes Jakarta to be the state, and the intentions of the centre to have been realised everywhere else. As studies from the margins show, the state looks different when viewed from, say, the Meratus mountains, Aru, Sulawesi or even Bali (Tsing 1993; Spyer 2000; Acciaioli 1997). Dictates from Jakarta existed as a system of 'Chinese whispers'. Sometimes they were misinterpreted, at other times deliberately reinterpreted, the intentions of control and totalitarianism being just another type of appearance.

THE NEW ORDER AND HISTORY

The New Order's state of appearances made no sense in the Southeast Asian context. It fitted neither with pre-colonial nor with colonial models, although it contained elements of both. Most other parts of Southeast Asia had seemed to be living more dangerously than New Order Indonesia, or were weaker.

The New Order based its territorial claims on continuities with the pre-colonial Majapahit and to a lesser degree Sriwijaya empires. It is reputed that when the Dutch government returned the Lombok manuscript of the *Nagarakertagama* (along with the famous statue linked in legend to Ken Dedes), Soeharto slept with it beside his bed. Majapahit was presented in Indonesian school history textbooks as a military kingdom that ruled the whole archipelago from Java, and this version of history was used, *inter alia*, to justify the invasion of East Timor. As with all the other New Order appearances, this one too seems hollow. A visit to the probable site of Majapahit, at Trowulan, would have found it fairly run-down and neglected by Jakarta. Supomo (1979) who, unlike Soeharto, can read the *Nagarakertagama*, has demonstrated how absurd was the equation of Majapahit tribute systems with New Order military domination.

Anderson (1990) (correctly) by-passes the pre-colonial state in order to argue that the New Order state was the colonial state reborn. This became something of a Cornell orthodoxy, and served its rhetorical purposes before 1998. However, the essays assembled by Cribb (1994) demonstrate that in key respects there was not necessarily such direct institutional inheritance. Van den Doel (1994) shows, for example, that the use of military officers for civil administration under the Dutch was not really a version of *dwifungsi* (the dual military and socioeconomic role of the military). It was resented by civil servants, who were in a stronger position than their New Order equivalents to oppose it, and in any case was not a product of the will of the government so much as of the shortage of civil servants. Likewise the Netherlands East

Indies' political intelligence service 'was never free of government and public supervision and its activities seem to have been free of torture and arbitrary detention' (Poeze 1994, p. 242), unlike Bakin, Kopkamtib or the other instruments of the security/criminal state. Moreover the Dutch military–intelligence apparatus could not go into business.

State relations with capital differed in the two eras, as the civil service functioned and was structured differently; most importantly the physical reach of the colonial state did not approximate that of the New Order because of slow and often nonexistent communications, particularly in outlying areas. There was the problem of relations between the parallel Dutch and indigenous civil services as thousands of Dutch attempted to rule over millions of 'Indonesians', and this was manifested in the opaqueness of village life to the colonial gaze (Onghokham 1978; Schulte Nordholt 1991). There is still, also, the theoretical problem of what constitutes a colonial state. Was the Netherlands East Indies a separate state, or an appendix of the Dutch state?

The New Order can be seen as a product of the Cold War, but I would argue that it was a historical aberration in lasting so long. The other dictatorships that existed during the Vietnam War period's focus of US anti-communism on the region – South Vietnam, Lon Nol's Cambodia, Thailand for a while, and the Philippines under a number of presidents up to Marcos – resembled Indonesia during its honeymoon period. But they did not maintain their particular forms of US client dictatorship beyond the end of the 1980s, and Indonesia's Stalinist period deviated from the pattern of military dictatorships elsewhere in the region. There has been only one military ruler in the region who has lasted as long as Soeharto, Myanmar's Ne Win, but Myanmar is an extraordinary country by any comparison. The close personal friendship between Soeharto and Ne Win, both of whom trained under the Japanese, is a remarkable feature of the dynamics of their respective rules. Malaysia's Prime Minister Mahathir is also long-reigning, but whatever else Malaysia's regime may be, it cannot be called 'military'.

The historically aberrant nature of the New Order is due to the longevity of its appearance of order and control under one man. At the same time as the institutions of the state were being run down and the bases of democratic participation removed, its appearances were being taken as reality by foreign governments, investors, and the World Bank and IMF.

My argument has implications for how we perceive and represent Indonesia. The media's play with 'Year of Living Dangerously' images implies that ethnic and communal tensions, separatism and occasional bursts of violence are not normal for Indonesia, but surprising and aberrant. Indonesia is heterogeneous, pulling and pushing in various ways, and so it was under the New Order. I remember being in Jakarta in 1978 when there was a bombing, but it was not reported in the newspapers. Today's bombings, anti-Chinese riots, church burnings, communal tensions and other spates of violence are not new; what is new is that we are now talking about them.

It is testimony to the collective Cold War mentality of Australia that we accept representations of 'security' and large states as meaning 'stability' and 'strong leadership'. Is Indonesia about a 'search for stability', as the subtitle of Adam Schwarz's revised edition of *A Nation in Waiting* tells us? The last thing Indonesia needs is another strong leadership figure. What is more urgently required is a group of people who can help Indonesians accept a more complex and even messy view of the state, and thus create a space for people to act for themselves. Gus Dur seems to be doing that, despite the New Order's best efforts at de-educating the Indonesian people.

NOTES

1   See, for example, Lindsay Murdoch's 'Religious Killing Fields Spread across the Ugly New Indonesia' (*Sydney Morning Herald*, 29 June 2000, p. 1). Ironically, Hamish McDonald, in an article on Australian–Indonesian relations in the same issue of the *Herald* ('How Warmth from the North Turned Cold'), attributes anti-Indonesian attitudes to the 'taxi-driver/talkback radio sub-current', when his own paper's stories and especially headlines about Indonesia under Gus Dur have consistently been negative.

2   Ali Moertopo was Minister for Information from 1978 to 1983 and a key New Order strategist. He masterminded most of Soeharto's political manoeuvrings in the 1970s, including the invasion of East Timor.

3   Goenawan Mohamad responded to the conference presentation of this paper with a story from the Soeharto years about sitting next to an Intel agent who had been sent to report on a speech by Abdurrahman Wahid. During the speech the agent asked Goenawan where Wahid was. Goenawan replied that that was him giving the speech, to which the agent responded, 'No it's not, that's Gus Dur' (Wahid's nickname). He added that during this period the best way to get rid of Intel tails in Jakarta was to take the toll road, because they would rather lose the person they were following than pay the toll.

4   I am drawing here on a series of papers presented in the late 1980s by Alfred McCoy on masculine cultures in the military of the Philippines.

5   Nowadays they are – in Bali at least – reduced to the more conventional sources of income: gambling, drugs and prostitution.

6   Analysts of the media in Indonesia have yet to examine the importance of newspapers in filling in the time of government employees. Civil servants were probably the major readers of the newspapers.

7   My thanks to Doug Martin for this example. This is not exactly unique to Indonesia, as anyone who knows anything about Sydney Harbour will tell you, but in Indonesia overlapping bureaucracy seems to have been raised to an art form.

8   More disturbing still is the reliance of foreign scholars on these statistics. These

same scholars failed to see the signs of economic collapse, which were obvious to anyone who looked at examples of banking and business practice from 1993 onwards.

9   Some of the most desirable areas for logging were in Indonesia's national parks. These forests were regarded as the 'property' of military groups such as Kopassus, who were supposed to protect them but in practice profited from massive logging operations in their areas of control. Businessman Bob Hasan and other Soeharto cronies were granted leases over large areas of rainforest in the national parks. Legal and illegal logging activities in the parks were carried out by Hasan in partnership with Indonesian or foreign firms, and also by foreign firms that would pay a percentage of their profits to Hasan or the military.

10 This helped keep land prices high, and meant that once the cronies had received a percentage of the building costs, the hotels could be sold on to foreign investors, usually multinational chains.

11 In 1985 or 1986 I heard Kim Beazley, then Australian Minister for Defence, give a speech at the University of Sydney that included comments on how Soeharto had 'saved Indonesia'.

12 Unfortunately it mattered a great deal to those involved in the actual exploration, since at least one of them ended up 'accidentally' falling out of a helicopter.

13 Another point of continuity: Ibnu Sutowo was not only never taken to court over his 'management' of Pertamina, but his wealth helped his son Ponco to become head of one of the largest conglomerates of the late New Order, and to survive in business even after the fall of Soeharto.

7

MIDDLE WAY LEADERSHIP IN INDONESIA: SUKARNO AND ABDURRAHMAN WAHID COMPARED

Angus McIntyre*

Sukarno (1901–70) and Abdurrahman Wahid (born 1940) each became president at a time when the integrity of the ethnically diverse Indonesian nation was threatened, and they each practised what Graham Little has called 'middle way leadership'. This conjunction was fortunate, for the core psychological assumption of leaders in this mould (and, indeed, of their followers) is that the self, far from having anything to fear from contact with different selves, will actually benefit from it.

In the case of nations, this issue of the relationship of the self to other selves is not only psychologically basic but also sociologically and politically complex, for the persons in question may speak a variety of languages, adhere to different religions and embrace a range of ideologies. The Indonesian motto, *Bhinneka Tunggal Ika* ('We Are Many but We Are One'), which was adopted on Independence Day, 1950 (Cribb 1992, pp. 57–8), shows how the leaders of the new nation attempted to deal with it. Indeed, there is a claim here that beneath such ethnic and ideological differences as there are between Indonesians lie more compelling similarities and likenesses. Therefore, the motto not only gives eloquent expression to the aspirations of Indonesia's civic nationalism but also shares the assumption of middle way leadership about the possibility of full mutuality between all manner of selves.

On the other hand, the core assumption of 'strong leadership', another of Little's categories, is that the self can only realise itself in opposition to other selves. This form of leadership claims to govern for all yet promotes 'righteous division'; it is pugnacious yet feels embattled; and it resists empathy with opponents, especially the weak (Little 1988, Chs 1–2). If former President Soeharto belongs anywhere in Little's scheme of things, it is plainly in the strong leadership category. Just as middle way leadership finds its match in civic nationalism, strong leadership shares its underlying assumption – that the self can only realise itself in opposition to other selves – with both ethnic nationalism and its political equivalent, where ideological criteria are substituted for ethnic ones. That is to say, although the strong leader may suppress what is for him a natural temptation to practise scapegoating, and maintain a commitment to ethnic tolerance, he will be inclined to construct shibboleths to distinguish the politically virtuous from their opponents; and this can be as ruinous for the integrity and well-being of the nation as any attempt to favour one religion, culture or language over another.

MIDDLE WAY LEADERSHIP

If strong leadership is characterised by moralism and divisiveness, middle way leadership embraces diversity, for its leader seeks a match for his own complexity and richness (as he sees it) in the variety of the world. Tolerant of differences, or impatiently discounting them, and seeing similarities and likenesses everywhere, the middle way leader forms friendships in many places, feels that he belongs everywhere, and attempts to draw diverse people together by negotiation and compromise, or by example. Middle way leadership thereby achieves a measure of inclusiveness. However, it is important to note that this inclusiveness is not a matter of institutional arrangements but very much hinges on the leader himself who, resisting routinisation, seeks to place himself at the centre of an expanding circle of friends and supporters. This process can appear extraordinary, exciting, inspiring – less a matter of compromise between groups than a transcendence of old constraints – and future-oriented; and the leader in its midst is sometimes regarded as charismatic (Little 1983a, 1983b, 1985, 1999a, 1999b).

Little's examples of middle way leaders are Franklin Roosevelt (who described his politics as 'just going down the middle'), John Alderdice, the former leader of the Alliance Party in Northern Ireland and now speaker of the Northern Ireland Assembly, Pierre Trudeau, Bob Hawke, Bill Clinton and Tony Blair. With the partial exception of Alderdice, they are all from established liberal democracies, and it is this fact, perhaps, which causes Little to leave this system of government out of account. In fact, a democratic system of government can bestow a number of advantages on this style of leadership. It is, of course, an intimate way of leading in which the leader is sensitive not only to the aspirations of various individuals and groups but also to the issues that agitate and divide them. However, if the leader's intuition should fail him in these matters or if he should lapse into solipsism, the machinery of democratic government – interest groups, political parties, representative institutions and the like – is there to keep him in touch with public sentiment. This system of government also makes the all too fallible leader less central to the process of building and maintaining a national consensus. Indeed, if he should become obdurate, it also has the means, whether by a vote in the party room, in the legislature or in the electorate, to remove him from office.

Finally, a democratic form of government can offer the leader an opportunity to contain his narcissism by transforming it into idealisation of the democratic process of which he is but a transient part. Authoritarian government, on the other hand, serves only to idealise the strong leader, thereby exacerbating his narcissism and fostering hubris. This is 'the pride of overconfidence', seen in Greek tragedy as a fatal flaw that eventually brings down the hero and visits disaster on his people (Abrams 1962, pp. 98–100; Frye 1990, p. 38, *passim*). Thus if middle way leadership works, as it did at least for a time with the above leaders, then it does so not only because of their expansive personalities and corresponding ability to bridge differences between individuals but also because of the resources of the democratic system within which they do their leading.

However, even democracy cannot prevent middle way leadership from retreating into a narrower version of itself in the face of adverse circumstances. As the middle way leader ages, becomes ill or encounters obstacles, he may end up communicating 'a dead version of the superlative vitality he began with' (Little 1985, p. 153). Or, where he was open and generous previously, he may subsequently become narrowly preoccupied and selfish, and friends and followers will discover in the end that the leader's love is only for himself. An extreme example of this trajectory, in which the end point can no longer be called middle way leadership, is to be found in the life of Sir Oswald Mosley, who began his political career by attacking Lloyd George's policy of reprisals in Ireland and ended it as leader of the British Union of Fascists (McIntyre 1988). Thus, although middle way leadership with its inclusive orientation and kinship with civic nationalism had much to offer Indonesia in the troubled circumstances of 1945 and 1999, it was also, as the above comments make clear, an unstable form of leadership that could easily degenerate into a lesser version of its former self or become something quite different. As the case of Sir Oswald Mosley shows, the comparatively benign, middle way caterpillar may end up as the wasp of strong leadership. And, to anticipate the argument of the next section, this pattern is discernible in the history of Sukarno's leadership.

SUKARNO

Sukarno came into his own as a middle way leader in the months before the Declaration of Independence on 17 August 1945, and continued to lead in this manner as head of state in the early democratic years of the republic. For example, in his famous Pancasila speech of 1 June 1945, Sukarno spoke of the aspiration to build 'a state of "all for all", "one for all, all for one"', 'a state built on mutual cooperation'. In seeking to realise this goal, he sought a compromise between Muslims and Christians in the form of a 'theistic state' and suggested that a representative body would be an appropriate place for them to advance their respective claims (Sukarno 1945, pp. 23, 29, *passim*). In these remarks and, indeed, in his subsequent involvement in offering concessions to disappointed Muslims – and then, with the sensibilities of Christians in mind, apologetically withdrawing them – we may observe a middle way leader working openly and generously to realise a civic form of nationalism at the birth of a new country (Reid 1974, pp. 19–20, 30).

In most of these activities the flamboyant, Javanese and nominally Muslim Sukarno was closely accompanied by the staid, Minangkabau and devoutly Islamic Mohammad Hatta, who served as both prime minister (December 1949 – August 1950) and vice-president (1945–49, August 1950 – December 1956). Although very different people, they had worked closely and cordially together since the beginning of the Japanese occupation, and by 1949 'it was ... customary to speak of ... [them] as one political force'. Indeed, they became known as the *dwitunggal* (two-in-one) signifying 'traditional ideas of the unity-in-duality of the cosmos' (Feith 1962, p. 51, *passim*). It is also possible to see in this expression and, indeed, in the close partnership of the two leaders that gave rise to it a realisation of the national motto and its ideal of full mutuality between the citizens of this heterogeneous nation. As stated above, it is the coming together of self and other, the transcendence of difference, that gives middle way leadership its excitement and ability to inspire, and the partnership between Sukarno and Hatta was a fine example of this phenomenon. Of course they fell out in the end, with Hatta resigning the vice-presidency in December 1956. Thereafter Sukarno's middle way leadership began to lose its plausibility as he came increasingly to be identified with ethnic and political groups within the nation rather than with the nation itself. As Hatta later commented, the *dwitunggal* (two-in-one) became the *dwitanggal* (doubly divided) (Rose 1987, p. 169).

By 1956 Sukarno was seeking alternatives to the liberal democratic government that had prevailed in Indonesia since late 1945 and which was, 10 years later, struggling ineffectually with regional disaffection and unrest within the army. In this troubled environment, the president first declared himself (in October 1956) to be in favour of the burial of the political parties (Sukarno 1956, p. 11). But we then observe him, in the face of strong opposition from the parties, drop this idea and struggle anew with the diversity of his country and the ways in which it might be represented at the centre. In a major speech of February 1957 he called for the formation of a cabinet of 'mutual cooperation' in which representatives of the major parties, including the Indonesian Communist Party (PKI), would sit, and suggested by way of justification that it was not practical to exclude from the processes of government a group that had received six million votes in the recent elections (of 1955). He also proposed the establishment of a National Council to serve as an advisory body to the cabinet. Revealing the recent influence upon him of corporatist ideas, he suggested that the membership of this body should consist of representatives of functional groups in society and, as he saw it, thereby reflect the composition of society, just as the cabinet would reflect the composition of parliament (Sukarno 1957, pp. 12–13; Bourchier 1996b, pp. 130–33).

Sukarno's proposals were still consistent with a middle way leadership approach to Indonesia's problems. But his claim in the same speech that he was 'the mouthpiece of the Indonesian people' implied that he was more able than either of these two bodies to give accurate expression to the wishes of the people (Sukarno 1957, p. 15). In subsequent years Sukarno returned to this theme, reformulating the nature of his link to the public in ever more solipsistic terms: 'the language which comes out of my mouth', he said in the following year, 'is already inscribed in the hearts of the Indonesian people themselves' (Sukarno 1958, p. 1). This substitution of himself for representative institutions (even corporatist ones) boded ill for his continuing application of middle way leadership in Indonesia. He may have liked to view himself as the mouthpiece of the Indonesian people – but the danger, of course, was that they would become his.

In 1960 Sukarno banned Masyumi, the modernist Islamic political party that had garnered almost eight million votes from a largely Outer Island constituency in the 1955 elections, on the grounds of its involvement in the regional rebellion of 1958 (Feith 1962, pp. 434–5). This may be seen as a turning point in the history of Sukarno's domestic leadership of the Republic of Indonesia for, after such a drastic act of exclusion, it no longer seems accurate to describe it as middle way. A year later his foreign policy began to show signs of a comparable transformation. Before that time Indonesia had pursued a global version of middle way leadership by adopting a position of non-alignment between the two rival blocs in the Cold War and even on occasion seeking, together with like-minded countries such as India, a lessening of the tensions between them. However, from 1961 Sukarno recast his map of the world. Where previously Indonesia had found a place between two competing groups, it now saw itself as a leading member of the 'new established forces' (NEFO) locked in conflict with their neocolonial and imperialist counterparts or 'old established forces' (OLDEFO).

But if the president's style of leadership in the early 1960s became increasingly divisive in some respects – leading us to drop the characterisation of it as middle way and think of it rather as a form of strong leadership – then in others it appeared at first glance to be recklessly broad in its embrace.

I am referring to his reintroduction into Indonesian politics in 1960 of his belief, first formulated in 1926, of the desirability of cooperation between Islamic, nationalist and socialist forces. At first this idea, now cast as NASAKOM unity – the unity of Nationalist (*Nasionalis*), Religious (*Agama*) and Communist (*Komunis*) forces – served to underpin his efforts to build a close working relationship with and between the Indonesian National Party (PNI), the Nahdlatul Ulama (NU) and the PKI as a way of balancing the power of the Indonesian army. Later, however, it acquired the position of a doctrine equal in status to the state ideology of Pancasila, and one which he sought to inculcate into the hearts and minds of each and every Indonesian.

In addressing an unruly meeting of the PKI's student front on 29 September 1965 – the students kept up a chant demanding that the government ban HMI, the modernist Islamic student organisation – Sukarno reiterated his confidence in NASAKOM and claimed that it had taken root in Indonesian society.

> Now, brothers and sisters, this NASAKOM, for which I say Thank God, has already become national property. By this I mean that it is already owned by all the Indonesian people. Except the false ones brothers and sisters. Except the people who are in fact traitors to the nation. Except the people who are in fact counter-revolutionaries. Now NASAKOM has become a national asset, the property of all the Indonesian people. Ninety-nine per cent of the Indonesian people hold NASAKOM in high esteem (Sukarno 1965b, pp. 4–5).

One can appreciate the president's wish that these three groupings should each enjoy a place in Indonesian society; and it is important to recall that, although he banned Masyumi, he resisted PKI pressure to follow suit with HMI, thereby leaving some space within Guided Democracy for modernist Muslims. Nevertheless, Sukarno's approach here was not a matter of like seeking like across social and political divides in the manner of middle way leadership. Rather, he held up NASAKOM unity not simply as a desirable political goal but also as a shibboleth that distinguished between revolutionaries and counter-revolutionaries, loyalists and traitors, true and false Indonesians. This last distinction – between true and false Indonesians – is particularly telling, and shows how strong leadership, even while remaining committed to civic nationalism, may, as suggested above, divide the nation.

The other point, of course, is how wrong Sukarno proved to be, as the murder only a few weeks later of *Kom* by *Nas* and *A* with the incitement, support and direction of General Soeharto and the army demonstrated. Indeed, to bring together groups of such diverse, indeed antagonistic, interests within an environment shaped by frantic political mobilisation, soaring inflation and serious food shortages, and to persist in such efforts amidst the violence stirred up in the villages of Central and East Java by the PKI's attempt to implement the Land Reform Law of 1960, seemed to be courting disaster. We have witnessed Sukarno's growing conviction that he was uniquely capable of giving voice to the aspirations of the Indonesian people, but what is striking about him at this late stage of his political career is not his intuitive rapport with the Indonesian people, but just how out of touch he really was. For all his charm and gregariousness, he seems at some point to have retreated into the autistic world of omnipotent fantasy, telling Cindy Adams that 'I'm constantly trying to subdue or remake circumstances so they can be vehicles to reach what I'm pursuing' (Adams 1966, p. 2). And perhaps we may see evidence of this retreat so far as NASAKOM is concerned as early as 1960. In this account by General Nasution of Sukarno arguing with the regional army commanders who had banned the PKI in South Sumatra, South Kalimantan and South Sulawesi, we observe him not turned outward to his people, but preoccupied with himself and his past.

> He then delved again into the origin of the national movement and the precision of Marxism as an analytical tool. ... He challenged those present, asking who amongst them had read and studied more Marxist books than him. In the final analysis he could not envisage the Indonesian national struggle separately from the former line whereby Nationalists, Religious People and Communists all played a part. He said that NASAKOM has been a tendency in our national struggle since former times. Saying this affected him and tears flowed down his cheeks (Nasution 1989, pp. 35–6).

This self-absorption led not only to remoteness and detachment from the people whose mouthpiece he claimed to be, but also, by 1965, to indifference to their suffering. In a speech of 23 May of that year, at the 45th anniversary celebrations of the PKI, he boasted there was so much food in Indonesia that the people actually used cassava to block up holes in the pavement (Sukarno 1965a, p. 7, *passim*).

ABDURRAHMAN WAHID

The similarity of leadership style between Sukarno and Abdurrahman Wahid provides us with a basis for comparison, and thereby the possibility of obtaining a deeper understanding of Abdurrahman's presidency. But, noting that the similarities extend beyond Sukarno's early middle way approach to his later narrow version of it, one fears that Abdurrahman has not been able to learn from the history of his predecessor's leadership style.

Abdurrahman Wahid's middle way leadership appears to have been shaped by a father who, in his own person, transcended the difference between traditional Islam and the modern world. According to Fealy (1998, p. 119): 'Not only was ... [Kiai Haji Abdul Wahid Hasjim] the son of its most revered *ulama*, Hasjim Asj'ari, he also epitomised the "new NU leader"; one who combined the training and cultural mores of traditional Javanese Islam with those of the modern, secular world'. His mother, Solichah, was not lacking in importance in NU circles either, possessing a political lineage almost as impressive as her husband's; and it was she, it seems, who stimulated the ambition of her eldest son by instilling in him a sense of calling as a future leader. Abdurrahman's survival unscathed in a car accident that killed his father (in April 1953), although a most traumatic event and undoubtedly striking him as an appalling tragedy, may also have led him to believe that he had been saved in order to continue his father's work (Barton 1996, pp. 191–2).

From this portentous background, Abdurrahman Wahid emerged as a man convinced of his own superiority and, although a devoted member of the NU, seeking a broader Indonesian – even world – stage on which to fulfil his destiny, and a more diverse circle of friends and followers in whom to discover himself. The consequence of this open, grand embrace of Indonesia and the world was a broad tolerance and an ability to see similarities where others could perceive only differences. A speech he gave as president on 27 December 1999 at a ceremony to celebrate Christmas gave expression to these attributes. Indeed, it could even be described as a credo of middle way leadership, so eloquently did it elaborate on its core sentiment that the way to full selfhood (both for the leader and his followers) lies via a close association with other selves. He said:

> I am a person who believes in my religion. But this does not prevent me from feeling kinship with people of other religions in this country, moreover with my fellow human beings. Since I was small I never felt that, although I remained in the circle of the *pesantren* and lived in the family of a *kiai*, I was even a little different from others (*Kompas Online*, 28 December 1999).

Acting on these middle way sentiments, Abdurrahman Wahid 'revoked [in January 2000] Soeharto's Presidential Instruction No. 41/1967, which restricted the observance of Chinese religious practices and traditions' (*Jakarta Post Online*, 19 January 2000). In the following month (29 February) he visited Dili and, after laying wreaths, offered apologies to the families and friends of those buried both at Santa Cruz cemetery and at the Seroja Heroes Cemetery (for fallen Indonesian soldiers) over what had happened in the past (*Kompas Online*, 1 March 2000). In March, after reiterating the apology he had made when leader of the NU 'for all the killings of alleged communists which had occurred [in 1965]', he proposed that Decision No. 25/1966 of the Interim People's Consultative Assembly (MPR) banning Marxism and communism be revoked (*Kompas Online*, 26 March 2000).

By acting in this way – by seeking to overcome the divisions between Christians and Muslims, between Chinese-Indonesians and their fellow citizens, between East Timorese and Indonesians, and between communists and

anti-communists, in short by insisting on the possibility of unity among heterogeneous selves – Abdurrahman showed middle way leadership striving for
inclusiveness. After the strong leadership of Soeharto, in which he both conducted a political pogrom and compromised his commitment to ethnic tolerance by scapegoating the Sino-Indonesian minority, the advantages of such an
approach to the harmony and integrity of the nation could not be gainsaid.

But if Indonesia has enjoyed the benefits of Abdurrahman's middle way
leadership it has also suffered as a result of its characteristic weaknesses.
Broadly speaking, these relate to its emphasis on general principles and a tendency to mistake the word for the deed, not to mention the self for the other
and the fantasy for the reality; and its corresponding failure to pay attention
to processes and implementation. In Abdurrahman's case this manifests itself
in many ways. His neglect of detail and failure to follow through has been
described by Feith (*Detak*, 4–10 January 2000), and there is a lack of proportion in his concern with world problems while pressing domestic issues
remain unresolved, if not neglected. Also, there is his assumption that good
government is simply a matter of dealing with friends in appropriate places
(*Tempo,* 24 October 1999; Mietzner 2001).

Notwithstanding such inherent weaknesses, the above account of some of
President Abdurrahman Wahid's words and deeds provides examples of middle way leadership at its most open and inclusive. However, as noted above,
it can contract into something less inclusive, generous and spacious on the one
hand, and more self-regarding, self-admiring and stifling on the other. The
usual sequence is for the middle way leader to begin openly but then, as obstacles, illness and ageing take their effect, to end narrowly. Certainly this was
the case with Sukarno. However, with Abdurrahman, who was felled by two
strokes before he became president, this order has been partly reversed. As we
shall see, he won the presidency by practising a very narrow version of this
style of leadership but, restored perhaps by the acquisition of high office and
the challenges it posed, he has on occasions since, such as the ones referred
to above, been able to practise the broad version (Fealy, pers. comm., 1999).

The steps Abdurrahman Wahid took to win the presidency may actually be
seen as a travesty of middle way leadership. In an extraordinary, strenuous act
of self-assertion and compensation, he rose from his sick bed to drive down
the middle, not with compromise and inclusiveness in mind, but in order to
divide and conquer (Mietzner, pers. comm., 2000). His main opponent was
Megawati Sukarnoputri. They had been friends for years and he had often
joined her on pilgrimages to her father's grave. On one such pilgrimage, on
the 91st anniversary of Sukarno's birth on 22 June 1992, he had spoken mov-
ingly of the cooperation and friendship that had existed between his father and
Sukarno on the eve of the Declaration of Independence. Also, he offered her
advice and such protection as he could when she was engaged in her danger-

ous challenge to Soeharto's leadership in 1995–96. Like Hatta and Sukarno before them, Abdurrahman and Megawati were, it seems, perceived as a *dwitunggal.* One a devout Muslim, the other less so, one male, the other female, they were an interesting pair that bridged the gap between *santri* and non-*santri* and between the genders; and they inspired hope amidst the thuggery and corruption of the late Soeharto years. But this close association did not survive Abdurrahman's aggressive bid for the presidency.

In March 1999 he advanced his presidential cause at Megawati's expense by claiming that 'a female president would be unacceptable to the majority of Indonesian Muslims' even though NU *kiai* had argued in the previous month that a female president would be acceptable to the *umat*; and this from a man who had adopted a feminist stance within the NU in the past (Mietzner 2000, p. 41, *passim*). Also, he claimed that Megawati's Indonesian Democratic Party of Struggle (PDI-P) was unfit for government because it did not understand Islam – and called one of her close supporters a Shi'ite – although he had argued most vigorously in the past that Islam should not be used for political ends. Finally, he accepted the support of those modernist Islamic groupings that he had previously condemned for what he believed were their sectarian inclinations, and solicited the support of the armed forces faction in the MPR by offering 'protection'and high office to its commander fresh from presiding over large-scale murder and massive destruction in East Timor (Fealy, pers. comm., 1999). In the end Abdurrahman got his majority in the MPR. However, as the television cameras revealed, Megawati was left in tears and (as we would later discover) she then complained of his treachery. Not only was the *dwitunggal* shattered, but Abdurrahman's victory had been achieved at considerable cost to his reputation for moderation, tolerance and decency. From the point of view of middle way leadership, this was not a promising beginning.

To complete this picture of the narrow version of middle way leadership as practised by Abdurrahman Wahid, I shall now turn to his claim to omniscience. Like Sukarno in 1957, he believes himself to have a profound, intuitive knowledge of the Indonesian people. It will be recalled that Sukarno made his claim at the very time he was promoting authoritarian government, and thus it was never tested at an election. Abdurrahman, on the other hand, was the presidential candidate of the National Awakening Party (PKB). He showed every confidence that this party would prevail in the parliamentary elections of 11 June 1999, claiming in early March of that year 'that more than half the people will support PKB' (*Far Eastern Economic Review*, 11 March 1999). This was an extraordinarily high estimate, especially if one recalls that the NU, the organisation from which the PKB had sprung, had received only 18% of the vote in the 1955 elections. In June, Abdurrahman's party garnered only 13% of the vote in the parliamentary elections whereas Megawati's obtained 34%. This result did not lead him either to question the democratic legitimacy of his bid for the presidency or to change his assessment of his understanding of the Indonesian people. In late January 2000 he claimed that he 'had the pulse of his people', adding, 'I know the people's mood' (*The Australian*, 20 January 2000).

As was the case with Sukarno, this presumed omniscience was accompanied by a certain insouciance. Indeed, we are left with the impression that this man who claims to know his people so well nevertheless seems only lightly touched by the suffering they are experiencing. As Budiman (2000, pp. 168–9) has observed, he appears to lack a sense of the seriousness of such events as the separatist movement in Aceh. Indeed, the thought and behaviour of the two leaders appear similarly detached. I talked above of Sukarno retreating into the autistic world of omnipotent fantasy. It would probably be an exaggeration to make the same claim of Abdurrahman Wahid, for he is working within the confines of a democratic system where a vigorous parliament and a free press make it more difficult for solipsism to flourish. Nevertheless, a similar tendency has been discernible in him for some time, to judge by the comment of a close observer who said that Abdurrahman 'did not see himself as an ordinary person bound by the "facts" or "truth". [Rather] ... he had to make the facts and truth work for him, because that's what people ... [of] destiny do'.[1]

CONCLUSION

The survival of the Republic of Indonesia as a voluntary association will depend on many factors. One of these is a form of leadership able to bridge the diversity and fissiparous tendencies at work within it. Strong leadership, as we have seen, promotes political division; although the leader may express a commitment to ethnic tolerance, scapegoating will always be a temptation. As we know, this was a temptation to which Soeharto succumbed. On the other hand, middle way leadership enjoys a close affinity with civic nationalism and is thus well suited to the nation-building task that remains incomplete in Indonesia. Therefore, it is distressing to note that Indonesia's incumbent president is seemingly unable to learn from the history of Sukarno's leadership, only occasionally practising this way of leading in its full, broad and inclusive form. At other times he leads after the manner of its narrower, more self-regarding version. But what is the lesson to be learned in this case? If it is that hubris may bring a leader and his people undone, then this is, of course, a difficult lesson for a proud leader to learn, especially when his pride has been tuned to a high defensive pitch in the aftermath of two strokes. But if it is, more specifically, that middle way leadership cannot long survive in an authoritarian system of government, then it may be said that this was a lesson Abdurrahman Wahid learnt years ago (although he would not have framed it in these terms) when he first sought to advance the cause of democracy in Indonesia. It may appear paradoxical that he now finds himself, as president, not altogether comfortable within a democratic system of government that restrains his actions and challenges his grandiosity. But we have this form of government, and Abdurrahman Wahid's original insight into its virtues, to thank for the fact that his middle way leadership survives at all.

NOTES

*   I am very grateful to Herb Feith, Greg Fealy and Marcus Mietzner for the information and interpretations concerning Sukarno, Megawati and Abdurrahman Wahid that they have generously shared with me.
1   These remarks were made by a close observer of Abdurrahman Wahid and the NU, Martin van Bruinessen, to Greg Fealy (pers. comm., 4 January 2000).

8

PARTIES AND PARLIAMENT: SERVING WHOSE INTERESTS?

*Greg Fealy**

Political parties and the parliament are key elements of Indonesia's democratisation. In the two years since Soeharto's downfall, the roles of both have changed dramatically. Parties have proliferated and been freed from state manipulation; they are now the central players in Indonesian politics where once they were either instruments of the New Order regime or largely impotent 'opposition' parties. Parliament has gone from a 'rubber stamp' institution that was compliant to the government's wishes to being an assertively independent legislature with the power to review and restrict executive actions.

The expanded role of parties and parliament has prompted heated debate in political, academic and NGO circles about the quality of their performance. Critics have questioned the commitment of major parties to consolidating democracy, claiming they are too focused on narrow electoral politics and the quest for power rather than creating a fair, open and stable political system (*Media Indonesia*, 17 May 2000). The growing tension between the Abdurrahman Wahid government and the parliament over issues of executive accountability to the legislature has also sparked widespread debate about the delineation of powers and the effectiveness of Indonesia's political institutions.

This chapter examines the performance of parties and the parliament from both a contemporary and a historical perspective. Historical comparisons have not featured prominently in the recent debate about political institutions and democratisation, but when they have been made, the usual period of comparison has been the New Order years (1966–98). I would argue, however, that it is more fruitful to compare the current parties and parliament with those of the 1950–57 period, when Indonesia had a liberal democratic system. This period more closely approximates present conditions than the authoritarian Guided Democracy (1957–66) and New Order regimes and thus provides a better vantage point for analysing political change and continuity. In joining this debate, I am mindful of how little research has been completed on the contemporary party and parliamentary systems. Although numerous scholars are currently studying aspects of these topics, few findings have been published as yet. As a result, much of my consideration of these matters rests on impressions and scattered anecdotal information rather than detailed research.

For the purposes of this chapter, discussion of parliament is restricted to the national legislature, the People's Representative Council (DPR), and does not include regional legislatures.[1] Indonesia's supreme decision-making body, the People's Consultative Assembly (MPR), is also excluded on the grounds that it has neither continuing overview of government activities nor a legislative function, two of the core tasks of a parliament.[2]

DEFINING THE FUNCTIONS OF PARTIES AND PARLIAMENTS

Before discussing the performance of Indonesia's parties and parliament, some consideration should be given to the normative roles of parties and legislatures in a properly functioning democracy, as well as the constitutional and legislative framework within which they operate in Indonesia. For political parties, the most obvious function is that of gaining or maintaining power through elections. This involves a range of activities, including the nomination of legislative candidates, the conducting of election campaigns and the persuasion of voters about the relative strengths of a party's candidates or policies and the relative weaknesses of its opponents'.

But it is the 'non-electoral' functions of parties that are of more interest to this discussion. Chief among them is the unification and representation of a range of interest groups. By articulating the demands of various interest groups, parties can bring them into the political system and act as a safety valve for grievances, thus ensuring political stability and order. A second important function is to serve as a link between government and the people, particularly by passing on demands of interest groups to the executive and explaining government policies to the community. Parties can educate and activate the electorate, reaching politically inactive citizens and leading to greater participation. Third, parties carry out political recruitment, not only of members but also of cadres to be groomed for leadership roles.

The main legislative framework for parties in the post-Soeharto era is the Political Parties Law of 1999 (Undang-Undang No. 2/1999). It defines the aims and roles of parties in Indonesian democracy and includes many of the elements referred to above. Parties, it states, are organisations formed voluntarily by Indonesian citizens to 'struggle for the interests of both their members and the people and state via general elections'. Furthermore, 'the sovereignty of political parties is in the hands of their members' (section 1). The function of parties (section 7) is to:

(a) undertake political education to foster and develop the people's awareness of their political rights and obligations in the life of the nation and state;
(b) absorb, channel and champion community interests in creating state policies via the mechanism of deliberative/representative bodies; and
(c) prepare community members to fill political positions in accordance with democratic mechanisms.

The new law also defines parties as 'democratic institutions' that are 'vehicles for stating support and demands in the political process' (Penerbit Sinar Grafika 1999, p. 5). While not fully comprehensive, the law provides a credible legislative basis for a democratic party system in Indonesia.

Parliament, as a forum for party representatives, has numerous functions in common with parties, including those of transmitting opinions between the executive and the community and representing and protecting a range of community interests. It can also resolve conflict over competing interests or ideologies. Its two primary functions, however, are overseeing and controlling the actions of the executive and creating legislation. For most parliaments, the legislative function is largely that of discussing, amending and passing or rejecting bills, rather than drafting bills. Supervising the government is achieved through a range of controlling rights, such as the power to reject budgets and the right to question, criticise, investigate and censure the government.

The functions and powers of Indonesia's parliament are spelt out in the constitution (discussed below) and in an array of statutes and parliamentary decrees. In general, though, it possesses a wide range of legislative and investigative powers such as can be found in many parliaments in well-established democracies, and it also has the authority to monitor and review the actions of the executive, the military and the bureaucracy through a system of specialised commissions and committees.

This chapter concentrates on two elements: political participation and interest representation. Indonesia's electorate endured almost four decades of authoritarian rule under Sukarno's Guided Democracy and more particularly Soeharto's New Order. The number of parties was limited to ten in 1961 and three after 1973. Under Soeharto's so-called 'floating mass' policy, most voters were able to participate in politics only during the brief, five-yearly election campaigns, and the political rights of a vast majority of Indonesians were severely curtailed. Moreover, there was widespread intimidation, vote buying and electoral manipulation to ensure large victories for the state party, Golkar.

Political discourse was severely restricted and ordinary Indonesians were not encouraged to be politically active in non-regime-sponsored organisations. If democracy is to flourish in Indonesia today, it must achieve genuine mass participation and the representation of a broad cross-section of interests. Parties and the parliament will be crucial to this process.

POLITICAL PARTIES

The rise of political parties since Soeharto's downfall has been a hallmark of Indonesia's embracing of democracy. More than 140 parties were registered in the first seven months of Habibie's presidency, 48 of which were later judged to have met the Interior Ministry's minimum requirements and went on to contest the June 1999 general elections. Of these, 21 parties won seats in the national parliament (Table 8.1). Despite (or perhaps because of) three decades of grassroots depoliticisation under the New Order, the public appeared eager to participate in party politics. Thousands of party branches were established across the country and millions of people flocked to join new parties and attend political rallies. That the campaign passed without significant violence was in part attributable to community determination to prevent incidents which might jeopardise the now free elections.

Despite the appearance of a successful and effective party system, there are strong grounds for arguing that Indonesia's parties are not fulfilling their intended role. To begin with, most of the major parties are not, to quote the 1999 statute, 'in the hands of the people' but rather are controlled by small numbers of elites, both at the national and local levels. Major parties tend to have poor internal communications: branches generally receive scant information about policy issues or higher-level decision making, and there is little consultation with rank and file members on such matters. Branch-level activity in most parties has slumped since the last election, prompting one senior advisor of a major party to observe wryly that hers was 'just a five-yearly party' that only came to life for the quinquennial elections (confidential interview with PKB activist, 3 December 1999). This lack of grassroots input allows local officials to control party affairs with only minimal accountability to members. In short, parties are failing in their task of aggregating and transmitting community interests to the parliament and the government. They are also not educating members about issues in a manner that would produce an informed and politically mature constituency.

A further problem is that, far from being subject to 'democratic recruitment', party cadreisation is poorly developed and prone to favouritism. Instead of cadres being inducted into parties through formal processes and rising through the ranks on their merits, recruitment and promotion often depend

TABLE 8.1 The 1999 General Election Results and Parliamentary Seats for Major Parties

Party	Votes (%)	Seats (no.)
1 PDI-P (Indonesian Democratic Party of Struggle)	33.76	153
2 Golkar (Functional Groups Party)	22.46	120
3 PKB (National Awakening Party)	12.62	51
4 PPP (United Development Party)	10.72	58
5 PAN (National Mandate Party)	7.12	34
6 PBB (Crescent Moon and Star Party)	1.94	13
7 PK (Justice Party)	1.36	7
8 PKP (Justice and Unity Party)	1.01	4
9 PNU (Muslim Community Awakening Party)	0.64	5
10 PDKB (Love the Nation Democratic Party)	0.52	5
Other 11 parties	7.85	15[a]

a This figure does not include the 38 parliamentarians representing the military and the police.

Sources: BHKPU (2000), p. 192; LSPP (1999), pp. 100–101; Kompas 2000, p. vii.

on personal contacts and access to networks of patronage. Many of those nominated as legislative candidates for the 1999 election owed their positions to high-level connections or to their presumed ability to 'deliver' blocs of votes from a community group or contribute generously to party coffers. Although parties usually had set criteria for the selection of candidates, these were often ignored or manipulated. As a result, there is limited opportunity for talented cadres to advance their careers without money or *koneksi*. The most notable exception to this is the Justice Party (PK). It has a small but highly committed membership, with strict rules and processes for promotion within the party. To a lesser extent, Golkar has also been able to maintain genuine cadreisation, though connections and financial resources still remain a major element of the party's culture.

Some conclusions can be drawn about the state of Indonesian democracy and party politics by comparing the current major parties with those of the 1950s. The first is that individual leaders dominate modern parties to a far greater degree than was the case 40 years ago: President Abdurrahman Wahid of the National Awakening Party (PKB), Vice-President Megawati Sukarnop-utri of the Indonesian Democratic Party of Struggle (PDI-P) and, to a lesser extent, Amien Rais of the National Mandate Party (PAN) are exemplars of this. They are revered figures in their respective parties and have immense power over decision making. Abdurrahman and Megawati in particular have almost cult status and attract unquestioning, often fanatical, loyalty from many of their grassroots supporters. Leaders of parties in the 1950s, such as Mohamad Natsir of Masyumi, D.N. Aidit, chairman of the Indonesian Communist Party (PKI), and Wahab Chasbullah of Nahdlatul Ulama (NU), were highly influential, but they were not iconic figures like Abdurrahman or Megawati; nor could they impose their will on their parties as their modern counterparts are capable of doing.

Another striking aspect is the declining importance of ideological and policy disputes in the post-Soeharto era. In the 1950s, ideological differences drove many of the factional disputes within parties; party meetings and publications often featured intense debates over core principles and concepts and how these were to be reflected in the party platform and in strategy. Serious cadres were usually well versed in such matters, and ideologues figured prominently in many large parties. In contemporary parties, ideological discussions are usually a minor part of their internal discourse. Few of the parties at the last election attempted to put forward cogent ideological statements, and most were content to build their platform around vague commitments to *reformasi* and the stamping out of corruption. Moreover, most of the major parties have striven to suppress debate on contentious issues, partly to avoid the appearance of internal division and partly to ensure that the views of the dominant leadership group are not challenged. For example, the PDI-P and PKB congresses in 2000 were notable for the absence of debate about ideology and controversial policy issues. They were highly stage-managed events in which most important decisions were made behind closed doors by a small group of leaders rather than on the floor of the congress after a thorough and open debate. Such processes do little to promote transparency or community understanding of important issues.

The ebb of ideology has been accompanied by the rising importance of money in party politics. Although patronage and the use of financial and employment rewards have been an ever-present element in Indonesian politics since independence, 'money politics' is far more pervasive in parties now than before the New Order period. The purchasing of strategic positions and the use of monetary inducements to influence decision making are commonplace in local and national party affairs. In the past two years, there have been numerous instances of party discipline being subverted by money politics. The most obvious manifestation of this has been the frequent failure of regional parliamentarians to vote for a party's official nominee for positions such as regent (*bupati*) or speaker because a rival candidate has won their support through bribery. The PDI-P has been particularly prone to this.

Physical intimidation also plays a far greater role in today's party politics than it did 40 years ago. All major parties have their own security forces, commonly referred to as *satgas* (*satuan tugas*). In the case of the four largest parties – the PDI-P, Golkar, the PKB and the United Development Party (PPP) – these are effectively paramilitary groups. Members receive military-style training and wear distinctive jungle fatigues in their party's colours; *satgas* organisational structures and leadership titles also mirror those of an army. The quality of these groups is varied, ranging from well-run units comprising highly committed party members to ill-disciplined gangs dominated by local hoodlums and criminals. The *satgas* are supposed to protect party members from outside threats and maintain order at internal party functions. There are numerous instances, however, of them becoming involved in unsavoury and often criminal activities such as petty extortion, racketeering and debt collection in order to generate income for the party and *satgas* members. *Satgas* have also been known to take a partisan role in internal party disputes, often involving a powerful local figure employing them to harass and intimidate rivals. This problem has been especially evident in the PDI-P, with more than a few of its candidates at the last election gaining their positions through the use of strong-arm tactics. Party 'security' forces were also used against other parties during the 1999 election, leading on occasion to violent clashes. I can find no evidence of major parties of the 1950s using paramilitary organisations or internal security units, and the reported use of intimidation by one party faction against another was relatively rare.

A final conclusion is that political parties in the 1950s were far more central to the intellectual life of the country than is the case now. At that time, the great majority of public intellectuals were affiliated with a party and were often active in promoting discussion within parties on ideological or policy issues as well as engaging in public debate with intellectuals from rival parties. The Indonesian Socialist Party (PSI) and the modernist Muslim Masyumi in particular were the focus of intense intellectual activity. In the post-Soeharto era, many intellectuals have remained aloof from parties, preferring instead to foster links with NGOs and independent think-tanks or serve as freelance academic commentators. The reluctance of intellectuals to join parties is in part due to a 1999 regulation preventing civil servants from becoming members or executives of a political party (PP No. 5 and No. 12, 1999). As a result, academics at state universities and government researchers must resign from their positions before they can become party members. No such prohibition applied during the 1950s. Another factor, though, is the low opinion many intellectuals have of major parties and their leaders.

The foregoing comparisons suggest that the party system of the 1950s operated more effectively than that of contemporary Indonesia. Parties functioned better then as institutions for informing the electorate and transmitting community views to the legislature and the government than do current par-

ties. There was a more open and robust discourse on matters of political substance, and party cultures were less idolatrous. Corruption and hooliganism
were also much less common that they are today. It must also be noted,
though, that the party system of the 1950s failed to provide stable government
and lost the trust of the public, thereby contributing to the downfall of liberal
democracy and the rise of Guided Democracy.

Undoubtedly, many of the 'undemocratic' features of Indonesia's present
party system are legacies of the New Order regime. The floating mass policy
disengaged a large section of society from grassroots-level politics. Although
there is now a high level of interest in politics, knowledge of democratic
norms and the willingness of ordinary members to assert their political rights
within parties is limited. Many political leaders have little motivation to
change this, as it affords them greater freedom to run their parties as they see
fit rather than in the ways that branch members and the party's constituency
dictate. Political corruption, intimidation and coercion were integral elements
of Soeharto's authoritarian rule, as was state manipulation of parties. Ridding
Indonesian politics of these elements will require a longer-term transformation of political culture.

PARLIAMENT

Parliament's change of role has been no less remarkable than that of the political parties. Since Soeharto's downfall, the DPR has greatly increased its
powers, especially in relation to the executive. The most obvious change is
that relating to its legislative powers. The constitutional amendments passed
by the MPR's October 1999 General Session and August 2000 Annual Session granted the DPR greater powers to initiate legislation. The original 1945
Constitution stated that the 'president holds the authority to create legislation
with the approval of the DPR' (section 5). The 1999 amendments place
greater emphasis on the DPR's legislative role, declaring that 'the DPR has
the authority to create legislation' and that 'DPR members have the right to
propose bills' (sections 20 and 21). The president was accorded the right 'to
submit legislation to the DPR' (section 5). Although criticised for not explicitly defining the parliament's powers, these amendments allow parliamentarians far greater rights to table bills than have existed since 1959. The
amendments passed in 2000 further strengthened the DPR's position with
regard to the executive by stating that a bill that does not receive presidential
approval within 30 days will automatically become law (section 20). This
effectively removes the president's right to veto legislation.

The second major change is greater DPR involvement in presidential
appointments. MPR Decree IV/2000 requires the president to seek DPR

approval before appointing or dismissing the chiefs of the armed forces and the police (sections 3 and 7). This sits oddly with section 10 of the constitution, which vests 'supreme authority over the armed forces' with the president. Furthermore, the 1999 constitutional amendments obliged the president 'to consider the views of the DPR' when appointing Indonesian ambassadors or accepting foreign ambassadors (section 13). It also required the president to consult with the DPR before granting amnesties or pardons (section 14).

The third element is the DPR's reassertion of its right to monitor the executive. In particular, it has begun exercising its powers of interpellation (that is, suspending normal parliamentary procedures to demand an explanation from the president or other high officials) and investigation (*hak angket*) into government activities, neither of which have been used by an Indonesian parliament in more than 30 years (Sekretariat DPR-GR 1970, pp. 183–4; Budiardjo 1994, p. 305). These rights were given constitutional force in the 2000 amendments (section 20A). The DPR also revitalised its system of parliamentary commissions to oversee specific areas of policy and government activity. Further moves to circumscribe presidential powers appear likely. The parliament is soon to consider a bill on presidential powers that reportedly sets out limitations on the president's prerogative rights and his ability to accept personal gifts and donations from domestic or foreign benefactors (*Kompas*, 3 October 2000).

In all, these constitutional amendments add up to a significant shift of authority from the executive to the legislature. Whereas the original 1945 Constitution set out a largely presidential system, the amended constitution takes Indonesia closer to a hybrid parliamentary and presidential system. This shift has been brought about by a number of factors, the most obvious of which is a desire to give parliament the power to protect the rights of citizens against arbitrary or oppressive government action. But practical political considerations have also driven this process. Fears that Abdurrahman Wahid would prove an erratic or irresponsible president prompted some of the parties within his initial governing coalition, such as Golkar and the Muslim Central Axis (Poros Tengah) grouping, to push through measures allowing the DPR and MPR greater control over him. This was, in effect, an insurance policy to ensure that Abdurrahman kept to his undertakings on policy issues and the sharing of political power.

How is the DPR exercising these new powers? For the most part, its performance has been patchy. For example, despite now having the authority to initiate legislation, only five bills have emanated from parliamentarians in the past year, four of which were relatively straightforward bills relating to the creation of new provinces; the other 41 bills to come before parliament originated from the executive (*Kompas*, 18 August 2000, p. 7). In some ways, this should not be surprising. Although there are dozens of lawyers in the DPR, no member has expertise in drafting legislation. Furthermore, the DPR Secretariat General has until recently had few staff available with the necessary expertise to assist MPs in drawing up bills. While it is true that in most well-established democracies, the executive rather than parliament is the source of most legislation, the DPR could assume a more proactive role than it is at present. DPR leaders and members have, to date, given priority to monitoring the executive and have neglected to develop parliament's legislative functions.

The DPR's use of its powers to probe executive action and provide input into government decision making has also fallen short of expectations. In deliberating on such matters, parliamentarians have often been ill-prepared and more inclined to seek political advantage than to adhere to due parliamentary practice. For example, members of the Special DPR Committee investigating alleged presidential corruption in the Bulog scandal (commonly referred to as Pansus Bulog-gate) have repeatedly breached the stipulations of the 1954 *angket* law by revealing to the media evidence given before *in camera* proceedings (*Media Indonesia*, 19 October 2000). Their actions, though contrary to the law and parliamentary ethics, appear calculated to embarrass President Abdurrahman Wahid and add to the political pressure on him.

Another committee inquiring into the actions of the military in Aceh during the period the province was under military control mishandled its public questioning of six senior generals last year and failed to extract useful additional evidence. Committee members seemed poorly briefed and coordinated. When the generals denied claims put by the committee regarding their complicity in military abuses, few members had follow-up questions to force them into more detailed rebuttals and some members lapsed into political rhetoric. The DPR Committee (Komisi Satu), which has responsibility for matters related to foreign affairs, also has a poor record of informed decision making. In early 2000, for instance, it urged the government to consider rejecting Richard Smith as the next Australian ambassador to Indonesia on the grounds that he was ill-equipped for the position having only served as ambassador to Mongolia; Smith had, in fact, been ambassador to China. The DPR has also been tardy on amnesty issues. In late 1998, Democratic People's Party (PRD) leader Budiman Sudjatmiko was forced to remain in gaol for almost two months after being granted clemency by the government while waiting for the DPR to approve his release (*Kompas*, 18 August 1999, p. 7).

The use of interpellation rights has also yielded mixed results. The DPR used these powers in July 2000 to summon the president to explain his dismissal of cabinet ministers Laksamana Sukardi and Yusuf Kalla. The interpellation session, however, resulted in a stand-off between the president and parliament. Abdurrahman refused to answer questions put by members, claiming that to do so would breach the constitutional principle that the president is accountable only to the MPR, not the DPR. Though Abdurrahman later tendered documents to support his actions, little new light was shed on the dismissals and the main outcome of the exercise was to heighten tensions between the executive and the legislature regarding the DPR's right to demand accountability from the president (*Suara Merdeka*, 21 July 2000; *Republika*, 12 October 2000).

Parliament's disappointing performance is partly attributable to the relative inexperience of its members. A large minority of parliamentarians are new to the legislature and thus lack familiarity with parliamentary practice. Analysis of the DPR in the 1950s suggests that parliamentary efficiency and professionalism tended to increase as members gained experience and developed conventions and practices to meet legislative demands (Budiardjo 1956, p. 17).

Still, many MPs evince a low commitment to their representational duties. Attendance at parliamentary sessions has been falling, and reached a low point in October 2000 when a plenary session could not be convened for want of a quorum (*Media Indonesia*, 18 October 2000). A recent study showed that only 65% of DPR commission members attended proceedings in the mid-year parliamentary sitting, a decline of 4% over the previous sitting (*Suara Pembaruan*, 16 July 2000). Although the DPR now has an independent Research and Analysis Unit (P3I), only a relatively small number of parliamentarians regularly use the service. A large number of MPs appear to give high priority to pursuing personal business and patronage opportunities, with many accepting offers of directorships, consultancies or partnerships in the commercial world. Personal observation indicates that MPs are more likely to be visited by people seeking to discuss business than constituent-related matters. Some initial studies suggest that the income of members from non-parliamentary sources leapt significantly after their election to the DPR (*Kompas*, 28 July 2000).

Comparing the performance of the current parliament with that of earlier DPRs provides some interesting conclusions, though account must be taken of the different political environments in which they operated. The 1950 Constitution enshrined a parliamentary system in which governments were fully accountable to the DPR. During the nine years of that constitution's operation, the legislature precipitated the downfall of three governments. The unamended 1945 Constitution, which was in force from 1959 to 1999, restricted the role of the parliament and ensured an executive-dominated political system. DPRs throughout this period were largely subservient to the Sukarno and Soeharto regimes. The present DPR, despite its enhanced powers, is unable to bring down a government as its predecessors of the 1950s were able to do; it can only, provided certain requirements are met, call on the MPR to convoke a special session to impeach the president.

There are several indicators of comparative performance. The first is the enactment rate, that is, the number of bills passed by a parliament in a given period (Table 8.2). The Provisional DPR (1950–56) passed an average of 30 bills per year; the 1956–59 DPR approved almost 34 per annum. The current parliament's rate is 27, a vast improvement on the annual average of less than 11 for DPRs from 1971 to 1997. A measure of the assertiveness of parliament may be found in the number of bills rejected or withdrawn. During the Provisional DPR, 64 of 237 bills (27%) were withdrawn, the rate falling to 16 of

TABLE 8.2 Comparison of Parliamentary Legislative, Investigative and Interpellative Activity

Legislature	Bills Passed	Average per Year	DPR-initiated Bills	Investi-gations)	Interpel-lations
1 KNIP (Aug 1945–Dec 1950)	133	28.3	15	1	2
2 DPR-RIS (Dec 1949–Aug 1950)	7	7.0	1	0	1
3 Provisional DPR (Aug 1950–Mar 1956)	167	29.9	5	1	16
4 DPR from 1955 Election (Mar 1956–Jul 1959)	113	33.9	3	1	3
5 Interim DPR (Jul 1959–Jun 1960)	5	5.0	0	0	0
6 DPR-GR (June 1960–Nov 1965)	117	21.6	0	0	0
7 DPR-GR Pancasila (minus PKI) (Nov 1965–Nov 1966)	11	11.0	0	0	0
8 New Order DPR-GR (Nov 1966–Aug 1970)	81	21.0	5	1	0
9 DPR from 1971 election	43	7.8	0	0	0
10 DPR from 1977 election	55	11.0	0	0	0
11 DPR from 1982 election	47	9.4	0	0	0
12 DPR from 1987 election	56	11.0	0	0	0
13 DPR from 1992 election	74	14.8	0	0	0
14 DPR from 1997 election	n.a.	n.a.	n.a.	0	0
15 DPR from 1999 election[a] (installed Oct 1999)	27	27.0	5	2	2

a All figures quoted for the current DPR are for the period October 1999 to October 2000.

Sources: Sekretariat DPR-GR (1970); Budiardjo (1994), p. 305; Sekretariat Jenderal DPR (2000a, 2000b).

113 bills (14%) for the 1956–59 parliament. During the New Order period, only two bills were withdrawn or substantially amended by the DPR. The current DPR has rejected only one of 41 bills (2%) presented to it.

Another interesting benchmark of legislative initiative is the number of bills proposed by the DPR. No post-1971 New Order parliament initiated legislation; the present DPR has put forward five bills. The Provisional DPR proposed five (mostly relating to internal DPR procedures), the 1956–59 DPR three and the 1966–70 DPR-GR five. Notably, the interim legislature of the revolutionary period, KNIP (1945–50), was the most impressive with 15 member-initiated bills (Budiardjo 1994, pp. 304–6). Though by no means conclusive, these figures suggest that parliaments of the 1940s and 1950s may have taken their legislative functions more seriously than the present DPR. It should also be mentioned, however, that parliament in the 1950s was, at times, notoriously slow, in some cases taking as long as three years to pass bills (Budiardjo 1956, p. 19; Logemann 1953, pp. 350–51).

It could be argued that the above figures do not take account of the quality of the legislation passed or of the thoroughness of the DPR's consideration of bills. Even here, there is much expert legal opinion suggesting that the quality of bills passed by the DPR in the past two years has been at best variable. Many bills were drafted with little attention to detail, were vaguely worded and, in some cases, contained clauses which contradicted other statutes. Examples include a bill giving police the power to investigate crimes committed by off-duty members of the Indonesian National Army (TNI) but which failed to revoke the earlier law granting military police exclusive authority over such inquiries, and the decentralisation laws that fail to define which government institutions will have authority for an array of income-raising and revenue disbursement tasks. This lack of precision provides the bureaucracy with opportunities to manipulate the interpretation of the legislation for its own purposes.

One final point of comparison between the present parliament and those of the 1950s is that relations with the executive and bureaucracy at that time were more constructive than is the case now. This is attributable to the fact that, until at least 1956, there was acceptance by both government and the legislature about the proper role of the DPR. As Herb Feith (1962, p. 320) wrote, 'parliament was respected and governments largely adhered to the rule of constitutional democracy' and 'cabinets were meticulous in relations with parliament'. Miriam Budiardjo (1956, p. 19) also concluded that exchanges between parliamentary committees and government officials were 'constructive', leading to mutual agreement about amendments to bills.

This sense of mutual respect and agreed delineation of functions has been lost. Since Abdurrahman Wahid became president there has been rising hostility between the executive and the parliament, at the core of which is fundamental disagreement over the nature of Indonesia's political system, namely over to what degree it is presidential or parliamentary (NDIIA 2000; PSHK 2000, pp. 8–12). In particular, does the DPR have the power to demand accountability from the executive, and especially the president? The constitutional uncertainty over this matter has led to high-stakes manoeuvring by the government and the DPR in order to gain political and moral advantage. Both sides appear to be caught in a cycle of testing each other's authority and resolve. Parliament, for example, is determined to use its interpellation powers to require the president to explain his actions, claiming that this is in keeping with the *reformasi* ideals of accountability and transparency; the president resists, saying that the DPR's actions are politically motivated and unconstitutional. The rhetoric from both sides is increasingly opprobrious.

This dispute carries two risks for the DPR. First, it may incline parliamentarians to use the legislature as an instrument in the battle for political power rather than developing a genuinely professional institution for representing their constituents and maintaining high standards of government accountability. And second, it may erode public confidence in parliament if DPR members are seen to be neglecting or abusing their position for short-term political or personal interests. One solution is to clarify the relationship between the executive and parliament in future constitutional amendments. Many of the recent amendments which strengthen the authority of the DPR vis-à-vis the president have been passed with minimal discussion about the fundamental structure of the political system. Unless such disputes are settled, the continued wrangling between the executive and the DPR could diminish the standing of the nation's key political institutions.

CONCLUSION

In the past two years, the Indonesian electorate has shown great faith in and commitment to democratisation. This has been evident in its ready embracing of political parties, in its discipline in achieving an overwhelmingly fair and non-violent election campaign in 1999, and in its interest in following parliamentary developments. For democracy to continue to develop, parties and parliament need to ensure that they actively involve and effectively represent community interests in the political process. Failure to do so would betray the faith shown in them by the community and undermine the current process of political reform.

NOTES

* In preparing this article, I was fortunate in being able to draw upon the expertise of Herb Feith, Angus McIntyre, Lance Castles and Ken Ward. Their ideas and suggestions, particularly in relation to Indonesian politics of the 1950s and 1960s, proved most helpful. I am also grateful to Rodd McGibbon for his comments on the functioning of the present parliament.

1 There are now more than 350 provincial and subprovincial parliaments (DPRDs). Assessing their role would require a far more extensive study than is possible here.

2 The MPR's main functions are to elect the president and vice-president, determine the Broad Guidelines of State Policy (GBHN) and amend the constitution. It also has the power to impeach the president.

9

CONSERVATIVE POLITICAL IDEOLOGY IN INDONESIA: A FOURTH WAVE?

David Bourchier

The exhilarating political reforms of 1998 and 1999 made many of the ideological mantras of the Soeharto decades (1966–98) seem inane and anachronistic. No longer did politicians speak of 'Pancasila democracy', *dwifungsi*, integralism and the disjuncture between Indonesian culture and liberal freedoms. The new catch cries were democracy, regional autonomy, human rights and civilian supremacy. This entailed what Budianta (2000, p. 109) referred to as a 'cultural identity crisis', a search for new ways to think about what it meant to be Indonesian. Old taboos were swept aside as it once again became possible to talk of the liberal democratic 1950s in positive tones, to advocate federalism and to call for the overhaul of the 1945 Constitution. But this public rethinking of the foundations of the Indonesian state and of national identity was only part of the story. More than a year after Abdurrahman Wahid was elected president, the power of the so-called 'status quo' forces has become increasingly apparent. It is clear that however Indonesian politics is going to unfold in the next few years, the forces of reaction and conservatism have to be taken more seriously. This chapter will reflect on the character of political conservatism in Indonesia. It will examine ideological devices used by past generations of Indonesian conservatives to counter democratic ideas and movements. This will help put current attempts to retard the democratisation process in perspective and perhaps assist the present generation of reformers to respond to them.

Conservatism is an imprecise and contingent concept. In this chapter I am using the term to signify something which in its extreme form resembles what Indonesia's first prime minister, Sutan Sjahrir (1968, p. 28), called 'hierarchical feudalistic solidarism' but which more broadly manifests as rejection (or suspicion) of ideological pluralism in favour of a more or less organicist conception of the polity. These conservatives, who in another context could be described as ultra-conservatives or reactionaries, regard political contestation as dysfunctional; as a problem to be overcome rather than a natural expression of a diverse society manageable through democratic negotiation. They have typically represented their anti-liberal and indeed anti-political outlook as culturally authentic, justifying this with reference to their own peculiarly paternalistic construction of indigenous tradition.

Broadly speaking, there have been three waves of conservative ideologising by Indonesian politicians in the 20th century: romantic traditionalism (1910s to 1945), corporatist anti-partyism (mid-1950s to early 1960s) and integralist developmentalism in Soeharto's New Order (1966–98), especially before 1988. While these initiatives share a family resemblance, each was shaped by its particular political and intellectual milieu. After looking briefly at how each of them rose and subsided, I will speculate on the shape and character of an incipient fourth wave of reaction in the post-Soeharto era.

ROMANTIC TRADITIONALISM

What I have called romantic traditionalism arose as a conservative response to the Muslim, communist and socialist nationalist movements in the first two decades of the 20th century. Its proponents were mainly members of the *pangreh praja*, the indigenous administrative elite that served the colonial government and joined organisations such as Boedi Oetomo or Parindra.[1] Many in fact thought of themselves as nationalists, but dedicated themselves to either cultural nationalism – in most cases Javanese cultural nationalism – or to a version of national independence that involved minimal disruption to the existing social hierarchy. Sukarno's brand of nationalism they saw as dangerously populist and a threat to the privileges they enjoyed as servants of the colonial state. It was only after Sukarno and other hardline nationalist leaders were arrested and exiled in the 1930s that they came to play a significant role in national politics, becoming the best represented Indonesian political party in the Volksraad (van Klinken 1997, p. 82). Their vision was of a monarchical or autocratic system in which a class of benevolent administrators presided over a country of grateful and obedient peasants.

The most developed attempt to translate the ideas of the romantic traditionalists into reality was Raden Supomo's contribution to the Japanese-sponsored constitutional debates in June 1945. Supomo was Indonesia's foremost expert on *adat* (traditional) law. As with several other representatives of this tradition, Supomo had been trained in Holland and was strongly influenced by the Historical School of Law, a stream of legal thinking associated with German romantic nationalism. One of the key lessons Supomo and many of his colleagues learnt from their Dutch training in the 1920s and 1930s under figures like Cornelis van Vollenhoven was a deep suspicion of liberalism and a strong belief that a country's legal system ought to be grounded in its indige-nous traditions. Supomo argued that village *adat* provided the best model for Indonesia's future legal and political system.

As Indonesia's highest ranking legal scholar, Supomo was assigned the task of drafting a constitution by the Japanese-appointed Committee for the Investigation of Indonesian Independence. In June 1945, in the dying months of the Japanese occupation, he spoke to that committee of the glories of Indonesia's traditional society and *adat*, and argued strongly for a constitu-tional framework based on the political values that he (and his Dutch teach-ers) regarded as embedded in traditional *adat*: namely harmony, consensus and a unity between rulers and ruled.

On this basis he rejected liberalism (as too individualistic) and commu-nism (as based on a theory of conflict) in favour of what he called integral-ism. Indonesia, he argued, should be an 'integralist state'. What he meant was a state in which the interests of the whole always came before the interests of individuals or groups. Unfortunately for him, though, the examples he chose to illustrate the idea of an 'integralist state' were Nazi Germany and imperial Japan. He advocated a totalistic (if not totalitarian) state in which he argued that there would be a close, familial relationship between the rulers and the ruled – as in his imagined harmonious village community. Any provision for political rights in the constitution, he maintained, would run counter to inte-gralist principles because it would imply a separation, and a lack of trust, between the government and the people.

Supomo was only partly successful in having his ideas incorporated into the constitution. While some members of the committee supported his ideas, others of a more democratic bent opposed them and managed to have some political rights (however ambiguously worded) and checks on executive authority written into it. By the end of 1945 romantic traditionalism was a spent force. The Japanese had surrendered, Allied troops were arriving and the spirit of revolution had spread across the country. Supomo's primary con-stituency, the *pangreh praja*, were prime targets of popular violence because of the part they had played in enforcing the vicious labour recruitment and requisitioning policies of the Japanese military administration.

However, some of the ideas promoted by Supomo and other Dutch-trained lawyers flowed into the mainstream of secular nationalist political thought. One was the principle that a country's legal and political system must be rooted in its customs and traditions. A second was the idea that traditional Indonesian patterns of social organisation were, essentially, communal, har-monious and cooperative, in contrast to the individualistic, conflict-ridden, litigious character of Westerners and Western capitalist society. These ideas were particularly strong among lawyers and were perpetuated via law schools in universities and military academies. Supomo's concept of 'integralism' was also to resurface four decades later.

CORPORATIST ANTI-PARTYISM

Under the parliamentary democratic constitution of 1950, political parties dominated the political process both at the centre and in the provinces. Among the groups most threatened by this was the territorial administrative corps, which had changed its name in 1946 from *pangreh praja* (translated literally, rulers of the realm) to *pamong praja* (guides of the realm). Its members resented the ballooning of the bureaucracy and the rapid influx of party appointees to fill administrative positions that had previously been their preserve. They were also unhappy with the disruptive effects of the proliferation of party organisations in 'their' towns and villages, especially in the 1953–55 period when the parties intensified their activities in preparation for the elections (see, for example, Kartohadikoesoemo 1965, p. 257). Old networks of patronage and obligation were undermined as villagers forged allegiances with unions, parties and other mass organisations.

Allied with these disaffected administrators were sections of the army leadership, who saw the democratic 1950 Constitution as having been foisted on the young republic by the Dutch. In 1954 a group of officers, including suspended army chief of staff General Abdul Haris Nasution, formed IPKI, the League of Supporters of Indonesian Independence, an 'anti-party' party that aimed to 'restore the spirit of the proclamation of 17 August 1945'. The IPKI and the two main *pamong praja* parties, the PIR and Parindra, were critical of emerging social and class antagonism and called on all groups to cooperate rather than compete.[2] Their dislike of parliamentary democracy intensified when their enemies, the Indonesian Communist Party (PKI), won 16.4% of the vote in Indonesia's first general election in 1955. The PIR, Parindra and IPKI were all but obliterated electorally.

As early as 1952, General Nasution held discussions with constitutional lawyers in an attempt to formulate a critique of parliamentary democracy. His key legal advisers throughout the 1950s were the Dutch-educated lawyer Djokosutono and Djokosutono's student Basaruddin Nasution. Drawing on European Catholic political thought, Nasution's advisers proposed a political system based on corporatist principles. Representation in parliament, according to these principles, would be based not on ideologically oriented parties but on occupationally defined 'functional groups' such as intellectuals, artists, farmers, youth, women, soldiers and so on. As in Europe, corporatism in Indonesia was associated with a vision of society as an organic whole, each of whose parts contributed to a putative 'common good'.

Corporatism had some appeal to President Sukarno, who had always stressed the need for unity and who, by 1956, had become openly hostile to political parties because of what he saw as their eternal bickering and indecisiveness. Although Sukarno's arguments with parliamentary democracy were quite different from those of the army, he was persuaded to experiment with the idea of corporatist representation and, in July 1959, conspired with the army to reintroduce the authoritarian 1945 constitution. The army leadership – again advised by Djokosutono – quickly took advantage of the new dispensation, representing themselves as a legitimate functional group and laying claim to a permanent role in the 'highest policy-making bodies, especially parliament, the National Council [Dewan Nasional], the National Planning Council, and the Cabinet' (Nasution, quoted in Penders and Sundhaussen 1985, p. 133). When it became plain to Sukarno in the early 1960s, however, that the military and their conservative allies were controlling the corporatist agenda, he reversed course. By 1963 he had revived the parties, and he became increasingly dependent on the most radical of them, the PKI, to mobilise the population behind his policies. Militant populism returned to the centre stage and conservative ideologies were pushed into retreat.

But, as was the case with the first wave, the formulas and doctrines developed by conservative politicians and army intellectuals in league with constitutional lawyers between 1955 and 1963 did not disappear. Corporatist ideas, a suspicion of political parties and antagonism towards political liberalism and communism alike had become a well-established part of conservative political thinking and were to have a profound influence on the way the military restructured the political environment after it seized power.

THE NEW ORDER: INTEGRALIST DEVELOPMENTALISM

'Conservative' hardly seems the word to describe a government that presided over the slaughter of half a million of its domestic enemies, turned Indonesia's foreign policy upside down and rapidly reintegrated the country with the global economy. But we are talking here about ideology and there is no question that Soeharto's New Order implemented an unprecedentedly comprehensive and sustained campaign to recast Indonesian political culture in a conservative mould.

I have proposed the clumsy label 'integralist developmentalism' to describe New Order ideology because it combined two different streams. The developmentalist aspect of government ideology grew out of modernisation and political order theory. The basic argument of its proponents was that political stability was the essential precondition of economic growth or, in the parlance of the students who supported the rise of the New Order, 'Development yes, politics no!' The government relied on this argument to justify a range of measures, including the centralisation of power in the office of the president, the dismantling of parties and mass organisations, the silencing of criticism and the granting of extensive political rights to the armed forces. Economic collapse under Sukarno, and of course fear of the military, saw most Indonesians go along with this narrowing of political space in the name of development (*pembangunan*). At the same time, realigning Indonesia with the West and with capitalism was going against so much that the country had stood for under Sukarno. Developmentalist discourse emanated from the heartlands of liberal capitalism and had few positive historical or cultural resonances.

In order to present the New Order to the wider public, especially the more nationalist elements, in a way that established its credentials as historically authentic, Soeharto called on the services of a number of ideologues linked to the coalition of anti-party forces in the 1950s (PIR, the *pamong praja* or Nasution's group). All were either lawyers or intellectuals connected with the Military Law Academy. One key strategy they used was to appropriate for the New Order the symbol of the Pancasila, which until that time had been closely identified with its creator, Sukarno. Soeharto's adviser Brigadier-General Sutjipto accused Sukarno of 'ideological deviation' and of 'betraying the Pancasila' (Sutjipto 1967, p. 1). Military Law Academy professor Soediman Kartohadiprodjo argued that Sukarno had been 'swallowed up by Western thinking' (Soediman 1970, p. 102). Individual *sila* or principles of the Pancasila were infused with new meanings: 'monotheism' became overtly prescriptive, 'internationalism' was rejected as communist, 'humanitarianism' took on overtones of charity, and 'national unity' was given the added connotation of unity between citizens and the state.

In appropriating the Pancasila, the emphasis was on a return to origins – not only to 1945 but to Indonesia's cultural roots. Although Sukarno had also linked Pancasila to a collectivistic notion of 'tradition', the New Order's representation of indigeneity was quite different. While Sukarno highlighted the dynamic, populist aspects of village culture, the 'indigenous values' promoted by pro-New Order ideologues were those that integralist lawyers and scholars associated with conservative anti-party forces had propagated since Supomo's time: hierarchy, harmony and order.

Linking Pancasila to this static, organicist image of tradition paved the way for the repudiation by the government of all political ideologies and practices with which it was declared inconsistent. The government's initial targets were all forms of Leftism as well as political Islam, but also many democratic principles and practices such as popular sovereignty, voting and the separation of powers. By the 1980s human rights had become another favourite target, as well as what the regime called 'dichotomous thinking' – namely the tendency of critics to highlight differences between rich and poor, civilian and military, workers and bosses. Opposition itself was deemed contrary to Indonesian culture.

The institution that did more than any other to marry integralist and developmentalist ideology was the Centre for Strategic and International Studies (CSIS), a high-level think-tank dominated in the 1970s by Soeharto's intelligence aide Ali Moertopo. CSIS brought together several recent graduates from US universities who had taken to heart the lessons of scholars like Seymour Martin Lipset and Samuel Huntington. Most of its senior staff, including Harry Tjan Silalahi and Jusuf Wanandi, were Catholics whose view of politics was strongly coloured by a particular brand of Catholic social theory, with its virulent anti-communism, its distaste for liberalism and its preference for corporatist formulas. When Soeharto put Moertopo in charge of reformatting the political landscape, it was the CSIS that supplied the blueprint and the ideological rationale. It was fully committed to 'accelerated modernisation', and had little wish to duplicate US-style democracy. Instead it advocated corporatist solutions and promoted the language of community, cooperation, partnership and family. One example of how developmentalism and integralism were neatly (and cynically) combined was in the doctrine of Pancasila industrial relations. Before the rise of the New Order, Moertopo argued, relationships between workers and employers were influenced by Marxist notions of class struggle and historical materialism. This approach, he claimed, with its emphasis on confrontational behaviour and contradictions, had no place in a Pancasila state based on *kekeluargaan*, or family principles (Moertopo 1982, pp. 210–11). In a situation where strikes were outlawed and workers could join only one, government-sponsored, union, the repressive implications of a doctrine emphasising joint endeavour and partnership between workers and employers are obvious.

The period between 1978 and the mid-1980s saw the Soeharto government become increasingly preoccupied with staking out and policing the boundaries of legitimate ideological discourse. The centrepiece of Soeharto's ideological project was an elaborate and expensive program of Pancasila indoctrination known as P4. A key theme of the courses was the glorification of a 'village tradition' in which duties came before rights, the good of the community took precedence over the individual, and decisions were made by wise leaders after consultation with the community. The Indonesian state was depicted as a village writ large, embodying the same values and requiring the same sense of commitment and sacrifice from its citizens. For Moertopo (1983, pp. 208–9) the purpose of P4 was to 'Indonesianise Indonesians', to instil into the populace a new understanding of their own identity and culture in such a way that it would make them 'impervious to communism and other ideologies'.

In the 1980s Soeharto grew even more obsessed with ideological purification. Legislation introduced in 1983 required all parties and social organisations to proclaim Pancasila as their sole philosophical principle (*azas tunggal*). Soon afterwards Soeharto's ideologues introduced a further refinement, bringing conservative ideology full circle. In response to growing criticism of the government on constitutional grounds, they began quoting Supomo's 1945 arguments, including his concept of integralism. By the mid-1980s Supomo was appearing in P4 textbooks as the spiritual father of the constitution, and integralism was being referred to for the first time as Indonesia's supreme constitutional principle (*Staatside*). This indigenist reading of the constitution was apparently intended to neutralise its provisions for political rights and other checks and balances on executive authority by casting them as divisive and un-Indonesian. Ironically the government's attempt to ensconce integralism as a kind of master concept received stinging criticism on account of its fascist associations, and was reluctantly wound back. But the fact that Supomo's ideas held such appeal for New Order ideologues in the first place is telling.

Ultimately Soeharto's New Order failed. Although Indonesia attained unprecedented levels of prosperity under Soeharto's rule, the government's corporatist strategy and its suppression of dissent failed to contain a rapidly expanding civil society. Decades of indoctrination about the virtues of 'Pancasila democracy' also appeared to come to little. As soon as they had the chance, Indonesians joined mass demonstrations against Soeharto and, once he had been deposed, had no hesitation about demanding a free press and a fully fledged multi-party democracy.

For all their differences, the three waves of conservative ideologising in 20th century Indonesia had certain features in common. Structurally speaking, they were the product of elite groups – usually including the upper reaches of the civil service and the military – hoping to stave off or wind back mass participation in politics. Each condemned ideological polarisation and appealed for unity with reference to an image of traditional Indonesian culture as harmony loving, communalistic and static. It was not coincidental that each was informed by lawyers in thrall to Historical School assumptions about the need for legal systems – and by extension political systems – to reflect indigenous norms. Catholic social teaching too had a real, if rarely acknowledged, influence at each juncture. And, as we have seen, each wave to some extent prefigured the next. This brings us to the question of a fourth wave.

A FOURTH WAVE?

Many of the conditions exist today for another conservative backlash. The euphoria that accompanied the overturning of restrictions on parties, the press and public protests had all but petered out by the beginning of 2000. Just as in the late 1950s, cynicism about parties and parliament became rampant. The press is routinely criticised for irresponsibility, and tolerance of street demonstrations appears to have declined. Perhaps most worrying is the commonly expressed perception that regionalism and ethnic–religious conflict are tearing Indonesia apart. The threat of national disintegration has always provided fertile ground for those who would like less argument, less politics.

The groups that have put up most resistance to democratic reform are those with the most to lose from it: the Soeharto family, the military, Golkar and, perhaps surprisingly, Megawati's PDI-P. Of these, the most outspoken has been the military. To its credit, the military played a neutral role in the 1999 general election and consented to some important curbs on its political role, including a reduction in its parliamentary quota and a ban on taking up civilian jobs while on active duty. But while paying lip service to *reformasi*, it has strongly opposed efforts to bring military affairs under civilian control and to make officers accountable for corruption and crimes committed against opponents of the New Order regime. Its old anti-party and centrist impulses were quick to resurface. Between the general election and Abdurrahman Wahid's election as president in October 1999, military spokespeople repeatedly called on parties to cooperate with one another and form some kind of a consensus government.[3] This style continued after Abdurrahman assumed power, sometimes involving veiled threats of a military coup if the civilian politicians did not do their job properly.[4] Senior officers have been vocal in their criticism of federal solutions to regional grievances, arguing for the retention of strong central control and the use of force and emergency powers where they see threats to the 'unity and oneness' (*kesatuan dan persatuan*) of the Indonesian state (Suh and McCawley 2000; 'Support for Ambon Martial Law Grows', *Jakarta Post*, 25 June 2000). Faced with domestic humiliation over the 'loss' of East Timor and the prospect of war crimes trials, the military leadership has also attempted to direct public anger against alleged foreign interference in Indonesian affairs ('Panglima TNI: Pemerintah Tolak Campur Tangan Asing', *Kompas*, 13 December 2000).

But the military would not have been nearly as successful in rebuilding a conservative platform had it not been for the support it received from some of the major parties. In one sense, *all* of the major parties to emerge from the rubble of the New Order's collapse were conservative. They were all led, as Jeffrey Winters (1999) has pointed out, by members of a 'floating elite' that feared 'a politically mobilised *rakyat* [people] more than anything else'. This was well articulated by Golkar's Marzuki Darusman after the general election: 'The parties have to be aware of the possibility of a new radical movement, or *people power*. So we, the parties, have to sit down and talk together, negotiate with one another' ('Wawancara Marzuki Darusman', *Gamma*, 7

September 1999). The parties not only sat down and talked to each other, they also talked to the military. This was, in part, because the military continued to control a strategic bloc of 38 seats in the People's Consultative Assembly (MPR). But the period after the elections was marked by a more general coalescing of interests both between the major political parties and between the parties and the military.

Conventional wisdom would have it that Golkar was the most conservative of the political parties, and perhaps on some counts this is valid. Its position in many of the debates about political and ideological reform was often close to that of the military. It supported the military on the question of representation in parliament in the 1998 MPR session, and in the 1999 session assented to an extension of the deadline for military representation in parliament from 2004 to 2009. Golkar also opposed federalism and argued against student and Muslim demands that the ideological apparatus of the New Order – including the P4 program and the *azas tunggal* legislation – be scrapped. But, perhaps because it was so obviously tarred with the New Order brush, and perhaps because it was deeply riven by factionalism itself, Golkar at times publicly distanced itself from the military and supported causes, such as wide-ranging decentralisation, that were at odds with the military's agenda.[5] Golkar can also be credited with passing a wide range of reformist legislation in parliament and with voting to abolish P4 during the 1998 MPR session when it realised the strength of opposition to it.

Megawati's PDI-P, on the other hand, which represented itself as the underdog in the 1999 election campaign, has consistently aligned itself with the military and may well inherit Golkar's mantle as the pre-eminent conservative party. Megawati made little contribution to public life during her years in parliament, and during the election campaign she famously exempted herself from a debate with rival party leaders held at the University of Indonesia, on the grounds that debates were 'not in accordance with *budaya Timur* [Eastern culture] or with the 1945 Constitution'.[6] This retreat into indigenist rhetoric betrays her debt to New Order political culture. Moreover, Megawati presided over the PDI-P's first congress in April 2000 in true New Order style, forcing other contenders for the position of party chair to withdraw in order that she could be elected by acclamation – avoiding the need for a vote. Observers at the congress noted the lack of expression of dissenting opinion, leading the *Jakarta Post* to editorialise that 'the party's democratic credentials have now been destroyed'.[7]

As well as these large parties, there were also small ones with intimate links to the military, including the Justice and Unity Party (PKP), formed by former Defence Minister General (ret.) Edi Sudradjat, and IPKI, resurrected as a party by the 79-year-old A.H. Nasution and headed by the former governor of Jakarta, Lieutenant-General (ret.) R. Soeprapto. A central concern of these parties was to preserve national unity against the threat of federalism. As with the secular nationalist Golkar and PDI-P, they were also committed to preserving important parts of the ideological legacy of the New Order, including the *azas tunggal* legislation.

One tactic the army leadership used in the late New Order period in an attempt to keep the reformist movement at bay was to build links with hardline Muslim groups such as KISDI, the Indonesian Committee for the Solidarity of World Islam. Following the fall of Soeharto, these alliances broke down to some extent over the issue of the Pancasila. While the army and its conservative allies wanted to preserve the Pancasila as the state ideology and require all parties to retain it as their philosophical basis, many Muslim groups used the opportunity provided by *reformasi* to demand that the *azas tunggal* be abandoned. Eggy Sudjana, for instance, a Muslim labour activist who had worked closely with the former Special Forces commander Lieutenant-General Prabowo Subianto, was among the most vocal proponents of scrapping the legislation. He argued as early as July 1998 that it was an affront to Muslims' faith and that it had been imposed in a manipulative and violent manner, resulting in the deaths of many Muslims who had opposed it in Tanjung Priok and elsewhere ('Pemerintah Didesak Cabut Asas Tunggal', *Republika*, 30 July 1998).

The issue that enabled these erstwhile supporters of the New Order to set their differences aside was President Abdurrahman Wahid's March 2000 call for the 1966 ban on propagating Marxist–Leninist teachings (MPRS Resolution XXV/1966) to be rescinded ('Ide Penghapusan Tap MPRS XXV', *Kompas*, 26 March 2000). Robert Hefner (2000) has argued that, together with the president's overtures to Israel and his move to launch human rights investigations into abuses by the military, the call to legalise communism 'handed Islamist hardliners the issue they needed to rebound from their electoral defeat by forging an alliance with old regime military officers'. This in turn paved the way, he argued, for their collaboration in inciting ethnic and religious violence in Maluku.

But the impact of Wahid's courageous but untimely attempt at reconciliation with the families of murdered or ostracised members of the PKI was broader. While it was welcomed by human rights groups in Indonesia and abroad, it was condemned by virtually all parties, including his own Minister for Law and Legislation, Yusril Ihza Mahendra from the Crescent Moon and Star Party (PBB) ('Geger Sekitar Tap MPRS XXV/1966', *Media Indonesia*, 9 April 2000). Its unintended effect was to provide Wahid's conservative opponents with a common platform from which to attack him. Abdul Qadir Jaelani, a Muslim member of parliament, declared that the president was a Marxist ('Mabes TNI Mendukung Gus Dur Soal Pencabutan TAP MPRS/XXV/1966', *TNI Watch!* 8 April 2000). Others took a more indirect approach. Amien Rais, the speaker of the MPR, stated that if the ban were lifted, the PKI would be back and there would be 'hammers and sickles everywhere' ('Pro-Kontra Penghapusan Tap XXV/1966, *Kompas*, 3 April 2000). Husni Thamrin, a senior United Development Party (PPP) politician, warned that conditions were now 'very favourable for a Communist Party wanting support from the poor' ('Komunis Harus Tetap Dilarang di Indonesia', *Media Indonesia*, 20 March 2000). The tabloid media also bought into the hysteria, carrying headlines such as 'Communism Returning to Threaten Islam' and 'Anticipating Communist Guerrillas' (*Tabloid Jurnal Islam*, 29 September – 5 October 2000).

The changed mood was evident in the commemoration of the 1965 coup attempt held at Lubang Buaya in Jakarta on 1 October 2000. In New Order times, this day was called Hari Kesaktian Pancasila (Supernatural Power of the Pancasila Day) and was regarded as the 'holiest' day on the national calendar. In 1999 members of parliament boycotted the ceremony ('Peringatan Hari Kesaktian Pancasila tidak Dihadiri Anggota DPR/MPR', *Suara Pembaruan*, 1 October 1999). One might have expected that it would fade away or be attended by a handful of military officers. In 2000, however, a host of dignitaries took part, including Vice-President Megawati and the speakers of the People's Representative Council (DPR) and the MPR ('New Theme for Pancasila Day', *Jakarta Post*, 30 September 2000). The Sekretariat Negara (State Secretariat) issued a decree changing its name to 'Day of Commemoration of the National Tragedy due to the Betrayal of Pancasila'. According to the State Secretariat, the change in theme was 'necessary to remind people of the essence of the 1965 coup attempt and that every citizen is entitled to prevent such incidents occurring in the future'.[8]

The first point of interest is that it was celebrated at all. The commemoration was an integral part of the foundation myth of the New Order – and its version of the 1965 coup. Its continuance can only be read as an endorsement of that narrative. Second, in endorsing that myth, the ceremony rehearsed the New Order's condemnation of communism, dramatically undermining Wahid's attempts to reconcile with former communists and reincorporate them into the national community. Third, the choice of the term 'betraying the Pancasila' is pure New Order rhetoric, illustrating how little effort has gone into developing new symbols and new ideologies in the post-Soeharto era. When Sutjipto used the term in 1966 it was as part of an effort to redefine Pancasila. What about now? Whose Pancasila was being betrayed?

CONCLUSION

Large sections of the old guard remain in place and present a significant challenge to reformers. Whether this is a 'fourth wave' is still an open question, because in almost all cases the actors are products of the political environment of the New Order. Chronologically they may constitute a fourth wave but there has in fact been little ideological innovation. If anything, conservatives post-Soeharto have been less imaginative than their forebears in the 1950s and 1970s, perhaps because the language of organicism and corporatism was largely discredited during the Soeharto years. This may be why some opponents of reform are resorting to destabilisation and xenophobic nationalism.

One lesson that can be drawn from history is that conservatives typically anchor their political ideologies and arguments to particular conceptions of tradition or indigeneity. In Indonesia the image of the harmonious, self-sufficient village has a history dating back to the 1920s that has been harnessed by successive waves of conservatives. President Sukarno tried to promote a more dynamic, socialist-oriented view of village culture as the basis of his political program, but this was largely extinguished by the efforts of New Order ideologues who went to great lengths to reconstruct a harmonious and hierarchical image of 'Indonesian tradition' which they tied in to interpretations of the Pancasila and the Indonesian personality. What the government of Abdurrahman Wahid has not yet come to terms with is that in the absence of a concerted effort of his own to redefine what it means to be Indonesian, these nativist interpretations of the national personality and of the Pancasila will continue to circulate and be available for use by those at the conservative end of the political spectrum. If the Pancasila is to remain as the state ideology, and this seems likely since it was reaffirmed as such in November 1998, the Wahid government needs to give it an overhaul to free it of the ideological baggage from the New Order and earlier times. If he can manage, in the words of Budianta (2000, p. 110), to 'construct a concept of nationhood that is more inclusive and open to heterogeneity', the kind of reactionary conservatism I have been discussing in this chapter will have less fertile ground in which to grow in the future.

NOTES

1   Boedi Oetomo (Supreme Endeavour) was a conservative Javanese 'cultural nationalist' organisation founded in 1908. Parindra (the Greater Indonesia Party) was first formed in 1936. A small party of the same name with several of the same members was formed in November 1949. Much of the following discussion is paraphrased from Bourchier (1996b).

2   The PIR (the Greater Indonesia Unity Party) was formed in December 1948 under Wongsonegoro. It had much in common with the pre-war Parindra. It split in October 1954 into Java and Sumatra-based parties, PIR Wongsonegoro and PIR Hazairin.

3   See, for instance, AFX-Asia (14 September 1999) and Bambang Yudhoyono's comments in *Kompas* (25 August 1999).

4   See, for instance, Defence Minister Juwono Sudarsono's warning in the *Jakarta Post* (23 November 1999). US Ambassador to the United Nations Richard Holbrook was also responding to coup threats when he issued a threat of his own to the military not to move against the government of Abdurrahman Wahid (Associated Press, Jakarta, 14 January 2000).

5   See *Antara* ('FKP: Limitasi Peran Sospol Abri di DPR Perlu Ditentukan', 8 November 1998).

6   See Detik.com, ('Debat Capres Dipindah ke Salemba', 26 April 1999), http://www.detik.com/berita/199904/990426-1523.html; and *Forum* ('Mega Bersembunyi di Balik Budaya', 3 May 1999).

7   See *Jakarta Post* ('"Democracy" vs Democracy', 3 April 2000), and also *Kompas* ('Hasil Kongres I PDI-P: Konservatisme Menguat', 3 April 2000).

8   State Secretariat Decree No. B-347/Sesneg/2000, signed by State Secretary Djohan Efendi and put into effect by Minister of National Education Decree No. 3/U/2000.

10

REMEMBERING THE LEFT

Goenawan Mohamad*

This chapter will explore the meaning, significance and relevance of 'the Left' in modern Indonesian political culture, and in Indonesian society in general. This idea, and its heritage, will be assessed both in the activities and statements of so-called 'dissidents' opposed to the authoritarian New Order rule imposed by President Soeharto, and in the light of efforts to deal with the legacy of the brutal 1965–66 massacres of members of the Indonesian Communist Party (PKI) and their suspected associates.

THE POLITICS OF MEMORY

The evening of 22 June 1996 began with a spectacle of red bandannas. About 70 people, mostly in their twenties, packed the neon-lighted conference room of the Jakarta Legal Aid Bureau's office. Almost everyone had a red scarf tied around the neck, almost everyone was skinny and emaciated, and the room had an air of excitement and of brazenness.

It was, quite obviously, an unusual evening. The young people were celebrating the birth of a new political party, the Democratic People's Party (PRD). In one bold stroke, they produced two acts of defiance against the Soeharto regime. The regime had declared it illegal to set up a political movement or party without the government's permission, and the PRD members and supporters challenged this openly. As a mechanism of control, the Soeharto regime created a widespread fear of anything 'leftist' and threatened anyone fostering opinions tainted with Marxism. Against this, the young people with red bandannas stood up in opposition. Under the watchful eyes of government spies, they openly hoisted the banner of the Left. The evening was also marked by an award-giving ceremony honouring people and institutions regarded by some as the enemies of the regime. The novelist Pramoedya Ananta Toer and *Tempo* news weekly were among those receiving awards.

Any Indonesian over the age of 40 who witnessed the events of that evening would likely be either moved or apprehensive, or both. What was moving was the courage of these young people: here was a group of people who, without restraint or inhibitions, rose up and threw off the cover of suppression forced on them for years. However, this episode was frightening at the same time. It was no secret that the Soeharto regime was quite capable of eliminating anything or anyone it regarded as supporting the return of communism. Everyone in that conference room was acutely aware of the violent backlash awaiting them. Such fears were turned into reality when on 9 August 1996 the government charged the PRD with having committed treason; its leaders, who had gone into hiding, were subsequently arrested. The PRD's chairman, Budiman Sujatmiko, was charged and sentenced to 13 years in prison. A number of PRD members were kidnapped and tortured, and one was murdered.

However, the New Order regime's strategy of attacking the Left had a serious flaw. Suppressed by the stifling control of the New Order, the Left evolved and developed into something different. It has become more than a strain of ideology, and no longer holds an orthodox and easily definable political view on a range of political, social and economic matters. It has become a badge of courage among the young and an enchantment for the uninitiated. To paraphrase the words of one of Graham Greene's characters on the nature of communism, there is both a 'mystique' and a 'politique' about the left.[1]

The Mystique of the Left

The mystique of the Left grew from various whispering voices passing on information and developing ideas. For instance, the banning of books on Marxism meant that they quickly became a new form of pornography: young people surreptitiously sought and avidly explored them. They also photocopied these books, thus multiplying them. Some of these people became publishers: 'We used to get them in photocopy [form], passed on from hand to hand', said an executive of Teplok Press Publishing, which published an analytical volume on *Das Kapital*. These activities, begun in 1989, continued with discussion groups held in unlikely places – while mountain climbing, for instance, or in rooms lit only by the kerosene lamps known as *teplok*, a word Teplok Press Publishing later adopted as its business name (*Kompas*, 15 April 2000, p. 7). It is not surprising, therefore, that barely one year after the fall of Soeharto, books with left-leaning tendencies should enter the market unhindered.

My own observation shows that, since 1999, around 40 titles associated with socialism and Marxism have been published in Indonesia. Among these are a translation of *Marx for Beginners* – a work by Mao Zhe-dong about contradictions – a translated work of Che Guevara and the writings of Tan Malaka. An introduction to Marxism sold more than 20,000 copies within a year and has entered its fourth edition. There are seven publishing houses (mostly managed by young people) actively publishing books, bulletins and journals in this genre (*Kompas*, 15 April 2000, p. 7). At least three left-leaning periodicals are in circulation at present: *Majalah Kerja Budaya, Kiri* and *Kritik*.

The expression 'left-leaning' is not restricted to literary publications, but resonates with considerable meaning in the arts as well. Since 1998, a group of young artists in Yogyakarta sporting punk hairstyles and tattoos, and calling themselves Taring Padi, or Fangs of Rice, have initiated a kind of art that opposes the business of art in galleries because of its obvious associations with capitalism. They produce images based on political themes and display them in public places. In cooperation with a number of organisations, they published a short-lived bulletin with the slogan title of 'opposing imperialism'. They appear to wish to be seen as more 'left', more 'collectivist' and more 'radical' than Apotik Komik (Cartoon Pharmacy), an organisation for artists set up in April 1997 that also aims to carry the message of social concern – without shouting about 'social realism' – and to bypass the galleries.[2] Many of Apotik Komik's paintings, set against a plain background of primary colours, depict carefully drawn images of human bodies in pain or anger, as if to represent, with a surrealistic touch, the grim realities of the New Order.

So, what does the Left signify for these young people? The Left ultimately is an issue of the politics of memory under the New Order. To be sure, for various groups of pro-democracy activists born and growing up after 1966 – the beginning of the New Order – the Left represents more a state of opposition to the New Order regime than an attempt to recapture movements and times past. However, it is this collective memory that was invaded by the powers that be, and it is the authority to weave that memory that the young people are today fighting to seize. The struggle was not always an open protest. Every year from the 1980s until the end of the New Order, Indonesia's youth had to watch a propaganda film about the murder of army generals in 1965, called 'The Betrayal of G30S-PKI'. In protest, they read with enthusiasm the works of Pramoedya Ananta Toer, who was accused of being a communist and whose works were banned. In various closed meetings, they welcomed former political detainees who had links with the PKI. The bandannas adorning the necks of PRD members on 22 July 1996 can be viewed as a deliberate act in the politics of memory – reminiscent of the political consciousness among some student and other groups, in the 1965–67 period in particular.

Thus, the important thing is not what the Left is, but how it is expressed. An English-language website featuring the leader of Taring Padi, Yustoni Volunteero, describes him as a reader of *Das Kapital* and the works of Bakunin as well as possessing the kind of appeal that lures 'womankind'. One prolific publisher, LKIS, which is managed by young Muslim intellectuals in Yogyakarta, publishes books that link ideas of social emancipation with Islam. There is a trace of bravado in all of this, but there is also an uninhibited desire to explore new territories of thinking that transcend the borders prescribed by society, religion and the state. While lured by the mystery of the repressed past, the new Left does not seek simply to emulate the old Left. The PRD, for years regarded with varying degrees of concern as a 'new generation of the PKI',[3] promotes in its political agenda the need for parliamentary democracy and a multi-party system (but says nothing about leadership by the proletariat). At a discussion about 'The Left in Asia' in Jakarta, PRD chairman Budiman Sujatmiko even attacked the conceptual mistakes of the PKI in its land reform programs in the 1960s.[4]

Kritik, a journal associated with the Left, expresses the need to explore new thinking for the 'renewal of socialism'. PRD activists as well as young intellectuals adhering to political ideas of 'democratic socialism' sit as members on the editorial board. It is not clear what unites or divides them. In the past, it was the Indonesian Socialist Party (PSI) that represented the 'democratic socialist' platform. Interestingly the PKI branded the PSI 'right-wing'.

The Politique of the Left

Despite its mystique and its aura of being the New Order's most feared enemy, the Left has not generated any coherent thinking about the current situation in Indonesian society and what should be done to meet the various challenges facing the nation. While communist and socialist parties of the past all produced precise Marxist analyses of the social and political condition of society – and formulated an official line on the strategic and tactical steps to be taken – only the PRD has indicated an awareness of the need to have a theory-based political platform. The problem is that it is not easy to formulate a left-wing political agenda in an era defined by the success of the market economy, both inside and outside Indonesia.

This may have an impact on the *politique* of the Left. Ideologically in retreat, the Left finds itself in uncharted water, unable to decide what should be done in response to the advance of the capitalist ethos in society. In this respect it has failed to make itself a lodestar for a new generation of thinkers capable of conceiving of solutions for Indonesia's ills. Despite the evident social disparity in Indonesia and the widespread and lingering resentment towards the legacy of Soeharto's regime and its links with 'big business', the presence of the Left remains negligible, in terms of both popular following and ideological prominence. In the 1999 election, the PRD amassed only 70,000 votes – not enough to gain a single seat in parliament (DPR). In the meantime the Justice Party (PK) – which like the PRD was founded and supported by young people, many of them members of underground discussion groups at universities – managed to obtain six seats. However, the PK has no connection whatsoever with Leftist ideology; it espouses Islamic ideas of the moral purification kind, reminiscent of the Ikhwanul Muslimin movement in the Middle East.

The 'winner' of the 1999 election, the Indonesian Democratic Party of Struggle (PDI-P), has a large constituency among the poor. During the elections its supporters carried banners of President Sukarno, a man of the Left and a hero of the PRD. However, the PDI-P did not promote ideas that would have been typical of the leftist, anti-government agenda during Soeharto's rule. On the status of East Timor and the role of the military in both the DPR and the People's Consultative Assembly (MPR), the PDI-P, led by Sukarno's daughter Megawati Sukarnoputri, had more in common with the Golkar Party, its political enemy. Indeed, it appears that ideology and class background figure little in the way Indonesian political parties choose their friends and enemies.

THE COMMUNIST PHOBIA

President Sukarno coined the word *komunistofobia* in the 1960s. It was designed to castigate Indonesian political groups who showed an aversion to the PKI and rejected any attempt to forge a 'united front' with the Marxist–Leninists. But in 1966, Sukarno and his ideas were wiped from the political constellation. Since then *komunistofobia*, or fear of communism, has indeed reigned supreme in the language and practice of Soeharto's New Order.

It began with the massacre in 1965–66 of at least half a million people accused of being members of the PKI, and it has not yet come to an end. In a recent opinion poll conducted by *Tempo* of over 1,000 high school students in three major cities, 57% of respondents said 'no' to the question of whether communism should be allowed to be taught and imparted to students as 'knowledge'. Almost 60% were opposed to the distribution of books on communism in Indonesia. Apparently three decades of the New Order's anti-communist campaign has embedded a strong and resilient thread in the national psyche. According to the poll, 97% of the respondents received their information on the G30S (the 30th of September Movement, involving the arrest and killing of army generals – a violent act provoking the 1965 anti-communist massacre) from their teachers and school books. More than 80% thought that the version of events portrayed in the New Order propaganda film of the incident was essentially true (*Tempo*, 8 October 2000, p. 14).

The persistence of memory may, in this case, play an important role in shaping, or in unsettling, Indonesia's democratic political agenda. Indonesia's traumatic past could push the nation towards the creation of a better practice and method of resolving conflicts. This traumatic history, and its unresolved status, also impacts negatively on the accumulation of social capital in Indonesia – that is to say, the development of the shared capacity to trust and the peaceable management of differences. President Abdurrahman Wahid's failure to achieve reconciliation on a broad scale in dealing with prosecuted PKI members is indicative of a deep-seated societal and political gridlock impeding progress towards more intelligible and institutionalised political reform.

It is typical of Gus Dur's style to make a bold presidential statement, not followed by any action. In March 2000, the president reiterated what he said he had always believed, namely the need to apologise to the victims of the 1965 anti-communist massacre. 'Since early on, I have always asked for an apology … I'd like to apologise for all the killings of those people said to be communists', he is quoted as having said on a public television talk-show on 13 March (*Kompas*, 15 March 2000, pp. 1, 11).

Remarkably, the president, who was formerly the chairman of Nahdlatul Ulama (NU), also admitted that many NU-connected people (*kalangan NU*) had taken part in the massacre. He said he was aware that there was a dispute about whether PKI members accused of being (but never proven to have been) involved in the 1965 murders of seven senior army officers deserved punishment. The case should be reopened, he said, and the dispute should be brought to court in order to achieve settlement.

The talk-show, named 'Secangkir Kopi' ('A Cup of Coffee'), had a rather convivial flavour to it, but the reaction to Gus Dur's words was intransigent. The main target was the president's suggestion that the 1966 MPR decision to outlaw the PKI and the dissemination of Marxist–Leninist ideology should be revoked.[5] Most Muslim political and religious leaders adamantly rejected the idea. The Indonesian Council of Islamic Scholars (MUI) issued an official statement expressing similar sentiments.[6] The first week of April 2000 saw thousands of supporters of the Indonesian Muslim Community Front (FUII) take to the streets, voicing their protest in front of the Presidential Palace and burning PKI flags and symbols (*Media Indonesia*, 8 April 2000). Even Gus Dur's natural constituency, the NU community, did not back him on this particular issue. His handpicked successor as chairman of the NU, K.H. Hasyim

Muzadi, told a reporter that a policy of reconciliation with PKI members should be gradual. He argued that for the time being the 1966 MPR decision should stand.[7]

The support Gus Dur enjoys comes mainly from members of his own party, the National Awakening Party (PKB), from human rights activists and from intellectuals; but they rank as a modest political influence in the Indonesia of today. Typically, President Abdurrahman Wahid, known for his contempt for parliamentarians, has done little to generate a more powerful following in the legislative body. It is small wonder, then, that nobody has raised their voice to urge the MPR to revoke the decree issued by the previous assembly in 1966.

PRAMOEDYA AND THE IDEA OF RECONCILIATION

One curious voice heard during this episode was that of the writer Pramoedya Ananta Toer, who has become an icon of the 1965 victims. He rejected Gus Dur's apology. 'How easy!' he said, with a spark of sarcasm, when commenting on Gus Dur's call for reconciliation. He said he did not trust President Abdurrahman Wahid, who in his view was one of those who should be held responsible for the massacre and the establishment of the New Order. 'Those who suffered from the beating still feel the pain, while the beaters remember no more. Reconciliation is a nonsense ... reconciliation is mere talk by the people in power' (*Forum Keadilan*, 26 March 2000, pp. 24–7).

Rather than reconciliation, Pramoedya insisted on the need for retribution; what is more, he wanted this to be done through legal means. For him, justice would be achieved by bringing the perpetrators to trial. However, he did not offer to tell the interviewer how the government would manage this, given the absence of a credible legal institution to deal with political crimes committed by a large number of people over three decades ago.[8] His recipe was simple: 'If the government cannot do it, it should step aside'.

Pramoedya's uncompromising voice (tinged with bitterness, I must say) is a lonely one. He has received no support even from his close friends. In my meetings with former political prisoners associated with the PKI, I discovered that many of them did not share Pramoedya's sentiments. Some even resented his open expression of these ideas, saying they would lend support to political groups spreading fear of a future pro-communist backlash. Some of them viewed Pramoedya as a political philistine, alienating would-be allies and strengthening existing foes. At least one told me that no one had a moral right to reject a public expression of apology from a person as well meaning as Gus Dur. Many of them believe in the president's sincerity, remembering that even before he became head of state, he often expressed his views on reconciliation in various private communications.[9]

For the present, however, the idea of reconciliation has disappeared from the scene, and it has yet to be seen whether anything will eventuate from the nation's effort to deal with its traumatic past. An NGO team prepared a draft to create the legal basis of a 'truth and reconciliation commission'. A drafting team comprising members of a number of departments, including the Attorney General's Office and the Ministries of Law and Legislation, Internal Affairs and Security, hopes to submit a final draft of the proposed legislation to the DPR for discussion. Beyond this, however, matters have progressed very little and no one is sure what might happen. Given the strong reaction against any reconciliatory gesture towards communists and communism, and especially considering that at the present time Indonesia is preoccupied with separatist movements in Aceh and Papua and continuing violence in Maluku, it is unlikely that the government will pay any further attention to this issue. In addition, Gus Dur's declining political support will make it difficult for him not to focus his efforts on making his presidential seat secure, to assure his political future.

'I am no Nelson Mandela ... and Indonesia is not South Africa', Pramoedya Ananta Toer said in an interview, in response to criticism of his position on Gus Dur's idea of reconciliation (*Tempo*, 16 April 2000, p. 22). Pramoedya is right: no one in today's Indonesia is a Nelson Mandela, and there are indeed major differences between the Indonesian and South African experiences.[10]

Indonesia lacks a pool of national leaders with the ability to provide credible moral guidance of the kind exhibited by Nelson Mandela and Desmond Tutu in South Africa. Unlike the ANC in South Africa, the new Indonesian political elite lacks coherence. It has no consolidated opponent comparable to the white political groupings in the South African state. Gus Dur, although persistently pursuing a policy of reconciliation, appears to have no allies truly committed to the establishment of procedures to work together and create visible and rapid change that will ultimately strengthen unity in Indonesian society. In other words, unlike South Africa, Indonesia has no unified and functioning political elite committed to investigating and dealing with past crimes as a means of paving the way to a better future.

The diversity of Indonesian grievances and crimes presents another difficulty. Whereas in South Africa reconciliation mainly occurred between two sides, in Indonesia multiple forms of reconciliation must take place. In the New Order's history of persecution, one cannot single out the victims of the 1965–66 anti-communist purge as the only witnesses of political terror. As a former communist student activist told me, the Indonesian communists were not entirely blameless in the outbreak of violence in 1965–66. It is morally questionable and politically fatuous to claim, 'the victim, that's me'. Failure to address all violations may give some victims the impression that they are being further discriminated against, and their complaints, however legitimate, disregarded. Such a perception would undermine both justice and reconciliation efforts in Indonesia.

In some cases reconciliation cannot be achieved without meeting at least some demands for justice. However, to advocate justice one has to be sure of an acceptable level of institutional capability. Indonesian legal institutions are very weak. It is not clear that they would be able to provide trials that all parties would consider fair, and that would be recognised as such beyond Indonesia's borders.

Given this, it is difficult to envisage the construction of a consistent method of dealing with the dark side of Indonesia's past. Ultimately, the nation must recognise its limitations honestly – for the foreseeable future at least – in dealing with such matters. This is particularly important in grappling with questions such as what constitutes justice when the case in question is a large-scale crime committed amidst widespread frenzy and horror such as occurred in the political cataclysm of 1965–66.

Much as I believe that justice is probably impossible to achieve, it is vital that Indonesia as a nation tries to come to terms with these issues. Even if the attempt to attain justice fails, the nation may well be able to resolve a number of problems along the way, or at least place a number of important issues on the table. In the end, one may have to settle for a 'selective justice' of one kind or another, leaving an unavoidable – and for many unacceptable – feeling of incompleteness.

My approach to these issues implies a certain degree of humility. In an open letter to Pramoedya in *Tempo* (9 April 2000), I wrote:

> In an age when the victim is easily sanctified, one who thinks himself of a higher degree of victimisation will, with ease, also believe in the right to become the ultimate arbiter of justice. But, as with every claim to sanctity, this too could give rise to arbitrariness. Mandela knew this … [He has] humbled [himself].

To be sure, there is a link between humility and the will to forgive. But for me, forgiveness does not mean absolving the guilt or the guilty. Forgiveness is in fact an affirmation of the existence of wrong. And with each affirmation of wrong, life can take flight again: with wound, with trauma, but also with hope. Revenge bears with it an element of justice, but there are those who will distinguish revenge from justice. In each act of revenge waits the turn of another victim.

NOTES

* I would like to thank Dewi Anggraeni for translating some parts of the text. I would also like to thank M. Nasiruddin from the ISAI Library for helping me in my research.

1 'Communism, my friend, is more than Marxism, just as Catholicism ... is more than the Roma Curia. There is a *mystique* as well as *politique* ... Catholics and Communists have committed great crimes, but at least they have not stood aside, like an established society, and been indifferent. I would rather have blood on my hands than water like Pilate' (from Dr Magot's last letter in Greene 1966, Part 2, Ch. 4).

2 On the difference between Taring Padi and Apotik Komik, see *Gamma* (27 June 2000).

3 See Human Rights Watch (1996). More recently, a statement by a deputy chairman of the MPR has suggested that the PRD's plan is to 'bring communism back to Indonesia' (*Media Indonesia*, 20 March 2000).

4 Notes from a seminar on 'Kiri di Asia' ('The Left in Asia') organised by *Jurnal Kalam* at Teater Utan Kayu, Jakarta, on 25 February 2000.

5 Gus Dur reaffirmed his position by stating that the decision violated the individual's legal rights (*Media Indonesia*, 1 April 2000).

6 See *Media Indonesia* (24 March 2000). It later published a quote by Hussein Umar, a United Development Party (PPP) member of the DPR, who mentions a judgement issued by the Congress of Islamic Scholars (Kongres Alim Ulama) in Palembang in September 2000 opposing Gus Dur's idea of reconciliation and declaring communists to be 'infidels' (*kafir*). Any bond with them would therefore be illegitimate, Hussein Umar says, quoting the Congress's statement.

7 See *Forum Keadilan* (9 April 2000, p. 72). Earlier, he was quoted as saying that 'communism should stay banned in Indonesia' and that 'MPR members should stay firm in refusing to revoke [the 1966 MPR decision]' (*Media Indonesia*, 20 March 2000).

8 Views differ on the killings in 1965–66. There is increasing evidence that they were part of a systematic and coordinated plan, but the historical record plainly shows that the pattern of action differed quite dramatically from place to place. Local political conflicts between parties – NU and PKI supporters in East Java, and Indonesian National Party (PNI) and PKI supporters in Bali – also played a significant role in the bloodshed. See, for example, Sulistyo (2000, pp. 232–47).

9 See an interview with Rewang, a former Politbureau member of the PKI, in *Forum Keadilan* (2 April 2000, p. 75). Gus Dur also met with D.N. Aidit's daughter, who lives in Paris, and regards himself as a friend of the woman whose father was the murdered chairman of the PKI. As president, he allowed his picture to be taken sitting next to her during his latest visit to Paris – a significant gesture considering she is an exile who cannot return to Indonesia (*Tempo*, 5 March 2000, p. 93).

10 I borrowed most of this argument from a draft document prepared by the International Crisis Group (ICG 2000a).

11

THE RISE AND FALL OF THE GENERALS: THE INDONESIAN MILITARY AT A CROSSROADS

Atmadji Sumarkidjo

This chapter records the involvement of the Indonesian National Army (TNI) in Indonesian politics from the late 1950s through to today. The army faces a number of dilemmas relating to its future, including its political role and its relationship with the executive arm of government. This chapter traces the evolution of the military's role in Indonesian politics; follows the rise of President Soeharto and his system of promotions and demotions of high-ranking officers; and covers the rise and fall of leadership groups within the Indonesian armed forces.

THE INVOLVEMENT OF THE TNI IN THE POLITICAL 'MIRE'

The TNI's involvement in Indonesian politics dates back to the late 1950s and has its origins in three key events. The first was the speech in 1958 by army chief-of-staff (Kasad) Major-General A.H. Nasution, which outlined his view that the armed forces should pursue a 'middle way' between the poles of Latin American military dictatorship and Western military political passiveness.

The second was the nationalisation of Dutch companies in 1957, which resulted in a number of army officers taking up key economic and business positions. Officers who became active in economic fields, such as Colonel Dr Ibnu Sutowo and Major Suhardiman, played an increasingly non-military role. The effect was two-fold: it prevented communists from seizing strategic positions in the economic and business fields, thus providing a means to prevent communist infiltration of labour movements; and it allowed army-controlled businesses such as Pertamina, the national oil company managed by Ibnu Sutowo, to become important sources of finance for the TNI.

A third and final element was President Sukarno's decision to restore the 1945 Constitution on 5 July 1959, and to appoint several military officers as ministers in his working cabinet formed on 10 July 1959. By 1960 the TNI found itself holding some of the most powerful political and non-military positions in Indonesia. Moreover, as both Secretary of Defence and Kasad, Nasution was established as the second most powerful man in Indonesia after the president.

Nasution then worked to strengthen his position within the TNI as well as at the broader national political level. His first move towards institutionalising his power was to ensure the loyalty of the officers' corps, the majority of whom, like Nasution, shared a solidarity and cohesiveness based on their experiences during the Indonesian revolutionary period. Nasution promoted many to important positions at the level of general staff in Jakarta. Having consolidated his position, he eventually appointed Lieutenant-General Gatot Soebroto to replace him as Kasad in 1963. Following the death of Soebroto, Major-General Achmad Yani was appointed as Kasad.

Nasution removed former comrades-in-arms who disagreed with him, such as Colonels Ahmad Husein, Dahlan Djambek, Simbolon and Zulkifli Lubis. In some cases this backfired, as many went on to lead rebellions against Jakarta: Somba, Ventje Sumual and Runturambi, for instance, went on to lead the PRRI rebellion in North Sulawesi. Their replacements were loyal to Nasution, notable among them being Colonel Achmad Jani, who (ironically) ran the successful military operation against the rebellions in Sumatra and North Sulawesi. Not only did Nasution shore up support among the officer corps but, by opening up various business positions, he created a pool of people who felt 'indebted' to him politically and financially. Nasution enlarged and broadened the armed forces' organisational structure so as to 'take good care' of more officers. In addition, after being promoted to the rank of general, Nasution was able to create a host of new officer ranks ranging from lieutenant to brigadier-general.

THE RISE OF SOEHARTO

On the night of 30 September 1965, members of the military – notably from the Diponegoro Division – and civilian members of the Indonesian Communist Party (PKI) launched an attempted coup. In the confusion, Major-General Soeharto of the Army Strategic Reserve Command (Kostrad) took command of the army (one of the three branches of the armed forces – army, navy and airforce). Concluding that the coup attempt had been a PKI plot, he manoeuvred to eradicate communist supporters from the army and wider political and social circles.

During his early days in power, Soeharto relied heavily on his staff at Kostrad, especially Major-General Umar Wirahadikusumah, Colonel

Wahono, Colonel Yoga Soegama, Lieutenant-General Ali Moertopo and Lieutenant Colonel L.B. Moerdani. Soeharto also turned to officers and troops from other commands who were loyal to him, particularly Colonel Sarwo Edhie Wibowo of the Army Paracommando Regiment (RPKAD) and troops from the Siliwangi and Brawijaya Divisions. He was suspicious of troops from the Diponegoro Division, given the communist links of many of them and their involvement in the attempted coup, and only trusted those under the command of Kostrad. He also brought in an infantry brigade from North Sumatra under Colonel Yasir Hadibroto to take over the Diponegoro's command in Central Java.

Soeharto was sworn in as Minister/Commander-in-Chief of the Army (Men/Pangad) in November 1965, both because of his strong support from the army and because Sukarno did not want Nasution to hold power again. From 11 March 1966, when Sukarno gave Soeharto authority to restore social order and government functions, Soeharto worked to undermine the president and his supporters in the Indonesian armed forces (known for the duration of the New Order period as ABRI). Daily tasks gradually shifted to two groups loyal to Soeharto: professional military officers such as Maraden Panggabean, Soemitro and Alamsyah Ratu Prawinegara; and the Special Operations group headed by Ali Moertopo and Sudjono Humardhani. Members of these two groups became close advisors to Soeharto on political matters following the death in 1967 of Major-General Soewarto, head of the Army Staff Command College (Seskoad), and were suspected of engineering the political elimination of a number of generals.

Soeharto sidelined officers who had given him strong support in the period after the attempted coup, particularly those with a rank similar to his own, such as Sarwo Edhie Wibowo, Achmad Kemal Idris and Hartono Rekso Dharsono. Between 1970 and 1972, all were posted to regional commands, and all ended their careers not as soldiers but as diplomats. The removal of Sarwo Edhie and others created a mini-vacuum under Soeharto, leading to a power struggle as Soemitro's career progressed from deputy commander of ABRI to deputy commander of the Operations Command to Restore Order and Security (Kopkamtib) and eventually commander of Kopkamtib in April 1973.

General Panggabean and General Soemitro were perceived as professional military officers loyal to Soeharto. Their involvement in the power struggle had more to do with efforts to tidy up the Department of Defence and Security (Hankam), to maintain control of the three forces that made up ABRI and to reinforce Soeharto's authority, rather than with a personal political agenda of their own. The reorganisation of Hankam – driven by Soemitro – witnessed the rise of a new generation of military officers. Some, such as Sayidiman Suryohadiprodjo, Julius Henuhuli and Himawan Soetanto, were generals who had graduated in 1948 from the National Military Academy in Yogyakarta;

others included Rusmin Noerjadin (who later became airforce commander) and Soedomo (naval chief-of-staff and later commander of Kopkamtib).

As a result, observers claimed that there were three powerful men at the top in Indonesia at that time – Soeharto, Soemitro and Ali Moertopo – the last two of whom were in competition for access to Soeharto. Given Ali Moertopo's loyalty to Soeharto, it was widely rumoured that Soemitro had ambitions to succeed the president. This was a reasonable assumption. Soemitro was the commander of Kopkamtib, an extra-judicial organisation capable of arrest outside legal procedures; he had a strong and outspoken personality; and he was Javanese, an advantage for a prospective national leader. It was therefore not surprising that Soeharto suspected Soemitro of having plans to remove him or at least to challenge or reduce his powers.

The inevitable show-down between the two men came about through the Malari events of 14–15 January 1974 in Jakarta. The fall-out from the Malari incident led to Soemitro's resignation, despite doubts about his true role in the disturbances. Soeharto then reshuffled the top military positions. Surono, who was Kasad, took on the concurrent role of deputy commander of ABRI; Yoga Soegama was recalled from the UN mission in New York to head the State Intelligence Coordinating Body (Bakin); and Soedomo became commander of Kopkamtib.

Soeharto had learnt a new lesson: not to place too much confidence in a man capable of becoming a rival. Such a 'prospective rival' would have the following characteristics: a strong leadership style, not a 'yes' man and not corrupt. From then on, generals who demonstrated those characteristics managed to retain their positions for only one term. The power accumulated by Soemitro was never replicated by his successors, and for a time the post of commander of Kopkamtib was occupied by Soeharto himself, leaving only routine daily tasks to be managed by Soedomo.

A NEW DIRECTION

In 1978 Soeharto changed tack again. General Maraden Panggabean was appointed Coordinating Minister of Politics and Security and Ali Moertopo was appointed Minister of Information, in what were essentially demotions. The position of Minister of Defence and Security/Commander-in-Chief of the Armed Forces (Menhankam/Pangab) was handed to General Andi Muhammad Jusuf. The powerful Kopkamtib organisation was given to Admiral Soedomo, who also became Jusuf's deputy. The positions of assistant intelligence commander at the Centre for Strategic Intelligence and intelligence assistant at Kopkamtib were given to Lieutenant-General L.B. Moerdani.

Jusuf and Moerdani were entrusted with the key posts in ABRI because they were not considered strong enough to pose a threat to Soeharto. Conventional wisdom said that potential successors to Soeharto had to be Javanese Muslims. Jusuf, although a Muslim, was not Javanese, and Benny, though Javanese, was a Catholic, whereas their predecessors Soemitro and Ali Moertopo had been both Javanese and Muslim.

Few military observers initially paid much attention to the role and impact of the appointment of Jusuf as Menhankam/Pangab. Many questioned whether a field general who had spent the previous decade as a cabinet minister rather than in the armed forces was capable of the job at hand. However, Jusuf managed to revive the people's love for the army, which had been lost as a result of its clamp-down on student movements and newspapers in 1977–78. Jusuf also promoted young graduates of the National Military Academy in Magelang to important positions. However, his increasing popularity among wider society, and among young military officers, began to so concern Soeharto that he was replaced by Benny Moerdani in April 1983.

SOEHARTO'S RECRUITMENT SYSTEM

Having either removed or witnessed the retirement of generals in his own age group, Soeharto began to institute his own system of recruitment. In a successful move, he turned to former signal officer Colonel Try Sutrisno, who had been his senior adjutant for three years. Try was appointed to regional and then Jakarta-based appointments during his rise to become Pangab in 1988. Try's loyalty, and his political impotence both within and outside ABRI, saw his eventual appointment as vice-president. Other choices of apprentices, such as Suryadi from Special Forces Command (Kopassus) and Soeyono, were less successful.

Soeharto then turned to another presidential adjutant, Wiranto, whose career had followed a similar path to that of Try. After 'passing his exams' as an adjutant – lessons had covered such topics as the philosophies of life and how to swing a golf club – Wiranto returned to the army. With an infantry background, Wiranto was given administrative training as chief-of-staff of the Regional Military Command (Kodam), then rose to become commander of Kostrad, assistant to the Kasad, then Kasad, and finally Menhankam/Pangab. The only difference with Try was that Wiranto had much shorter assignment periods in an attempt to fast-track his rise through the ranks.

Running parallel to this, Soeharto took advantage of family connections in ABRI to secure a loyal senior officer. One such was his own son-in-law, infantry Major Prabowo Subianto of Kopassus and son of the distinguished economist Prof. Dr Soemitro Djojohadikusumo. While Prabowo stressed that he was a professional soldier rather than an officer with political ambitions, he himself acknowledged that his professional and familial relationships with the president were difficult to distinguish.

The systems of promotion, tours of duty and regional commands used by the army organisation eventually broke down in the face of Soeharto's increasingly tight personal control over the promotion of officers. By 1998 the independence of the armed forces was at an all-time low, as witnessed by the weak leadership of Major-General Feisal Tanjung as Pangab.

Soeharto's long-term strategy had been to install an armed forces commander who would be able to protect his own and his family's interests on a long-term basis. But Soeharto had to choose a number of officer graduates from the National Military Academy as fillers or 'gap-stops' to hold the positions of Kasad and Pangab until the man he 'developed' was ready to come forward. That person turned out to be Major-General Feisal Tanjung, who for a long time had been commander of Seskoad. Although General Edi Sudrajat was Kasad for longer than anyone else under Soeharto, it did not mean that he was trusted by him – Soeharto was simply 'out of stock' when Try became Pangab in 1988 and Edi was chosen because he did not have any political ambitions.

What about the other high-ranking officers? M. Yogi Suardi Memet, onetime commander of Kowilhan II, commander of Kodam Siliwangi and commander of Kopassandha (Kopassus), while trustworthy, could not be relied on to protect the Soeharto family's interests. Wismoyo Arismunandar, commander of Kostrad, deputy Kasad and eventually Kasad, was considered by outsiders to be a possible successor: he was a reliable officer, he was very loyal, and, most important, he had a family tie (through marriage) with Ibu Tien Soeharto. However, Soeharto and Wismoyo never got along, and the closer Wismoyo came to the centre of power and decision making, the more Soeharto felt threatened by his policies, particularly after some of his children complained to their father that he 'was not cooperative' when it came to their business dealings with the army. When Wismoyo's 55th birthday came around, the president did not extend his time of service (for only the president was entitled to decide an extension of active service for officers above the rank of colonel).

By that time it was clear that Soeharto had another successor in mind, although it was not someone he had identified early on. General R. Hartono was a high-ranking officer who had begun his career as regional military commander of Brawijaya before becoming commander of Seskoad and governor of the National Defence Institute, neither of which were significant positions. When he was promoted to the position of head of ABRI's Social–Political Affairs Unit, Hartono developed a close relationship with Siti Hardyanti Indra Rukmana, the eldest daughter of Soeharto.

Many people saw the rise of Hartono as evidence that ABRI's promotion system lay in ruins. Indonesia now had a Pangab who would not contradict Soeharto and a Kasad whose career reportedly took off as a result of his close relationship with the Soeharto family. There had always been an unwritten regulation to obtain the president's approval for positions such as commander of Kostrad. However, this was a request for approval, not a request for names, and Soeharto was only informed orally about appointments to the position of regional commander. Soeharto began to meddle more and more in army personnel issues, and the old convention had well and truly disappeared by the time he appointed Hartono. Clearly this was due to generational and age differences between Soeharto and his top brass, and the fact that Soeharto was becoming increasingly authoritarian. Few were prepared to challenge his decisions and those who did usually fell from grace. One such victim was the chief of the general staff (at that time), Lieutenant-General Soeyono.

Whether or not Soeharto was aware of it, the role played by his son-in-law Prabowo was crucial to the 'new' system built in order to control the promotion of generals within ABRI. A big gap had appeared between Soeharto and the younger generation of officers – Soeharto did not know them individually and was not fully conversant with their track records, even though he based his decisions on such information. Thus the presence of a son-in-law as a senior military officer provided Soeharto with a second opinion about names put before him by the Pangab.

The close relationship between father-in-law and son-in-law ended as a result of the events of May 1998. Prabowo was suspected of 'planning' to betray his family, while ABRI suspected him of holding another political agenda. Prabowo was subsequently dismissed from military service with an early pension. Soeharto met a worse fate – he was forced to resign as president.

THE NEW 'REFORMISTS'

While Soeharto's recruitment system and power structures ended with his resignation, one of his students did survive: Wiranto managed to keep his job under the presidency of B.J. Habibie. There was some debate about the armed forces' role in the new cabinet, and consideration was given to separating the function of Pangab from that of Menhankam. In the end Habibie entrusted the dual position of Menhankam/Pangab to Wiranto.

Wiranto's record was mixed. His ability and leadership in dealing with the critical situation on 13–14 May 1998 in Jakarta was questionable, and he failed to investigate thoroughly the riots in Jakarta and the shootings at the Trisakti University where four students were killed. However, in September 1999 he did accede to pressure from a number of ABRI officers, including Lieutenant-General Susilo Bambang Yudhoyono and Major-General Agus

Widjojo, to consider internal reform of ABRI, eventually 'packaged' as the redefinition, repositioning and reactualisation of ABRI. One result was the name change from ABRI to TNI; as well, the police force was separated from the umbrella of ABRI and the Department of Defence, and the military's political–social structures were abolished completely. General Wiranto almost became Habibie's vice-presidential candidate at the General Assembly of the People's Consultative Assemby (MPR) in October 1999, but rejected the offer at the last moment. Wiranto was appointed Coordinating Minister of Politics and Security in the first cabinet of the new president, Abdurrahman Wahid, where he was also able to secure a number of his own candidates as ministers. After a protracted episode, made more so by the president being away on an overseas trip, Wiranto was replaced as minister in mid-February 2000 and later resigned from the military.

The new atmosphere of freedom and openness created by the removal of Soeharto and the democratic elections that brought Abdurrahman Wahid to the presidency led a number of TNI officers to come out in support of Major-General Agus Wirahadikusumah. He had, among other things, written a book outlining his views on the need for internal reform of the TNI, stressing in particular the political and very public processes required. This group of officers had a common mission: to speed up the reform process that had begun in September 1999; to reduce domination of the combined armed forces by the army in order to create a more balanced organisation; to liquidate the socio-political functions of the TNI, particularly Kodam, that encouraged its involvement in the political sphere; and to wipe out corruption in the TNI.

This did not sit well with a number of other high-ranking officers, who formed an opposing camp headed by Lieutenant-General Agus Widjojo, chief-of-staff of Kodam, who rejected the radical types of changes envisioned by his younger opponent. He was vehemently opposed to the liquidation of Kodam but in favour of a reorientation of its role. He was a strong supporter of the TNI's current structure and status, while acknowledging the need for subtle but internally initiated modification and change carried out over a longer time-frame.

In between the two sat the Wiranto camp, which included Lieutenant-General Djadja Suparman who, controversially, was installed as commander of Kostrad by Wiranto on his last days in office. This group conservatively acknowledged the need for change, but only as necessary, not simply for the sake of change.

These three groups have experienced fluctuations in their fortunes. The internal power struggle has, in a sense, further weakened the TNI's status in relation to the executive arm of government and the parliament. Internal bickering and attempts to discredit or eliminate members of opposing camps (in the case of Agus Wirahadikusumah, by character assassination) even led to the resignation of Bondan Gunawan, an aide close to President Abdurrahman Wahid. With this dismissal the reformists around Agus Wirahadikusumah lost much access to the president. He was further weakened by the release of the so-called Bulakrante document, which appeared to be a report on a meeting – held at the house of Major-General Saurip Kadi – at which a plan to facilitate his ascension to the post of Kasad and, ultimately, TNI commander was apparently discussed. This document was 'anonymously' circulated to the media and various political figures. Reform of the TNI, however, remains at the core of divisions within the military and, despite the forced retirement of Agus Wirahadikusumah, will continue to dominate internal and public debate about its future role.

ON THE WAY TO A BETTER TNI?

There remains the question of whether the TNI will change in the newly democratic Indonesia, particularly with regard to its promotional system, organisational structure and future political role. Considering events since the election of President Abdurrahman Wahid in October 1999, it is difficult to say whether the TNI will become an independent institution, disconnected from the intrigues of government and able to resist internal and external pressures, since the TNI elite itself is not independent. In other words, since promotion to senior positions is in the hands of the president, prospective candidates inevitably align themselves with influential individuals and groups outside the military structure.

The president's decision to make the historic first-time appointment of a naval officer, Admiral Widodo AS, as TNI commander led many to point to a new organisational trend, notwithstanding the goodwill demonstrated by the army in accepting a commander from another force, a positive response in itself. However, the president's decision to seek advice from Bondan Gunawan and L.B. Moerdani about a replacement for General Subagyo HS as Kasad was disconcerting, not only because the eventual replacement was General Tyasno Sudarto, who had links with both Moerdani and Wiranto, but because the president sought counsel from outside the armed forces. That it took several months before he took up the appointment suggests that some at army headquarters were not too keen on Tyasno.

As long as the TNI elite continues to play politics in order to strengthen its own position, this will have negative repercussions for a genuine system of promotion based on professional merit. It is no secret that General Tyasno, whose election was endorsed by President Abdurrahman, is now close to Vice-President Megawati.

One way to regulate and control the TNI is to implement the Law on

National Defence (Undang-Undang Pertahanan Nasional), the bill for which is currently being drafted by parliament. If the bill becomes law, defence policy will be placed in the hands of the Minister of Defence, while the TNI commander will be responsible to the president through the Minister of Defence. The law will hopefully be followed by further regulations on internal reforms of the TNI and a timetable for their implementation.

Military doctrines must be reconstructed in the context of both new and future challenges and in accordance with the new Law on National Defence. The New Order doctrine focusing on the supremacy of the army in the combined armed forces is now outdated, as it does not accommodate the specific character of the forces today. Moreover, the armed forces needs to consider its public reputation seriously; otherwise it will face a shortage of suitably qualified cadets willing to join military academies.

Important also is the provision of sufficient funds for the TNI, in order to remove extra-budgetary sources of revenue created to fund military operations and supplement the salaries of soldiers. During the years of the New Order, these institutions and corporate business bodies distorted the genuine mission of the military and were subject to corruption and misuse. A professional army will only be possible if its personnel are adequately paid and not overworked – the reason for former Minister of Defence Juwono Sudarsono's tolerance of the existence of these institutions until wages and other day-to-day conditions improved.

A better TNI can be achieved in the coming five to ten years. Reforms are certainly necessary, as are their consistent application and implementation, but there should be optimism that the TNI will be able to fulfill its role in the new Indonesia.

12

THE CHANGING DYNAMICS OF REGIONAL RESISTANCE IN INDONESIA

Richard Chauvel

'Papua, Aceh and Riau reject the 17th.' Indonesia's National Heroes weep. Fifty-five years of Indonesian independence is a ruse. In three days time, on 17th August 2000, not all the people of the remaining 26 provinces are going to commemorate the proclamation. In Riau and Papua the people who want to celebrate are afraid, threatened by others who want independence.
(Bangkit Online, 2000)

In much of the discussion of the regional challenges Indonesia has confronted in the post-Soeharto era, there is the implied question of why, after over half a century of independence, Indonesia is still concerned with threats of territorial disintegration. Regional rebellions and separatist movements have been one of the reoccurring features of post-independence politics. John Legge has argued elsewhere in this volume that the struggle for national unity and the accommodation of diversity has been one of the defining themes of Indonesian history over the past century. Given the ethnic, cultural and religious complexity of Indonesian society, together with the very uneven distribution of human and natural resources across the archipelago, we should not be surprised that tensions between the provinces and the central government have had such a strong influence on Indonesia's political dynamics.

The persistence of strong regional identities and resistance to central authority in Papua, Aceh and Maluku suggest that historical experience and primordial loyalties remain important fixtures of the political landscape. Yet, it must also be remembered that there are many regions of the archipelago where there is little or no history of resistance. In this chapter I argue that while history, ethnicity and religion may be invoked by regional protagonists in how they articulate their cause, they are not immutable.

The changing political, economic and cultural contexts also shape the forms and dynamics of resistance to Jakarta's authority. Ambon was the location of one of the first attempts to secede from the republic. It has also been the centre of the most protracted ethnic and religious violence of the post-Soe-harto era. The rhetoric from certain quarters notwithstanding, the contemporary battle for Ambon is not separatist in inspiration. However, the government's inability to provide security might induce some Ambonese to see no other alternative but secession. Aceh provides the counter-example of where a region's resistance in the 1950s was not separatist, but from the 1980s became so. This chapter will examine the transformation of regional revolts and separatist movements from the revolution to the present day.

RELATIONS WITH JAKARTA

Regional rebellions and separatist movements are also about Jakarta. The central government's policies, its ability to impose its authority on the rest of the country, its ability to mobilise resources, the dynamics of political competition and dispersal of decision-making power, and the ideological constructions of the nation and state are all key 'Jakarta' factors that influence the changing dynamics of centre–periphery relations. The revival of regional resistance since the economic crisis and the fall of Soeharto suggests that a weak centre is the other side of the coin. Jakarta's authority has become weaker relatively, but regional movements have not necessarily become stronger in absolute terms.

Indonesia in the 1950s was a period when a newly independent government was establishing its authority and when political power was widely dispersed among competing groups and institutions. During the subsequent period – from the establishment of Guided Democracy through to the New Order – Indonesia became one of the most highly centralised large multi-ethnic states. Although the New Order state was not able to eliminate regional resistance, its control was never threatened by separatist movements in Papua (Irian Jaya), Aceh and East Timor. Authoritarian centralised governance went hand in hand with forthright assertions of national unity, perhaps disguising a nagging doubt that this might not be the case. If national unity was so strong and innate, why were such authoritarian methods required (Bourchier 1996b, p. 10)? The New Order style of governance of the regions, instead of promoting a sustainable model of national unity, formed the context for the contemporary revival of regional resistance.

THE INTERNATIONAL ENVIRONMENT

Indonesia's regional unrest and separatist movements have not simply been domestic affairs to be understood within the framework of centre–periphery

relations. Indonesia's strategic importance in Southeast Asia and its enmesh-
ment in the Cold War from the mid-1950s has meant that the international
environment has also impinged on regional conflicts in Indonesia. East Timor
is the most obvious example, but many of the other regional rebellions have
had important international dimensions.

The leaders of the 1950 rebellions had close relations with the departing
Dutch. There was direct involvement of senior Royal Netherlands Indies
Army (KNIL) officers in the Westerling APRA affair (Chauvel 1990, p. 325).
While active Dutch participation was a less important factor in the Andi Azis
affair and the Republic of the South Moluccas (RMS), these three revolts and
the associated struggle between supporters of a unitary state and the federalists were an issue of considerable importance in Indonesia–Netherlands relations during 1950 and contributed significantly to the rapid breakdown of
post-colonial relations.

The transportation of some 12,000 Ambonese KNIL soldiers and their
families to the Netherlands in 1951 and the establishment of an RMS government in exile in the Netherlands has given the contemporary Ambon violence
an international dimension (Chauvel 1990, p. 396). Audrey and George Kahin
have documented the extensive involvement in the PRRI–Permesta rebellions
of the United States and some of its allies. The rebellions illustrate the complex interactions between the Eisenhower Administration's Cold War objectives in Indonesia and the narrower regional and national agendas of the rebel
leaders themselves (Kahin and Kahin 1995).

Part of the history of the Papuan desire to separate from Indonesia has its
roots in the Indonesian struggle with the Netherlands for the sovereignty of
the territory. The administration in Netherlands New Guinea did much to
encourage a sense of separate Papuan identity. It established representative
institutions for the territory as the first stage towards self-government and
eventual independence. The Dutch fostered a Papuan elite, as Australia was to
do a decade later in Papua New Guinea. The resolution of the Indonesia–
Netherlands struggle was managed under the auspices of the United Nations;
the controversial 1969 Act of Free Choice was conducted under UN supervision and its results ratified by the United Nations. As in the case of the
PRRI–Permesta rebellions, the US desire to contain communist influence in
Indonesia was an important motivating factor in the resolution of the dispute.

Indeed, much of the contemporary Papuan pro-independence rhetoric is a
critique of the process of negotiations that culminated in the 1962 New York
Agreement and the conduct of the Act of Free Choice in 1969 ('Pernyataan
Sikap Politik', *Tifa Irian*, 15–22 November 1999, p. 6). Many Papuan pro-
independence leaders seek to internationalise their cause, framing their argument in the context of the history of international involvement in Papua's
integration in Indonesia. With reference to the case of East Timor, it has been

argued that because Papua became a part of Indonesia through a decision of the United Nations, it can separate through the same channel, and not as a result of a decision from the People's Consultative Assembly (MPR). The presence of Theys Eluay and other Papuan leaders at the UN Millenium Summit and the support the Papuan cause received from the presidents of Vanuatu and Nauru highlight the importance of the international context from the Papuan pro-independence perspective ('Dari Gedung BPD Hingga ke Gedung PBB', *Tifa Papua*, 18–28 September 2000, p. 3).

In the case of East Timor, the international context derived from its history as a Portuguese, rather than a Dutch, colony. Many of Indonesia's neighbours recognised Indonesia's annexation of the territory, but the United Nations and a majority of its members did not. The Habibie-initiated consultation with the East Timorese on autonomy within Indonesia or independence was conducted by the United Nations, the subsequent international intervention was sanctioned by the Security Council, and the post-separation transitionary administration was run by the United Nations.

The transformation of Indonesia's relations with the world following *krismon* (the financial crisis) – from a state largely able to set the terms on which it interacted with the rest of the world to one in which it has become dependent on the international community for financial survival and any hopes of economic recovery – has implications for how Jakarta deals with the regions. It is difficult to overestimate the impact on Jakarta's political elite of the international intervention associated with the separation of East Timor. World Bank President James Wolfensohn's letter to President Abdurrahman Wahid linking the Bank's continued financial support to Indonesia's ability to control its own military and militia in West Timor is a more recent example of the sort of international pressure that has created an intensely nationalistic atmosphere in Jakarta (Mufson 2000, p. A22). The separation of East Timor has prompted concern about further territorial disintegration and strengthened the resolve throughout the Jakarta political elite to draw a line in the sand after East Timor.

It is interesting to note that a *Tempo* survey of a well-educated and relatively well-off sample of Jakarta residents on attitudes towards the Papuan struggle for independence found them to be unsympathetic and strongly supportive of the government's efforts to maintain the unitary state and Papua as an integral part of it.[1] Despite repeated statements of support for Indonesia's territorial integrity from foreign governments, some senior ministers have alleged the involvement of outside powers in Indonesia's internal affairs. In October 2000 the Defence Minister, Mohammad Mahfud, accused a US 'spy' of involvement in the violence in Wamena (Papua). Although the government withdrew the accusation for want of any evidence, the affair did illustrate the great sensitivity some sections of the government and the political elite feel about foreign influence ('Government Dismisses Allegations of American Espionage', *Jakarta Post*, 28 October 2000).

The nature of regional governance, the behaviour of the military and the government's limited ability to control the military and its associates in some regions have made Indonesia vulnerable to international scrutiny. The dilemmas posed for foreign governments are acute. They want to support Indonesia's first democratically elected president and the processes of democratisation. Indeed they have a strategic interest in maintaining the territorial integrity of the Indonesian state. However, by applying pressure on Abdurrahman Wahid to control the military and resolve the regional challenges by non-violent means, the international community is risking inflaming national sentiment and undermining the democratising government it seeks to support. Such are the tensions between the democratic and nationalist imperatives in Jakarta and such is the nature of relations with the international community in the current climate.

RESISTANCE AND REBELLION

Regional revolts and separatist movements in the 1950s evolved from the revolution and the struggle against the Dutch around issues left unresolved by that campaign. These movements were led by people who participated in the revolution, but who opposed or felt threatened by political developments in Jakarta under republican-dominated governments. Some, like the leaders of the Andi Azis affair and the RMS, sought to preserve their status and influence. They were motivated by fears about what Indonesia might become and their own position and that of the regions they purported to represent in an independent Indonesia. Others, such as the leaders of the Darul Islam movements in West Java, South Sulawesi and Aceh, as well as the PRRI–Permesta regional rebellions of the late 1950s, sought to change the ideological and political character of the state. Although the separatist movements of the New Order and post-Soeharto periods have long histories, they are fundamentally forms of resistance to what Indonesia has become and to how central governments have sought to impose their authority on the regions.

Ambon and Aceh

To explore the dynamics of the 1950s rebellions, I have taken the examples of the RMS and the Darul Islam movement in Aceh. On the surface of it, Aceh and Ambon could not be more different culturally, religiously and in terms of historical experience in the colonial past and during the revolution.

Many Ambonese soldiers in the colonial army won their military decorations helping the Dutch subdue Aceh (Chauvel 1990, p. 45). The Acehenese have a proud history of resisting Dutch domination. They have provided Indonesia with more than their fair share of national heroes. During the revolution, Aceh was the only region to remain under republican control for the entire struggle. It is this history that makes Aceh so important for the Indonesian national enterprise. Nevertheless, there was something of a paradox about the Acehenese during the revolution. This paradox is crucial to our understanding of the revolt that followed. Aceh fully supported the republican cause, politically, diplomatically and financially, yet it enjoyed almost complete autonomy from the republican government (Kell 1995, p. 10).

The republican government exercised almost no administrative influence in Ambon during the revolution, but for very different reasons than in Aceh. The Moluccas were firmly within the region of unchallenged Dutch administrative and military control. Ambon was part of the Dutch-created Federal State of East Indonesia and developed strong local institutions of representative government. Without wanting to oversimplify an understanding of the RMS, for key groups of the Ambonese elite their commitment to an independent Indonesia, and Ambon's part in it, was conditional. The State of East Indonesia and the extensive autonomy that Ambon enjoyed within it were the important preconditions for membership of the Indonesian nation.

The struggle between unitarists and federalists in the State of East Indonesia during the early months of 1950 and the failure of the Andi Azis affair to defend the State of East Indonesia against Jakarta destroyed that conditionality. The key leaders of the RMS – Manusama and Soumokil – had not been separatists prior to the transfer of sovereignty. They had supported the State of East Indonesia, but saw with the collapse of that state a threat to Ambonese society, their position within it and their political careers. It was then, and only then, that they considered the option of an independent state. From their perspective, the collapse of East Indonesia and the sending of Indonesian National Army (TNI) troops to occupy the eastern half of the archipelago changed the terms of engagement for Ambon as part of an independent Indonesia (Chauvel 1990).

If some of the Ambonese elite were ambivalent and conditional about their commitment to an independent Indonesia, their Acehenese counterparts considered that they had made a particular contribution to the national struggle. They had fought the Dutch on the neighbouring east coast of Sumatra. They had contributed funds to enable the republic to purchase two aircraft. They had rejected the approach from the Federal State of East Sumatra for Aceh to become a federal state. The Acehenese were proud of their role in the revolution, which was understood as a continuation of their struggle against Dutch domination. It was a struggle in support of Aceh being part of an independent Indonesia and not as a separate state of Aceh. At the time of the transfer of sovereignty Aceh had the status of an autonomous province. Acehenese disillusionment with Jakarta began with the abolition of Aceh's status as a province and its becoming a residency within the province of North Sumatra (Ali 1999, pp. 7–9). The Acehenese *ulama* had been concerned during the revolution that Indonesia had not been created as an Islamic state. Their anxieties about religious autonomy were heightened when Aceh became part of North Sumatra and were exacerbated by Jakarta's measures to reduce their control over the administration and armed forces in Aceh (Kell 1995, pp. 10–11). Abdulla Ali considers the outbreak of Daud Beureueh's Darul Islam rebellion in 1953 a direct result of the feeling of disappointment and injustice in Aceh at the encroachment of Jakarta's authority (Ali 1999, p. 8).

Unlike the RMS, the rebellion in Aceh did not seek to establish an independent state, but rather an Islamic state in Indonesia. In this endeavour Aceh joined West Java and South Sulawesi. Daud Beureueh's commitment to Indonesia was not conditional in the way that Manusama and Soumokil's was; rather, his rebellion was an attempt to create a republic more to his liking. Aceh and Ambon were at opposite ends of the nationalist political spectrum, but they shared the desire to maintain local autonomy. They wanted, in varying measures, to be part of Indonesia, but they also wanted to maintain something of themselves – a cultural and political autonomy. What triggered the rebellions was the encroachment of Jakarta's authority.

In the negotiated resolution of the Daud Beureueh rebellion in 1959, the Acehenese secured some of their objectives. In 1965 Aceh became a province with the status of a Special Region (Daerah Istimewa). It had autonomy in the areas of religion, customary law (*adat istiadat*) and education (Ali 1999, p. 8). Robinson (1998, p. 130) argues that the resolution of the rebellion with limited loss of life was possible because the rebels had not sought to separate from Indonesia and their loyalty to a united Indonesia was not doubted.

The Establishment of Jakarta's Control and the Transformation of Governance in the Regions

Nazaruddin Sjamsuddin has labelled the Aceh rebellion of the 1950s as the 'Republican Revolt' (Sjamsuddin 1985). The description is also appropriate for the PRRI–Permesta regional rebellions of the late 1950s in parts of Sumatra and Sulawesi. Both the civilian and military leaders had fought with the republic against the Dutch. Their rebellion was in many respects a continuation of the parliamentary politics in Jakarta, by other means. The regional military commanders had somewhat different agendas in resisting Army Chief-of-Staff General A.H. Nasution's assertion of the central Army Command's authority. The economic interests of the rebellious, resource-rich, exporting provinces would be better served by a more favourable distribution of resources and revenues with the central government rather than severing the relationship altogether. Although the PRRI–Permesta leaders' nationalist credentials were tarnished through their association with the Americans, for whom the dismemberment of Indonesia may not have been in conflict with their Cold War objectives, the ideological, political, military and economic issues at stake were concerns of the Indonesian nation state.

The manner in which the regional rebellions were brought to a conclusion suggests that the nation was still inclusive, open and reasonably accepting of those who had strayed from the path. The leaders of the rebellions were permitted to 'return' to the republican fold. Of the Darul Islam soldiers in West Java, Nasution wrote: 'the TNI remembered that they were also our people, our family. It was our responsibility to help them return and become useful members of society' (Nasution 1985, p. 249). Nasution considered that the revolts and regional unrest of the 1950s and 1960s would not have occurred if national life, democracy and regional autonomy had been developed from the beginning, so that groups and particular regions could have sought the desired changes and reforms through political institutions and not felt it necessary to take up arms (Nasution 1985, p. 250). The regional unrest was born of issues left unresolved from the revolution. The rebels were nonetheless regarded as fellow Indonesians, however misguided.

By 1962, Nasution thought that security and unity had been achieved throughout Indonesia. Nearly all the rebel leaders had been either captured or 'returned' to the national fold – only Soumokil was still at large in the interior of Ceram. Security and unity was the TNI's achievement. Only the TNI stood above all groups and parties in the society, neither manipulated nor influenced by sectional interests (Nasution 1985, pp. 238, 249). This, at least, was the image that the TNI wished to convey.

Nasution felt that he had brought the rebellions of the 1950s and early 1960s to an end in such a way that many of the rebels, including their principal leaders, were welcomed back into the Indonesian family. The political and administrative positions assumed by military officers and the access to economic resources the TNI gained through control of the old Dutch enterprises were one of the factors in the transformation of governance in the regions that came to fruition in Soeharto's New Order. The integration in, if not dominance of, the executive and bureaucracy by the military went hand in hand with greater central control from Jakarta.

A second factor was the institutionalisation of violence, or what Ben Anderson (1999) has called the 'process of brutalisation' through which, in a systematic manner, enemies of the state were no longer regarded as fellow Indonesians – however misguided – but rather as 'animals', 'devils', 'objects' and 'possessions'. Anderson argues: 'A culture has developed in the military according to which in "security" matters every element of human decency can be set aside, with complete impunity: provided "the boss" gives them the order' (p. 8). The massacres of 1965–66 were the first example of this process of brutalisation, on a massive scale. In Aceh, Papua and East Timor this approach was systematically applied. Anderson contends that Papuans were simply not thought of as fellow Indonesians, but rather as possessions. Instead of welcoming the East Timorese into the Indonesian family, the military sought to 'subjugate' them, just as van Heurtz had the Acehenese (pp. 5, 8).

A third factor was the elaboration of Pancasila and the reformulation of the Indonesian nation, reflecting organicist arguments, to promote the image that Soeharto's New Order was 'the exemplar of Indonesian cultural tradition' (Bourchier 1996b, p. 295). Bourchier emphasised that the function of Soeharto's Pancasila and the accompanying P4 indoctrination campaign was 'to Indonesian-ise Indonesians' – to purge the remnants of the culture of conflict and competition and replace it with a discourse of harmony and obedience. By excluding alternative discourses – Marxism, social democracy and some strands of Islam – it placed their followers outside the Indonesian family (pp. 238, 240). It is suggested here that the process of exclusion also applied to regional discourses about Indonesia. The organicist arguments on which Soeharto drew had their origins in Dutch *adat* law scholarship, which contended, inter alia, that the archipelago constituted a discrete and coherent cultural area (Bourchier 1996b, p. 31). The unity, oneness and harmony of Soeharto's Indonesian culture in effect excluded the diversity from the unity, sanitised it and consigned it to Taman Mini.[2]

Aceh and Papua

Aceh is crucial to the central argument of this chapter. It is the region where rebellions occurred both in the 1950s and in the New Order and post-Soeharto periods. How was Acehenese resistance transformed from seeking to maintain local autonomy and secure a state in which Islamic values and laws were more important, to a rebellion that sought to separate from Indonesia? The transformation of Acehenese resistance under the New Order is particularly germane in the context of Habibie's and Abdurrahman Wahid's endeavours to implement regional autonomy. Special Region status for Aceh was an important part of the settlement with Daud Beureueh. Under Soeharto, the only thing special about Aceh was the extent of economic exploitation and the scale of institutionalised violence.

Kell (1995) and Robinson (1998) argue that the causes of the revival and transformation of resistance in Aceh are to be found in the policies, structures, and political and military practice of Soeharto's Indonesia, rather than in Aceh's rich history of resistance and strong sense of identity. In particular, this involved the combination of Jakarta's economic exploitation of Aceh's natural resources with the institutionalised and sanctioned terror of the DOM (Military Operations Area) period that began in 1989. Kell notes the importance of the provincial leadership to Jakarta's control of Aceh's economic resources. A new technocratic elite assumed provincial leadership from the *ulama* (Islamic religious leaders), who had dominated Acehenese society since the revolution. However, whereas the *ulama* found the basis of support within their own society, the Acehenese technocrats were beholden to Jakarta for their positions. The highly centralised nature of decision-making meant that they could do little to effect a more equitable distribution of the revenues generated by the exploitation of the province's resources (Kell 1995, p. 84; Robinson 1998, pp. 146–7).

As with Aceh, Papua is resource-rich and was governed by Soeharto with the same forceful military and political controls. Papuans experienced just the last two chaotic years of Guided Democracy before the 1965 coup brought Soeharto to power. Resistance started almost as soon as the Indonesian administration was established in 1963, with the Organisation for a Free Papua (OPM) formed the following year and the first substantial revolt occurring in Manokwari in 1965 (Djopari 1993, pp. 100, 109–10). The small Papuan political elite at the time of being 'returned' to Indonesia was divided. It included a group that had since the revolution favoured integration with Indonesia. The similarity between Aceh's and Papua's resistance and desire to separate is in their common experience of the dominant features of New Order Indonesia, namely economic exploitation, political repression and cultural exclusion.

The public Papuan nationalist discourse has two main parts. First, it involves a critique of the process of international negotiations in the 1960s through which Papua became part of Indonesia – a process in which Papuans had no say. Second, it is propelled by the suffering of more than 30 years of Indonesian occupation. Benny Giay (2000), the leading Papuan intellectual and theologian, has called it the 'suffering of the Papuan people during 35 years of *Pembangunan* [Development]' – a Memoria Pasionis (narrative of suffering). It is this experience which motivates the struggle for separation and independence. The experience of being treated as stupid, incapable and drunk, the intimidation involved in the acquisition of land for development, systematic discrimination in work and educational opportunities and access to health services together with the institutionalised abuse of human rights, gave birth to anti-Indonesian sentiment and a contempt for Indonesian culture and civilisation as that was represented in the New Order (Giay 2000, pp. 55–8). Closely related to the disdain for New Order cultural values – often unfavourably compared with those of the colonial Dutch by older generation Papuans – is the demand for Indonesia to respect their Melanesian cultural values. At its 2000 general assembly, the Gereja Kristen Injil di Tanah Papua (GKI, the principal protestant church in Papua) called for the implementation of Melanesian cultural values at all levels of government and in social, cultural and educational development (GKI 2000a, p. 68). During the assembly, the GKI's conservative moderator, the Reverend Herman Saud, stated that Papuans have been treated as if they were not Indonesian citizens. Their rights as Indonesian citizens were not respected (GKI 2000b, p. 100).

Papuan armed resistance to Indonesian control was sporadic, localised, but nonetheless persistent. The OPM suffered from factional disputes and failed to mobilise much international support. Although it kept alive the ideal of independence, it never posed a threat to Indonesian control (Djopari 1993). The military's campaign against the revival of Acehenese resistance under the Independent Aceh Movement (GAM) between 1989 and 1992 worked in the short term because the population was successfully terrorised and divided (Robinson 1998, p. 154).

In the turbulent political constellation that has emerged following the economic crisis and the fall of Soeharto, the relationship between Jakarta and the rebellious provinces has been transformed. This is due more to a decline in Jakarta's authority than an increase in strength in absolute terms of the resistance movements. Those in Papua and Aceh, alienated by institutionalised violence, cultural exclusion and economic exploitation, have tended not to join the *reformasi* movement of their fellow Indonesians in Jakarta and elsewhere in the struggle for a more democratic and inclusive Indonesia. Rather they have used the new political space created by a weak centre and *reformasi* political values to advance Papuan and Acehenese national aspirations.

In *reformasi* there should be much optimism for a peaceful resolution of regional resistance. Indeed, there have been many positive signs. Military abuses in Aceh have been exposed, and in May 2000 24 army personnel were tried for the killing of a pro-independence religious leader and some 50 of his followers. Although the senior officers involved were not charged – a captain was the highest ranked officer on trial – perhaps a small dent has been made in the impunity enjoyed by the military (ICG 2000a, p. 21). President Abdurrahman Wahid has resisted military pressure to impose a military emergency in Aceh and his government in May 2000 negotiated a humanitarian pause with the GAM (ICG 2000a, p. 18).

In Papua, new urban-based pro-independence leaders initiated a 'national dialogue' with President Habibie in February 1999. President Abdurrahman Wahid legitimised some of the new political space during his visit to Jayapura in December 1999, when he indicated his support for the use of 'Papua' – the name preferred by those supporting independence – over 'Irian Jaya'. He also gave his blessing to the flying of the Morning Star – the Papuan national flag. The president was invited to open the Congress of Papua (Kongres Papua) in May 2000, and while he was unable to accept the invitation, the government funded the event to the tune of Rp 1 billion ('Setahun Pemerintahan Abdurrahman Wahid Bara Disintegrasi Itu Masih Menyala', *Kompas*, 20 October 2000). The success of Kongres Papua with its straightforward demand for independence caused concern in Jakarta. To deflect criticism, the government initiated a program of special assistance – the Crash Program ('Crash Program: Redam Aspirasi "M"?', *Tifa Papua*, 4–9 September 2000).[3] At the August 2000 meeting of the MPR, President Abdurrahman Wahid's approach to the pro-independence movements in Aceh and Papua was subjected to strong criticism from across the parties. The MPR decreed that the president should take stronger measures against the separatist movements. It also refused to endorse his decision to change the name of the province from Irian Jaya to Papua (*Indonesian Observer*, 21 August 2000).

In the following months, there were progressive attempts by the central government to close the political space that Presidents Habibie and Abdurrahman Wahid had permitted. Jakarta endeavoured to prevent the Papuan flag from being flown, to disband Satgas Papua, the pro-independence militia, as well as restrict, if not prevent, the celebrations of the anniversary of the 1961 'independence day' on 1 December 2000. Key pro-independence leaders were imprisoned in the days before the anniversary. Jayapura was placed under military occupation and the greatly curtailed celebrations took place under the close guard of hundreds of riot police. When the Papuan flag was pulled down forcefully, there was violence and loss of life, most tragically in Wamena on 6 October 2000. During the weeks leading up to 1 December 2000, substantial troop reinforcements were made in Papua. The tone of statements from Coordinating Minister for Security and Political Affairs Susilo Bambang Yudhoyono became increasingly strident, warning that if there were celebrations of the 'independence day' anniversary, 'it will be considered an act of treason and the government will take stern actions based on the Constitution' (AFP 2000).

CONCLUSION

The criticism from across the political spectrum in the MPR of Abdurrahman Wahid's more open and inclusive approach to the pro-independence movements in Aceh and Papua during his first nine months in office suggests that Robinson was premature in his optimism about the influence of changes in the political climate since the fall of Soeharto on Jakarta's approach to regional problems (Robinson 1998, p. 155). The members of the MPR are the most representative parliamentarians since the mid-1950s and yet their capacity, as well as that of the government, to imagine ways other than the application of force to deal with regional resistance seems little greater than that of the Soeharto government.

Whether there is the space in post-East Timor Indonesia to renegotiate the terms of engagement – the national compact – so that the diversity can be brought back into the unity and so that Papuans, Acehenese, Ambonese and others can feel part of the Indonesian family is a critical issue. The tensions between the democratic and nationalist imperatives are acute. Whether Indonesia can become democratic and stay united remains to be seen.

NOTES

1 See 'Papua Membara, Jakarta Kecewa' (*Tempo*, 29 October 2000, p. 12); and the opinion poll on 'The Best Solution for Papua' (*Tempo* Jajak Pendapat, 'Penyelesaian Terbaik untuk Papua', 16–23 October 2000, www.tempo.co.id).

2 Taman Mini is a theme park on the outskirts of Jakarta constructed to display Indonesia's 'diversity in microcosm'. It was a project of Soeharto's late wife, Ibu Tien.

3 The Crash Program is a form of financial assistance given to local government in Papua to dampen criticism of Jakarta and redirect Papuan political energies away from support of the separatist movement and towards issues of economic and social development. Jakarta hopes the program will convince Papuans that the central government supports economic and social development in Papua.

PART III

ECONOMIC HISTORY

13

BRIEF REFLECTIONS ON INDONESIAN ECONOMIC HISTORY

Howard Dick

Until quite recently very little attention was paid to Indonesia's economic history. During the New Order period of government under President Soeharto, economists focused their attention on economic development and, like policymakers, looked to a better future. There seemed to be nothing to learn from the economic failures of the Old Order under President Sukarno, while the Dutch colonial era had become so remote as to be of interest only to historians. The fact that few non-Dutch scholars, even Indonesians, could read Dutch-language sources was a further discouragement. Ignorance of economic history, however, did not mean that it was irrelevant. Policies do not arise out of thin air but are based on reasonings of the time. Statistics and trends have little meaning without baselines.

Over the course of the 20th century, failure to pay heed to economic history gave rise to a sequence of poorly judged assessments of the Indonesian economy, alternatively too pessimistic and too optimistic. At the turn of the century, the preoccupation was with the diminishing welfare of the Javanese, but by the time the voluminous reports of the Welfare Commission came to be presented at the end of the first decade, the economy was booming and the crisis had passed. Even the severe 1930s Depression was followed by economic recovery and structural change in the form of nascent industrialisation. Yet despite ample colonial evidence to the contrary, by the 1960s economic development had come to be seen as almost unachievable: Indonesia was a poor, underdeveloped country trapped in a vicious cycle of poverty and held back by incompetent and ineffective government and bureaucracy.

Lo and behold, after 30 years of the New Order, rapid economic growth was being hailed as a natural and self-sustaining process – the norm. Such optimism was supported by a proliferation of statistics which gave the comforting illusion that growth and development could be measured and controlled. There were vested interests in maintaining that illusion – 'national development' justified authoritarian rule, rewarded policy advisors and returned well-connected businessmen a profit on their investments. Then suddenly in 1998, regardless of 'economic fundamentals', Indonesia fell into economic and political crisis. After the collapse of Soeharto's authoritarian government, experts boldly criticised the New Order for its authoritarianism and corruption. As the prospects for sustained economic growth receded, the pessimism of the 1960s seemed to return. Objectively, however, these assessments were not based on well-grounded analysis but rationalisations of prevailing moods.

Fortunately a new curiosity as to how the New Order sits in historical perspective coincides with the coming of age of the field of Indonesian economic history. As recently as a decade ago, very few English-language materials on 20th century Indonesian economic history existed – bar the magisterial study of Furnivall (1944) – and little recent work had appeared in Dutch. There were contemporary works, such as those of Higgins (1957) and McVey (1963) as well as the publication from 1965 of the *Bulletin of Indonesian Economic Studies* which, by passage of years, has now become a historical record. However, it was not until 1975 that there began to appear a valuable series of source publications – the *Changing Economy of Indonesia* series – that made edited and annotated colonial statistics available to a much wider audience.

In the 1980s scholars began to revisit Indonesia's economic history. A workshop convened at the Australian National University in 1982 on Indonesian economic history in the colonial era gave rise to the volume edited by Booth, O'Malley and Weidemann (1990) at almost the same time as that by Maddison and Prince (1989). In the 1990s economists and historians held conferences in Indonesia, the Netherlands and Australia to explore not only Dutch colonial economic history but also its relevance to Old Order and New Order economic development. Important issues have been debated, such as the origins of poverty, long-term trends in agricultural development, the origins of industrialisation, the economic content of the colonial Ethical Policy, the reasons for the failure of economic development after independence, and the nature of national integration. These debates have been brought together in several edited collections, such as Lindblad (1993, 1996). Publication of Booth's (1998a) thematic economic history, *The Indonesian Economy in the Nineteenth and Twentieth Centuries*, was a milestone. It will soon be supplemented by a chronological account (Dick, Houben, Lindblad and Thee 2001).

This collection of papers on Indonesian economic history contributes to the solid research of recent years and provides a succinct overview of the New Order in historical perspective. The papers demonstrate that development is a path-dependent but unstable process in which the interaction of economics and politics may be productive, or destructive.

14

REFLECTIONS ON THE NEW ORDER 'MIRACLE'

Thee Kian Wie*

Indonesia experienced rapid economic and social development under the New Order government of President Soeharto, and this contributed to rising standards of living for the Indonesian population. However, focus on the economic achievements at the expense of the negative aspects of the New Order gives a biased view of the era. Given the current tendency in Indonesia to look upon the New Order as an unmitigated disaster, this chapter attempts to record both its positive economic and social achievements as well as the negative aspects of economic development under the New Order.

FROM CRISIS TO 'MIRACLE' TO CRISIS

After recovering from the severe economic crisis and the wrenching political dislocations of the mid-1960s, the Indonesian economy embarked on a period of unprecedented growth from the late 1960s. This was, in general, sustained for the next three decades. Rapid economic growth during this period transformed Indonesia from the 'prime economic underperformer' in Southeast Asia in the early 1960s into a newly industrialising economy (NIE) by the early 1990s. It also transformed Indonesia from a largely agrarian economy into one in which the manufacturing sector contributed more to gross domestic product (GDP).

As a result, Indonesia was classified in 1993 as a 'high-performing Asian economy' (HPAE) by the World Bank in its famous but controversial report on the East Asian 'miracle' (World Bank 1993, p. xvi). The HPAEs were made up of Japan, South Korea, Taiwan, Hong Kong, Singapore, Malaysia, Thailand and Indonesia. While other developing countries also grew quickly, none were able to sustain high growth rates for as long as the HPAEs. The growth of the HPAEs was underpinned by high rates of capital investment, including investment in human capital (World Bank 1993, p. 8).

Rapid economic growth in Indonesia during the New Order was accompanied by steady improvements in social welfare, as reflected in a decline in the incidence of absolute poverty and considerable improvements in primary health care and education. Moreover, unlike in many other developing countries, Indonesia's rapid economic growth was not accompanied by worsening income distribution.

However, by July 1997, only two months after the release of a cautiously upbeat World Bank report on Indonesia's medium-term prospects (World Bank 1997a), perceptions about the Indonesian economy suddenly changed for the worse. The Indonesian rupiah began to depreciate, first gradually and then rapidly, as foreign creditors and investors scrambled to reduce their exposure.

The Indonesian government turned to the International Monetary Fund (IMF) for financial assistance to counteract the currency crisis. The government hoped that the availability of a large IMF standby loan backed by a credible domestic economic reform program sanctioned by the IMF would restore confidence in the rupiah (Sadli 1999, p. 17). Thus, as at the beginning of its reign in 1966, the Soeharto government again came under the tutelage of the IMF. But whereas in 1966 IMF assistance was aimed at combating hyperinflation (Booth 1998b, p. 178), in 1997 it was to stem erosion of market confidence in the rupiah.

The IMF's involvement failed to restore market confidence because of political uncertainty about President Soeharto's health and because of his reluctance to implement the economic reform program faithfully. As the rupiah continued to depreciate – by 80% in January 1998 alone – inflation rose to more than 50% and the economy contracted sharply. Absolute poverty, which had declined steadily during the New Order era, began to rise. Indonesia was also hit by a severe El Niño drought, which damaged the rice harvest, and by falling oil prices, which reduced government revenues.

Within less than 12 months, Indonesia was transformed from a 'miracle' economy, extolled by the international aid community and many foreign economists as a development model worthy of emulation by other developing countries, into a 'melt-down' economy dependent on the charity of the international aid community and donor countries for its very survival. The deepening and protracted economic crisis caused the economy to contract by almost 14% in 1998 – far worse than the 3% economic contraction in the mid-1960s (World Bank 1998, p. 2.1). The economic distress caused by the 1997–98 economic crisis led to serious political and social unrest, forcing the resignation of President Soeharto after a reign of 32 years. Thus Soeharto's New Order regime, which emerged in the mid-1960s during an economic and

political crisis left behind by President Sukarno's government, ended igno-
miniously in another, more serious, economic and political crisis.

ECONOMIC AND SOCIAL DEVELOPMENT IN REGIONAL PERSPECTIVE

Economic Development

The rapid and sustained economic progress achieved during the three decades
of New Order rule enabled Indonesia to graduate from the ranks of the poorest low-income countries in the mid-1960s into the ranks of the lower middle-
income countries by the early 1990s. With the economy growing at an average
annual rate of 7% over the period 1965–97, Indonesia's real gross national
product (GNP) roughly doubled every 10 years. Due to a successful family
planning program introduced by the government in the early 1970s, population growth over the period 1965–97 slowed to an average annual rate of 2%,
one of the lowest among developing countries. With average economic
growth exceeding average population growth by almost 5%, Indonesia experienced a rapid increase in per capita GNP. This was much higher than in most
other developing countries, and compared favourably with levels in the other
HPAEs. GNP growth led to rising standards of living, reflected in a high average growth rate of private consumption (Table 14.1).

Indonesia's economic growth was underpinned by the fast and sustained
expansion of gross domestic investment (GDI). Although Indonesia's GDI
compared favourably with that of other HPAEs, its export performance was
inferior. This can be attributed to the fact that Indonesia, unlike the other
HPAEs, relied greatly on primary exports, particularly of oil and gas. Indonesia only made serious efforts to promote manufactured exports when the oil
boom ended in 1982. The resulting surge in manufactured exports from 1987
slowed in 1993 to a level that persisted until the crisis of 1997–98. Many
observers attributed the slowdown to the relatively low international competitiveness of most Indonesian manufacturing firms.

During the New Order, the pace of economic growth led to considerable
economic and social structural change (Table 14.2). These structural changes
were reflected in a shift of production from agriculture to manufacturing and
modern services; a reduction in the agricultural labour force and growth of
urban centres; an enhanced role for trade in the economy; an increasing role
for the central government in the economy; and monetisation of the economy
as a result of stable economic management (World Bank 1999, p. 31).

Table 14.2 shows that Indonesia's economic transformation stood out even
among the HPAEs, particularly as it had been the most dependent on agricul-

TABLE 14.1 Average Annual Growth in Seven HPAEs of GNP, Population, Value Added, Private Consumption, GDI and Exports of Goods and Services, 1965–97 (%)

Country	GNP[a]		Population[b]	
	(total)	(per capita)	(total)	(labour force)
NIEs				
Indonesia	7.0	4.8	2.0	2.7
Malaysia	6.8	4.1	2.6	3.1
Thailand	7.4	5.1	2.1	2.7
Three 'Tigers'				
South Korea	8.2	6.7	1.5	2.6
Hong Kong	7.6	5.7	1.8	2.6
Singapore	4.4	6.3	1.9	3.1
Japan	4.4	3.6	0.8	1.1

a Total GNP is the sum of value added by all resident producers plus any taxes (less subsidies) that are not included in the valuation of output plus net receipts of primary income (employee compensation and property income) from non-resident sources. Growth is calculated from constant price GNP in national currency units. Per capita GNP is GNP divided by mid-year population.
b Average annual growth of total population and labour force is calculated using the exponential end-point method. The labour force comprises all those who meet the ILO's definition of the economically active population.
c Value added is the net output of a sector after adding up all outputs and subtracting intermediate inputs. It is calculated without making deductions for depreciation of fabricated assets or for the depletion and degradation of natural resources. The industrial origin of value added is

ture in 1970. Structural change in the occupational distribution of the labour force was far less rapid. This is reflected in the far higher percentage of the labour force employed in agriculture in 1997 than the share of agricultural value added in GDP. During this period Indonesia became a more urbanised society, with more than one-third of its population living in urban areas. Foreign trade, too, became much more important to the economy, accounting for more than half of GDP by 1997.

The relative size of the central government in the Indonesian economy – represented in Table 14.2 by the ratio of central government revenue to GDP – is far smaller than in the other two Asian NIEs, Malaysia and Thailand,

TABLE 14.1 (*continued*)

Value Added[c]			Private Consump-tion[d]	GDI[e]	Exports of Goods & Services[f]
(agriculture)	(industry)	(services)			
3.9	9.1	7.9	7.2	9.2	5.7
3.7	8.5	7.1	6.1	10.1	9.7
4.0	9.7	7.5	6.3	9.0	11.3
2.0	12.3	8.2	7.4	12.4	16.0
–	–	–	8.0	7.7	11.9
–1.4	8.6	8.3	6.7	9.6	12.2
–0.1	4.5	4.7	4.2	4.7	7.7

    determined by ISIC, revision 2. Agriculture is the value added of ISIC major divisions 1–5; industry is the value added of ISIC divisions 10–15; and services is the value added of ISIC divisions 15–37.
d Private consumption is the market value of all goods and services, including durable products, purchased or received as income in kind by households and non-profit institutions. It excludes purchases of dwellings but includes imputed rent for owner-occupied dwellings.
e GDI consists of outlays or additions to fixed assets of the economy plus net changes in inventory.
f Exports of goods and services refers to the value of all goods and market services provided to the rest of the world.
Source: World Bank (1999), Table 1.4, pp. 16–19.

owing to the relatively poor taxation efforts of the government. Before 1983, income tax collection in Indonesia was complicated and weak, allowing for 'tax haggling' between taxpayer and tax collector (Glassburner 1983, p. 30). Although the tax reforms of 1984–85 were fairly successful in raising non-oil taxes, Indonesia's ratio of non-oil tax revenues to GDP of 17% is still relatively low. This is partly because of the narrowness of the tax base, but also because the tax office is inefficient and the political will to increase tax compliance levels is lacking (Asher and Booth 1992, p. 49).

    Although the Indonesian economy was far more monetised in 1997 than in 1970, it was less monetised than Malaysia and Thailand in particular. The

TABLE 14.2 Indonesia's Long-term Structural Change in Regional Perspective, 1970–97

Country	Agriculture Value Added[a] (% of GDP)		Labour Force in Agriculture[b] (% of total labour force)		Urban Population[c] (% of total population)		Trade[d] (% of GDP)		Central Government Revenue[e] (% of GDP)		Money and Quasi-money[f] (% of GDP)	
	1970	1997	1970	1997	1970	1997	1970	1997	1970	1997	1970	1997
NIEs												
Indonesia	45	16	66	55	17	37	28	56	13	17	8	50
Malaysia	29	12	54	27	34	55	80	187	20	23	31	97
Thailand	26	11	80	64	13	21	34	93	12	18	27	84
Three 'Tigers'												
South Korea	27	6	49	18	41	83	38	77	15	22	29	45
Hong Kong	–	0	4	1	88	95	181	267	–	–	–	206
Singapore	2	0	3	0	100	100	232	358	21	24	62	82
Japan	6	2	20	7	71	78	20	19	11	–	69	112

a Agriculture value added is the sum of outputs of the agricultural sector (including ISIC major divisions 1–5) less the costs of intermediate inputs, measured as a share of GDP.
b Labour force in agriculture is the percentage of the total labour force recorded as working in agriculture, hunting, forestry and fishing (ISIC major divisions 1–5).
c Urban population is the proportion of the total population living in areas defined as urban in each country.
d Trade is the sum of exports and imports of goods and services, measured as a share of GDP.
e Central government revenue includes all revenue to the government from taxes and non-repayable receipts (other than grants), measured as a share of GDP.
f Money and quasi-money comprises the sum of currency outside banks, demand deposits other than those of the central government, and the time, saving and foreign currency deposits of resident sectors other than the central government. This measure of the money supply is called M2.

Source: World Bank (1999), Table 1.5, pp. 28–31.

importance of the agricultural sector (a significant part of which was not yet commercialised) in the economy up to the early 1970s may account for Indonesia's low rate of monetisation relative to other East Asian countries.

Social Development

Rapid economic growth during the Soeharto era was accompanied by equally fast-moving social development. The indicators used to measure progress towards the development goals for the 21st century – per capita private consumption, net primary enrolment ratio, infant mortality rate, maternal mortality rate and access to safe water (World Bank 1999, p. 19) – all point to considerable progress having been made (Table 14.3).

Per capita consumption levels, an indicator of the effect of economic development on the welfare of individuals, rose steeply in Indonesia over the period 1980–97. Although positive growth rates are generally associated with a decline in absolute poverty, the poor may not share equally in, or may gain less from, the improvement of welfare if income distribution is highly unequal (World Bank 1999, p. 19). But after correcting for the degree of income inequality, private per capita consumption growth in Indonesia is still high – even the highest among the ASEAN-4 countries.

Indonesia made rapid progress in education, as shown by the increase in net primary enrolment ratios for both male and female students. In 1980, these ratios were already quite high as a result of large government investments in the expansion of primary education, particularly in rural areas. These were made possible by the oil boom income gains of the 1970s (Jones 1994, p. 164). Table 14.3 shows that in the 1980s the goal of universal primary education had largely been achieved, assisted by slower growth in the primary school age population due to successful family planning programs.

Progress in the expansion of primary health care is reflected in a steep decline in infant mortality rates over the period 1970–97 and the improved provision of safe drinking water. Indonesia's record is less impressive when compared with that of the other ASEAN-4 countries, and less impressive still when compared with that of the three Asian 'Tigers'. Indonesia had by far the highest infant and maternal mortality rates, and the percentage of the population with access to safe water was much lower than in both the other ASEAN-4 countries and the Asian 'Tigers'.

Table 14.3 shows that, in general, Indonesia's achievements in social development, while considerable, were less impressive than its economic achievements, and overall compare unfavourably with the gains made in Malaysia, Thailand and the Asian 'Tigers' (Hill 1996, p. 7).

TABLE 14.3 Indonesia's Development Progress in Regional Perspective, 1970–97

| Country | Average Annual Growth in per Capita Private Consumption[a] | | Net Primary Enrolment Ratio[b] | | | | Infant Mortality Rate[c] (per 1,000 live births) | | Access to Safe Water[d] (% of population) |
	(uncorrected, %) 1980–97	(corrected, %) 1980–97	(males) 1980	(males) 1996	(females) 1980	(females) 1996	1970	1997	1996
ASEAN-4									
Indonesia	4.5	3.0	93	99	83	95	118	47	65
Malaysia	3.1	1.6	–	102	–	102	45	11	89
Philippines	0.7	0.4	95	–	92	–	67	35	83
Thailand	5.5	2.9	–	–	–	–	73	33	89
Three 'Tigers'									
South Korea	7.0	–	104	92	105	93	46	9	83
Hong Kong	5.2	–	95	88	96	91	19	5	
Singapore	4.9	–	100	–	99	–	20	4	100
Japan	2.9	–	101	103	101	103	13	4	96

a Growth in per capita private consumption is the average annual rate of change in private consumption divided by the mid-year population. Distribution corrected growth is 1 minus the Gini index multiplied by the annual rate of growth in per capita private consumption.

b Net primary enrolment ratio is the ratio of the number of children of official school age (as defined by the education system) enrolled in school to the number of children of official school age in the population.

c Infant mortality rate is the number of deaths of infants under one year of age during the indicated year per 1,000 live births in the same year.

d Access to safe water is the percentage of the population with reasonable access to an adequate amount of safe water (including treated surface water and untreated but uncontaminated water, such as from springs, sanitary wells and protected bore-holes).

Source: World Bank (1999), Table 1.2., pp. 16–19.

TABLE 14.4 The Decline in Absolute Poverty in Indonesia, 1976–96
(% of people under the official poverty line)

Year	Urban Areas	Rural Areas	Total
1976	38.8	40.4	40.1
1978	30.8	33.3	8.3
1980	29.0	28.4	28.6
1981	28.1	26.5	26.9
1984	23.1	21.2	21.6
1987	20.1	16.1	17.4
1990	16.8	14.3	15.1
1993	13.5	13.8	13.7
1996	9.7	12.3	11.3
1998 (adjusted estimates)	15.4	17.6	16.7

Sources: For the period 1976–96, see BPS (1999), Table 12.1, p. 576; for 1998, see Booth (1999).

ABSOLUTE POVERTY AND RELATIVE INEQUALITY

Absolute Poverty

One of the more remarkable achievements of the New Order government was its success in combining rapid growth with a sustained reduction in the incidence of absolute poverty, while keeping relative inequality, that is, the pattern of income distribution, at moderate levels. Estimates indicate that the incidence of absolute poverty declined steadily from 40% of the population in 1976 to 11% in 1996 (Table 14.4). This fall took place in both urban and rural areas. The corresponding number of people in poverty fell from around 54 million in 1976 to 23 million in 1996 (BPS 1999, p. 576). A comparative World Bank study on poverty alleviation in a number of developing countries concluded that over the period 1970–87, Indonesia had been the most successful in reducing absolute poverty (World Bank 1990, p. 45).

In the 1970s this achievement could be attributed to the successful stabilisation of food prices which, particularly in Java, meant that the poor experienced a lower rate of inflation than the rich. The growth in agricultural production during the 1970s and early 1980s was made possible by the government's commitment to broad-based rural development, reflected in the successful dissemination of new production technologies in the food-crop (particularly rice) sector and in the generation of new employment opportunities in production, processing and marketing. The oil booms of the 1970s also spurred rapid growth in the non-tradeable sectors, including construction and trade, thus creating new employment opportunities for large numbers of unskilled workers (Booth 2000, p. 81).

The incidence of absolute poverty continued to fall even when the government was forced to pursue tight fiscal and monetary policies at the end of the oil boom period. One important reason why the budget cuts after 1982 did not prevent a further decline in poverty was that the most drastic cuts were made to the capital-intensive sectors (including energy), the transmigration program and subsidies of state-owned enterprises (SOEs), with little effect on employment (Booth 2000, p. 85). With the resumption of rapid growth in 1987–96, largely spurred by the surge of low-skill, labour-intensive manufactured exports, poverty declined at a slower rate than during the immediate post-oil boom period, particularly in rural areas. This development may largely be due to the fact that, during the late 1980s and early 1990s, the agricultural sector was relegated to a secondary role, reflected in its falling share of budgetary allocations. With greater priority given to manufacturing and modern services, it could be argued that government policies became less pro-poor from 1987 (Booth 2000, pp. 89–90).

Despite the steady downward trend in absolute poverty during the Soeharto era, poverty estimates based on the official poverty line do understate the incidence of absolute poverty. Indonesia's official poverty line is not only far lower than those used in neighbouring countries – such as the Philippines, which has almost the same level of per capita income as Indonesia – but even lower than those used to estimate poverty in the poorest countries in the world (Booth 1992b, p. 637). Even though a higher poverty line would still show an unmistakeable downward trend in the incidence of absolute poverty, it would also naturally show a higher incidence of absolute poverty than estimates based on the official poverty line. The steep fall in absolute poverty according to the official poverty line may have made the Indonesian government complacent about poverty at a time when many people above the line were leading a precarious existence with inadequate access to basic wage goods and services.

Since various countries use different poverty lines, it is difficult to make international comparisons of the incidence of absolute poverty. To solve this problem, the World Bank has developed an international poverty line, which can be set at either US$1 or (better to show the depth of poverty) US$2 per day at 1985 international prices, adjusted for purchasing power parity. Based on the US$2 per day international poverty line, in 1996 the incidence of absolute poverty in Indonesia was more than 50%, the second highest among ASEAN-4 countries after the Philippines, and almost five times higher than indicated by the official poverty line (Table 14.5).

TABLE 14.5 Incidence of Absolute Poverty in the ASEAN-4 Countries
Based on an International Poverty Line (%)[a]

Country	Year of Survey	Population below $1 per Day	Poverty Gap at $1 per Day	Population below $2 per Day	Poverty Gap at $2 per Day
Indonesia	1996	7.7	0.9	50.4	15.3
Malaysia	1995	4.3	0.7	22.4	6.8
Philippines	1994	26.9	7.1	62.8	27.0
Thailand	1992	<2	–	23.5	5.4

a 'Population below $1 per day' and 'population below $2 per day' are the percentages of the
   population living on less than $1 and $2 per day respectively at 1985 international prices,
   adjusted for purchasing power parity. 'Poverty gap' is the mean shortfall below the poverty line
   (counting the non-poor as having zero shortfall), expressed as a percentage of the poverty line.
   This measure thus reflects the depth of poverty as well as its incidence.

Sources: World Bank (1999), Table 2.7, pp. 67–9.

Using the concept of the *poverty gap* – that is, the mean shortfall below
the poverty line (counting the non-poor as having zero shortfall) expressed as
a percentage of the poverty line – the data in Table 14.5 show that the *depth*
of poverty in Indonesia is the second highest among the ASEAN-4 countries,
again after the Philippines.

Table 14.5 therefore indicates that, from an international or even from a
regional perspective, Indonesia was a relatively poor country in 1996, with
over half the population living in absolute poverty despite steady improvements in the standard of living during the New Order era. Consequently, many
of the poor and nearly poor were left economically vulnerable to large external shocks, as the 1997–98 crisis so clearly showed.

Relative Inequality

Another indicator of social welfare is relative inequality, which refers to the
degree of inequality in the distribution of income in an economy. This is
reflected in the percentage share of either income or consumption accruing to
segments of the population ranked by income or consumption levels. The segments ranked lowest by personal income receive the smallest share of total
income (World Bank 1999, p. 73). The extent to which the distribution
of income (or consumption expenditure) deviates from a perfectly equal

distribution can be provided by a summary measure, the Gini index. This indicator reveals that income distribution in Indonesia remained fairly constant during the New Order era (Table 14.6).

In South Korea and Taiwan, by contrast, the Gini indices were not only lower than in most other developing countries, but declined during their long periods of rapid economic growth. Indonesia's higher Gini index may be due to the greater importance of large-scale, capital and resource-intensive industries during the early phases of industrialisation. Since these industries require a higher proportion of highly skilled and professional employees, one might expect a more unequal income distribution in Indonesia than in South Korea and Taiwan (Manning 1995, p. 76). The fact that Indonesia received more foreign direct investment (FDI) flows than these two countries may also have contributed to a less equal income distribution, through the effects of high remuneration paid to expatriate employees and flow-on effects on domestic managerial and professional manpower (p. 77).

Despite the statistical evidence of constant Gini indices, many Indonesians hold the view that economic growth, particularly during the late New Order era, created gross inequalities. This perception was strengthened by the rise of large conglomerates, many of them owned and controlled by relatives and cronies of former President Soeharto, and by the opulent lifestyles of the rich elite.

TABLE 14.6 Distribution of Income or Consumption in Indonesia, 1964/65–1996

Year	Gini Index[a]
1964/65	0.35
1976	0.34
1987	0.32
1993	0.32
1995	0.34
1996	0.37

a The Gini index measures the extent to which the distribution of income (or consumption expenditure) among individuals or households within an economy deviates from a perfectly equal distribution. A Gini index of zero represents perfect equality, while an index of 1 implies perfect inequality.

Sources: For the period 1964/65–1987, see Hill (1996), Table 10.1, p. 193; for 1993, see World Bank (1997b), Table 2.6, p. 55; for 1995, see: World Bank (1998), Table 2.8, p. 69; for 1996, see World Bank (1999), Table 2.8, p. 71.

In so far as an unequal income distribution reflects an unequal distribution of wealth or productive assets (Ahluwalia and Chenery 1974, pp. 43–4), Indonesia's rapid economic growth may indeed have led to greater relative inequality if asset concentration occurred over time, as might be expected during a period of rapid economic growth. This asset concentration could have included both physical assets (land, ownership of companies, factories, banks and other economic entities) and non-physical assets (educational opportunities, particularly elite secondary and tertiary education, including opportunities to pursue tertiary education overseas). However, in the absence of reliable data on wealth or asset distribution, the view of 'unequalising growth' may simply be impressionistic.

Urban–Rural Income Disparities

Urban–rural income disparities are another aspect of economic inequality. One study has argued that the development process in developing countries is often characterised by a strong 'urban bias'. In most developing countries the allocation of scarce resources between urban and rural areas, and within the urban areas themselves, often reflects urban priorities rather than equity or efficiency (Lipton 1978, p. 13).

Using expenditure data as a proxy for income data, Booth and Sundrum (1981) found evidence of a rising urban bias over the period 1970–76, especially in Java. While average urban incomes in 1970 were 42% higher than average rural incomes, this disparity had increased to 84% by 1976 (p. 202). Urban–rural income disparities stabilised throughout the 1980s and early 1990s, but the gap between average incomes in the Jakarta Capital City Region and those in rural areas widened further. By 1993, average urban incomes were 92% higher than average rural incomes, but those in Jakarta were 205% higher (Booth 1998b, pp. 10–11). Thus average incomes grew *not only* much faster in Jakarta than in rural areas, but also faster than in other cities (p. 11). Indonesia's development during the 1980s and early 1990s was therefore characterised by both an urban bias and a pronounced capital city bias. This capital city bias was strengthened by the preference of domestic and particularly foreign investors to set up large and medium-scale manufacturing plants in the Jakarta Capital City Region, where amenities, physical infrastructure and access to domestic and foreign markets were generally much better than in other regions.

Regional Income Disparities

Another aspect of relative inequality concerns the disparity in average incomes between the various provinces in Indonesia. Estimates by the World

Bank have indicated that per capita GDP and consumption in all Indonesian provinces improved during 1983–93, a period for which consistent regional accounts are available. Indicators on social development showing an improvement in all provinces, including a steady decline in the incidence of absolute poverty, confirm this development (World Bank 1996, p. 92).

Despite generally rapid growth of gross provincial product (GPP) in the poorer provinces (World Bank 1996, p. 92), by the mid-1990s Indonesia still faced the problem of persistent regional income disparities. The degree of disparity in per capita GPP between the various provinces was high by international standards, due to the concentration of some of the country's most valuable natural resources – oil, natural gas, minerals and timber – in just a few sparsely populated provinces (Booth 1992a, p. 41). While poor provinces in eastern Indonesia, including West and East Nusa Tenggara, were growing more slowly than the national average, Jakarta continued to surge ahead (Hill 1998, p. 32).

One problem related to regional income disparity was that, although the resource-rich provinces with large export surpluses – specifically Aceh, Riau, East Kalimantan and Papua – were among the richest in terms of per capita GPP, living standards in these provinces in terms of per capita consumption expenditures were generally lower than the GPP levels would suggest (Booth 1992a, p. 41). This was because a considerable portion of these provinces' GPP was transferred to the central government, which subsequently redistributed part of it to the poorer provinces (pp. 41–2). The transfer of huge financial resources from the resource-rich provinces understandably led to serious discontent, giving rise to separatist movements in Aceh and Papua.

Intra-regional income disparities also emerged, particularly in Java, where large concentrations of manufacturing industries sprang up within and around the urban centres of Jakarta and Surabaya and, to a lesser extent, Bandung. The emergence of these industrial centres was an inevitable consequence of the ongoing process of industrialisation. It also contributed to the pace of urbanisation, as people living in relatively stagnant rural areas sought better-paying jobs in the urban manufacturing and modern service sectors (Booth 1998b, p. 10).

THE ENVIRONMENTAL IMPACT OF ECONOMIC GROWTH

During the first decade of the New Order, the Indonesian government placed a high priority on rapid economic growth without regard to the adverse environmental consequences. The degradation of land and water resources was very serious, as it involved a process of ecological adjustment from an originally stable level to a lower and often less stable level of productivity (Hardjono 1994, p. 179). This was accompanied by the depletion of both non-renewable resources such as minerals and renewable resources such as timber. Because of the indiscriminate felling of trees and burning of Indonesia's tropical hardwood forests, one of Indonesia's most valuable natural resources has been seriously depleted.

By the late 1970s, rapid industrialisation and the increased use of motor vehicles had resulted in worsening air and water pollution, particularly in larger urban areas, causing serious health problems and imposing significant costs on the economy. To deal with the environmental consequences of economic growth, in 1978 President Soeharto appointed Professor Emil Salim as Indonesia's first Minister for the Environment. Salim was instructed to find a path of sustainable development in which economic development would be combined with protection of the environment (Salim 1997, p. 62). As Minister of State, he was not an executive agent and had to work through other ministers, many of whom were mainly concerned with their own sectoral interests. They were often indifferent to Salim's views on environmental protection, and were rarely inclined to implement them (p. 64).

To deal more resolutely with air and water pollution, the Environmental Impact Management Agency, Bapedal, was established in 1990. In the early 1990s, the Minister for the Environment also launched the Prokasih (Clean Rivers) project, which required industrial polluters to install sewerage treatment facilities. Bapedal's task was facilitated by growing public awareness and support for the right of Indonesians to live in a healthy environment. Despite this, the depletion of Indonesia's valuable renewable natural resources might well have proceeded without hindrance under the authoritarian and corrupt New Order regime, because of the profitability of forest exploitation in particular.

THE GRADUAL MORAL DECLINE OF THE NEW ORDER GOVERNMENT

The New Order government's political legitimacy was based on its economic performance, in particular its ability to deliver rising standards of living for the people. This required fast and sustained economic growth, and the opening up of new employment and business opportunities as a means of escaping poverty.

Rapid and sustained economic growth seemed to be assured in the late 1980s, following the restoration of macroeconomic stability and the wide-ranging deregulation measures taken in response to the end of the oil boom in 1982. However, from the early 1990s many observers and academic economists began to voice growing concerns about economic and social issues that in their view threatened to undermine not only long-term growth, but also the cherished national goal of establishing a 'just and prosperous society' (*masyarakat adil dan makmur*). Many of these issues were interrelated. They included the massive scale of corruption at all levels of the government bureaucracy and the embezzlement of public funds for private gain, collusive relationships between political power-holders and their business cronies, many of them Sino-Indonesian tycoons, and the proliferation of policy-generated barriers to domestic competition and trade.

These restrictions on domestic competition were of particular concern to Indonesian economists, as they adversely affected the business environment for bona fide, particularly small, entrepreneurs. Unlike Indonesia's trade regime – which had been subject to several deregulatory measures in the 1980s that had greatly reduced its anti-export bias – domestic competition faced numerous regulations and restrictions, particularly in the agricultural sector. Restraints on domestic competition included cartels, price controls, entry and exit controls, exclusive licensing, dominance of SOEs in certain industries and ad hoc interventions by the government in favour of specific firms or sectors (Iqbal 1995, p. 14).

The restrictions on domestic competition were justified on various grounds, such as the 'essential' nature of certain commodities, the distribution of which was too important to be left to the market; the promotion of infant industries or domestic value-added processing activities (for which restrictions on domestic competition were combined with restrictions on international trade); the exploitation of Indonesia's market power in world markets (plywood being a case in point); and revenue raising for the local government (World Bank 1995, p. 46). In fact, however, these were merely excuses for blatant rent-seeking activities that conferred huge monopolistic or monopsonistic rents on politically well-connected businessmen and their political patrons in both the central and local government bureaucracies. Among the benefits such businessmen received were preferential access to credit provided by state-owned banks, protection against import competition, and tax and duty exemptions.

Not surprisingly, restrictions on domestic competition and the preferential treatment accorded politically well-connected businessmen adversely affected the incentive system for private business – including small and medium-scale enterprises – by raising the cost of doing business (thus giving rise to long-standing complaints about Indonesia's high-cost economy). The restraints on domestic competition reduced both economic efficiency and the economic opportunities available to small businesses lacking in political and administrative connections (Thee 1998, p. 119).

The corrosive effects of KKN (corruption, collusion and nepotism) greatly damaged public morale and confidence in the government. Such practices gave rise to widely held views about the 'widening economic gap' between rich and poor, and between non-indigenous (mostly Sino-Indonesian) and indigenous Indonesians, undermining the social cohesion required for political stability and national development. The fact that many of President Soeharto's business cronies were wealthy ethnic Chinese businessmen fuelled resentment at the perceived economic domination by a Sino-Indonesian minority. The preferential treatment accorded to a number of such tycoons further aggravated latent anti-Chinese feelings. By the mid-1990s, this resentment erupted into anti-Chinese riots in various parts of the country, particularly in Java, and culminated in the violent May 1998 anti-Chinese riots in Jakarta and Surakarta.

Economists have expressed concern at the erosion of economic considerations in policy formulation, the ascendancy of the so-called 'technologists' at the expense of the economic 'technocrats', and the attendant promotion of costly 'high-tech' projects of questionable economic viability (Nasution 1995, pp. 4–5). Although some of the senior technocrats, including Professor Widjojo Nitisastro and Professor Ali Wardhana, remained as economic advisers to President Soeharto, they had no executive power from 1993.

In the end, the abuses of the increasingly corrupt and oppressive New Order regime removed its political legitimacy; its ruthless suppression of any overt opposition, by violence if necessary, ultimately led to its infamous downfall. Ironically, President Soeharto's downfall was precipitated not so much by a people's revolt as by the 'invisible market forces' behind the steep depreciation of the rupiah, which Soeharto failed to comprehend and effectively rectify. Thus the New Order regime came to its inglorious end amidst the misery of a gravely damaged economy, heavily reliant on large infusions of foreign and domestic loans. The costs of this hugely enlarged foreign and domestic debt will be borne by many generations to come.

CONCLUSION

Leaders in many developing countries including Indonesia have claimed that political freedoms and rights hamper rapid economic growth. Since growth was considered essential for raising the standard of living of the population (as well as raising the international status of the country), demands for more political freedom were suppressed, often ruthlessly. However, Amartya Sen was undoubtedly right when he stressed the importance of the 'protective role of political democracy' in the event of an economic crisis (Sen 1999, pp. 157–9).

While things were going well as, with a few exceptions, they did during the 32 years of New Order rule, the important role played by democracy may not have been badly missed. However, once Indonesia was hit by the serious economic crisis of 1997–98, the protective role of democracy to push the government, and more specifically President Soeharto, to take speedy and effective action to meet the crisis was sorely lacking.

As the implementation of several important economic reforms – particularly fiscal and structural reforms as mandated under the agreement with the IMF in return for a standby loan of US$43 billion – was perceived by the president as eliminating generous preferential treatment given to the businesses of his children, Soeharto was reluctant to introduce them. The protracted tug-of-war between the president and the IMF further undermined market confidence and led to more outflows of capital. In the repressive and increasingly paranoid political environment of early 1998, no one dared urge the president to take the economic medicine prescribed not just by the IMF but by many Indonesian economists as well.

In the end, President Soeharto's inability or unwillingness to avert a deepening economic crisis led to a full-blown political and social crisis which led to his inglorious fall in May 1998. This also heralded the beginning of a transition to a more democratic Indonesia which, however promising at this stage, remains brittle. The lack of a decisive shift to a more robust democracy in the face of strong opposition from the still-entrenched interests of the New Order regime has also held up a major restructuring of the economy, so crucial to a sustainable economic recovery.

NOTE

*   Some parts of this chapter are based on Chapter 7 of the book by Howard Dick, Vincent Houben, J. Thomas Lindblad and Thee Kian Wie, *The Emergence of a National Economy: An Economic History of Indonesia, 1800–2000* (Allen & Unwin, 2001, forthcoming). I would like to acknowledge the valuable comments of Professor Howard Dick on an earlier draft of this paper. Naturally, I alone am responsible for any errors or shortcomings.

15

INDONESIA'S ECONOMY AND STANDARD OF LIVING IN THE 20TH CENTURY

Pierre van der Eng

Until 1998, Indonesia was on its way to becoming a middle-income country, even though it often seemed that the high rates of economic growth enjoyed since the late 1960s had not lifted the standard of living for all Indonesians. A common explanation was that this was a consequence of increasing income inequality. Another explanation was that it was not widely appreciated that rapid economic growth started from a very low base in the 1960s. In fact, what may have changed was not necessarily the degree of inequality but general perceptions of poverty.

By taking a long-term perspective, this chapter aims to instil some appreciation of the fact that the Indonesian economy has actually developed quite rapidly and that standards of living improved very significantly over the course of the 20th century. This process did not begin in the late 1960s, nor when the country became independent in the late 1940s, but closer to 1900. The chapter aims to provide several broad proximate explanations for Indonesia's process of development and assesses the extent to which economic growth has lifted the standard of living.

THE DEVELOPMENT RECORD

National accounts data are generally used to trace changes in the size and composition of an economy. One indicator is gross domestic product (GDP) per capita, which is a rough indicator of the standard of living. Figure 15.1 shows the development of per capita GDP in constant prices. It illustrates that the Indonesian economy increased faster in size than the population during the periods 1900–30 and 1967–97. There were temporary setbacks in both periods but, on balance, economic growth was quite significant.

There were significant fluctuations during the intermediate period of

FIGURE 15.1 Per Capita GDP in Indonesia, 1900–2000 (1993 Rp thousand)

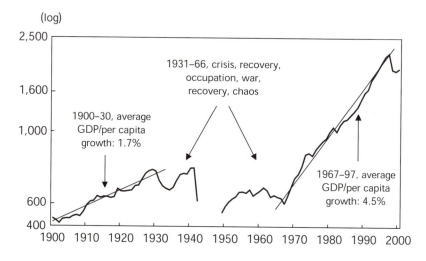

Source: van der Eng (2001), with data converted to 1993 prices.

1931–66. The global depression that caused a downturn in the early 1930s was followed by significant recovery until 1941, then by another downturn during the Japanese occupation. The economy recovered in the late 1940s and early 1950s before stagnating in the late 1950s, and ultimately experienced negative growth in the early to mid-1960s.

Figure 15.1 illustrates that the recent crisis resulted in a fall in per capita GDP to the 1993 level, contracting by 17% in 1997–99. This is comparable to the per capita GDP decreases of 16% in both 1929–34 and 1961–67, although the recent crisis spread much faster. However, if the crises of the 1930s and 1960s provide any guidance, the Indonesian economy should soon recover.

Table 15.1 shows that from 1900 to 1997 the Indonesian economy grew at an average annual rate of 3.3%, and that per capita GDP increased by 1.7% per year. This may seem like a low rate of change but, from a comparable level, it took Western Europe more than 400 years to achieve what took Indonesia only 100 years. This reflects the fact that, for most of the world, economic growth has tended to be a long-winded process complete with upturns and downturns (Maddison 1999a). Moreover, Indonesia achieved this with a population growth rate four times higher than that of Western Europe.

Indonesian economic growth during the 20th century was low compared with that of Asia's most successful performer, Japan, which had average

TABLE 15.1 Comparison of Economic Growth in Western Europe and Indonesia

	1500	1913	Average Annual Growth (%)
Western Europe			
Population (million)	57.3	261.0	0.4
GDP (1990 int. $ billion)	43.9	903.0	0.7
Per capita GDP (1990 int. $)	767.0	3,460.0	0.4

	1900	1997	Average Annual Growth (%)
Indonesia			
Population (million)	42.7	201.4	1.6
GDP (1990 int. $ billion)	31.0	728.0	3.3
Per capita GDP (1990 int. $)	726.0	3,615.0	1.7

Sources: Calculated from Maddison (1999b) and van der Eng (2001).

annual growth of per capita GDP of 3% between 1900 and 1997. However, Japan was the exception; on average, per capita GDP in the rest of Asia increased by an annual 1.2% in 1900–97, significantly lower than in Indonesia (calculated from Maddison 2000).

By Western historical standards, and in the context of 20th century Asia, Indonesia's rates of economic growth have been high. The key question is, however, 'Why has economic growth in Indonesia been so fast during the 20th century and has this led to an improvement in the standard of living?'

SOME BROAD TRENDS AND EXPLANATIONS

Structural Change

Investigation into the sources of economic growth starts with the output side of the economy. Figure 15.2 illustrates structural change in Indonesia's economy. As services are highly heterogeneous we can conclude that, until the 1970s, agriculture was the single most important sector of the economy. Its

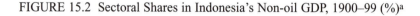

FIGURE 15.2 Sectoral Shares in Indonesia's Non-oil GDP, 1900–99 (%)[a]

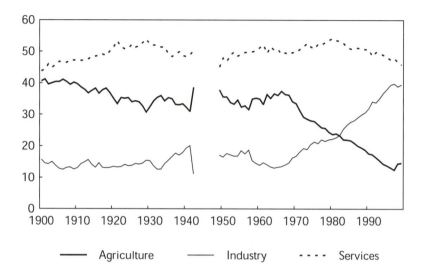

a Calculated from output data in 1993 prices.

Source: van der Eng (2001).

share decreased only slightly during 1900–30, largely because of the gradual commercialisation of agricultural production by farmers and large-scale plantations, which stimulated economic activity in non-agricultural sectors and was the main cause of economic growth during the period. This brought about a concomitant increase in the total share of the services sectors.

The industry sector (manufacturing, non-oil mining, utilities and construction) began to expand from the late 1930s, mainly due to the growth of manufacturing output caused by policies pursuing import-replacing industrialisation. These were continued in the 1950s and 1960s, but industrial growth was not sustained and the economy's reliance on the agricultural sector increased. Hence, the slowdown of economic growth was caused by a reduction in agricultural growth.

Only after the 1960s did the structure of the economy change drastically, with a consistent increase in the share of industry and an accompanying decline in the share of agriculture. The share of the services sector decreased slightly. This suggests that economic growth during 1967–97 was due to the industrialisation of the economy, based largely on import substitution and, from the mid-1980s, on export orientation.

TABLE 15.2 Contribution of Key Inputs and Total Factor Productivity to GDP Growth, 1940–97[a]

	Labour Force (million)	Capital Stock (1983 Rp billion)	GDP (1983 Rp billion)	Labour and Capital (%)	Total Factor Productivity (%)
1940	26.7	45.6	22.8		
1967	32.6	60.5	26.8		
1997	88.3	634.8	208.9		
Average annual growth (%)					
1940–67	0.7	2.8	1.2	115	−15
1967–97	2.7	8.1	7.1	61	39

a Labour and capital contribution to GDP growth has been calculated assuming income shares of 70% and 30% respectively in GDP; total factor productivity is a residual.

Source: Calculated from van der Eng (2001).

Labour and Capital Inputs and Productivity Change

Another way of dissecting economic growth is through investigation of the role of resources used in the production process, these chiefly being human labour and capital goods. Table 15.2 shows that the growth of capital stock has greatly exceeded the growth of GDP. A rough calculation suggests that for 1940–67, the growth of the labour force and capital stock explains the low rate of GDP growth. In other words, economic growth was simply due to the fact that more people entered the labour force and more capital was invested in the reconstruction and expansion of the stock of capital goods.

During 1967–97, expansion of the labour force and capital stock explains about 60% of GDP growth, meaning that about 40% was due to more pro-ductive use of available labour and capital. This is not surprising given that the expansion of industrial output explains a large part of economic growth. Industrial expansion was largely based on the employment of new imported production technology (embodied in capital goods such as machinery and equipment) and the improvement of the education and skill levels of human resources, which also contributed to productivity growth.

TABLE 15.3 Contribution of Exports to GDP Growth, 1900–97[a]

	GDP (1983 Rp billion)	Exports (1983 Rp billion)	Average Ratio of Exports to GDP	Direct Contri- bution	Total Contri- bution
1900	8,339	989			
1930	18,511	4,760			
1967	26,762	7,027			
1997	208,941	57,598			
Average annual growth (%)					
1900–30	2.7	5.4	0.209	42	54
1930–67	1.0	1.1	0.103	11	14
1967–97	7.1	7.3	0.227	23	30

a Direct contribution is [(av. ratio × export growth)/GDP growth × 100%]; total contribution
   assumes a multiplier of 1.3.

Source: Calculated from van der Eng (2001).

The Role of Foreign Trade

Another way of thinking about economic growth is to distinguish between
foreign and domestic demand for Indonesia's products. Table 15.3 shows that
the index indicating export volume increased by 5% per year during 1900–30
and 7% per year during 1967–97. The direct contribution of export growth to
economic growth was around 40% for 1900–30 and around 25% in 1967–97.
Taking account of backward linkages of export production, the total contribution of exports was more than 50% in the first period and about 30% in the
latter. The contribution of exports for the period 1930–67 was minimal.

   These calculations suggest that the role of exports became significant
when the Dutch colonial government, in reaction to the 1930s Depression,
introduced a policy of import-replacing development that affected both agricultural production, particularly rice, and manufacturing. This policy was
broadly continued during the 1950s and 1960s, and only changed with the
advent of the 1970s oil boom and the expansion of export-oriented manufacturing in the 1980s and 1990s.

   There are several explanations for why high export growth during
1900–30 did not result in higher rates of economic growth. First, most of
Indonesia's export earnings were used to finance merchandise imports. Until

FIGURE 15.3 Barter Terms of Trade, 1900–99 (1913 = 100)

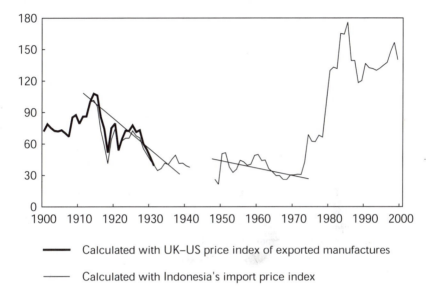

━━━   Calculated with UK–US price index of exported manufactures

─────   Calculated with Indonesia's import price index

Source: van der Eng (2001).

the 1930s these consisted mainly of consumer items (50–60%). The share of these products gradually decreased to around 5% by the 1990s, when most imports consisted of industrial raw materials and capital goods. This is evidence of the impact of import-substituting development policies and an autonomous expansion of production for domestic consumption. Imports of industrial inputs contributed more to economic growth than imports of consumer items.

Second, Indonesia's commodity exports exceeded imports by an average 36% during 1900–30, compared to 15% during 1967–97. In the first period, these net export earnings were used to finance overseas remittances. This largely reflected the fact that Indonesia was a net importer of the services of foreign-owned productive resources, particularly shipping, Western entrepreneurship and investment capital and, to a lesser extent, ethnic Chinese wage labour and entrepreneurship (van der Eng 1998, p. 30).

Third, Indonesia experienced a structural drop in its barter terms of trade from 1914 to 1972 (Figure 15.3). The price of exports fell relative to the price of imports because Indonesia's exports were dominated by primary products – sugar, rubber, copra, tin – that were also produced by other less-developed countries. This only changed as a consequence of rising international oil and gas prices during 1973–85, and a subsequent increase in the share of manufactures in exports.

The Role of Domestic Demand

The contribution of expanding domestic demand, consisting of public and private consumption and capital formation, to economic growth was quite significant, much more so during 1967–97 than during 1900–30. Public expenditure was on average about 10% of GDP in 1900–29, and double that in 1968–97 (Table 15.4). This expansion was largely owing to increases in public revenues from oil and gas exports and an inflow of overseas development assistance, which together contributed 50–70% of total public expenditures in the 1970s and 1980s. More than half of this revenue was used for public investment.

Total capital formation averaged 21% of GDP during 1968–97. Accurate estimates of private investment before the 1960s are not available, but they are likely to have been around 5% of GDP. Public expenditure and private investment accounted for only about 15% of GDP until 1968, after which they

TABLE 15.4 Average Annual Shares of Categories of Expenditure on GDP, 1900–97 (%)

	1900–29	1930–67	1968–97
Net exports, goods only	6.9	3.1	4.6
Net exports, goods and services	–0.9	0.0	2.2
Public expenditure			
Consumption			8.9
Gross capital formation			10.7[a]
Total	9.7	12.1	19.6
Gross capital formation			
Private	c. 5.0	c. 5.0	10.7[a]
Total			21.4
Total expenditure accounted for	13.8	17.1	32.5
Private consumption[a]	86.2	82.9	67.5

a Residual.

Source: van der Eng (2001).

doubled. Consequently, private consumption was about 83% of GDP expenditure in the period 1900–67, declining to 68% in recent years. The expansion of consumption of both imported and domestically produced products explains most of the economic growth of 1900–29 and 1968–97, as well as the lack of growth during 1930–67.

The expansion of domestic consumption, and therefore increased production for domestic consumption, was a significant cause of economic growth. This is likely to have been a consequence of the development of domestic transport and communications infrastructure throughout the 20th century, which furthered economic integration and the development of a national economy. A national economy did not exist in 1900 – the Dutch colonial government was established in Java, but was only nominally effective in the rest of Indonesia, which was more self-sufficient and more reliant on trade with contiguous parts of Southeast Asia.

The gradual development of the national Indonesian economy had three dimensions for transport: (a) an increase in the volume of goods and the number of people transported; (b) the expansion of the transport and communications network across the country, first in Java and gradually encapsulating other islands; and (c) a change from one means of transport to another, depending on the relative economic viability of transport technologies. This process was not continuous. It ebbed and flowed according to the availability of funds for public infrastructure, chiefly railways and roads. It was interrupted during the 1940s, when the Japanese military government requisitioned transport facilities and when the war for independence caused further losses to transport equipment. It stagnated in the 1950s and 1960s but accelerated significantly during more recent years.

Improvements in transport and communications enhanced the mobility of people, products, finance and information, and facilitated the gradual integration of markets in Indonesia. Reduced transport costs opened markets for a wide range of producers and encouraged specialisation of production. In so far as specialising producers were able to generate economies of scale, market integration may have reduced production costs and advanced production for domestic consumption.

CHANGES IN THE STANDARD OF LIVING

There is no unambiguous definition of the 'standard of living' – it is generally associated with changes to personal income and wealth or consumption. GDP encompasses much more than that, and per capita GDP is at best a broad indicator of the standard of living. It does not take account of non-market activity, the value of non-material aspects of consumption (education, health,

FIGURE 15.4 Net Food Supply, 1900–96 (Kcal per capita per day)

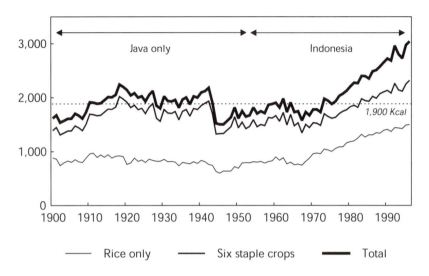

Source: van der Eng (2000a).

leisure, art and entertainment) or the cost of negative externalities such as pollution and crime. Three further indicators of the standard of living are discussed below.

Food Consumption

Food consumption can be gleaned from information on the production and foreign trade of foodstuffs (van der Eng 2000a). Figure 15.4 shows trends in the per capita availability of food in Java until 1953, and in Indonesia as a whole since then. The pre-World War II situation in Java is important, as Java has long been regarded as an overpopulated island that would experience difficulties in feeding itself, while per capita food supply in other islands has been significantly higher than in Java.

In terms of consumption levels, it appears that rice has been the single main source of calories (50%). However, this figure also underlines the importance of non-rice foods. Estimates of total calorie supply do not include a range of small food items (for example, eggs, poultry, fruit, vegetables) and are too low by about 110 kilocalories (Kcal) (van der Eng 2000a, p. 596).

Average food requirements are difficult to specify because they depend on the age–sex distribution of the population, average levels of physical activity and average body size. An approximation of the minimum requirement, being 1,900 Kcal per day, is illustrated by the dotted line.

The Japanese occupation was the most critical period in Java. Unlike earlier food shortages, restrictions on transport and the marketing of food triggered a disastrous fall in food production in Java. Dependence on wage labour saw food entitlements disappear, causing widespread poverty and resulting in the deaths of as many as 2.4 million Javanese in 1944–45 (van der Eng 1994, p. 40).

In terms of trends, the chart reveals four broad phases. First, during 1905–20 the Engel effect increased the demand for food. A shortage of irrigated land and the unavailability of suitable seed-fertiliser technology inhibited an expansion of rice production. Consequently, non-rice crops, particularly cassava, were produced in greater quantities to meet the growing demand for food. Second, in 1920–40 food demand stabilised and there was a shift towards demand for non-food items. In the third phase, from 1950 to 1970, population growth accelerated at a time when stagnating and declining export revenues made it difficult to meet shortfalls in domestic food production. Consequently, average food consumption was at, or just below, average requirements. Fourth, from the late 1960s food consumption rose to levels well beyond minimum requirements. Government support for rice farmers increased rice production; cheap low-quality rice replaced cheap non-rice foods; and a rise in per capita rice consumption drove the increase in calorie consumption. In the 1980s and 1990s, demand for food shifted away from basic foods towards luxury food items.

Educational Attainment

Good estimates of average educational attainment are only available for the years of the postwar population censuses. Figure 15.5 presents annual estimates based on school enrolments that approximate the census results well.

The level of education increased from less than 0.1 years of education per person in 1900 to 0.5 years in 1930 and 1.3 years in 1960. The main gains have been made since 1960, with an increase to 5.5 years in 2000. These have mainly been achieved in primary education, but increasingly also in secondary and tertiary education. This places Indonesia among those countries with a medium level of human development (UNDP 1993, pp. 136–7). Population census data confirm these trends, with the literacy rate of people older than 10 years increasing accordingly from 8% in 1930 to 39% in 1961 and 84% in 1990.

FIGURE 15.5 Educational Attainment, 1900–2000 (years of schooling per capita)

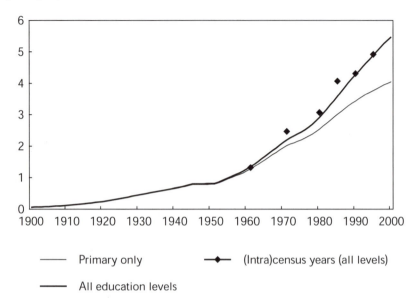

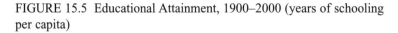

Source: van der Eng (2001), updated with enrolment data for 1997/98 – 1999/2000.

Infant Mortality and Life Expectancy

Figure 15.6 gives data on the infant mortality rate (IMR) and life expectancy at birth for key years. In 1930, the IMR was very high – almost one in four children did not survive infancy and life expectancy at birth was 30 years. Since then it has decreased by a factor of almost five and life expectancy has more than doubled. More and more children survive infancy and live longer than ever before as a consequence of improvements in public health care facilities and hygiene awareness, and increases in the affordability of health care.

Each of the indicators discussed above suggests that the Indonesian standard of living increased significantly throughout the course of the 20th century. It is not easy to strike a balance between these and other indicators. Per capita GDP, life expectancy, literacy rates and school enrolment are key components of the UNDP's human development index (HDI), which is widely hailed as a measure of the standard of living. In 1992, Indonesia's HDI was broadly equivalent to that of today's developed countries in 1913, and of Japan in 1950 (Crafts 1997, pp. 310–11). This suggests that in terms of

FIGURE 15.6 Life Expectancy (in years) and Infant Mortality Rate (per 1,000 births), 1930–95

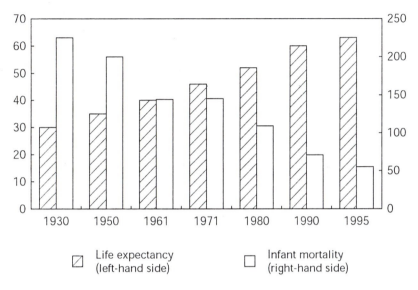

Sources: Hugo et al. (1987), pp. 373–4; BPS (1996), *Indikator Kesejahteraan Rakyat 1995*, pp. 130–31.

improvements in living standards, Indonesia is following the developed world, albeit with a delay.

THE DISTRIBUTION OF INCOME

GDP and other indicators discussed above relate to per capita averages, but the distribution of factors such as food consumption or education across different income groups is difficult to assess because of the lack of data available for the entire period in question.

For the pre-World War II period, reference is often made to the 1930 income estimates showing significant differentials in average income between the main ethnic groups (Table 15.5). These results should be viewed with caution. First, the total income of Indonesians was significantly underestimated. Second, per capita averages reveal nothing about the size distribution of income, which may have been more uneven among Indonesians than among other groups. Lastly, 66% of 'other Asians' (including ethnic Chinese, Indians

TABLE 15.5 Population and per Capita Income by Ethnic Group, 1930

	Population (thousand)	Per Capita Income (guilders)
Indonesians, Java	40,891	55
Indonesians, other islands	18,247	66
Other Asians, Java	635	309
Other Asians, other islands	714	214
Europeans, Java	193	2,321
Europeans, other islands	48	3,198
Total (average)	60,728	73

Sources: Calculated from Kantoor voor de Volkstelling (1938), Table 1; Polak (1943), p. 70.

and Arabs) and 71% of 'Europeans' had been born in Indonesia and should be regarded as residents of Indonesia rather than as foreigners.

Information to approximate the size distribution of income has been available since the first national household budget survey was conducted as part of the National Socioeconomic Survey (Susenas) in 1964/65. The Susenas surveys record household expenditure. This results in a bias towards equality, as higher-income groups are likely to save more of their income. The surveys are also believed to be biased towards the urban poor and to underestimate nonfood expenditure, particularly spending on consumer durables such as television sets and cars. This causes a progressively increasing degree of underestimation (van der Eng 2000b).

Figure 15.7 shows the Gini ratios that can be calculated from the household expenditure data. They provide a broad indication of the degree of inequality and range from 0 (perfect equality) to 1 (perfect inequality). Except for a peak in 1978, the Gini ratios of household expenditure appear to be low, leading many observers to suggest that income distribution in Indonesia is relatively even. This is confirmed by the distribution of income for 1984 and 1990 in Java from the unpublished Susenas data. These two Gini ratios are indeed much lower than those for, say, England in the 18th and 19th centuries and the United Kingdom in the 19th century (Lindert 2000, p. 175), when per capita GDP was comparable to levels in Indonesia in the 1970s and 1980s but income Gini ratios were between 0.49 and 0.59.

FIGURE 15.7 Gini Ratios of per Capita Household Expenditure and Wage
Income, 1964–97

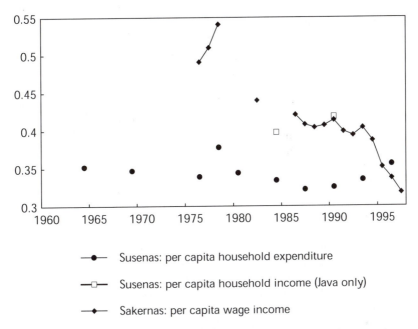

—●— Susenas: per capita household expenditure

—□— Susenas: per capita household income (Java only)

—◆— Sakernas: per capita wage income

Sources: Susenas expenditure Gini ratios are calculated from BPS (1976–78), *Survei Sosial
Ekonomi Nasional: Pengeluaran untuk Konsumsi Penduduk* and *Keadaan Angkatan Kerja di
Indonesia*; Sakernas income Gini ratios are calculated from BPS (1982, 1986–88), *Keadaan
Buruh/Pekerja di Indonesia*, BPS (1989–94, 1996–97), *Keadaan Pekerja/Karyawan di Indone-
sia* and BPS (1995), *Penduduk Indonesia: Hasil Survei Penduduk antar Sensus 1995, Seri S2*;
Susenas income Gini ratios for Java are from Cameron (2000), p. 157.

Another source of data on income distribution is the National Labour
Force Survey (Sakernas), conducted since 1976. Its income data are restricted
to wage labourers and employees, who constituted about 28% of the labour
force in 1986 and 35% in 1997. It does not take account of the majority of
income earners, mostly self-employed in the agricultural and informal sectors
(van der Eng 2000b). The Sakernas Gini ratios in Figure 15.7 are significantly
higher than those based on expenditure data, particularly in the 1970s. Access
to salaried jobs was constrained in the 1970s, but many more such jobs
became available as a consequence of deregulation and export-oriented development in the 1980s and 1990s. This helps to explain the decrease in inequality in wage income.[1]

The next indicator of inequality is the regional distribution of GDP. In the
first half of the 20th century, two countervailing processes took place that

were part and parcel of the development of Indonesia as a national economy and a nation state. These were, first, an increasing reliance of the economy on exports generated in the Outer Islands; and second, administrative and political centralisation in Java, despite a late colonial change towards greater provincial autonomy (van der Eng 1999, pp. 188–9).

The late conversion to decentralisation was reversed after independence. Indonesia's foreign exchange policies heavily taxed export producers in the Outer Islands and goods had to be shipped through ports in Java, adding to handling costs. Such centralising tendencies fed allegations that import-consuming Java was 'milking' the export-producing islands, and contributed to regional secessionist uprisings in 1956–58, which were subdued using military force. Since then the provinces outside Java have generated growing foreign exchange and revenues for the national government through the growth of natural resource-based industries such as petroleum, natural gas, mining and logging.

Since the late 1960s, provincial GDP data have consistently indicated significant differences in per capita GDP between provinces that are well endowed with natural resources and those that are densely populated and/or sparsely endowed with natural resources. Table 15.6 provides some indication of the considerable regional economic differences, with East and West Nusa Tenggara at the lower end of the scale and oil-rich East Kalimantan at the higher end. The table reveals significant regional dynamics – South Sumatra, Maluku, Bengkulu, North Sulawesi, Jambi and Southeast Sulawesi have witnessed a decline, while Irian Jaya, Bali, West Sumatra and most provinces in Java have experienced an improvement relative to the national average. The inequality of regional GDP has increased slightly over time, although the degree of inequality was still low in 1997.

GDP data in Table 15.6 exclude value-added oil and gas production, which significantly reduces the level of GDP in the provinces of Aceh, Riau, East Kalimantan and Irian Jaya. The central government benefits most from the revenues generated by these activities and redistributes them to the poorer provinces, particularly in Java. The fact that public revenues have in recent decades been channelled into the development of manufacturing industries in Java articulates the economic dichotomy between it and other islands, and arguably has prolonged the existence of significant interregional inequalities in non-mining per capita GDP (Akita and Lukman 1995).

CONCLUSION

This chapter has demonstrated that Indonesia's economic development during the 20th century was fast, although the development trajectory did fluctuate.

TABLE 15.6 Inequality of Regional per Capita GDP, 1971, 1983 and 1997[a]

Province	1971		1983		1997	
	National Av.= 100	Rank	National Av.= 100	Rank	National Av.= 100	Rank
Jakarta	247	(1)	328	(1)	371	(1)
East Kalimantan	247	(2)	218	(2)	246	(2)
Irian Jaya	99	(14)	108	(8)	163	(3)
Riau	139	(6)	116	(6)	135	(4)
Central Kalimantan	116	(8)	130	(4)	127	(5)
Bali	107	(11)	98	(11)	122	(6)
Aceh	96	(15)	119	(5)	107	(7)
North Sumatra	158	(4)	103	(9)	100	(8)
South Kalimantan	111	(9)	109	(7)	97	(9)
West Kalimantan	101	(12)	90	(13)	97	(10)
East Java	88	(19)	99	(10)	93	(11)
West Sumatra	89	(18)	97	(12)	91	(12)
Yogyakarta	75	(22)	75	(21)	89	(13)
West Java	87	(20)	81	(18)	88	(14)
South Sumatra	201	(3)	143	(3)	87	(15)
North Sulawesi	122	(7)	85	(16)	75	(16)
South Sulawesi	79	(21)	77	(20)	75	(17)
Central Java	74	(23)	74	(22)	71	(18)
Maluku	106	(10)	88	(14)	66	(19)
Jambi	150	(5)	84	(17)	65	(20)
Bengkulu	91	(17)	86	(15)	59	(21)
Lampung	92	(16)	57	(24)	55	(22)
Southeast Sulawesi	99	(13)	81	(19)	54	(23)
West Nusa Tenggara	52	(25)	51	(25)	44	(24)
Central Sulawesi	56	(24)	73	(23)	43	(25)
East Nusa Tenggara	48	(26)	48	(26)	40	(26)
Gini ratio[b]	0.18		0.21		0.24	
CVw[c]	0.42		0.55		0.66	
Ratio highest/lowest	5.1		6.8		9.8	

a GDP excludes gross value added from oil and gas, and is not corrected for price differences between provinces.
b Calculated with provincial totals of population and GDP, ranked by per capita GDP. The implicit assumption is that income is distributed equally within each province.
c Coefficient of variation weighted by population.

Sources: Calculated using population data from *Statistik Indonesia*, and GDP data from BPS (1980), *Pendapatan Regional Propinsi-Propinsi di Indonesia, 1971–1977*, BPS (1992), *Pendapatan Regional Propinsi-Propinsi di Indonesia menurut Lapangan Usaha, 1983–1990* and BPS (1998), *Produk Domestik Regional Bruto Propinsi-Propinsi di Indonesia menurut Lapangan Usaha, 1993–1997*.

As far as can be gauged, economic growth was accompanied by significant improvements in the standard of living; despite continued inequality of income, these improvements were broadly shared.

Indonesia's experience is not unique – today's developed countries have all undergone a similar process. What does set Indonesia apart is the very pace of economic change and development, which involved the forging of a national economy and nation state inclusive of diverse peoples and spanning an area equivalent to the size of Western Europe.

In Western Europe, budding nation states and national economies in past centuries were much smaller than the Indonesia of the 20th century. This gave the people of these states the opportunity to forge a common identity, although the process was marred by occasional setbacks due to war. Only during the last 40 years have European nation states striven to achieve a higher degree of economic integration, and only recently have they started to hand some of their sovereignty to a supranational body.

Although there are significant differences with Western Europe, the process of establishing a nation state spanning such a large number of disparate peoples, and of achieving economic integration, took place at a much faster rate in Indonesia during the 20th century. A supranational body was imposed from the start in the form of the Dutch colonial government and the succeeding government of the Republic of Indonesia, incomplete as it was. The process was bound to lead to tensions: the economic stagnation of 1930–66 was caused in part by a transition of regime and a nationalistic development ethos.

Why was economic development in Indonesia so fast in the 20th century? A major factor was that Indonesia was a latecomer to economic development. Gerschenkron (1962) has drawn attention to the 'advantages of backwardness' that latecomers enjoy. They have the opportunity to absorb technological knowhow from more advanced countries, without having to bear the cost and time of research involved in the development of new production technologies. However, they also require access to technologies, which presupposes the export earnings and foreign investment to pay for them, and they need to have the capacity to absorb such technologies.

Indonesia's phases of per capita GDP growth – 1900–30 and 1967–97 – were characterised by relatively high exposure to foreign markets. At the same time, the country had governments that took a 'developmentalist' stance as far as the means to do so were available. This led, for instance, to an expansion of investment in public infrastructure, which was conducive not only to export growth, but also to market integration and the expansion of production for domestic consumption and investment.

NOTE

1 Gini ratios have been calculated from the published Sakernas data. In the 1990s these have become sensitive to the average for the highest income bracket (those earning over Rp 300,000 per month), which has to be assumed. For the calculations in Figure 15.7, the average was estimated at Rp 400,000. A higher average increases the Gini ratio but does not affect the downward trend.

16

THE CHALLENGE OF SUSTAINABLE DEVELOPMENT: ECONOMIC, INSTITUTIONAL AND POLITICAL INTERACTIONS, 1900–2000

Howard Dick*

Economic development used to be thought sufficient both to improve material conditions and to pave the way to a more open and democratic society. Until recently, the progress of the West, the collapse of communism and the rise of Asia appeared to justify this confidence. The Asian crisis sowed doubt because in several countries, including Indonesia, spectacular economic development could not be sustained by fragile institutions and political systems. Economic development was therefore judged to have been too narrowly based. In the new 'conventional wisdom', political and institutional development should proceed simultaneously with economic development.

This chapter begins by periodising Indonesia's economic and political development during the 20th century and identifying periods of synchronised and of lopsided development. It then focuses on the dynamic interaction of economics and politics within and between periods, in particular drawing out the comparison between the New Order and the late colonial period.

TRENDS AND PERIODISATION

Political Periodisation

Conventional historiography proposes a neat sequence of political periods by which to consider Indonesia (Table 16.1). Each of these periods has its own events, dynamics and sources and almost invariably they are studied independently, thereby avoiding many potentially interesting questions about continuity and change. Nevertheless, a periodisation determined by political rather than economic events may not be the best way to approach economic history, or to study the interaction between economic and political development.

TABLE 16.1 Political Periodisation

Year	Period
To 1942	Colonial rule
1942–45	Japanese occupation
1945–49	Revolution
1950–66	Old Order
1966–98	New Order
Post-1998	Reformation

Economic Periodisation

The best way to determine an economic periodisation is to use a consistent long-term time series. A series for Indonesian GDP constructed back to 1880 has been compiled by van der Eng (1992, 2001) based on constant 1983 prices. Here I will use the series for GDP per capita with a shadow price of oil to prevent the OPEC effect from distorting the price deflator. The series clearly shows the main long-run trends, which show up as alternating upswings and downswings in Figure 16.1.[1] The peaks and troughs are marked by arrows. Ignoring minor business cycles, we can distinguish the following main periods.

1884 to 1902: Stagnation
A world depression resulted in falling commodity prices for Java's huge, export-producing plantation sector, magnified by coffee blight and sugar cane disease. GDP per capita peaked at Rp 188 in 1884, briefly rising in 1899 and 1900, and falling back to Rp 186 in 1902. Prolonged stagnation gave rise to official concern about the diminishing welfare (*mindere welvaart*) of the Javanese population.

1902 to 1929: Upswing
Economic growth accelerated up to the eve of World War I, boosted by rising commodity prices. GDP per capita levelled off at around Rp 229 during the war (1914–18), surged in 1918–19, fell back during the sudden postwar recession of 1920–22, then advanced again to a peak of Rp 290 in 1929.

1930 to 1934: Downswing
The worldwide depression of the 1930s saw income per capita contract sharply from Rp 290 in 1929 to just Rp 244 in the trough of 1934.

FIGURE 16.1 GDP per Capita, 1900–2000 (Rp thousand at 1983 prices, oil at shadow price)

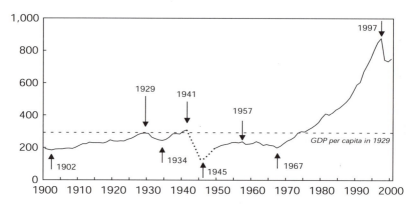

Sources: For 1900–41 and 1948–2000, van der Eng (2001); for intermediate years, van der Eng (1992).

1934 to 1941: Upswing
From the trough of 1934, economic recovery was rapid to 1937, slackening to 1939, before the surge in wartime demand pushed GDP per capita to a new high of Rp 309 in 1941. This phase of recovery and expansion was different from the preceding period because of the contribution of import-substituting manufacturing.

1942 to 1945: Catastrophic Decline
The Japanese occupation combined with drought saw GDP per capita fall to less than half its 1941 level and about a quarter below its 1880 level.

1945 to 1957: Upswing
From the all-time trough of 1945, GDP per capita recovered to a peak of Rp 237 in 1957, slightly exceeded (at Rp 238) in 1960. Nevertheless, this upswing was only by way of economic recovery. Because of population growth during the interim, the peak of Rp 237/8 was barely above the Depression trough of 1934.

1958 to 1967: Downswing
Economic stagnation and decline in the later years of Guided Democracy were followed by the sharp credit squeeze of 1966–67, reducing GDP per capita to just Rp 200 in 1967, which was below the independence level of

1950 and even below that of 1910. The New Order therefore had to catch up 57 years of lost economic growth.

1967 to 1997: Upswing

Growth accelerated quickly after 1967, and in 1976 GDP per capita at last exceeded the previous peak reached in 1941 – in 1972 if the deflator included the full oil boom effect. By 1997 GDP per capita was almost three times that of 1941. As is well known, this upswing was driven first by the oil boom and then by industrialisation, which after the 1980s looked to export markets.

1997–99: Downswing

GDP per capita contracted sharply in 1998 before levelling off in 1999. The loss of GDP per capita was equivalent to about three years of pre-crisis growth.

Joint Periodisation

Allowing for some rounding of years to get a reasonable fit, the result of combining the political and economic periodisations is set out in Table 16.2. Periods of marked political reform or economic progress are marked in bold.

This cross-periodisation shows that in only three periods has political reform coincided with economic development, namely 1901–20, 1950–57 and 1966–73, in all just 32 years, or one-third of the 20th century. None of these periods was long enough to build solid institutions and inculcate new patterns of behaviour. The other two-thirds of the century divides into periods

TABLE 16.2 Joint Political and Economic Periodisation

Period	Politics	Economy
1901–20	**Ethical era**	**Expansion and boom**
1920–30	Reaction	**Expansion** (after 1923)
1930–42	Repression	Depression and recovery
1942–45	Occupation	Catastrophic decline
1945–49	**Revolution**	Uneven recovery
1950–57	**Parliamentary democracy**	**Rehabilitation**
1957–66	Guided Democracy (1959)	Stagnation and decline
1966–73	**Modest reform**	**Economic recovery**
1974–98	Repression	**Rapid development**
1998–	**Democratisation**	Crisis and stagnation

of economic development without political development, and vice versa. The last two decades of colonial rule were periods of tightening political repression, as was the New Order period from 1974 to 1998. Conversely, the 1940s and the period of Guided Democracy, as again since 1998, were periods when society was preoccupied with politics and the consequent instability put paid to economic expansion. Is there a pattern to these alternations, and if so, how is it to be explained?

POLITICAL AND INSTITUTIONAL DEVELOPMENT

Political and institutional development can be subdivided into four broad categories. *General political rights* are about representative institutions and freedoms. *Legal rights* refer to what is often known as 'rule of law', which involves not only good laws but also a capable and honest judiciary to mediate between state and society. *Property rights* (including intellectual property rights) are the basis for private business. They depend upon protection at law from encroachment by competitors or the state, as well as a stable business environment and a sound banking and financial system. *Social rights* refer to the basic human needs of adequate nutrition and public health, clothing, housing and mass education, without which there can be no social justice.

Why does economic and political development so often diverge? The problem can be illustrated by a simple matrix.

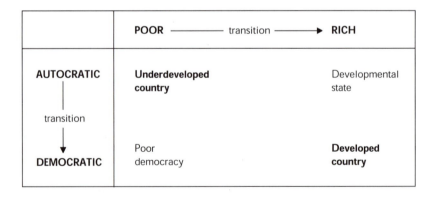

Countries seeking to move from underdeveloped to developed country status face the challenge of a double transition: an economic one from poor to rich and a political one from autocratic to democratic. Countries that complete the double transition become a modern, Western country, typically a member of the Organisation for Economic Cooperation and Deveopment (OECD), like the nations of Europe, North America, Japan, Korea and Australasia. It is in theory possible for a nation to achieve a transition to democracy while remaining poor. India and the Philippines may perhaps be cited as examples, but typically power is not shared in such countries and there is no tradition of rule of law and dissent. More common are countries that achieve an economic transition but remain autocratic. These may be called developmental states, of which Singapore and until very recently South Korea may be taken as examples. Countries may also get stuck in an intermediate zone where lack of economic progress frustrates political reform and lack of political reform frustrates economic progress. Albeit at different stages of development, various African, Asian and Latin American countries would appear to fall into this amorphous intermediate zone.

The challenge of the double transition may be viewed in terms of the relationship between state and society. The state may be the main agent of change or the greatest obstacle to change. Where there are open processes of expression and participation, state and society may engage in a productive struggle for change, ultimately enhancing social cohesion. Where such processes are repressed, as in late colonial or late New Order Indonesia, society reacts by denying the legitimacy of the state and institutional development may languish. To explain the pattern of economic and political change, we must therefore try to understand how political choices were made and enforced.

ECONOMICS AND POLITICS: THE PATTERN OF INTERACTION

1901–20: State Formation, Economic Development and Institutional Reform

In the first decade of the 1900s, the high tide of global imperial expansion, a modern state took shape that would become Indonesia. Hitherto effective colonial rule had been confined to Java. The Outer Islands were a patchwork of Dutch port settlements, semi-autonomous kingdoms and vast areas of tribal lands. After conclusion of the long-running Aceh War, the colonial government launched a series of small military campaigns that brought the whole of the Outer Islands firmly under Dutch rule. This was followed by installation of colonial administration, extension of regular shipping and telecommunications services, and imposition of the Netherlands Indies guilder as the official currency (Dick, Houben, Lindblad and Thee 2001, Ch. 5).

State formation and economic growth were linked and given a particular trajectory through a new policy approach known as the Ethical Policy. Announced in the Queen's speech to Parliament in 1901, the Ethical Policy targeted the specific policy initiatives of irrigation, education and emigration (Dick, Houben, Lindblad and Thee 2001, Ch. 5). However, it may more usefully be viewed as combining administrative reform, infrastructure and social welfare measures. Administrative reform was fundamental because it put flesh on the very bare bones of colonial rule.

In 1900 the colony had been managed by a very small European civil service (Binnenlands Bestuur), while day-to-day rule was in the hands of the 'native' civil service (Sutherland 1979). During the 1900s new functional departments were set up, including agriculture, industry and trade (1904), public works (1908) and education (1908), as well as specialist agencies such as the Public Health Service (1911) and People's Credit Banks (1912). The Decentralisation Law (1903) led to the formation of urban municipalities and, later, rural regency councils. By the 1920s the colonial state had become a sophisticated, multi-functional bureaucracy that reached down to the village level and across the entire archipelago. Unlike the 'nightwatchman state' of the 19th century, this was an energetic bureaucracy that sought to achieve results, the origins of the developmental state familiar in New Order Indonesia. Driving this was the education at Leiden University of a cadre of Dutch officials committed to a noble colonial task (Fasseur 1993).

Infrastructure spending, which is to say physical development (*pembangunan*), was the domain of the powerful Department of Public Works. The prime task was irrigation works to boost agricultural output, but infrastructure also encompassed ports and harbours, the railways, roads, bridges, drainage and flood control, and public buildings. The two specific social welfare measures announced in 1901 under the rubric of the Ethical Policy were emigration and education. Emigration (that is, transmigration) was intended to redistribute population from land-scarce and apparently poverty-stricken Java to the land-abundant Outer Islands. The modest program had minimal effect on the distribution of population and was not pursued again on any large scale until the New Order. Education reforms had more far-reaching effects, not because of any significant progress towards universal literacy or any general expansion of secondary or tertiary education – those achievements awaited the New Order – but because secondary education, including Dutch-language education, was opened selectively to Indonesians. Before 1900 there had been few secondary schools in the entire archipelago and only a handful of Indonesian aristocrats gained access. Wider opportunities now allowed the emergence of a Westernised, intellectual elite that in the 1920s became the core of the nationalist movement (van Niel 1960).

1920–30: Economic Growth, Political Reaction

Appointment of the ultra-conservative Governor-General Fock in 1921 coincided with the postwar recession and ushered in a period of contractionary budgets and political reaction. Economic growth soon revived but the momentum of institutional reform was lost. The Ethical Policy had envisaged the advancement of the 'native' but not nationalism. A Western-educated elite had been expected to behave as grateful 'brown' Dutchmen, not to demand political rights. At first the colonial government tolerated the rise of Indonesian nationalism, but mass political radicalisation during the 1910s alarmed the local Dutch population and put liberal reformers on the defensive (Shiraishi 1990). Unrest among the Indonesian population increased after 1918 as poor harvests, rapid inflation and falling real incomes led to hardship – fertile ground for the organisation of trade unions and subsequent strikes (Ingleson 1986).

Sutherland (1979, p. 87) identifies a three-fold political strategy of colonial *realpolitik*. First, the censorship, surveillance and repressive apparatus was strengthened. Second, efforts were made to enhance the authority of 'traditional' leaders among the local aristocracy and in particular officials of the indigenous civil service, the *pangreh praja*. Third, 'responsible' nationalist leaders were to be given a legitimate outlet to express their views through the advisory parliament (Volksraad), and through residency and regency councils. Institutional – or rather administrative – reform continued, albeit at a slower pace, but the political process remained firmly under bureaucratic control.

The watershed in colonial policy was 1926–27. The young Indonesian Communist Party (PKI) was implicated in rebellions in West Sumatra and West Java, and in 1927 Sukarno founded the Indonesian Nationalist Party (PNI), committed to independence from Dutch rule. Political repression intensified, culminating in the arrest and gaoling of nationalist leaders, including Sukarno and Hatta, and the banning of the PNI. The colonial government was now on the defensive and sought to apply the age-old tactic of divide and rule. With the intention of isolating Western-educated nationalists from the people, much greater attention was now paid to 'tradition', 'native custom' (*adat*) and local ethnic identity (Benda 1966). Decentralisation and indirect rule were means to isolate impressionable 'natives' from dangerous modernising influences. Educated Indonesians were either actual or potential troublemakers. The 'natives' were to remain 'natives' and had best stay in their well-ordered villages. Stability (*rust en orde*) now took precedence over development (advancement) (Sutherland 1979).

1930–42: Repression, Depression and Recovery

The 1930s were a period of depoliticisation. The term *beamtenstaat* has been much cited to identify the late colonial Netherlands Indies as an apolitical bureaucratic state *par excellence*. The colonial bureaucracy did not just administer the state; it was the state. Dick, Houben, Lindblad and Thee (2001) argue that the emergence of this modern state after the 1800s was one of Indonesia's fundamental historical parameters. The Ethical Policy may be seen in its political aspect as an enlightened but cautious strategy to graft this state onto society, so that it would no longer rule by might but by broad consent. The consent of the people was to be gained by material advancement of the elite by education and position. Politics, let alone democracy, was not on the agenda, except to a very limited extent for the very small European minority. However, it was placed on the agenda by Indonesian nationalists, who harnessed the empowering force of Western ideology, especially democracy, socialism and communism. This set of moral claims, which challenged the legitimacy of Dutch rule in Western terms, in turn called forth a bitter and highly racist political reaction from Europeans, whose power and privileges were threatened by presumptuous 'natives'. Europeans then jettisoned the 'do-gooder' Ethical Policy and turned to a strong state to protect their privileges. More than token politics could not be tolerated because it allowed the state to be challenged.

The last opportunity to legitimise Dutch rule, to graft state onto society, was presented in 1936 by the Soetardjo petition to the Volksraad, seeking agreement in principle to eventual self-government (Abeyasekere 1976). This coincided with the achievement of self-government in the Philippines. The Dutch rejected the petition. When the Japanese threat became imminent in 1940, the Dutch refused to arm the Indonesian population, and few Indonesians stood willing to defend the colony on Dutch terms. Many welcomed the Japanese invasion as it revealed the unexpected weakness of Dutch rule.

The late colonial period, which combined rigid political stability with a form of economic development, thus set up a highly destabilising dynamic for the period after independence. First, because economic expansion had rested on capitalist foundations, free trade and private/foreign ownership were discredited as exploitative and unjust. The socialist alternative was protection and state enterprise: the economy should be subordinate to the state. Second, like forbidden fruit, politics was a right that could now be indulged. The problem was that acceptable institutional mechanisms to resolve conflict hardly existed. Formal law, which had been the instrument of harsh repression, was not respected; informal *adat* law was tainted by colonial manipulation.

1945–49: Occupation and Revolution; Catastrophic Economic Decline and Recovery

The Japanese occupation, though traumatic and destructive, released long pent-up political energies. The Dutch were swept into captivity and Indonesians took over civil government under Japanese tutelage. Political and economic mobilisation meant that the state now organised the population down to the level of neighbourhood cell in village and *kampung*. Ultra-nationalism involved rituals of loyalty to the Japanese emperor, but Indonesians learned how to adapt these new institutions and organisations to their own national purpose. The capital stock was run-down, but the main cause of the collapse of output was the virtual suspension of international trade and the imposition of local autarky (Sato 1994). Crop failures in 1945 added to the misery (van der Eng 1994).

The three and a half years of Japanese tutelage provided the irresistible momentum for Indonesians to resist by armed struggle the reimposition of Dutch rule. While the Dutch tried to counter by introducing limited self-government under a federal system, only in parts of the Outer Islands did this find much popular support. In Java, Dutch authority was fragile and popular loyalties continued to flow to the republic. The revolution was therefore a time of contending systems. Economic hardship was widespread. Both the Dutch and the republic destroyed or mortgaged economic assets in the struggle for control and there were huge movements of displaced people.

1950–57: Parliamentary Democracy and Rehabilitation

As the colonial regime disintegrated in the 1940s, Indonesians reclaimed politics and identity. Authoritarian rule gave way to mass political mobilisation led by the first president, Sukarno, and Vice-President Hatta. The early years of independence witnessed dramatic political and institutional development (Feith 1962). Sovereignty was transferred from the Dutch crown to the people of the new nation, and ways had to be found to graft the radical constitution, ideology and institutions of the republic onto the conservative laws, bureaucracy and institutions of the colonial state. The state apparatus and the body of colonial law and practice remained fairly intact, but the style of government changed profoundly. Indonesians now claimed the democracy and equality that had so long been denied them.

At the same time, the centralising tendency of the state became more apparent. To limit the influence of republican nationalists, in 1949 the Dutch had imposed a federal political system with a weak centre. Once in control of the state, in 1950 republicans struck back by reorganising a unitary state that was more centralised than the colonial model. In theory the state and the people had both won, but a democratic centralised state could not easily be sustained in a politically immature society and this would be a source of ongoing strife.

A virtuous cycle of economic recovery and political development was broken by political crisis. After a decade of occupation, war and revolution and without a supportive fabric of the informal institutions of civil society, the unfamiliar divisions and tensions of party politics were hard to accommodate. Frequent changes of cabinet gave a sense of instability, which contrasted sharply with the stability, however repressive, of the colonial period. Tensions intensified when no clear victor emerged after the 1955 national election. In 1956 Vice-President Hatta's resignation aligned party divisions with a split between Java and the Outer Islands. Declarations of autonomy by regional military commanders threatened national unity.

1957–66: Stagnation and Decline under Guided Democracy

Hatta's resignation and the regional challenge shifted power decisively towards the centre, and very specifically to President Sukarno and the central army command. In March 1957, Sukarno signed a declaration of martial law, transferring de facto power to General Nasution and the army (TNI) to deal militarily with the regional challenges. The cabinet was forced to resign and the president appointed a new extra-parliamentary cabinet. In 1959 he cited delay in ratifying the permanent constitution as an excuse to issue a decree suspending parliament, to restore the original authoritarian 1945 Constitution (which granted almost unlimited powers to the president) and to introduce 'Guided Democracy' (Nasution 1992; Bourchier and Legge 1994).

Under this new 'guided' political system, Sukarno allowed mass political mobilisation through the political parties, known as 'functional groups'. However, in the absence of national elections, Sukarno determined the level of representation that each functional group would enjoy in parliament and in cabinet. In theory, there was discussion (*musyawarah*) and consensus (*mufakat*), but these did not translate into alternative institutional mechanisms of conflict resolution. In practice Sukarno played groups off against each other to maintain his personal rule. Sukarno was not granted his mandate by any democratic vote. He claimed it by right as 'Leader of the Revolution', an ultra-nationalist assertion of the will of the people, and solved the political problem of the relation between state, nation and people by embodying them all in himself. This solution had no independent institutional form. It worked only as long as Sukarno remained in good health and neither the armed forces nor the PKI was prepared to bid for power in its own right.

The outcome was a society of high expectations, intense struggles for power, high conflict and declining social capital. The well-established state and judiciary atrophied in functional capability and integrity. Although Sukarno's PNI claimed to represent the aspirations of civil servants – and indeed the number of civil servants grew enormously – salaries were so eroded by hyperinflation that civil servants were forced to take other forms of paid employment. In the struggle for survival, commitment and integrity were hardly to be expected. The judiciary was similarly compromised. The nominally powerful centralised state became bloated and dysfunctional, prey to the short-term interests of the political parties and Sukarno himself.

Guided Democracy was accompanied by Guided Economy (Tan 1967). When independence failed to usher in the socialist ideal, the original nationalist equation of $x = sovereignty$ was respecified as $x = political + economic sovereignty$. Dutch nationals were expelled, and soon all other foreign-owned business was taken under state control. Nationalisation of the modern sector subordinated capitalist economy to a nominally socialist state and society. In the name of neocolonialism, Indonesia turned not only against the white rulers but also against the faceless economic regime that was seen as having been the substance of oppression. Low wages, long hours and poor conditions were the product of colonial exploitation, not impersonal labour markets. There was seen to be no need to maintain an economic discipline and way of thinking because that too was part of colonial oppression.

However hastily conceived and clumsily applied, the nationalist and revolutionary politics of Guided Democracy and Guided Economy were logical responses to the contradictions of the colonial order and the tensions of the 1950s. Nevertheless, the populist-autocratic experiment lasted barely six years. Its weaknesses were both economic and political. Disengagement from the world economy carried a high price in terms of economic dislocation. Artificial political stability was bought for a while by huge budget deficits and soaring inflation but rested on no more solid foundations than Sukarno's health (Mackie 1967). Both the Western powers and the communist nations manoeuvred to secure advantage in this vital Cold War struggle. Beyond Sukarno, there was no longer any institutional means to resolve the crisis short of violence.

1966–73: Modest Reform and Economic Recovery

When Sukarno's health failed in the mid-1960s, the revolutionary tide turned amidst a bloody showdown between the army and the PKI. A traumatised country accepted the army-sponsored, broad-based New Order alliance led by General Soeharto against the PKI, whose members were either arrested or murdered. This alliance represented the interests of the military, urban middle class, Chinese business, broad-based Islam and, at its cutting edge, students. Reflecting the interests of this alliance, the new government of President Soeharto began with political reform, an attack on corruption and a program for economic recovery led by enlightened technocrats. A liberal economic regime was quickly restored, and as markets were freed of their regulatory shackles, capitalist society reassembled itself.

However, political reform combined with economic recovery for only a brief period. By 1972 it was apparent that there would be no sanctions against corrupt high officials. Student protests against the business interests of the president's wife, Tien Soeharto (Madam Ten Percent), led to arrests. In January 1974, the Malari riots against visiting Japanese Prime Minister Tanaka and Indonesian-Chinese business magnates (*cukong*) provoked a harsh crackdown of arrests, closure of the crusading newspaper *Indonesia Raya*, and the banning of the Indonesian Socialist Party (PSI). General Ali Moertopo, presidential advisor and intelligence head, increased his power and influence and set the regime down the path of manipulation and repression. Economic development accelerated, boosted by the OPEC-induced oil boom, but under a regime of tightening political repression.

1974–98: Repression and Rapid Development

The post-1974 New Order government was more ruthlessly repressive than the colonial state. The power of coercion was greater and the scope for evasion less. The colonial state had intervened in *kampung* and village life, but only on the margin. Not until the Japanese occupation did the writ of the state penetrate to the *kampung* and only under the New Order did it become effective. At the *kampung* and village level, 'stability' and 'development' were not just goals but a top-down process of rule. Stability began in 1966 with the arrest and murder of communists. Military officers and non-commissioned officers were brought in to stiffen the local bureaucracy, so that there would be a smooth chain of command from the Ministry of Internal Affairs in Jakarta to each neighbourhood. Development policies and ideological education could then be implemented with a clear line of authority. Anyone who protested stood to be accused of being a communist remnant, with potentially fatal consequences. The same applied to anyone foolhardy enough to challenge local officials for their petty embezzlements.

By the end of the New Order, the state had thus been grafted onto society from top to bottom but through a thoroughly corrupt and autocratic model. This graft was achieved not by participatory politics but by administrative decree, sanction and fear, backed by the brute force of the armed forces and police. There had been institutional reform but it was very narrow. The state was retooled as an effective – though hardly efficient – instrument of rule, and centralised to the highest degree the country had known as either independent nation or colony. The army and its intelligence operations – the state within the state – were developed to a historic level of capability (Tanter 1991). Parliament, the legal system and civil society languished.

Probably without being conscious of the parallel, the New Order found itself reinventing the past, not as colonial rule by an *ethnic* minority, but as indigenous authoritarian regime as handmaiden to development. The parallels were striking. Anderson (1983) recognised the similarity, even continuity, between colonial and New Order states, but the comparison can be broadened. Colonial *rust en orde* with an Ethical Policy, and the New Order's stability and national development, were imposed by force and legitimised as good government, involved capitalist development with open trade and investment regimes, were supported by an urban middle class, and were maintained by systematic repression.

The New Order stumbled sooner against the contradictions of authoritarian rule because power became ever more concentrated in the person of Soeharto. He could no more liberalise the political system that entrenched the power of his family and the armed forces than the colonial government could share power with the nationalists. Neither system could evolve in any other way than to become more repressive.

If the resemblance between late colonial and New Order Indonesia seems remarkable, it is because nationalist historiography conflates the pre-war Netherlands Indies with colonial rule, instead of analysing it in the context of the economic system in which colonial rule and colonial society were embedded. In both cases the primary fault-line was between the state and people, 'them' and 'us'. Village and *kampung* dwellers recognised much sooner than the middle-class bureaucratic elite that the New Order did not represent their interests.

CONCLUSION

Over the course of the 20th century Indonesia has experienced a repeating cycle of reaction and revolution. The struggle for independence is invariably explained as the rejection of colonial rule, but it was also a rejection of a particular pattern of globalised, capitalist economic development. Likewise, collapse of the New Order involved popular rejection not only of corrupt, highly centralised and repressive rule by the Soeharto family and the military, but also of the New Order pattern of economic development. During the intervening period of populist government, Indonesia disengaged from the global economy. Since the Asian crisis, the Indonesian polity has made another sudden lurch. The period since May 1998 has seen political reform not much less dramatic than that which followed the transfer of sovereignty in December 1949, and the outcome so far has been a similar mixture of elation, confusion and disappointment.

One of the lessons of the Asian crisis is that economic development needs to be supported by institutional development. Political repression may help to accelerate economic development, but it does not ensure sustainability. The tragedy of both the late colonial period and the New Order is that political and institutional development were not tackled while there was the opportunity and resources to do so. The colonial government abandoned the Ethical course and turned to repression in the 1920s; Soeharto ceased to compromise and turned to military repression after the Malari riots of January 1974. Neither regime could tolerate politics because of the challenge to those in power. Conflict was suppressed but legitimacy was forfeited. In the process, the path was blocked towards peaceful political evolution. The consequences have been fateful.

Nevertheless, the old argument is still being made that politics is ruining the country. The new developmental paradigm seems to be to insulate economic *and institutional* development from politics. Nevertheless, without a return to the 'anti-politics' of repression by a new military regime (Loveman and Davies 1978), it is hard to see how a new national consensus can be crafted and embodied in institutions and organisations except by a great deal of messy politics. Institutions do not arise out of thin air but out of conflict. The key question is whether Indonesia has enough skilled political leaders to do this crafting before conflicts fomented by anti-democratic vested interests overwhelm a still fragile democratic system.

A critical issue in the stability of the new political system is the role of the urban middle class. In the late colonial period the *European* middle class held sway, believing that soft repression was a better way to retain its privileges than meeting Indonesian demands for increased popular representation. Under the New Order an *Indonesian* middle class made a very similar political choice for material welfare over political rights. At the end of the New Order, that class saw its material welfare under threat and found the courage for a democratic transition. However, the demand for rule of law is subliminally a demand for rule by the class that would administer the laws, namely the middle class, not necessarily a call to enfranchise the people. Rule of law would allow the people to be protected by enlightened civil servants, which harks back to the late colonial paradigm. The middle class is the class that knows what is best for the rest of society. Whether it will continue to be willing to trade off material welfare for political freedoms is an open question. If economic stagnation and political conflict persist, autocratic government may again have seductive appeal. Whatever the nature of the new emerging polity, it will still be an urban middle class polity and it will still be 'corrupt'. Ameliorists who pin their hopes on institutional reform and good governance are bound to be disappointed.

NOTES

*   This paper draws on the forthcoming book by H. Dick, V. Houben, T. Lindblad and Thee Kian Wie (2001), especially Chapters 5, 6 and 7. I am very grateful to Pierre van der Eng for allowing me access to his updated GDP series in electronic form, to him and Elizabeth Maitland for comments on an earlier version, and to Catherine Maguire for assistance with Figure 16.1.

1   A more complex logarithmic scale would eliminate the marked increase in absolute annual growth increments under the New Order as a result of the compounding effect.

17

THE LATEST CRISIS OF REGIONAL AUTONOMY IN HISTORICAL PERSPECTIVE

Wihana Kirana Jaya and Howard Dick

The recent radical changes to legislation governing the relations between central and local government in Indonesia are the latest in a series of reforms and experiments dating back to the Dutch colonial government's Decentralisation Law of 1903. However, rather than a steady and maturing evolution, the process has followed what Mackie (1999, p. 2) has referred to as a 'zigzag' pattern between decentralisation and centralisation. Modest decentralisation in the late colonial period became the basis for a federal Republic of the United States of Indonesia, but soon after independence the republic was reconstituted as a unitary state. The degree of centralisation reached a peak under the New Order government of President Soeharto, and this eventually triggered a 'crisis' in centre–region relations, leading to the introduction of new laws on regional autonomy. These laws will shift functions and fiscal resources from central to local government over a two-year implementation period (Jaya, Mardiasmo and Matfatih 2000). Law No. 22/1999 is an attempt to democratise the local government, and to devolve certain powers. Law No. 25/1999 is designed to support that shift of power to the local government by providing more fiscal resources (Brodjonegoro and Asanuma 2000).

This chapter will survey how this recent shift towards regional autonomy compares with Indonesia's past experience. We examine three interrelated aspects of relations between the centre and the regions over the course of the 20th century: political, administrative and fiscal. After a brief discussion of the various forms of regional autonomy and decentralisation, we summarise the features of each main phase in the evolution of centre–region relations, and then examine the fiscal aspects of regional autonomy.

REGIONAL AUTONOMY AND DECENTRALISATION

Fundamental to the study of regional autonomy is the issue of political power. Centre–region relations are concerned with the distribution of power between levels of government (Davey 1989). This division of power arises in any democratic system, unitary or federal (Zariski and Rousseau 1987). One form of decentralisation is federalism, in which the constitution divides power between national and local levels of government and in which each level of authority retains some exclusive powers. Another form is regional devolution, in which national power is paramount over regional powers and in which a central government agent can appeal against regional legislation.

Decentralisation theory recognises four types of decentralisation: political, administrative, fiscal and market (Rondinnelli 1999). This chapter will focus on the first three of these. Political decentralisation is the mechanism by which the central government transfers political power to local governments. Administrative decentralisation is the delegation of administrative authority from central to local government. Its three forms are de-concentration, delegation and devolution. De-concentration exists when the central government disperses responsibility for the delivery of services to the local level; delegation and devolution relate to the balancing of central and local interests. Fiscal decentralisation essentially involves increasing the financial responsibility of local government.

A review of decentralisation literature suggests several criteria for achieving decentralisation (Litvack and Seddon 1999). In the case of political decentralisation these include redistribution of power, democratisation and greater local participation. Administrative decentralisation involves the redistribution of administrative authority and responsibility and an emphasis on strong local administration, while fiscal decentralisation incorporates self-financing, expansion of local revenue and authorisation of municipal borrowing and expenditure. Table 17.1 presents a simple classification of the decentralisation criteria.

According to Hidayat (1999), the process of decentralisation serves both political and economic objectives. The political goals are to strengthen local accountability, nurture political skills and consolidate national integration. Economic decentralisation is required to enhance the ability of local government to provide public goods and services (Rondinnelli 1999; Oates 1999). The administrative goal of decentralisation is to transfer planning, decision-making and administrative authority from the central government to field organisations and local administrative units. Attention will now focus on Indonesia's experiments during the 20th century with structural change of the kind outlined above.

TABLE 17.1 Criteria for Decentralisation

Political	Administrative	Fiscal
Delegation of political power	Redistribution of authority	Self-financing or cost recovery
Greater local participation in politics	Shift of responsibility	Co-financing or co-production
Democratisation	Strengthening of local administrative capability	Expansion of local revenue
Strengthening of local legislature	Delegation to lower-level units	Intergovernmental transfers for block grants
Development of pluralistic political parties	Establishment of new public enterprises	Authorisation of municipal borrowing
Effective public control	Increase in discretionary power	Autonomous expenditure

Source: Litvack and Seddon (1999).

PHASES OF DECENTRALISATION AND CENTRALISATION

Table 17.2 summarises the main phases of decentralisation and centralisation between 1903 and the recent laws passed in 1999. Rows in bold indicate the main phases of decentralisation, excluding the post-1974 New Order (Law 5/1974) period of nominal devolution but actual administrative and fiscal centralisation. The table supports Mackie's (1999) view of a zigzag pattern of decentralisation and centralisation. Modest delegation of power in the late colonial period laid the basis for the short-lived federal Republic of the United States of Indonesia. The main trend in the period from the Japanese occupation (1942–45) to the end of the New Order in 1998 was towards a highly centralised unitary state. This eventually triggered another crisis in centre–region relations, leading to the recent introduction of new laws on regional autonomy. These phases will now be examined in greater detail.

Until the end of the 19th century, colonial administration in the Dutch East Indies consisted of a simple top-down territorial structure. Within this administration a skeleton staff of around 300 Dutchmen in the Binnenlands Bestuur (Department of the Interior, now Departemen Dalam Negeri) managed the

TABLE 17.2 Decentralisation and Centralisation Measures, 1900–2000

Period/Law		Political	Administrative	Fiscal	Indicator
Dutch Colonial (1900–42)	**Law 1903**	**Delegation of power to local government**	**Delegation of authority to local government**	**Delegation of powers to levy own taxes**	**Decentralisation**
	Law 1922	**Delegation of power to provincial government**	**Delegation of authority to the 'native' in Java**		
Japanese Occupation (1942–45)		Centralisation of formal power	Shifting of responsibility to central government	Fiscal centralisation	Centralisation
Revolution (1945–49)	1945 Constitution	Unitary republic			Centralisation
	Law 22/1948	Delegation of democratic principle	Delegation of authority	Fiscal devolution	
	Dutch Policy 1948–49	**Federal states**	**Administrative decentralisation**	**Fiscal decentralisation**	**Decentralisation**
Old Order (1949–65)	Unitary	Unitary state	Administrative centralisation	Fiscal centralisation	Centralisation
	Law 1957	Division of powers	Administrative devolution	Fiscal centralisation	
	Presidential Edict 1959	Guided democracy	Administrative centralisation	Fiscal centralisation	
New Order (1965–98)	Law 18/1965	Devolution of power	Administrative centralisation	Fiscal centralisation	Centralisation
	Law 5/1974	Centralisation of power under army and civil bureaucracy	Administrative centralisation	Fiscal centralisation	
Reform Order (1999 – present)	**Law 22/1999**	**Devolution of power; democratisation; strengthening of local legislation**	**Redistribution of authority and responsibility**	**Expenditure devolution; revenue centralisation**	**Decentralisation**
	Law 25/1999				

main functions of government in Jakarta (Batavia) and Bogor and staffed the territorial administration down to the level of residency and regency/district (*kabupaten*) (Furnivall 1944, Ch. 9). Local administration below the *kabupaten* level was in the hands of the indigenous aristocracy (*pangreh praja*) (Sutherland 1979). Of the entire numerical strength of the colonial administration, about three-quarters was located in Java, then firmly under colonial rule, and the balance situated in the Outer Islands, then still being brought under Dutch control. A larger number of Chinese were involved in collecting taxes under various 'subcontracting' or revenue-farming arrangements (Diehl 1993, p. 201).

By 1900, it was apparent that this ad hoc skeleton structure no longer met the demands of efficient and modern government. The conquest of the Outer Islands was expanding the area under colonial control and requiring closer administrative integration with Java (Dick, Houben, Lindblad and Thee 2001). Tax farms were phased out in favour of a system of direct tax collection (Diehl 1993). Moreover, the expanding European communities in the main towns sought a measure of local autonomy. The inauguration of the Ethical Policy in 1901 provided a framework for administrative reform and greater local autonomy (see also Dick, this volume). The Decentralisation Law of 1903 established a legal basis for autonomous local (urban) government. Based on this the Municipality (Gemeente) of Batavia was formed in 1905, followed by Surabaya in 1906 and other towns throughout Java and the Outer Islands (Kerchman 1930). These municipalities became, in effect, government 'by Europeans for Europeans' (Furnivall 1944, p. 291). 'Native' *kampung* remained nominally self-governing under the authority of the local regent (*bupati*) (Sutherland 1979).

After years of vigorous debate, in 1922 the colonial government passed a more far-reaching Decentralisation Law, which proved a victory for conservatives over liberal reformers (Furnivall 1944; Sutherland 1979). It firstly provided a legal basis to merge the intermediate administrative unit of residencies (*gewesten*) into larger provinces with enhanced powers, beginning with West Java in 1926 and followed by East Java in 1929 and then Central Java in 1930. Second, it sought to delegate powers to the regency level and to activate new regency councils. An important motivation was to strengthen the conservative *pangreh praja* as a bulwark against the growing nationalist movement. In fact the provinces were not significantly empowered, as one observer noted: '[A]uthority was to devolve from Provinces to Regencies and the colonial regime was to remain in total control' (Sutherland 1979, p. 106). Administrative reforms during the 1930s sought further to strengthen indirect rule and traditional local authority, especially in the Outer Islands, on the basis of *adat* law (traditional law) (Benda 1966).

The Japanese occupation (1942–45) had a radical effect on this whole process. When Dutch officials were interned, the dividing line between the European Binnenlands Bestuur and the *pangreh praja* disappeared. Indonesian officials moved up into senior administrative positions and nationalist leaders, including Sukarno, became part of the government (Cribb and Brown 1995). At the same time, the Japanese extended the authoritarian bureaucracy down to the level of hamlets and household (neighbourhood) associations (*tonarigumi*, now *rukun tetangga*). Thus 'every household, neighbourhood association, hamlet and village, all of which had previously fallen outside the formal administrative structure, was incorporated into the all-encompassing single administrative pyramid dominated by the Japanese Army' (Sato 1994, p. 28). Although wartime necessity forced the Japanese to decentralise authority to the provincial and local levels, the long-term effect was towards increased centralisation.

Between 1945 and 1949, sovereignty and authority were contested. Seeking to restore their authority but with some popular legitimacy, the Dutch pushed ahead with decentralisation in areas under their control. Indonesia was to be broken up into autonomous states (*negara*), led by administrators responsible to assemblies made up of representatives from local regency councils (Yong Mun Cheong 1982). In the Outer Islands, where the Dutch were fairly successful in re-establishing control, the *negara* acquired some substance, most notably in East Indonesia, South Sumatra and East Sumatra, while other territories (*daerah*) relied heavily on the authority of traditional rulers and the local aristocracy. In Java, where the republic survived, the Dutch sought to hive off units such as Pasundan (the highlands of West Java), East Java and Madura where they thought they could gain the support of aristocratic and religious leaders.

Meanwhile, in revolutionary territory, nationalist leaders sought to apply a republican model of a unitary state under the new 1945 Constitution. The new cabinets inherited from the Japanese a single top-down bureaucracy, notably still based on Dutch law and practice, but sought to graft onto this elements of local participation and representation. The republic's first local government law (No. 22/1948) maintained a fairly centralised approach. However, because of the exigencies of war, few permanent administrative reforms could actually be implemented. Authority and decision making necessarily had to be even more highly decentralised than during the Japanese occupation.

On the transfer of sovereignty from the Dutch in December 1949, the republic was forced to accept the compromise of a federation, a Republic of the United States of Indonesia, that combined the republic with the various Dutch-sponsored states and territories. The Dutch claimed that this arrangement was the only way to protect the diverse regional interests of the country. In republican eyes, however, these states were Dutch puppet states and the 'ramshackle' federation had no legitimacy (Feith 1962, pp. 58–71). In 1950 agreement was reached whereby the states and territories would merge with the republic into a unitary Republic of Indonesia. In the case of East Indonesia, armed resistance led to military intervention from the centre.

The regional problem that emerged during the 1950s involved a contradiction between the need to satisfy regional aspirations and the need to establish stable and strong central government (Legge 1961). Between 1953 and 1962 there were a number of attempts to topple the central government in West Java, Central Sumatra, North Sumatra, South Sumatra, Makassar and even Jakarta. Mackie (1999) argues that the conflicts that polarised the central government and the regions could eventually be settled only by armed force. The principal causes were divergent economic interests between the Outer Islands and Java, which aligned with splits within the army.

In response to rising political pressure, the central government enacted a basic law on regional government (Law 1/1957), which allowed much greater local autonomy (Legge 1961, p. 53). Had the law been implemented a year or two earlier it might have accommodated regional aspirations and avoided the outbreak of regional unrest. In any event, it was passed in 1957 on the eve of the declaration of martial law and of military action against the PRRI–Permesta rebellions in the Outer Islands. In 1959 it was overtaken by a presidential decree suspending parliamentary democracy in favour of Guided Democracy based on the restored 1945 Constitution. The legal framework thereby returned to a highly centralised form that greatly disadvantaged local government.

The New Order government of President Soeharto enacted a new basic law (*undang-undang*) on regional autonomy (Law 5/1974) that purported to introduce 'real and responsible local autonomy'. Three principles were set out: decentralisation, de-concentration and the idea embodied by the Dutch term *medebewind*. Decentralisation meant transfer of authority from central government to the provinces (Daerah Tingkat I, the highest tier of local government) or from provinces to *kabupaten/kotamadya* (Daerah Tingkat II). De-concentration meant delegation of authority from central government to its agencies at the local level. The Dutch term *medebewind* meant delegation of policy implementation from central government offices to local government (Davey 1989). The most notable reform was the establishment at the provincial level of Regional Development Planning Boards (Bappeda), followed in 1979 by similar *kabupaten*-level bodies (Bappeda II) (MacAndrews, Sibero and Fisher 1982). East Java was one province that took advantage of this greater local planning capability (Dick, Fox and Mackie 1993).

However, despite initial high expectations, Law 5/1974 did not reverse the trend towards the centralisation of political and financial power. First, the president held the formal power to appoint provincial governors, while the

Minister of Home Affairs, acting under presidential authority, possessed the power to appoint *bupati* and mayors. In this respect at least, nothing much had changed since the Decentralisation Law of 1903. Second, tighter central administrative controls, combined with military secondments to the civilian bureaucracy under the doctrine of dual function (*dwifungsi*), pegged back some degree of de facto local autonomy. Third, the central government was able to draw on oil revenues to make tied revenue grants down to the village level, most notably through the Inpres programs.

The New Order government applied central control over provincial and local civil servants in various other ways. Control of civil service appointments was in the hands of the Minister for Utilisation of the State Apparatus (Menteri Pendayagunaan Aparatur Negara) and the Civil Service Administration Agency (Badan Administrasi Kepegawaian Negara). Administrative intervention occurred through various means, such as circulars (*surat edaran menteri*), guidelines (*petunjuk menteri*) or implementing guidelines and technical guidelines (*juklak* and *juknis*). Budgetary control was shared between the Ministers for Home Affairs and Finance and the National Development Planning Board (Bappenas).

The fall of President Soeharto in 1998 opened a new chapter in the history of decentralisation in Indonesia (Hull 1999). In May 1999, the Reform Order government under President Jusuf Habibie formulated a new approach to political decentralisation with Law 22/1999. In the context of the democracy and *reformasi* movement, the stated aims were to democratise local government and devolve specific central government powers to the *kabupaten/kota* (Brodjonegoro and Asanuma 2000, p. 3). However, rather than redistributing power and revenues from the central government, the intent of Law 22/1999 is to redistribute these from the provinces. The central government has retained strong political and administrative powers, especially fiscal powers, but undermined the power of the provinces which, as much larger units, are less amenable to central control (McLeod 2000a, p. 28). In that regard the situation now approximates that of the late colonial period when the provinces were still new and poorly funded.

If legislative reforms suggest a zigzag pattern of evolution in centre–region relations, an overview of administrative hierarchy suggests continuity. Table 17.3 summarises the long-term evolution of the administrative hierarchy from the Javanese kingdom of Mataram to the present Indonesian system. (Rows in the table do not always denote exact equivalence, as for example between *patih* and resident/governor or between *wedana* and *camat*.) Two points stand out.

First, there has always been a supreme ruler, whether sultan, governor-general or president. Second, and more importantly, the local ruler or chief official (regent or *bupati*), and his area of authority and seat (*kabupaten*), has

TABLE 17.3 Evolution of the Administrative Hierarchy

Mataram (Yogyakarta)	Colonial		Indonesia
	Native Civil Service	European Civil Service	
Sultan	Governor-General	President	
Patih	Resident/Governor	Governor	
Bupati	Bupati	Assistant Resident	Bupati
Assistant Bupati	**Wedana**	**Controleur**	**Camat**
	Assistant Wedana		Lurah

over several centuries remained the basic territorial unit of government. There have been many shifts in the balance of power between supreme ruler and *bupati*, and also reforms to intermediate levels of government (the residencies or provinces). Individual *bupati* have from time to time been murdered, exiled, imprisoned, dismissed or humiliated. Nevertheless, the institution of district government has remained essentially intact despite the evolution from patrimonial to rational, bureaucratic government. Unlike residents and governors, who have remained dependent upon central government patronage, the *bupati* and *kabupaten* have survived because they are rooted in grassroots Javanese society and thereby, even more than the army, are fundamental to social stability.

Examined from this perspective, the thrust of the recent decentralisation measures is not particularly surprising. The supreme ruler cum central government has surrendered few of its real powers but has allowed some resurgence of local authority under the guise of local autonomy and democracy. This clever feat has been achieved at the expense of the provinces, whose governors and military commanders were seen as powerful princes of the realm and a prime potential threat to the stability of the central government. They were vulnerable because, unlike *bupati*, they tended to lack a strong local constituency.

It is a moot point whether the new centre–local government relations embodied in Laws 22 and 25 are 'modern' or 'traditional'. On the one hand, the reforms are consistent with trends elsewhere in the world towards decentralisation or devolution of power. Highly centralised administration is seen as being remote and undemocratic. There is a precedent in the reforms of the late colonial period, even if Dutch residents were the prime beneficiaries of these measures. On the other hand, it could be argued that the reforms take the system back more towards its 'Javanese' origins. Rohdewohld (1995) and Mardiasmo (1999) argue that Indonesia's administration has been influenced by traditional Javanese concepts of power and hierarchy, accentuating centralisation of power, patrimonial attitudes and top-down decision making. In the time of Mataram, loyal *bupati* were assured that the office would remain in their family for a period of at least 'seven generations'; to maintain their power, status and prestige, *bupati* had to spend freely on a conspicuous lifestyle and be conscious of meeting social obligations (Sutherland 1979). Colonial officials turned *bupati* into salaried officials, but social pressures ensured that the old style of behaviour continued, giving rise to financial abuse and indebtedness. Since independence, networks of exchanges and mutual accommodations between *bupati* and executive patrons, the military, local legislators and local businessmen have sustained a culture of corruption, collusion and nepotism. Mehmet (1994) argues that rent seeking and corruption resemble Javanese cultural traits in handling power and wealth. While cultural generalisations should be treated with great caution, there can be no question that bureaucratic culture is culturally embedded and cannot readily be changed by legislative reform.

THE EVOLUTION OF FISCAL POWERS

Centre–local government financial relations are concerned with distribution, and are highly political, since they determine how much weight is exercised by local government within the total system of government (Davey 1989). These relations also reflect the tension between centralising and decentralising pressures, and between a political and functional view of the role of local government (p. 176). From this perspective, we may compare local government finances in 1997/98 with those in the late colonial period under the Decentralisation Law (1922). Table 17.4 compares 'own-revenue effort' for (rural) regencies and (urban) municipalities in Java.

The results are intriguing. Rural regencies, whose own-revenue effort was minimal in the 1920s, have gained a greater degree of financial autonomy. By contrast, municipalities (*kota*) had clearly lost much financial autonomy by the end of the New Order in 1998. Across Java, the average municipal own-revenue effort appears to have fallen from 38% in the 1920s to just 23% in 1997/98. Under the New Order, Indonesia possessed one of the most centralised taxation systems in the world (Shah et al. 1994). Most regional and local government revenues in Indonesia were highly dependent on central

TABLE 17.4 Comparison of Revenue Ratio of Regencies and
Municipalities in Java, Dutch Colonial versus New Order (%)

Region	Dutch Colonial (1925–27)		New Order (1997/98)	
	Regency	Municipality	Regency	Municipality
West Java				
Bogor	2.5	38	3.8	25
Sukabumi	2.1	38	13.9	22
Bandung	4.7	37	14.0	26
Central Java				
Tegal	7.5	33	12.2	19
Pekalongan	8.7	37	18.8	13
Semarang	3.6	39	20.5	27
East Java				
Madiun	6.7	49	11.5	21
Mojokerto	7.1	32	20.5	18
Surabaya	2.1	34	–	33
Java average	5.0	38	14.0	23

Sources: Ruckert (1930); BPS (2000).

government transfers. Regional and local tax revenues were derived from a
small tax base and the very modest collection capacity of local administration
(Mahi 2000).

The new decentralisation reforms only partly redress this situation. Under
Law No. 25/1999 the central government has retained full control of high-
yielding taxes such as income tax, value-added tax, export taxes and import
duties, while agreeing to transfer 25% of central government revenues to the
regions by way of general grants (*dana alokasi umum*). Regions also gain
increased shares of natural resource revenues and a small (20%) share of personal income tax. The regions have therefore gained access to greater revenues, but without significantly greater taxing powers. This can be seen from
Law 34/2000 (Local Taxes and Charges) of 20 December 2000, which
updates the rules for levying and distributing local taxes and charges (*ret-
ribusi*). Provinces may levy taxes on vehicles (with 30% passed on to districts), motor fuel (70% to districts) and water resources (70% to districts).

Districts may levy taxes on hotels, restaurants, entertainment, public advertising, street lighting, quarrying and parking and must pass on 10% of the revenues to villages (*desa*). This miscellany of provincial and local taxes, most inherited from the colonial era, remains a very narrow tax base. To boost own-tax effort, provinces and districts without natural resource revenues have little choice but to impose a miscellany of ad hoc charges (Dick 2001). This reverses the intent of the previous Law No. 18/1997, which had sought to bring about greater uniformity by reducing the number of user charges levied across Indonesia from 192 to 30 (McCarthy 2000).

The central government has retained ultimate decision-making power in national budget policy. Under the old system there was a formal process of consultation from the subdistrict (*kecamatan*) level upwards to provide input into the budget-making process (Shah et al. 1994). In practice, however, informal lobbying for projects and budgetary assistance determined the size of monetary allocations (Mardiasmo 1999). Some regional government activities followed set norms; others paid more regard to informal guidance and unofficial guidelines. At the local level, budgets were often decided by informal meetings between the *bupati* and the regional assembly (*rapat setengah kamar*). These informal processes are likely to continue in the post-Soeharto era, but under Law 25/1999 will involve over 300 local governments directly lobbying Jakarta.

CONCLUSION

Since the colonial government's Decentralisation Law of 1903, Indonesia has followed a zigzag pattern between decentralisation and centralisation (Mackie 1999). The Decentralisation Law of 1903 established municipalities and the Decentralisation Law of 1922 established provinces as a larger coordinating unit than residencies. Now, after more than 50 years of centralisation, the new Decentralisation Laws of 1999 diminish the powers and revenue-raising capacity of provinces and restore some powers and revenues to the *kabupaten/kota*. However, Laws 22 and 25 of 1999 suggest that the central government in the reform era may be no more committed to delegating power – especially fiscal power – to local government than its colonial predecessors. The principles behind the new reforms are good ones. Bringing government closer to the local people through political, administrative and fiscal decentralisation should in theory make government more responsive, accountable and democratic. On close inspection, however, the new laws are revealed to be less radical than they appear. As in 1903 and 1922, they are biased towards administrative rather than political reform.

Moreover, reforming the habitual culture and practices of centre–region relations and local administration involves more than new laws. *Bupati* and *walikota* (mayors) are now subject to election and accountable to regional legislatures, but their administrative powers and resources have been increased. Exposed to all the temptations of money politics, and in the absence of the rule of law, members of local legislatures may collude with vested interests and with local and central power-holders, giving rise to concern at the possible emergence of local kings (*raja-raja kecil* or *Soeharto-Soeharto kecil*). Reform therefore also requires ongoing monitoring by civil society, including the media and anti-corruption groups. This supporting institutional development will be a slow process. It does not help that such changes are happening at a time when Indonesia is faced with wide-ranging political, economic and social problems.

PART IV

SOCIAL HISTORY

18

BRIEF REFLECTIONS ON INDONESIAN SOCIAL HISTORY

Robert Cribb

Only 30 years ago, the dominant view of the social history of the Indonesian archipelago was one of transition to modernity.[1] The societies of the region, it was widely believed, were undergoing a process of being ripped from their stable and supportive traditions to be deposited in a modern world in which increasingly uniform values, norms, intellectual conceptions and political and economic forces were at work. In many areas of Indonesian social history, this approach remains analytically highly effective. Changes in the status of women, in religious practice, and in conceptions of money and of the natural world seem to have a strongly directional trend.

This view of Indonesian social history has been attacked from two directions. At one end, post-modern relativism denies that there is any consistent direction in social change anywhere in the world.[2] At the other end, there is a growing realisation that the history of the archipelago has been one of relentless social and cultural change for at least two thousand years, and that the apparent transition to modernity of the 20th century has counterparts of equal importance in earlier centuries. Some social changes that once seemed to be strongly directional, such as the emergence of a dominant, pan-archipelagic cultural identity generally called 'Indonesian', now seem less securely rooted than they once did.

Instead of imagining that Indonesian history has only followed some teleological path towards the modern Indonesian nation, it has now become useful also to imagine the archipelago's social history as a series of struggles to place the society and societies at particular points on at least three key axes. The first of these axes stretches from mobility to immobility, the second from social rigidity to social flux, and the third from isolation to cosmopolitanism.

Deep-rooted habits of mobility are reflected in the settlement of the archipelago by Austronesians between three and four thousand years ago, in the tangled pattern of language affinities which everywhere in the archipelago suggests major population movement over time, and in the historical record of independent and state-sponsored migration since the 17th century. On the other hand, all who are familiar with Indonesia know the strong attachment to place, to *kampung halaman*, which most Indonesians feel, and are aware of the spiritual importance of local geography in traditional Indonesian religions. The tension between mobility and immobility became more acute in the 20th century as travel became easier and cheaper, while the growing commodification of land added an economic incentive to claim a spiritual link with the land at national (*Tanah Air*) and local levels.

Second, scholars have become increasingly aware of the extent to which Indonesian societies are status-driven.[3] There has been a powerful, often political, tension between strong state-sponsored ideologies which maintained that specific rigid hierarchies between lords and peasants, between Europeans and natives and between technocrats and citizens are the natural order of things, and those who have sought to open new channels of social mobility in religion, education, marriage, commerce and the armed forces. One of the consistent sources of dynamism in Indonesian societies has been the creation of new institutions to act as vehicles for the social mobility of new elites. The whole Indonesian enterprise itself can be understood as a vast new channel of social mobility for those who found their way to power and status blocked within the colonial order and within older indigenous societies. Equally consistent, however, have been the attempts of established elites to install social, cultural and political devices for thwarting the emergence of rivals.

This struggle has been reflected especially in the continuing tension between individualism and community in Indonesian society. On the one hand, the scramble for status places enormous emphasis on individual achievement. On the other hand, there is a very strong belief in the power of collective action within the village community, in cooperatives, and indeed in the Indonesian nation as a whole.

Third, since the earliest academic analyses of Indonesia, scholars have commented on the archipelago's openness to cultural influences from outside.[4] We have long ago overcome the inclination to believe that these influences were simply imposed by outsiders, and we now understand that there has been a continuing process of cultural selection by Indonesian societies. Although much cultural change took place for instrumentalist reasons, we can also identify a dynamic interest in cultural novelty, a cosmopolitan intellectual restlessness and a lack of interest in preserving cultural traditions in their precise initial detail which gives a distinctly modern air even to early societies in the region. Yet we can also identify strongly xenophobic inclinations in Indonesian society, a suspicion of outsiders, their intentions and their ideas, and a cultural conservatism which means that we can see, in today's Indonesia, structures and cultural assumptions that can also be found in the earliest descriptions of society.

Historians were once fond of the paired concepts of continuity and change, but in social history this opposition has become difficult to sustain. As well as following clear directional trends, societies move to and fro along axes defined by major social values. As the political and social assumptions of the Soeharto era rapidly vanish, the challenge for social historians will be to identify just where these changes are taking Indonesia.

NOTES

1   See, for example, Wertheim's (1956, 1959), *Indonesian Society in Transition*, probably the most influential analytical survey of Indonesian social change within a modernisation paradigm.

2   See, for example, Stoler's (1985) *Capitalism and Confrontation in Sumatra's Plantation Belt*. This was one of the first works in which post-modern theory began to shift the analysis of Indonesian society away from the modernisation paradigm, with its emphasis on social forces and social processes, and into the realm of ambivalence registers of discourse.

3   See Anderson's (1972a) 'The Idea of Power in Javanese Culture'. Anderson emphasised culture as the key to understanding politics and society in Java and, by extension, Indonesia. Scholars reacting to his exuberant conclusions uncovered a vastly more complex range of cultural attitudes to power and authority.

4   See, for example, van Leur's (1955) *Indonesian Trade and Society*, a landmark statement refuting the idea that Indonesian societies were no more than the passive recipients of foreign culture.

19

INDONESIAN VIEWS OF THE FUTURE

M.C. Ricklefs

This topic – assigned to me, not chosen – is highly speculative, as readers will recognise. It does, however, have the potential to direct analysis to the centre of Indonesia's present crises and dilemmas. One's imagining of the future powerfully shapes what one does today. There is inescapable difficulty in the topic, however, for there has never been a single view – Indonesian, Ambonese, Acehenese, Javanese, Balinese, Christian, Muslim, Hindu, young, old, educated, middle-class, peasant or whatever – of the future. It would even be wrong to say that there have been as many views of the future as there have been ethnic, class and religious groups in Indonesia. In fact, there have been as many views of the future as there are individuals in Indonesia, as is true for the rest of humankind. Moreover, the records of life and thought in Indonesia rarely include anyone's views of the future, except implicitly in their actions and, more often, problematically in the pronouncements of politicians. Nevertheless, we may speculate usefully on the topic, and bring history to bear on its implications.

Examination of views of the future in Indonesia from a historical perspective raises several recurrent themes. Notable among these are (1) the belief that the past was better than the present and that a better future must in some measure revive the benefits of the idealised past; (2) frequent and sometimes violent dispute over how that better future might be achieved; and (3) the failure of successive leadership groups to deliver the better future which they promise. These recurring patterns have bequeathed to today's citizens of Indonesia widespread cynicism about political leadership, a distrust of institutions and a willingness to try radically alternative forms of leadership and ideology.

In other words, volatility is a legacy of Indonesian searches for a better future, and over a long time. Given the patterns noted above and the general stage of Indonesian socioeconomic development, it is not surprising that the most potent and convulsive searches for a better future have been driven largely by an intellectual restlessness among the elite combined with the volcanic force of peasant radicalism.

The period since the revolution in Indonesia is the most familiar and the easiest from which to draw out patterns. It is important to recognise, however, that the themes discussed here have deeper historical roots, and are thus part of longer Indonesian experience and of more deeply rooted Indonesian expectations – and thus that they carry the authority of folk knowledge, of intergenerationally transmitted expectations and presumptions about the future. The history of countries such as the United States or Australia leads their citizens to believe that, however corrupt, foolish or incompetent their leaders may prove to be, the institutions of society and the state make it unlikely that citizens' property, beliefs or liberties will be taken from them. Even intense controversy thus rests upon a bedrock of shared expectations about the future for the mainstream of those societies. No such history exists in Indonesia. Rather, history and memory tell people in Indonesia that their leaders will prove corrupt, foolish and/or incompetent, that their property, beliefs and liberties are constantly under threat, and that it has always been so. Yet the urgent, painful search for a better future goes on.

Speculation about past expectations of the future in Indonesia also emphasises the importance of religion. It is not surprising that religion should play a central role in the search for greater justice and morality, that messianism provides promises that desperate people are willing to embrace, or that mysticism provides solace to those who lose hope. One might observe that this reflects the recurring failure of any other form of leadership, but religious leaders have also failed their followers. No one has yet delivered the 'Just King' (*Ratu Adil*) of Javanese messianic tradition, or the Mahdi of Islam, to Indonesia. Despite the manifest failure of religion to provide Indonesians with the future they sought, however, as other ideas have fallen by the wayside – the embracing of colonialism and its culture, leftist radicalism, secular nationalism, democracy *à la* Indonesia, Pancasila, this or that – religion has retained its capacity to mobilise hope.

Examples from the period before independence, revolution or colonial rule will illustrate the depth of these patterns in the Indonesian experience. It is only in a few cases from before the 20th century that historical records are sufficient to support speculation about views of the future and their outcomes, but those cases are of considerable interest.

Sultan Agung of Java, who reigned from 1613 to 1646, was the greatest of the warrior–saint–monarchs of the Islamic Javanese royal tradition, the very model of what a king should be, and his reign provides an instructive episode of conflicting views of the future (Ricklefs 1998). In 1625, he completed the conquest of the Javanese-speaking heartland of central and east Java. This was the culmination of some three decades of bloody armed struggle by which the Mataram dynasty defeated and largely destroyed the harbour cities on the north coast (*pasisir*) of Java and the dynasties that governed them, paramount among them being the kings of Surabaya. These wars brought much devastation and disease to Java. In 1625–27, the Dutch East India Company (VOC) reported that in some regions up to two-thirds of the population had died from epidemic diseases. This was exacerbated by an El Niño weather and climatic period. Presiding over this creation of a new empire stood Sultan Agung, evidently the agent of an invincible force which could only be the power of God working on the earth through His regent the king: the *wawayangan ing Allah* of Islamic Javanese tradition – the shadow of God upon the earth. Agung's invincibility was proof of his supernatural protection.

But in 1628–29 Agung overreached his logistic capacity and, in defeat, brought into question his standing as the agent of God. He decided to expel the VOC from its new headquarters in Batavia (taken by the VOC in 1619), which was booming as a Chinese trading town governed by a tiny European elite, and which Agung regarded as a threat to his hegemony over the island of Java. He twice besieged the VOC's fortified city, in 1628 and 1629. Batavia was truly threatened, in particular by the first siege, but it survived. The Javanese armies suffered terribly during these sieges, conducted at a distance of some 500 kilometres from the capital of Mataram. After the first siege the army executed its commanders as it withdrew, leaving the Dutch to count 744 unburied bodies. The 1629 siege was a disaster, for the VOC found and destroyed the Javanese army's rice stockpiles on the *pasisir* even before the attackers had reached Batavia, thereby sealing their fate. As the Mataram army withdrew it disintegrated, and doubtless the survivors who managed to reach their homes in Agung's domains brought with them tales that were inconsistent with the idea that God could be guiding the hand of the king.

Agung was demonstrably not invincible, and thus doubts naturally arose about whether he could truly be the shadow of God upon the earth. A series of rebellions in several parts of the empire followed during 1631–36, most of them not well documented and all of them ultimately put down by Agung. Enough, however, is known about the rebels near his court in central Java to make relevant observations about their and Agung's views of the future. According to VOC reports, this rebellion was led by wandering religious leaders. Evidently the holy grave site of Sunan Bayat, whom tradition identifies as the saintly Islamiser of central Java, was the focal point of the rebellion. Thus it seems that local people, concluding that Agung was not invincible, turned to an alternative religious elite for leadership and inspiration. Some might observe that 1998 seems unremarkable in the light of such a precedent. Unlike Soeharto, however, Agung successfully used the tools of state suppression to crush his opponents.

But Agung did not just put down his enemies, he also acted to co-opt the supernatural power and vision that had inspired them. In 1633, the rebellion safely destroyed, he made a pilgrimage to the Sunan's holy grave at Tembayat. While some of his doings are of uncertain date, it seems that during this period, and perhaps while he and his court were at Tembayat for an extended period, he undertook major ritual acts that established him – and not the wandering mystics of central Java – as the heir to the sanctity and power of Sunan Bayat's spirit. He erected and inscribed a ceremonial gateway which still stands there to mark his pilgrimage; he abandoned the Hindu quasi-solar calendar then in use in the court and adopted the lunar Islamic calendar of months (but continued the Javanese enumeration of years to produce the unique *Anno Javanico*); he reconciled his dynasty with that of Surabaya (descended from the *wali* Sunan Ngampel-Denta) by bringing the last prince of Surabaya to his court and uniting the two dynasties through marriage; and he introduced from Surabaya major works of Islamic literature into the Javanese canon (*Serat Yusup*, *Serat Iskandar*, *Kitab Usulbiyah* and perhaps others). According to legend, Agung communed with the spirit of Sunan Bayat, who taught him the mystic arts of kingship, lessons possibly encapsulated in the work known as *Suluk Garwa Kancana*, admonishing the monarch to be an ascetic Sufi. In all these acts, Sultan Agung was reshaping the future by invoking the supernatural sanctity of the past age of the *wali*.

In this episode, one sees perceived failure of Agung's leadership in defeats at Batavia, leading to popular embrace of an alternative religious leadership. In this case Agung's leadership survived, partly by physical repression of the opposition and partly by Agung reinventing himself as the Islamising Sufi king. The rebels' view of the future was presumably of a more just, more peaceful, more devout Java. Although they were crushed, their vision of the future was fulfilled in part by Agung as the saintly monarch reviving the power of the past, of the age of the apostles of Islam.

If one turns to the 19th century, one sees many episodes of local resistance to established power structures, often inspired by religious ideas. This was, in particular, an age of Islamic renovation across the world, including in Indonesia. Wahhabi-style puritanism, Naqshabandi-style Sufism and the early stages of Islamic modernism all found sympathetic echoes and followers in Indonesia. In all of these episodes, an idealised past played a role in imaginings of the future.

One of the most dramatic and best-known cases was the Padri reform movement of Minangkabau, known through Dobbin's fine work (Dobbin 1983). By the late 18th century, the Minangkabau system of three kings was losing its economic foundations, for the gold resources upon which the monarchical system depended were running out. Meanwhile new crops were increasing in importance, notably coffee, salt, gambier and textiles, which were being traded with American and British traders in the region, especially after the British foundation of Penang in 1786. These crops were from regions of Minangkabau more remote from the system of royal control. The booming trade stimulated lawless conditions, which threatened the lives, freedom and fortunes of Minangkabau traders in particular.

In this fluid and turbulent environment arose the Padri reform movement, a devout Islamic movement which shared many of the ideas of the Wahhabis and was similarly prepared to use violence to achieve its ends. To Minangkabaus it promised relief from the royal system and a more stable and just society resting upon strengthened Islamic law and the justice of the *tuanku* (religious leaders). In 1803–04 fighting broke out in support of the Padris' revolution, which encapsulated a view of a future Minangkabau society that was more just, more secure and more pious. Thus the Padris and their followers were generally seeking a vision of the future similar to that which appears to have been cherished by the opponents of Sultan Agung nearly two centuries before.

In 1815 most of the royal family were murdered, signalling the near-victory of the Padris. But this revolution was aborted by the intervention of Dutch colonial forces from 1821. At the end of the Padri War (1821–38) the Padris were defeated, but they left behind a powerful legacy. In the fluid balance of indigenous custom (*adat*) and Islam which constituted the rules and structures of Minangkabau society, the weight of Islam was significantly strengthened.

As the 20th century opened in Indonesia, there was tension between those who thought the key to a better future, especially one free from Dutch rule, lay in finding a way back to an idealised past and those who thought it was to be found in embracing the modernity represented by the Europeans and their science. Offering both answers was Islamic modernism, which sought to purify Islam from medieval obscurantism so as to return to the original revelation of the time of the Prophet, and with that foundation to embrace what modern learning had to offer. Thus, the past was better than the present, and offered the key to the future. A century after the Padri revolution began, Islamic modernism began to take off in Minangkabau, and subsequently it spread across much of Indonesia. Here was a vision of the future as a more pious Islamic society, one that could regain the strengths implicit in the original, pure Islam as God's final revelation to humankind, and thereby resist Christian rule.

Sarekat Islam was founded in 1912 in Java. Its leadership – derived from urban commercial and educated 'lesser *priyayi*' circles – had links with urban, educated modernism more than with the Orthodox (Shafi'i) Islam of the countryside. Its promise of the future evidently depended upon who heard it. For some the organisation, and particularly its most famous leader Tjokoroaminoto, promised the *Ratu Adil* of Javanese messianic tradition. In general, Islam was a label of identity to the followers of Sarekat Islam, who were drawn principally from those who felt disempowered by the existing structure of authority. Their enemies were mainly the Chinese, the governing *priyayi* elite, local people who did not join Sarekat Islam and the Dutch. Their vision was of a more just, less exploitative society, resting upon solidarity among indigenous people who were identifiable by their Islamic identity.

Sarekat Islam tapped the potential of peasant radicalism. In 1913–14 a wave of violent anti-Chinese actions spread across Java. In 1919 a Dutch lower official was murdered at Tolitoli in North Sulawesi, and Sarekat Islam was blamed for the killing. That same year a secret revolutionary cell within the organisation, called Afdeling B (Section B), was discovered. After 1917, many Sarekat Islam members joined the radicals who eventually founded the Indonesian Communist Party in 1920. But ultimately Sarekat Islam was a failure. It disintegrated in the early 1920s and was overtaken by other organisations promising new leaders and new visions of the future. It played little role in the eventual overthrow of Dutch colonial rule, but it exemplified for a time the power of an alliance between the educated urban elite and peasant radicalism.

During the Indonesian revolution, the violent conflicts among Indonesians themselves reflected in large measure conflicting views of the future. There were Indonesians who thought that Dutch rule would be restored; others who thought that the Allies would support the republic; those who believed that armed revolution was the only way to independence; those who imagined that social revolution would bring an end to social ills; others who believed that social revolution diminished the very prospect of independence; those who believed that national unity and a unitary state must be the goals; others who were convinced that local autonomy and a federal state were the keys to the future; those who believed that an Islamic state was the natural answer; those who believed that a secular state was the only answer; and still many others who held different views. These differences were not the stuff of abstract debate. People died because of them, among them Amir Sjarifuddin, Amir Hamzah, Tan Malaka, Musso, many of the aristocratic *uleëbalang* of Aceh and many local village heads, policemen, moneylenders, officials and others. At the transfer of sovereignty in 1949, the most credible view of Indonesia's future saw the nation as independent, secular and unitary, embodying the goal of social justice and based upon freedom of religion.

Even before the Dutch conceded sovereignty to the republic, dissenting views of the future had led to rebellion. The outbreak of the House of Islam (Darul Islam) rebellion in 1948 rested upon a view of the future state as properly based on Islamic law, ruled by *ulama* and led by the charismatic Kartosuwirjo. Darul Islam was linked to the resistance movements of Kahar

Muzakkar in South Sulawesi and that in Aceh. Its aspirations for an Islamic state eventually disintegrated into chronic banditry in West Java. Ultimately it collapsed with the recognition of Aceh as a Special District in 1959, the surrender of the Kahar Muzakkar rebels in the early 1960s, and the capture and execution of Kartosuwirjo in 1962. Again, radical religion-based appeals had, for a time, mobilised mass support.

The history of independent Indonesia since 1949 is more familiar to students of Indonesia, who will readily recognise the pattern of failure by successive elites, along with their programs and their views of the future. In the early 1950s the Dutch-educated secular elite saw Islam as a private matter of faith and the state as a secular and moderate democracy *à la* the Netherlands, led by an educated urban elite who must guide (and needn't much listen to) the uneducated masses. Much of this program consisted of restoring the best aspects of Dutch rule, but with indigenous rather than foreign leadership. This view of the future ended in corruption, maladministration, incompetent government, regional rebellion and the declaration of martial law in 1957.

A new vision of the future was conveyed by Sukarno, the army and the radicals who supported Guided Democracy. Here was the state as the agent of the ongoing revolution, and the people as participants rather than mere followers, thereby attempting to tap the force of mass revolutionary spirit. The future was consciously presented as a return to something more originally and truly Indonesian, in place of the imported ideas of parliamentary democracy. This vision ended in chaos: economic disaster, internecine political violence and ultimately the massive slaughters of 1965–66.

Twenty years after the outbreak of the revolution, by the mid-1960s it was not unknown for Indonesians to look back to the days of Dutch colonial rule with nostalgia. That was *jaman normal*, the normal times. The past was better than the present. Was it the key to the future? At least the leadership of Soeharto's subsequent New Order regime seems to have thought so, for many of its policies echoed the emphases of Dutch rule in the first three decades of the 20th century. The parallels may, however, have been more accidental than intended.

Soeharto's New Order viewed the people as grateful followers again, not as participants in the affairs of government. The state was the servant of the ruling elite, not of the people. And religion was a private matter, not an affair of state or a proper influence in politics. Yet the economic and social developments of the New Order were such that these ideas – tenable in the context of colonial rule – became increasingly untenable in modern Indonesia. As prosperity, literacy and urbanisation increased, more people believed that they had a right to be involved in the life of the nation as participants, that they should contribute to the direction of affairs. Many acquired the idea that the state should serve them and that the elite had no right to pilfer from the nation for their own advantage. And Islam became a public as much as a private issue, as the Islamisation of the society rapidly advanced. In the end, the New Order ended in extravagant corruption, oppression, economic and ecological disaster, and the violence of 1998.

What of Indonesia today? The government of Abdurrahman Wahid began with hope and vision. Here was a liberating view of the future for many Indonesians: a nation free of a corrupt, oppressively hierarchical elite, free of religious sectarianism but nevertheless devoutly Islamic at its heart, and committed to justice and honesty, based on the sovereignty of the people represented through truly elected legislative organs. This was a return to the democracy of the 1950s, but this time Indonesia would get it right. The elections of 1999 were, for the first time since 1955, truly a 'festival of democracy' rather than the largely empty rituals of the Soeharto years. A year later, that government seems surrounded by corruption, of doubtful competence and with too few leaders who, in the dreadful circumstances of contemporary Indonesia, might be able to convert vision into reality. Both members of the middle class and the less privileged are sometimes heard to say that things were better under Soeharto: the past, yet again, is better than the present.

So what are Indonesian views of the future today? It is well to recall the opening caveats of this discussion. There has never been a single Indonesian view of the future and such views as have existed are rarely recorded, so it is presumptuous even to try to describe them. But that is what I was invited to do, so the speculation must proceed. At the risk of losing a sense of the contingent individuality of Indonesian experiences and views, one may speculate about the vision of certain identifiable groups in Indonesia.

The civilian urban middle class has a major role to play in Indonesia's future. Its view of the future must be shaped above all by its sense of uncertainty. The future holds the prospect of generalised chaos, in the midst of which the middle class nevertheless must hope that the institutions of representative democracy will take root and that the urban poor can be restrained, while fearing that neither will be possible. They may suspect that, after all, a reformed, more moral, less grotesquely avaricious and violent version of the New Order would have served them better. But they may reasonably doubt that there are any institutions which could now deliver such an outcome. A major question, given the history of various leadership groups in Indonesia, is whether there are those among the civilian urban middle class who are prepared to embrace radical alternatives. Would some be prepared to return to authoritarian rule or to embrace radical Islamist or other extreme ideologies? It is relevant here that members of this class must recognise that the military failed them in the New Order, that radical Islam failed them in the early years of independence, that the radical left failed them in Guided Democracy, and

that middle-class democracy of the kind familiar in more established democracies has yet to take root in Indonesia. Their dilemma is thus profound.

Greater powers of imagination and speculation are required to guess at the
views of the urban poor of Jakarta, the prime source of cannon fodder for any
violent upheaval. For them there is reasonable certainty that things are not
going to get much better than they are now. They must be suspicious of all
recent forms of authority, especially of the representatives of state authority
such as the police, military and judiciary. History suggests that their views –
resting as they do on the reasonable belief that no conventional leadership has
the capacity to improve their lives greatly – will allow for radical alternatives,
particularly radical Islamic alternatives. There is here, as in many parts of
rural Indonesia, potential for millenarian-like radicalism to be unleashed, with
attendant invulnerability cults and promises of a freer and fairer future, where
the wealth of the Chinese, the elite and indeed the middle class would be
shared among all. A radically egalitarian Islamic order could prove to be the
most attractive vision of the future for the urban poor.

Turning away from the capital city, what vision of the future drives the
dissident elite and their followers in Aceh, the people who lead and support
the Independent Aceh Movement (GAM). That at least is easy to answer: for
the GAM, the vision of the future is one of war against Indonesia until independence is achieved. Then of course the vision supposes that social, economic and political problems can be solved by having the reins of power held
in local hands. The prospects of any solution short of this diminish daily. It
might be worth remembering that the Dutch colonial army which the Acehenese fought for 40 years was commanded by Europeans but consisted
largely of people from other parts of Indonesia. No doubt some Acehenese
feel that their people have been here before, a century ago.

As a final example, what is the vision of the future among the people of
Ambon and Maluku more generally? Violence along religious lines over the
past two years has claimed thousands of lives and displaced tens of thousands
of people, in the nation that once regarded itself as an example to the world
of interreligious tolerance. What can the Christian and Muslim combatants
imagine the future to be? Do they actually intend a confessional version of
'ethnic cleansing' in their region? Since the coexistence of religious and ethnic identities lies at the heart of Indonesianness, do the combatants in Maluku
think their future to be in any sense 'Indonesian' at all? It seems clear that the
Balinese Hindu soldiers of the Indonesian army who have deserted their posts
in Maluku and fled home to escape the cross-fire, as their comrades desert to
join the fighting, do not imagine that the future of Maluku has a role and place
for them: it is not, at least in the immediate future, a part of their Indonesia.
Where the killings of 1965–66 took place, people required a long time to
recover, and perhaps have never really recovered. Even if the religious

violence in Maluku comes to an end, the memories, the hatreds, the social scars will be long-lasting. It may be that Maluku has crossed a watershed that will leave it, like Northern Ireland, with a legacy of intractable confessional hatreds.

A recurrent pattern is evident in this discussion. A leadership group, with its ideology and style of governance, fails to meet the people's aspirations, fails to persuade the people of its legitimacy, rectitude or potency, and fails to perform satisfactorily. So an alternative, countervailing leadership arises and promises to rectify society. Frequently, these alternative leaderships are associated with alternative ideologies that promise to revive some better past as the key to a better future. And these leaderships and ideologies are often religious in character and prepared to embrace violence.

There is much to be hoped for by Indonesians, and by their friends, because there is much to be feared. Territorial disintegration of Indonesia is expected by some observers, and in the case of Aceh it seems possible. But widespread, endemic social violence may be a greater threat, leaving no one on the ground caring much whether the flag which flies over that violence proclaims Indonesian or some other identity. And of course such violence may invite military counter-violence and the overthrow of the nation's floundering democracy, a scenario probably central to the hopes of the Soeharto family and its cronies. Whatever the longer-term outcome, it is safe to predict that Indonesia will long bear the scars of the violence and hardship that attended the final failures of the New Order and the subsequent transition.

The list of leadership groups who have failed the nation, and in doing so discredited the ideas with which they were associated, is discouragingly long and comprehensive. The Dutch discredited federalism by using it as a ploy to prolong their influence, but it seems that Indonesians now feel enough time has passed to try it again. The secular elite of the 1950s discredited the democracy of party politics; the renewed experiment with it in the last two years may again be bringing it into disrepute. Darul Islam discredited the idea of an Islamic state, but there are new partisans of the idea willing to try again for that goal, and just as prepared to use violence as Kartosuwirjo and his followers. Sukarno and the communists discredited radical left politics, and so far there is little sign of that being revived. Soeharto discredited Pancasila by presuming that he, his family and his cronies embodied it, so that the term has disappeared from Indonesian political discourse with remarkable speed. Many Indonesians, and their friends elsewhere in the world, must hope that the cumulative effect of this series of failures and discreditings has not been to discredit the very idea of Indonesia. What lies ahead, it may safely be assumed, is a test of the relative force of Indonesian nationalism and of more parochial identities. The outcome of that contest will shape the future of Indonesia, of which none of us can yet have a clear vision.

20

THE PROSPECTS FOR ISLAM

Greg Barton

Just how important is Islam in modern Indonesian life? For a long time many observers of Indonesian affairs seemed to believe that Islam was of peripheral importance, an impression reinforced by the relative paucity of academic studies of Islam in Indonesia (Hefner 1997a). Compared with most other large Muslim countries, and Indonesia is after all the world's largest Muslim country, Islam in Indonesia has been surprisingly little studied. It was as if there was an unspoken assumption that Islam was on the decline, and that as Indonesia modernised and urbanised it would also secularise. Now, at the start of the 21st century, it is no longer tenable to hold such a view. Not only does Indonesia's most influential Islamic leader, Abdurrahman Wahid, now occupy the presidential palace, he acceded to this position with the backing of a coalition of Islamic parties. This chapter will examine the importance of Islam in contemporary Indonesia and evaluate its prospects for the future.

As far as the international media is concerned, Islam in Indonesia continues to be framed by suspicion and misunderstanding. Indeed, to the extent that the Western media paid any attention to Islam in Indonesia in the past, it was usually to point to its backwardness or to the dangers of fundamentalism – a view recast in academic terms in Samuel Huntington's *The Clash of Civilisations* (Huntington 1996). Hence from the moment the news of his ascension to the Indonesian presidency was flashed around the world, Abdurrahman Wahid was described negatively as 'the frail, half-blind Muslim cleric'. Sadly, in the events of the following year it was easy to find evidence to support Huntington's thesis. Indonesia's troubled society has struggled to come to terms with the consequences of essentially communal conflicts. First Ambon became Indonesia's wartime Beirut, a once cosmopolitan city reduced to warring enclaves, and then the conflict rippled outwards as Christians and Muslims turned on each other throughout Maluku. Even in Jakarta the regular appearance of radical Islamic groups protesting in the streets, or rampaging through nightclubs and bars in the early hours of the morning, has been difficult to ignore.

ISLAM AS AN ANTI-MODERN FORCE

There are at least three separate aspects to recent developments that suggest, at face value, that Islam is not only reasserting its influence in Indonesian society but that it is doing so as an anti-modern force – threatening progress and clashing with the liberal democratic ideals that it was hoped would take root in the post-Soeharto era.

The first phenomenon, not all that recent in origin, is the '*santri*fication' of Indonesian society. Increasing numbers of Indonesians, specifically urban middle-class Indonesians, are becoming more pious and observant in their faith, and more *santri* (originally the name for students of the *pesantren,* or Islamic boarding schools, and now also used to identify any conscientiously observant Muslim). Before the mid-1980s it was considered unfashionable to be seen to be too earnest about one's faith. Some urban professionals were persistent in carrying out the orthodox requirements of their faith – fasting during Ramadan, praying at the five appointed times through the day, being careful to avoid non-*halal* food and so forth – but they represented the exception to the rule. For most public servants or executives in private firms to be seen to be 'too *santri*' was to risk ridicule and perhaps to jeopardise their careers.

That all began to change during the 1980s as the worldwide resurgence of Islam aroused fresh enthusiasm for their faith among increasing numbers of Indonesian Muslims. It was the formation of the Indonesian Association of Muslim Intellectuals (ICMI) in December 1990, however, that marked a sea change (Hefner 1997b). Soeharto not only agreed to the formation of the first significant new Islamic organisation targeted at urban professionals, but also indicated his willingness to sponsor the new association by placing it under the generous care of B.J. Habibie, one of his most trusted ministers. It is difficult to know to what extent ICMI and Soeharto's policy shift contributed to this change and to what extent it was simply the product of it, but there seems no doubting the fact that Soeharto had decided that it was time to woo those whom he had for decades regarded as his enemies. It suddenly became not merely acceptable but desirable to be seen to live a *santri* lifestyle and urban professionals began to pray regularly, to fast, to make the *haj* pilgrimage and to attend Islamic study classes and discussion groups in increasing numbers. Indeed, in 1991 President Soeharto made his first *haj* pilgrimage to Mecca and returned home to Java styling himself Haji Muhammad Soeharto. Soon his ministers and senior bureaucrats were following suit and no one dared suggest that *santri* behaviour was parochial or undesirable.

From the outset ICMI represented a means of reinforcing the dominance of Soeharto over the military and of Golkar over its two rivals, the Indonesian Democratic Party (PDI) and the United Development Party (PPP). There was no question that Islam appeared to have become more 'popular' but the real test of Islam's popular appeal came only after the fall of Soeharto. The 7 June 1999 national elections in Indonesia were the first free and fair elections since 1955 and they provided a reasonably accurate barometer of public sentiment. In any case, Indonesia does not have a strong history of public polling so the elections were the first really objective indication of how deeply the *santri*-fication of society had taken root. Early signs that Islam was going to play an important role came well before the election. Within weeks of Soeharto's res-ignation – well before the Habibie interim government had a chance to process the changes in legislation that would permit the formation of new par-ties – dozens of new parties were being formed, and a great many of these were Islamic parties. By the time the campaign proper had begun the follow-ing year, the newly drafted eligibility requirements resulted in the number of parties able to contest the June polls being culled by 50%. Even so, 21 of the remaining 48 parties could be described as Islamic parties. When they were finally put to the test, these 21 parties gained 38% of the national vote. Com-pared with the 1955 elections this suggests a slight decline (depending on how the comparison is made) but it certainly does not indicate a significant wan-ing of Islam's political significance. Of course confirmation of the importance of the Islamic parties came with the success of the Poros Tengah (Central Axis) alliance of Islamic parties in propelling Abdurrahman Wahid into the presidency.

Second, and rather ironically, Islam has since proven to be of continued importance in Indonesia's political life, not so much because of its initial backing for the Wahid presidency as for its current criticism of the belea-guered president. The harshest critics of the government today are drawn largely from these Islamic parties. In particular, the man who more than any other helped engineer Wahid's victory, National Mandate Party (PAN) leader Amien Rais, quickly became his leading public critic. Even more importantly, behind Amien Rais are powerful figures such as Fuad Bawazier. In 1999 the wealthy Soeharto associate helped finance both the PAN and Wahid's National Awakening Party (PKB) and encouraged Wahid's accession to the presidency. In early 2000 his commitment to the president began to wane, however, and he quickly became a driving force behind the attack upon the Wahid government. This was seen dramatically on the second day of the August 2000 People's Consultative Assembly (MPR) annual session when the Fraksi Reformasi (Reform Faction) replied to President Wahid's opening speech to the assembly with a stinging critique of his first 10 months in government. Bawazier was said to have personally scripted the Reform Faction speech. Most of the responses from the 11 factions were critical, some very strongly so, but the Reform Faction's response stood out for the way in which it harangued the president, laying the blame for every conceivable social ill at his feet in the language of a fiery Friday sermon. Interestingly, Bawazier is also said to have helped finance the militia group known as Laskar Jihad (Aditjondro 2000).

Third, communal unrest and violence has become an unhappy reminder of the importance of Islam in Indonesian society. Not surprisingly, one of the cases most often cited in the foreign media is the conflict in Aceh, the so-called 'Veranda of Mecca'. Those familiar with the Acehenese situation point out that the problems in Aceh primarily have to do with years of trauma and a strong sense of grievance. Given the level of brutality and harassment suffered by the Acehenese throughout the 20th century – and particularly over the past decade – at the hands of governments from Java, this is understandable. It is injustice, not religion, that is the source of Acehenese anger, and in fact many Acehenese *ulama* are involved in efforts to end the conflict. Even so, the coincidental fact that Islam forms an important part of Acehenese identity seems to prey upon the mind of the international media, and reports on the ongoing violence in Aceh rarely fail to mention Islam.

A much more convincing case for the role of religion in furthering conflict can be made for Maluku and Central Sulawesi, where sporadic violence has clearly transmuted into communal conflict (ICG 2000b). The origin of the conflict in Ambon and Poso is difficult to determine, but there seems to be a general consensus that it did not begin as an ethnic or religious conflict. Nonetheless, it is hard to deny that this is what it has become. The fact that in these parts of eastern Indonesia Christians and Muslims live side by side in roughly equal numbers seems to have contributed both to the way in which the violence has developed and to the perception that 'religion' is part of the problem. This perception is accentuated by the manner in which both communities speak about the conflict. In appealing for help in halting the violence, it is understandable that both Christians and Muslims speak about their desire to stop the killing of their co-religionists. What is unfortunate, however, is the way in which this religiously coloured perception of the conflict tends to feed back into the conflict itself.

One of the most dramatic examples of this is the presence in Maluku of more than 3,000 militiamen from the Java-based Laskar Jihad (Aditjondro 2000; Fealy 2001b; Forum Keadilan 2000). Laskar Jihad (Holy War Paramilitary Troops) was formed in January 2000 as a direct response to the violence in Maluku and the plea from Muslims there for help. There are no equivalent Christian groups on its scale but there certainly has been Christian vigilante activity as well. There is much speculation about the role of Laskar Jihad in the violence and about its sponsors, and how it is that some members of this group have come to be armed with military assault rifles. Apprehensions about Laskar Jihad are difficult to dismiss when the group itself speaks of its desire to avenge the spilling of Muslim blood by attacking Christians. There are also worrying signs that it may extend its theatre of operation. Although Laskar Jihad has yet to send large numbers of fighters to Poso in Central Sulawesi, the organisation's leaders have spoken about their desire to do so. There are even some suggestions that they might travel to Irian Jaya to protect Muslim transmigrants against attack by Christian locals.

Needless to say, the entrance of this sort of well-organised militia group into these troubled regions is extremely disturbing. The situation is exacerbated by the suspicion that the government is being undermined in its efforts to rein them in. This is suggested by the fact that Laskar Jihad was able to ship thousands of fighters to Maluku despite the president's command that they not be allowed to depart the port of Surabaya. The fact that earlier in the year Laskar Jihad held a series of demonstrations in the centre of Jakarta – with its 'young warriors' turned out in their distinctive white, Arab-style uniforms and with some wielding swords – reinforces the sense that the government is hamstrung in acting against them. That the police took a long time to close down the Laskar Jihad camp just outside Jakarta compounds these suspicions, especially given claims by the organisation that those training the militiamen include returned fighters from Pakistan and Afghanistan as well as members of the Indonesian military (TNI).

For all this, it might still be possible to dismiss Laskar Jihad as an aberration were it not for the fact that in Indonesia there are literally dozens of Islamist groups involved in low-level harassment and confrontation. Their activities include regular raids on nightclubs and, in November 2000, an attempt to drive out American tourists staying at international hotels in the central Javanese city of Solo. Groups such as Front Hizbullah (Army of God Front) and Front Pembela Islam (Defenders of Islam Front) operate largely unchecked. At this stage these raids have resulted chiefly in damage to property but it is not difficult to see how the situation could rapidly become bloodier. Even before groups such as Laskar Jihad, Front Pembela Islam or Front Hizbullah emerged, other groups such as the Indonesian Committee for World Islamic Solidarity (KISDI) and elements within the Indonesian Islamic Preaching Council (Dewan Dakwah Islamiyah Indonesia) had earned notoriety because of their xenophobic rhetoric.

Given the increased *santri*fication of Indonesian society, at least among urban professionals, the ongoing importance of Islam in politics and the links between radical Islamists and communal violence, is there any way in which a more sanguine view about the prospects for Islam in Indonesia can be sustained? It is easy to appreciate why many non-Muslims in Indonesia, particularly those from eastern Indonesia's troubled provinces, might be feeling apprehensive about the prospects for Islam in Indonesia. After all, more than 85% of the Indonesian population is officially Muslim and the rhetoric of the hard-line Islamists suggests a complete intolerance for minority groups playing a decisive role in national life. Crude attempts at ethnic cleansing in parts of Maluku illustrates clearly why many (Christians in particular) see things as deteriorating. It needs to be remembered, however, that the issues raised above reflect only a fraction of the story. Looking at the larger picture, there are compelling reasons suggesting that Indonesian Islam will remain largely moderate and tolerant – at least as long as political and social stability is maintained. The situation in Maluku is a striking illustration of how bad things can become when governance breaks down and social order is overturned.

ISLAM AS A MODERATING FORCE

One of the grounds for adopting a positive outlook about the role of Islam in Indonesian society is that even the process of Islamisation itself seems to produce results consistent with Indonesian Islam's longstanding reputation for moderation and pluralism. Those urban professionals who have become steadily more *santri*fied seem, for the most part, to have become not just more pious and observant in their faith but also more knowledgeable about it in a way that encourages them towards tolerance and open-mindedness. This is most clearly seen in groups such as Nurcholish Madjid's Islamic educational non-government organisation (NGO), Paramadina, where the process of growth in religious commitment goes hand in hand with a deepening knowledge of Islam that encourages an open-minded approach to the faith and its application in modern society.

However, when young people in particular from a non-*santri* background decide to become more observant in their faith, they often come to see the world and the teachings of their faith in black and white terms. It is also the case that many of the people who join such Islamist groups come from disadvantaged socioeconomic communities and are partly motivated by the desire to find certainty in a seemingly incomprehensible world. Considering the established links in other societies between urban unemployment among young men and radical Islamism, it is significant that these groups have not become more popular. When a group such as Front Pembela Islam holds a rally of 5,000 or 10,000 neatly uniformed demonstrators in the centre of the national capital, it makes for quite a spectacle. But with the greater Jakarta area housing some 20 million people, and with thus literally millions of young men who are either unemployed or underemployed, it is significant that these groups have not been able to attract greater numbers. In cities such as Karachi or Cairo radical Islamist groups have been much more successful. An examination of those new *santri* who continue to be most influential in Indonesian life – the urban middle-class *santri* – indicates that *santri*fication appears a much more benign phenomenon than the antics of the Islamists might suggest. The overwhelming majority seem to have no desire to embrace a more narrow-minded understanding of their religion, although not all are liberal and tolerant.

More objective evidence of this can be seen in the results of the June 1999 general elections. It is true that as many as 38% of the voters voted for Islamic parties, that is to say, parties with either an Islamic platform or at least an Islamic mass base. However, when the figures are evaluated closely, it is clear that very few of these people want to support a narrow Islamist understanding of Islamic politics. A distinction can be made between parties such as the PKB and PAN – which appeal to an Islamic mass base through their connections to Nahdlatul Ulama (NU) and Muhammadiyah respectively, but which also have an expressly pluralistic charter – and other parties such as the Crescent Moon and Star Party (PBB) and the Justice Party (PK), which state explicitly that they are Islamic parties and that their ideology is based on Islam or on the Qur'an and Sunnah. Analysing the figures on the basis of this division, it is clear that the greater portion of the votes was awarded to the pluralistic Islamic parties, which gained 22% of the overall vote, whereas the formalistic parties gained just 16% (Fealy 2001a). The situation in terms of seats won in parliament is a little different. The pluralists with 22% of the vote gained 92 seats, but they were nearly matched by the formalists, who gained as many as 81 seats with their 16% of the vote. (This success had in part to do with the appeal of the more doctrinaire Islamic parties in the Outer Islands and the way in which they were able to coordinate an alliance of small parties and fruitfully pool their results.)

The situation becomes even clearer when a distinction is made between parties that can properly be called Islamist (that is to say, combining a narrow understanding of Islam with a narrow political agenda in which Islam is the central issue) and those parties that have an Islamic orientation but are known to be much more general in their aspirations. For example, parties such as the PPP are known to be essentially conventional multi-issue parties whereas the PBB and PK are much more single-issue Islamic parties. Specifically, the Islamist parties tended to argue strongly in favour of replacing Pancasila with *shari'ah* (Islamic law), or for *shari'ah* to be accorded a place in state legislation. These parties were also inclined to adopt an exclusivist approach to communal relations and to view with suspicion all outside of their orbit, seeing the world very much in terms of 'us and them'. They are therefore susceptible to conspiracy theories about Christians, Jews, Chinese and other non-Muslim groups, as can readily be discerned from publications such as *Sabili* and *Media Dakwah*. Some of Indonesia's most outspoken Islamist figures have backed the PBB, including labour leader Achmad Soemargono and activists Fadli Zon, Farid Prawiranegara and Abdul Qadir Djaelani.

Parties such as the PBB tend to style themselves as modern-day heirs to the legacy of the popular Sukarno-era modernist party Masyumi, which gained almost 21% of the vote in the 1955 elections. It is interesting to note, however, that these parties enjoyed very limited success in the June 1999 polls. Together, the radical Islamist parties were unable to garner 4% of the national vote. Presumably, in the 2004 Indonesian general elections, the majority of these parties will be unable to contest the election because only one of them, the PBB, was able to muster the requisite 2% to qualify as a party for the next election. This means that these small parties will be forced to coalesce into one larger radical Islamist party. Their share of votes gained at the 1999 election is not insignificant and a consolidated Islamist party would be a force to be reckoned with. But given that they gained less than 4% of the national vote, even when they claimed the mantle of Masyumi, it is clear that the overwhelming majority of Indonesians are not drawn to radical Islamist politics. This suggests that Indonesian Islam remains essentially moderate and tolerant and that when people vote for an Islamic party they generally choose not to vote for those with an Islamist agenda.

These election results also indicate that, despite the phenomenon of *santri*fication, the overall increase in the number of people prepared to vote for Islamic parties – an approximation of the proportion of the population that is *santri* – has not changed greatly in the last four decades. Just as importantly, the majority of *santri* Muslims attracted to Islamic parties voted for moderate Islamic parties.

If the generally liberal and tolerant orientation of Indonesian Muslims was solely due to cultural conditioning or national character, whatever that means, it would in itself be grounds for confidence that Islamism of a more radical form is not likely to escalate in Indonesia. As it happens, there are related structural factors that make concrete the vague but nevertheless significant notion of cultural orientation. One is that the overwhelming majority of *santri* in Indonesia are affiliated either with Muhammadiyah or the NU. This is highly significant as both of these organisations are essentially moderate in character (Nakamura 1983; van Bruinessen 1996).

It is true that Islamism is more likely to find support among modernists than among traditionalists. Even though some of the Islamists behind parties such as the PBB have a Muhammadiyah connection (as do right-wing Islamic elements in the PAN such as Amien Rais and A.M. Fatwah), Muhammadiyah itself has steadfastly refused formal relations with any political party. Since the fall of Soeharto, the softly spoken Gadjah Mada University academic and chairman of Muhammadiyah, Syafi'i Maarif, has shown great statesmanship in preserving the moderate and inclusive character of the organisation from political contamination. The great majority of members have been happy to display their faith through charitable endeavours manifested in schools, hospitals, health clinics, orphanages and so forth, and are generally not attracted to more radical understandings or demonstrations of Islam. The election results suggest that a significant number of Muhammadiyah members voted for the PPP, but it is likely that many of these voted out of habit as much as ideological conviction given that the PPP was one of the three old established parties.

The NU, for its part, is no less moderate and tolerant than its modernist counterpart. It is true that the NU *ulama* are a rustic and eccentric group, being drawn primarily from rural stock. And it is also true that a number of NU *ulama* are strongly conservative. The Sufistic core to NU belief and practice, however, means that a degree of flexibility and accommodation permeates its traditionalist core. Progressive intellectual *ulama* such as Abdurrahman Wahid are not typical of NU *ulama*, but nor are they uncommon, particularly among the younger *ulama*. During his 15 years at the head of the NU, Abdurrahman Wahid fostered the social and political development of numerous like-minded intellectuals. Significantly, the most penetrating critiques of Wahid's behaviour and ideas, particularly in the political sphere, have emerged from within the ranks of the NU.

One of the reasons why there are a growing number of liberal intellectuals from *pesantren* background is that, having gained a sound foundation in Arabic and Islamic scholarship in the *pesantren*, many proceed to the more technical faculties of the State Institute for Islamic Studies (IAIN), where they are encouraged to think critically about their faith working from primary sources. For several decades now IAIN Syarif Hidayatullah in Jakarta and IAIN Sunan Kalijaga in Yogyakarta have consistently produced good intellectuals. These institutions have benefited from a series of progressive Ministers for Religious Affairs – in particular Mukti Ali in the 1970s and 1980s and Munawir Sjadzali in the 1980s and 1990s – and key senior academics such as Jakarta's Harun Nasution, Azyumardi Azra and Nurcholish Madjid. Promising young faculty members were encouraged to go to Western institutions to undertake postgraduate studies in the social sciences in order to develop critical thinking skills. As a result, over the past two decades, a culture of critical thinking within the leading IAIN departments has been nurtured carefully and has borne fruit in the form of hundreds of liberal Islamic thinkers now working as officials in the Department of Religious Affairs, as Islamic teachers, preachers and *ulama*, as university academics, as NGO activists and as journalists (Barton 1994, 1997a).

Ironically, in many ways the authoritarian nature of the Soeharto regime meant that liberal Islam was protected through the 1970s and 1980s from forces that might otherwise have retarded it, as has been the case in countries like Egypt, Pakistan and Malaysia. The result was that liberal Islam in Indonesia has developed into a broadly based movement that today is able to hold its own. This means that young people searching for insight into Islam's engagement with the modern world have plentiful material to draw upon from within their own society in the form of the writings and public presentations of liberal intellectuals. This suggests that the majority of *santri* Muslims in Indonesia are committed to a tolerant and moderate understanding of their faith, with most finding radical Islamism unappealing. A small but significant minority have embraced a sophisticated and thoughtful understanding of Islam that is in every respect both progressive and liberal (Barton 1995, 1997b).

RADICAL ISLAM

Is there any reason, then, to be anxious about the potential for radical Islamism to negatively influence political developments or for communal violence to break out on a broader scale across the troubled archipelago? The short answer is yes. This is not to say that radical Islamism is about to enjoy a sudden spurt of popularity in Indonesia, but rather to acknowledge the dangers latent in what is presently a minority movement representing a very outspoken and radicalised section of society. The first reason to be concerned is that the doctrines of the radical Islamists are indeed dangerous. This is clearly seen in the formation of Laskar Jihad with a specific goal of engaging in combat against the Christians in Maluku. Even if it is ultimately found that Laskar Jihad has not played a decisive role in furthering the violence in Maluku, it is nevertheless a matter for concern that such a group has trained warriors for a 'holy war' against another community within its own society. A more insidious, and perhaps ultimately more dangerous, phenomenon is the willingness of political leaders at an elite level to buy into intercommunal disputes in such a way that they effectively condone and encourage sectarian violence. Perhaps some of the leaders who engage in this sort of provocation do not intend to worsen the conflict. Whatever their intentions, however, they are playing with fire.

What is behind the appeal of radical Islamism? First, it is clear that there are some Islamist activists who are genuine idealists and deeply convinced of the truth of their doctrine. It is likely that in time many of these people, who are mostly aged in their twenties and early thirties, will grow out of these ideas as they mature. Some of the youthful romantics involved in radical Islamism, however, are not so much drawn to the Islamic ideology of these groups as much as they are to the drama of protest itself. It is typical of such romantic activists that the majority do not have a carefully considered position; they are simply stricken by the realisation that the world is not as they believe it should be and are seeking to strike out against something or someone. Consequently, they are easily persuaded to target certain demonised enemies who are said to be the source of society's woes. In the current circumstances of regime change in Indonesia, it is clear that many of the people manipulating Islamist sentiment are doing so in order to protect themselves and their interests from the demands of reform.

The conflict in Ambon, Halmahera and Central Sulawesi is significant because it does not appear to have been started by religious activism on any side, and nor does it appear to have begun with religious or ethnic violence. Loosely attributed, the violence in these areas is probably the product of social tensions caused by socioeconomic cleavages that are partly the product of large-scale migrations during the Soeharto era and partly the result of the current economic crisis. What is significant and of concern about this conflict is the way it has quickly inflamed intercommunal relations. The violence that broke out in Poso in Central Sulawesi in late 1998, for example, was followed by more violence in April 2000 and then a third wave in May 2000. This third wave was apparently driven by Christians seeking revenge on Muslims whom they accused of having burned down their homes and villages. Today the future of the region remains uncertain, partly because of the cyclical nature of the violence exhibited. It will take a lot of work before the refugees return home and begin to forge a stable and harmonious society again. This is a reminder of just how vulnerable Indonesian society is at the moment and it is for this reason that any signs of organised sectarianism, such as radical Islamism, need to be taken very seriously.

THE FUTURE OF ISLAM

So what is the future of Islam in Indonesia? This chapter has primarily discussed radical Islamism and questioned whether we should be concerned about its appearance in Indonesia and its contribution to communal violence. It would have been just as easy to explain why we should feel optimistic and positive about the contribution made by Islam throughout the history of independent Indonesia. Islam has enormous potential to contribute positively to the building of a democratic society in Indonesia. This is one of the reasons why it is so important that the Wahid government should succeed. Abdurrahman Wahid's failings as a manager are well known and are frequently discussed. The difficult circumstances of regime change in which he finds himself are much less well understood and are certainly less frequently discussed. While the performance of his government remains under a cloud, there is no doubting that the liberal democratic ideals he stands for do have the potential to make an enormous contribution to Indonesian society. His personal commitment to a humanitarian, negotiated, political settlement of the Aceh and Papua issues, for example, represents a slim ray of hope. Significantly, it is clear that Islam has played an important role in the development of his liberal ideals (Barton 1996; Ramage 1995).

The success or failure of Wahid's government depends upon the president's recovery of a modicum of political capital in the Indonesian parliament as well as his rebuilding of social capital within Indonesian society. This in turn depends upon his alliance with Megawati Sukarnoputri and her Indonesian Democratic Party of Struggle (PDI-P). There remains good reason to believe that this alliance can work, even though it has been severely stressed by Wahid's seemingly cavalier approach to the relationship and Megawati's sense of betrayal by her old friend. One of the underlying reasons why this relationship is viable is that there exists a shared cultural orientation between traditionalists in the PKB and non-*santri* Muslims and non-Muslims in the PDI-P together with liberal modernist *santri* outside of these two parties. If this secular–moderate alliance can be consolidated, there will exist a good foundation for ensuring that Indonesian politics does not succumb to the forces working to drive it in the direction of communalism and sectarianism. At the same time, however, the experiences of eastern Indonesia remind us of how vulnerable Indonesian society currently is and how easily it can be tipped over the edge. Now is not the time to take anything for granted.

21

AFTER THE BANS: MODELLING INDONESIAN COMMUNICATIONS FOR THE FUTURE

Philip Kitley*

The mediascape in post-New Order Indonesia has changed dramatically. Under the unexpectedly liberal approach of Information Minister Muhammed Yunus Yosfiah, the Department of Information cancelled the requirement for press publication permits and issued more than 1,200 new licences. As many as 912 new radio licences and five new television broadcast licences have been issued (Masindo 2000, p. xiii). Whereas for years there was only one officially sanctioned professional association for journalists, Persatuan Wartawan Indonesia (PWI), there are now 24 (Suranto, Setiawan and Ginanjar 1999, pp. 24–5). Parliament (DPR) enacted a new Press Law in September 1999 that guaranteed freedom of the press (articles 2 and 4). The Abdurrahman Wahid government dissolved the former media regulatory authority, the Department of Information (*Far Eastern Economic Review*, 11 November 1999), and has put the state radio and television broadcasters Radio Republik Indonesia (RRI) and Televisi Republik Indonesia (TVRI) on notice that they should become self-funding within two years (*Jakarta Post*, 27 November 1999).

What struck me most forcibly in looking back over many years of reporting and scholarly analysis of the media in Indonesia was the recurring story of bans and repression of the media. My brief in this chapter is both to look back at critical events and to assess future developments in the Indonesian media. My discussion of the model and theoretical assumptions that guided media development and the political culture of media in the New Order will present a synoptic view which interprets what has gone on as the outcome of particular practices of governmentality. It will show that the repressive action against the media produced a whole range of practices which, taken together, have – ironically – prepared Indonesian audiences, readers and producers for a new and different alignment of power relations that are likely to be increasingly supportive of civil society. My focus will largely be confined to the press and television.

A BRIEF SURVEY OF MEDIA BANS IN INDONESIA

Media bans can be traced back to colonial bans on Malay and Chinese-Malay language newspapers in the 1930s (Hill 1994, p. 26). During the Japanese occupation Dutch radio stations were abolished, the Dutch language was banned on air and Dutch personnel in charge of the stations were either murdered or thrown out of their jobs, to be replaced by Indonesian operators and broadcasters (Wild 1991, p. 37). In the 1950s the politically partisan press suffered from more or less continuous harassment and bans. In October 1965, 75 papers were banned for their assumed links to the Indonesian Communist Party and its allies (Hill 1994, p. 34). Following the Malari demonstrations in 1974, 12 dailies were banned, and four years later, following campus riots, seven dailies and an equal number of student papers were banned. In the 1980s a wide range of high-quality papers and magazines were banned for content that conflicted with the Pancasila system. The publisher Kompas-Gramedia banned the very successful weekly, *Monitor*, to appease community sentiment, and *Monitor's* editor, Arswendo Atmowiloto, was gaoled for offending against conservative religious sentiment. In 1994, Information Minister Harmoko banned the major weeklies *Editor* and *Tempo* and the highly critical tabloid *DeTIK* – an action he was forced to defend in court and on appeal.

In the case of television, the bans have been fewer and have never threatened the enterprises themselves, which is understandable given that TVRI[1] is a state broadcaster, and that the licencees for the commercial television stations were Soeharto family or friends (Kitley 2000, p. 230). But even so, from time to time news editors such as Khrys Kelana of Rajawali Citra Televisi Indonesia (RCTI) have been caught up in the insidious *budaya telepon* ('telephone culture' of threatening phone calls) for screening images that were 'unnecessarily graphic' (Kitley 2000, p. 262). Most famously, Wimar Witoelar's talk show 'Perspektif' was taken off the air by station management at Surya Citra Televisi (SCTV),[2] Surabaya.

Advertising on TVRI was banned in 1980, when Acting Information Minister Sudharmono advised the president that the service would be better able to represent national development priorities without commercial interference (Kitley 2000, pp. 63–72). G.M. Sudarta's cartoon in *Kompas* (4 April 1981) suggested that this ban was especially cruel, as in banning commercials the minister was banning the most entertaining programs on TVRI! The desire to preserve intact a *national* system of broadcasting informed a ban on foreign investment in the media enforced by Information Minister Harmoko (Hill 1994, p. 152). Surprisingly, as recently as 3 August 2000, President Abdurrahman Wahid continued the repressive tradition when he decreed that foreign capital would not be permitted in broadcast television and radio, cable television, print or multimedia services (*Suara Pembaruan*, 5 August 2000). And finally, foreign languages were banned on television, the 1997 Broadcasting Law introducing a bizarre regime of dubbing all non-English dialogue into English before subtitling in Indonesian.

Then there were the bans that never happened, because editors, owners, journalists and broadcasters took care that they did not write or say things that might lead to a ban, or because policy prevented them from doing what their professional instincts urged them to do. This was a process of self-censorship, of giving in to Miss SARA's[3] insistent nagging and to other menacing voices over the telephone in a practice that became so widespread that *budaya telepon* came to be understood as a distinctive feature of the media in Indonesia. This regime of threat and intimidation was utilised without hesitation against those media institutions which the government perceived to threaten its power and reputation.

Indonesia has experienced a history of direct repression of the media and its people on the grounds that the bans helped to maintain national law and order and Indonesian cultural values and identity. The foundation of this repression was a particular model and theory of communications.

COMMUNICATIONS THEORY IN NEW ORDER INDONESIA

The communications model that informed media development after 1945 was associated with American sociological ideas about the integrative effects of communications in society and information theory as exemplified by the Shannon and Weaver model (1949), which understood communication as a linear transfer of messages between senders and receivers. Evidence for the influence of this theoretical paradigm in Indonesia, especially in the Sukarno period, is not readily available, as media practitioners are not usually explicit about their normative foundations. Further, the experience of the late colonial period and the Japanese occupation also had an important influence on media practices, journalists and broadcasters (Maladi, personal interview, 30 January 1992). The Japanese introduced to Indonesian radio broadcasters a practical understanding of the persuasive and integrative power of (Indonesian) language, and the power of simple, direct propaganda messages (Wild 1987, 1991). Even so, under the watchful eyes of their Japanese instructors, broadcasters soon learnt the art of inserting anti-Japanese messages and comments into their vernacular broadcasts.

Evidence of the transmission model that informed media practices in post-war Indonesia is explicit in Sukarno's description of the press as a 'revolutionary tool' (Hill 1994, p. 62). Sukarno used this phrase again when he authorised the establishment of television, which he saw as a 'tool for nation building, revolution, and the formation of Indonesian socialist humanity' (Presiden Republik Indonesia 1963). This functionalist 'message orientation' of the media was further exemplified in Decree No. 29 of March 1965 that all newspapers and periodicals had to be affiliated with political parties, mass organisations or functional groups (Minister for Information 1965).

In Soeharto's state addresses and in official sources such as the five-year plans, there is a shift away from the revolutionary focus of the Sukarno years to a discourse of 'development communications'. Development media theory is associated with American ideas of social transformation and development through economic growth, and understands the role of the media as fostering a sense of national integration and the inculcation of values supportive of industrialisation and modernisation (McQuail 1994, p. 131).[4]

This passage from the Second Five-year Development Plan provides an explicit statement of the development communications approach.

> The objective of information policies is to create a climate which will instil in the community understanding of the objectives of national development generally and of specific development programs. This is done through information and communication to increase their consciousness of the need to participate in achieving the targets of development programs (Republik Indonesia 1974/75, pp. 28–9).

A similar perspective was presented by Boediardjo, Minister for Information from 1968 to 1973, on the occasion of TVRI's 10th anniversary. He wrote that

> TVRI worked with a philosophy of information which was the foundation of every government information activity, namely to stimulate all the potential the community possessed to participate in the operation of each national program and activity by motivating the community through education and persuasion (Direktorat Televisi 1972, p. 17).

The writings and research projects of scholars and researchers of Indonesian communications also provide insights into the theoretical foundations of media and information programs. Communications scholars Astrid Susanto (1978) and Alfian (1979) cite approvingly the development and communications approach associated with pioneering American theorist Wilbur Schramm in work from the 1970s. Alfian collaborated with Godwin Chu and Wilbur Schramm in a major longitudinal study of the impact of satellite television on rural audiences (Alfian and Chu 1981; Chu, Alfian and Schramm 1991).

Wonohito (1977) argued for an indigenous, distinctively Indonesian theory of the press in his widely used text *Teknik Jurnalistik: Sistem Pers Pancasila* [Journalistic Technique: The Pancasila Press System]. TVRI staff member J.B. Wahyudi published a text with a similar focus titled *Jurnalistik Televisi: Tentang dan Sekitar Siaran Berita TVRI* [Television Journalism: Commentary on TVRI's News Broadcasts] in which he argues that TVRI worked within the guideline of a 'free and responsible press' in its news reporting (Wahyudi 1985, p. 17). TVRI staff member Sumita Tobing's doctoral thesis also focused on the development journalism paradigm, and concluded that TVRI news bulletins in 1990 were based on the development communications paradigm (Tobing 1991).

The view that communications planning was an important aspect not just of development but of cultural relations as a whole was supported by Ali Moertopo, Minister for Information from 1978 to 1983 and a key New Order strategist (Ramage 1995, p. 28). He argued that Indonesian society was characterised by three modes of thought or 'mental outlooks' – the peasant, the *priyayi* (civil servant) and the transitionalist – that hindered development planning. With this characterisation Moertopo targeted the objectified Indonesian population with well-planned information programs designed to produce subjects who wanted to change their regressive outlooks and contribute to the success of development.

By the mid-1980s, however, the focus on the role of the media as motivating the mass audience for development had shifted to an ideological emphasis on the inculcation of Pancasila values. Soeharto's state addresses from 1984 to 1994 and the Fourth Five-year Plan provide evidence of an ideological makeover of the media function: 'development communications' was mentioned less frequently and the 'Pancasila press' became the preferred term for describing the press and more generally the Pancasila media project in Indonesia.

Official sources pay more attention to the press than to electronic media.[5] This is understandable in the sense that RRI and TVRI were government broadcasters and could be relied upon to fulfil their designated development roles. But the press belonged to the private sector, and had to be won over to support the government's priorities. The press was urged/coopted to become the government's 'partner in development'. Arguably the repetition of this message, in the president's state addresses, operated as a means of subtle coercion and surveillance. This discourse was supported by other strategies of surveillance, such as the corporatisation of professional journalists into one officially recognised body and the requirement that all television and radio stations broadcast official news bulletins on the hour simultaneously across Indonesia. State authorities extended their communications infrastructure to cover the national space, as another mechanism for extending the disciplining and normalising power of the state's communication project. The bans cata-logued earlier, however, are evidence that the hegemonic policy had to be strengthened by more direct, repressive force on a regular basis, a clear sign of the ideological space separating media producers and publishers from the idealised role constructed for them by state authorities.

There is no doubt, then, that the media function in Indonesia has been shaped by development communications theory. But I want to emphasise that this paradigm rests on another, more fundamental, assumption that has been productive of the power relations surrounding the media in the New Order period. This is the assumption that, given the idea of linear transmission of messages, the media is powerful in producing effects, and that the media func-tion therefore needs control and responsibility in its use. It is this assumption, and not the adoption of development communications theory, that has largely shaped discourse on the media in New Order Indonesia.

NEW ORDER MEDIA DISCOURSES

In one sense the bans catalogued in the introduction above were not surpris-ing: the New Order was an authoritarian regime that was quick to eliminate any perceived challenges to its political and cultural authority. But to under-stand the bans as simply repressive is wrong, for it overlooks the political and cultural assumptions about the media that informed development in the Indonesian mediascape. Indeed the history of the media during the New Order can be understood as a discursive project that facilitated the penetration of social and self-disciplinary regimes into the domain of public, but more importantly *private*, life in Indonesia.

Official New Order discourse represented Indonesia and its people as a nation/family, an integrated whole where the government was understood as the head of the family and held a natural right to direct national development and establish a culture of modernisation and development (Reeve 1985; Ram-age 1995). At the heart of the regime's sensitivity about the media is a mono-logical imagining of the union and unity (*persatuan dan kesatuan*) of Indonesia. Because the media was theorised as a powerful instrumentality of publicity, it was precisely the site where the discourse of integralism, of the organic state, was most vulnerable to alternative, counter-discourses of national identity. And so over time New Order media discourse became increasingly preoccupied with Pancasila values and a concern with what it was proper to say about the nation/family.

The shift away from the discourse of development communications to the discourse of the Pancasila media project in the early 1980s can also be under-stood as anti-West, or better, post-colonial, in its emphasis on indigenous values. The metaphor of the 'watchdog press' in Western theory was turned against it when the former Director General of Press and Graphics said 'ours is not a watchdog press in the Western fashion. A watchdog must stand guard outside the house. We prefer to keep our press inside along with the rest of the family' (Romano 1999, p. 58). The Pancasila press is represented as erasing differences, or the appearance of differences, between sections of society. The nine o'clock World News bulletin on TVRI ('DUNIA dalam Berita') provides another illustration of the way the ritualised construction of a discourse of inside/outside served the state's hegemonic cultural project. Each night World News circulated the 'bad news' that the Pancasila model considered so destructive of social harmony. The Late News then returned viewers to the supposed calm of domestic affairs, folding them back into a social order in which everyone has a clearly defined place, and where the state's key role is the betterment of the people's welfare.

The Pancasila media project preserved the transformation of the population as a key goal, but reimagined the relationship between the state and population as a paternalistic, altruistic relationship of a parent doing what was best for a family member. The Pancasila model papers over the government's urge to control and direct the population by dismantling the target, erasing the distinction between itself and the wider population and, in that way, removing the very possibility of a divisive us/them relationship with the national population. The inclusiveness of the discourse makes alternative discourses and resistance unnatural because they challenge the idea of an inclusive family to which all speakers belong.

THE PRODUCTIVITY OF NEW ORDER MEDIA DISCOURSE

The apparatus of the New Order Pancasila media project was productive of a wide range of strategies that operated to discipline media practitioners and normalise media practices. Examples included the lack of a regulatory apparatus (especially for electronic media), the weak development of journalism, film and television and communication studies, the comparatively stronger development of development communication studies (*komunikasi pertanian*, or 'rural communications'),[6] self-censorship and compliance with official directives (Makarim 1978; Article 19 1996), and the corporatisation of the journalism profession. The prohibition on news production meant that radio journalism had little scope to develop (Kathleen Reen, personal interview, 15 June 1999). In the television field, newly established stations were considered to be part of the TVRI team rather than independent enterprises (Kitley 2000, p. 239). The 80,000 discussion groups (*kelompencapir*) established by the Department of Information in rural villages assisted media-deficient rural communities to process government information. As George Quinn (1996, p. 1) argues, these groups were 'important instruments in a strategy to manage public debate and sustain government authority'. The Department of Information's final draft for the 1997 Broadcasting Law showed that the department had paid too much attention to its cultural role and had not kept up with contemporary communications developments. The draft did not mention the globalised communications environment, and the possibility of digital convergence of services was not even considered (Kitley 1999). In this regard, the cultural politics of the media has inhibited the development of state-of-the-art facilities in Indonesia, putting it far behind neighbouring Malaysia and Singapore, which have highly developed convergence systems and legislation in place.

THE MEDIA AND NATIONAL UNITY/COMMUNITY

One of the most striking aspects of the Indonesian mediascape is the contradictory significance of the idea of the nation in the development of different media. Because the population of Indonesia was seen as a *national* family, it became a long-term imperative to deliver media services throughout the country. The plans for extension of facilities imagines the communities on the margins and in far-flung places not as a frontier inhabited by strangers, but as a part of the national family out of reach, waiting to be written back into the national cultural space. This was especially true of electronic broadcasting, and was best exemplified in the dramatic launch of the satellite Palapa which, in one bold stroke, promised through its information programs to capture in the net of state power and surveillance even the most distant segments of the national family (Thomas 1994, p. 111). Government programs that distributed newspapers and television sets to rural villages and the requirement that the media use the national language can be understood in the same way as the imperative for covering the national space. The language policy works to suppress regional and ethnic differences, giving more emphasis to *tunggal* (unity) rather than the idea of diversity in the national motto *Bhinneka Tunggal Ika* ('Unity in Diversity').

However, an ambivalence developed about the access the national family should have to media services. For as long as the state could dominate the channels, it promoted the idea of national communications and normalising power. But when it could not, it fell back on discourses of diversity and regional differences. For fear of circulating conflicting messages from Jakarta in the provinces, for a long time state authorities did not permit the print media to take advantage of long-distance printing technologies that would extend the reach of national dailies, but preferred to promote the regional press (Hill 1994, p. 120). Commercial considerations reinforced the pattern, as newspapers, and later television stations, saw few opportunities for expansion beyond major cities.

Commercial radio was always designated by state authorities as a 'local medium', which ironically has extended its life and significance in the post-Soeharto period. New Order policy required Indonesia's 700 commercial radio stations to apply for annual frequency permits, and restricted medium-wave commercial radio transmitters to just 500 watts (PPPI 1997/98, p. 64). The low power limited broadcast range and ensured that no one station would dominate in too wide an area (McDaniel 1994, p. 237). A similar desire to inhibit the national development of commercial television is evident in a series of ministerial decrees that originally imagined commercial television as a dispersed regional system (Kitley 2000, pp. 224–5). By 1994, however, all television operators were located in Jakarta and broadcasting to a national audience.

The emphatic mapping of the government media over the national territory was challenged in the early 1980s when Indonesian viewers in regions bordering on Malaysia began to enjoy Malaysia's first commercial channel, TV3. The flow of content from neighbouring countries brought Indonesian audiences face to face with alternative visions beyond the borders, which authorities had limited capacity to resist. The introduction of commercial television in this context in 1990 can be understood first as a pre-emptive strategy to domesticate the global, in the sense of bringing global television services within the management of local service providers, and second, in terms of taming global content by adapting it to an essentialised construct of Indonesian culture. This history of tightening up, letting go and compromising in the face of intrusive technologies bears out Nicholas Thomas's argument that the business of sustaining the kind of media project and governmentality I have described is 'often ... like repairing an old car: the cost and energy absorbed into surgery is never reflected in results ... and sooner or later the whole effort has to be abandoned' (Thomas 1994, p. 106).

COUNTER-DISCOURSES AND PRACTICES

The power relations created by New Order media discourses are also relations of resistance. I have in mind the widespread practice of writing, speaking and reading between the lines as a way of working within the guidelines of the sanctioned regime of truth (Heryanto, quoted in Kitley 2000, p. 227). There are a host of other modes of creative non-compliance, such as radio stations' reporting of news by picking up topics published in newspapers as a way of getting round the restriction on producing their own news bulletins (Saiful Azwar, Radio Trijaya, personal interview, 7 July 1999). Also banned from producing news, commercial television stations described their news broad-casts as current affairs or soft news, and regularly out-rated TVRI bulletins. When the popular chat show host Wimar Witoelar lost his program 'Perspek-tif' from SCTV, because station management was concerned about what Wimar's guest Mochtar Lubis might say on air, he took the show on the road and onto radio, opening up 'Perspektif' to audiences in town halls and other public venues (Wimar Witoelar, personal interview, 18 June 1999). His strat-egy created an interview road show, challenging the mass media's power to normalise how media events should be produced, managed and located.

The larger press companies that had suffered from bans chose to armour-plate their existence by diversifying across a whole range of non-core busi-ness activities (Sen and Hill 2000, pp. 57–8). Their financial diversity was both a protection against and a strategy for resisting the normalising practices of official policy. Audiences were equally creative. Tired of the insistent developmentalism and didactic quality of development communications pro-gramming, they read official programs against the grain (Kitley 2000, Ch. 5) and developed a great interest in new media experiences. Their enthusiasm for alternative media experiences involved consumption tactics such as media piracy, underground video, spillover broadcasts from Malaysia and, for the better-off, satellite television and sophisticated use of the internet.

Many journalists overtly resisted the norms of the Pancasila media system by not joining the official journalists' association, which they were required by law to join. Romano reported that only about 60% of journalists were members of the PWI, and even those who were believed that the organisation regulated journalists on behalf of the state and favoured state interests in cases where the interests of the two conflicted (Romano 1999, p. 166). Two-thirds of the 65 journalists Romano surveyed in 1996–98 argued that the 'Pancasila press' was a form of ideological control (pp. 64–5). One of the most direct strategies of resistance to the hegemony of the Pancasila project was the establishment of the non-official, independent journalists' association Aliansi Jurnalis Independen (AJI) in opposition to the PWI following the banning of *Tempo*, *DeTik* and *Editor* in 1994 (AJI 1995). The appearance of the banned *Tempo* on the Web in March 1996 as *Tempo Interaktif,* and the circulation of *Tempo Interaktif* 'books' for those who were not online, was testament to the creative exploitation of gaps in legislative control (Ridwan 1997).

THE LIMITS OF NEW ORDER MEDIA STRATEGY

The history of repression of the media and the widespread dissatisfaction with TVRI and RRI programming are evidence of a general failure of New Order media strategies (Siregar 1995, p. 107; Wardhana 1997, p. 81; Mulyana 1997,

p. 31). Given the intense ideological investment in the development of a complex system of information services designed to support national development and cultural projects, the question of why the project failed to dominate is pressing. After all, the idea of development communications is not obnoxious and has obvious utility in developing countries. The Pancasila media project failed because of resistances articulated across both production and consumption practices. First, commercial media producers remained unconvinced by the model, and while appreciating and working within its normalising disciplines, they reserved the right to write against the dominant paradigm. Their reservations about being a 'partner of government' (Soeharto 1989, p. 134) and their daily interaction with wire services and global programming put them in touch with an ever-present counter-discourse to the stultifying earnestness and evasions of the Pancasila model. Second, the model paid insufficient attention to the audience and failed to recognise the inevitability that the audience would read (in the general sense) media messages from its own historical, ethnic, cultural and values perspective (de Certeau 1998).

PROSPECTS

This analysis has tied the shape of the media scene to a particular model of communications, and to related ideas and discourses of power over the New Order period. Will things be different from now on in Indonesia's mediascape? The initial signs of change reported above look promising. But this effulgence is like the merry antics of a kinked hose that, untwisted, showers everything in range. The media function in Indonesia needs to be rethought in terms of two powerful constructs: a model of communications that gives far more attention and importance to audiences in the interpretation of media significations; and the idea of the public sphere, which, as John Keane (1998, pp. 169–70) puts it, 'has the effect of desacralising power relationships'.

These constructs need legislative support in which prime consideration is given to the idea of the citizen/subject as a discerning, critical media consumer/user who has the right to access, use and disseminate information; a competitive industry protected from market dominance; and a media environment where the public and industry players meet together to develop and change media policy on such matters as content, technical standards and access to services. These matters may best be managed through self-regulatory processes that interact with a regulatory authority set up at arm's length from government. Malaysia's recent Communications and Multimedia Act 1998 may provide a useful reference point.

Indonesian Press Law No. 40 of 1999 is a progressive piece of legislation and should assist the press in performing the role envisaged above. The Press

Council should also help in resolving disputes at arm's length from government. There is a need, however, to strengthen the concept of the public's 'right to know', and the Press Council is addressing this issue. Broadcasting Law No. 24 of 1997 has not been repealed and is the subject of current debate in the DPR. A 'draft initiative' proposed by 26 members of parliament in June 1999 is before the house and seeks to establish similar rights of access, expression of opinion and dissemination of information through broadcast media as provided for in Press Law No. 40. There is much of merit in the bill, but its emphasis on issues of freedom of the media have meant that insufficient attention has been given to pressing developments in electronic communications and to the changing character of the information and communications industry.

Despite the fact that it could be as influential as Palapa, the convergence of digital technologies is given insufficient attention, and the implications of convergence across telephony, interactive PCs, the print media, and radio and non-broadcast television services (video, cable, satellite and data services) are not considered. The incorporation of Indonesian broadcasting in a transnational or global ecology is also left out of consideration. I fear that the proposed legislation will quickly be overtaken by industry developments, as it is not technology-neutral and is cast in terms of specific technologies and legacies from an outdated, segmented industry approach.

CONCLUSION

As the semiotician Umberto Eco writes, all mass communication is 'aberrantly' decoded, not in line with the intentions of the producer (cited in Hartley 1999, p. 179). This means that the media can be taken far less seriously than it has been. Media diversity will be productive, censorship needs to be tapered off, and the system needs to open itself up to more participatory and interactive practices.

Rethinking the relations between media production and audiences will produce a different media studies curriculum in which the emphasis shifts from what *effects* the media has on audiences to how audiences use and interact with media, which is understood as central to cultural and political processes (Hartley 1999). The counter-imaginary, which I link to an alternative understanding of communication processes and an invigorated public sphere, will be productive of a different web of power relations. Indeed, new interpretative communities are developing, facilitated by the media, in the face of many authoritarian regimes around the world (Eickelman and Anderson 1999).

If the public broadcaster TVRI gives greater autonomy to regional stations in a 'back to the future' reorganisation,[7] regional television may come into its own, not because it delivers *regional content* (it may not), but because it may diversify and multiply opportunities for people in a particular region to interact with the media. As I see it, the old geography of local–regional–national spaces and allegiances is probably unsuited to the growth of the public sphere in Indonesia in a globalising world. Any signs that commercial television might join TVRI are not promising, however: the new stations are being built in Jakarta, not the provinces.

And finally, freedom of the press needs to be understood broadly as a practical right to access information, to ask questions and to publicise complex and confronting issues. It is not just freedom from being banned – that is like describing being well as not being sick. As for media consumers, they look forward to making their own choices, not having them made for them. The prescriptive mode of medicine assumes that patients have little idea or capacity to nurture their own health. But the years of bans against courageous reporters and publishers and the clever tactics of worldly consumers in Indonesia have shown that audiences and many practitioners have a very clear idea of what is good for them.

NOTES

*   Thanks to Robert Dixon and Angela Romano for their helpful comments on an earlier draft of this chapter, and to John Milne and Kirk Coningham who assisted me with sources.
1   TVRI, the state television service, was established in 1962.
2   RCTI and SCTV were Indonesia's first free-to-air commercial television licencees. They came on air on 24 August 1990.
3   The acronym stands for *menghasut, insinuasi, sensasi, spekulasi* (MISS) and *suku, agama, ras* and *aliran* (SARA), and refers 'to anything deemed seditious, insinuating, sensational, speculative or likely to antagonise ethnic, religious, racial or class tensions' (Hill 1994, p. 45).
4   See Anderson (1982) for insights into ideas on modernisation in American research on Indonesia in the 1950s to 1970s.
5   Soeharto discussed the role of the press in 12 out of 22 state addresses (*pidato kenegaraan*) over the period 1967–88. The mass media was mentioned in two speeches and radio and television were mentioned in five.
6   See Table A21.1, which lists communications, journalism and media studies programs in Indonesian universities. Film and television is taught at only two institutions (PDAT 1997).
7   Before 1965, TVRI's provincial stations were given considerable autonomy. Emergency regulations following the 1965 attempted coup, and later Palapa, put paid to a decentralised television system.

APPENDIX

TABLE A21.1 Tertiary Education Courses in Communications, Agricultural Extension Communications, Journalism, Film and Television, 1997

Program	Faculty	Universities Offering Program (no.)
Communications (*ilmu komunikasi*)	Sociology/Politics (14)	14
Communications in agricultural extension (*penyuluhan dan komunikasi pertanian*)	Agriculture (15)	15
Business communications	Communications (1)	1
Journalism (*ilmu jurnalistik*)	Communications (4); Sociology/Politics (2)	6
Film, television	Film and Television (2)	2

Source: PDAT (1997).

22

GENDER RELATIONS IN INDONESIA: WHAT WOMEN WANT

Susan Blackburn

Indonesia, in common with most Southeast Asian countries, has long been regarded as according a relatively high status to its women. For centuries observers have commented on the prominent role of women in the economy, the equality conferred by the bilateral kinship system found in much of the archipelago, and other indicators of status.[1] Measuring the status of women is a specialised and controversial field, and it gives us little feel for how women themselves consider their position compares with that of men. My aim in this chapter is to present what Indonesian women have been saying about their wants and needs over the last century, how those voices have been changing and where the trends might be heading. The purpose is to give an insight into the status of Indonesian women from the point of view of the subjects rather than the observers.

Before embarking on an analysis of women's views, it is worth noting that, at the end of the 20th century, Indonesia did not rank highly on international measurements of gender relations. On paper its record looks quite impressive. Since independence its governments have legislated for equal rights for women and ratified relevant international conventions, notably the Convention for the Elimination of All Forms of Discrimination against Women (CEDAW). In practice Indonesia's performance has been mediocre. The United Nations Development Program (UNDP) produces a gender-related development index (GDI), based on life expectancy, literacy, education and gross domestic product (GDP) per capita, that ranks Indonesia below the world and Southeast Asian and Pacific averages (see Table 22.1). The UNDP also computes a gender empowerment measure (GEM) concentrating on economic, political and professional participation of women compared with men. According to statistics from the 1990s, Indonesia ranked 56th out of 116 nations, slightly below Malaysia (UNDP 1995, p. 84).[2]

My purpose here, however, is not to evaluate Indonesian gender relations

TABLE 22.1 Indonesia according to the GDI[a]

	Female	Male
Life expectancy at birth, 1998 (years)	67.5	63.7
Adult literacy rate, 1998 (%)	80.5	91.1
Combined primary, secondary and tertiary gross enrolment ratio, 1997 (%)	61	68
GDP per capita, 1998 (PPP US$)	1,780	3,526

a With a GDI of 0.664, Indonesia ranked 90th out of 174 nations; it was below the world average of 0.706 and the Southeast Asia and Pacific average of 0.688 (UNDP 2000, pp. 163–4).

Source: UNDP.

by some international yardstick – a difficult task in any case, since the statistical data are often lacking, inadequate or debatable.[3] Rather, it is to try to assess them according to what Indonesian women want. Of course most women want many of the things that most men do: a reasonable income, good health for themselves and their families, a peaceful environment and so on. What I am investigating here is what women feel *qua* women about their position in society compared with that of men. I refer to this as gender relations because what is being discussed is how the societal expectations of men and women and of the interactions between the sexes have been constructed over time. A key issue in such debate is gender equality, chiefly whether the expectations and treatment of men and women should be free from discrimination on the basis of gender.

I realise there are pitfalls in my path. For a start, which women could be said to represent the views of all Indonesian women, given that women, like men, form such a heterogeneous category? However, this does not seem to me to be any more problematic than studying what certain foreign observers deduce from their own observations, limited and biased as they must always be. There is an intrinsic interest in hearing what Indonesian women themselves feel about their situation that outweighs the risks involved, and it is worth doing so long as one bears in mind the limitations of 'representation', as I shall try to do in this chapter. Second, there can be no such thing as pure or unmediated subjective views. What women say they want is influenced by prevailing attitudes, by their changing circumstances, by their knowledge of alternatives, by their age and experience of life and by a host of other factors.

This in itself is worth studying: we need to know what the factors are that influence women's perspectives on themselves as women at any particular time.

The views that I present to you are those of organised women, women who have chosen and are able to speak out as to what they think Indonesian women want and need in order to change their situation. Their willingness to comment on gender relations, as opposed to those who just accept their situation – 'The fish don't talk about the water' as one author (Risseeuw 1988) puts it – already tells us much about them as women. They are the most articulate and aware of the ways in which women are affected by prevailing gender relations, and as such, whatever their bias, they are worth listening to as being at the forefront of the public critique of gender relations. They have been the women trying to bring about change, both in social attitudes and in state policy and practice. In this respect the following questions interest me. Which women have been organised at different times and which women have they claimed to represent? What particular concerns have they articulated and how have these changed over time? Have those concerns been addressed? How are women's expressed needs and wants likely to be different in the 21st century?

In investigating these questions I am aware of the importance of a number of contextual matters that affect the way that women express their needs in an organised fashion. These include socioeconomic changes such as levels of literacy and employment, cultural changes like religious revivalism and international influences, and political changes like state control, regime change and the influence of nationalism and political parties. In addition one would have to take into account diversity among women, including racial, ethnic, class, regional, age and religious differences.

It would clearly be too big a task to try to cover all aspects of the issue in a short paper, so I have chosen to focus on a few major areas of change in women's articulated wants and needs. In brief, I consider that for most of the 20th century the major concerns of women's organisations as far as gender relations were concerned focused on education and marriage. Great improvements were made in both these areas and now the debate has moved on to new issues that are likely to dominate the next few decades, notably work, violence, political roles and more localised concerns. I will discuss how and why the discourse has shifted, which will entail some analysis of women's organisations and their relations with the Indonesian state over time.

INDONESIAN WOMEN'S ORGANISATIONS

In taking women's organisations to be a voice for women, I recognise that in the 20th century they were dominated by better-educated women living in

Java. There is nothing surprising about this, since the majority of the population and of educated Indonesians inhabit that small island. Organisations tend to be run by and to recruit members most easily from among people of greater wealth and higher education who have the time and skills to gather information, express their views publicly and attend meetings. Consequently, organisations tend to overrepresent the interests of such women and to be more ignorant and unconcerned about the needs of poorer women and those in more remote rural areas. Moreover, the profile of women's organisations has been dominated not just by Javanese but even more restrictedly by those based in Jakarta, because they have had better access to the government and to the mass media.

In addition we have to acknowledge the role of the state in Indonesia in controlling women's organisations. Governments during the colonial period and the New Order followed remarkably similar policies that came, under Soeharto, to be referred to as the 'floating mass' notion that the rural population should be kept out of politics. Hence the only women's organisations that were really free to flourish at the village level were those considered apolitical, such as religious organisations and, during the New Order, the state-controlled Family Welfare Program (PKK), which was intended to promote 'family welfare' and more generally helped implement the government's development plans, especially family planning. Except during the 1950s and early 1960s, it was politically difficult for women's organisations to organise rural working women. Radical organisations that tried to do so were suppressed, first by the colonial government before World War II and later by the New Order. Only during a relatively few years of the 20th century, therefore, was it possible to organise working women in rural areas independently. And in the urban areas, under the eagle eye of the colonial and New Order regimes, it was also made extremely difficult for women's organisations to reach out to ordinary working women.

While one might criticise women's organisations in Indonesia for not representing the vast majority of Indonesian women, the fact was that throughout the 20th century few organisations that were not purely religious in orientation have managed to attain a mass base. Those that did, such as the Indonesian Communist Party (PKI) and Gerwani in the 1950s and early 1960s, did not last long in the face of New Order repression. Moreover, as Wieringa (1995) has shown, Gerwani soon sold out its concerns for women in favour of submission to the communist agenda. It is hard enough for the urban educated women who inevitably run women's organisations to organise women from other backgrounds even in the best of times; for Indonesia in the 20th century the times have scarcely ever been propitious for such endeavours.

For most of the 20th century, therefore, the kinds of public demands put forward by women, reflecting concerns about their situation, were voiced by women's organisations largely representative of urban, better-educated and wealthier women. But some of their concerns were shared by many other women. The two issues I am going to discuss – education and marriage – seem to have met with widespread support among a range of women.

THE DESIRE FOR EDUCATIONAL EQUALITY

From the start of the 20th century, Indonesian women were voicing their dissatisfaction about not having the same access to modern education as men. What was at stake here was of far-reaching significance. Women wanted education for a variety of reasons. Access to better-paid, modern employment was an obvious attraction of schools, and although such work is by no means guaranteed by schooling, it is certainly restricted to those with the right educational qualifications. It was also hoped that staying at school longer would provide girls with more autonomy in the selection of a husband, since parents customarily arranged the marriage of daughters at very young ages. Finally, women hoped that with an education they would be better mothers and able to hold their own with educated husbands.

The colonial state, while well disposed to the notion of education for girls, did little in practice to advance girls' schooling. It was, however, responsible for planting the seeds of the desire for education, as women like Kartini eloquently attested.[4] At first, since parents were reluctant to send daughters to co-educational schools, it was important to have separate schools for girls. Women themselves in a private capacity did as much as the colonial state to establish schools for girls: the record includes the secular schools founded by Dewi Sartika in West Java and the Islamic school system founded by Rahma El Yunusia in West Sumatra.

Since independence Indonesian governments have seriously attempted to expand educational opportunities for girls. As the state's revenue grew and as personal wealth also increased, particularly in the New Order period, the number of public and private school places available for girls massively increased. In the course of the century, governments responded by expanding educational opportunities for women, with the result that by the 1990s equality had almost been attained at primary school level, although inequality increased with the level of schooling.[5] Of course levels of education for both men and women are relatively low, and much improvement is still needed, but education of girls is no longer prominent on the agenda of women's organisations. As the need for education reform in the post-New Order era gains support, it is likely, however, that more attention will come to be focused on the curricula and pedagogy of schooling rather than just on enrolments: the gendered aspects of the education system will come under increased scrutiny from women's organisations, which are now free to raise such matters publicly.

THE DESIRE FOR EQUITY IN MARRIAGE

As with education, reform of marriage laws was a high priority with Indonesian women's organisations for most of the 20th century, until the Marriage Law of 1974. This issue has been of greatest concern to Muslim women (around 90% of the female population), since previously Muslims married according to Islamic law, and family law matters such as divorce were determined by religious courts run entirely by men with virtually no supervision by the state. Marriage law was often implemented in ways that discriminated against women and appeared arbitrary and unpredictable. Moreover, the custom of parents marrying off their daughters at very early ages, before or immediately upon the onset of puberty, was a matter of great concern to women's organisations generally.

From the founding of the first women's organisations in the early 20th century, attempts were made to change social attitudes on marriage and to draw the state into taking measures against early marriage and arbitrary treatment of wives by husbands under Islamic marriage law as practised at the time. Both colonial and post-independence governments were reluctant to pass legislation on these matters, preferring instead to rely on attitudinal change, which they believed was promoted by schooling, by the example and leadership given by the civil service and by the campaigns of women's organisations themselves. And indeed the phenomenon of child marriage did decline without much overt interference from the state (see Blackburn and Bessell 1997).

After a long struggle by women's organisations, the 1974 Marriage Law was finally passed. It provided a uniform marriage code that set guidelines for all marriages and introduced greater security and equity for Indonesian wives. Minimum ages for marriage were set; it became easier for Muslim women to achieve divorce; greater restrictions were put on husbands' rights to divorce and take multiple wives; and the state reformed the Islamic court system, including the appointment of women judges.

Despite its flaws, the 1974 Marriage Law satisfied most women as the best that could be achieved under the circumstances, which included strong opposition by Islamic organisations to perceived interference in their affairs. A few prominent women (such as Nursyahbani 1993) continue to criticise the law on the grounds, for instance, that it was based on a patriarchal view of marriage, and recently the Minister for Women's Empowerment, Khofifah Indar Parawansa, announced that the law would be revised because she said

it 'domesticated' the role of women ('UU No. 1/1974 Segera Direvisi:
Karena tidak Berperspektif Gender', *Media Indonesia*, 10 February 2000).
So far, however, there appears to be no groundswell for change. The whole
context of marriage now offers greater autonomy for women: marrying later,
with better education as well as greater legal protection, women can feel
more confident about their ability to deal with their husbands on a more
equal footing.

NEW ISSUES: VIOLENCE AGAINST WOMEN

Equality in education and marriage was felt by women across the board to be
their due, and they could feel considerable satisfaction about progress made.
By the last decade of the 20th century, new issues were beginning to gain
attention from the wave of organisations established since the 1980s by
younger women outside the control of the state-dominated women's movement led by the federation known as Kowani.[6] They raised issues that challenged existing gender relations and focused on women's rights in a way that
was unacceptable to the consensus-oriented regime. With the fall of Soeharto
these issues can be promoted more easily, and the increasingly uncertain situation in the country also makes them more urgent. The socioeconomic context for women is more promising for the organisation and representation of
women's interests: most women are now literate; there is a much larger pool
of well-educated women from whom to draw leadership; and communications
throughout the archipelago are far easier than as little as 20 years ago.

An increasing source of influence on women's organisations comes from
external forces such as aid donors and the international women's movement.
Indonesian women leaders are well connected to United Nations and other
conferences on women, and are supported by funding from a variety of outside sources. The Ford Foundation, for instance, has been very active in promoting notions of women's reproductive health rights, especially in Islamic
organisations.[7]

One of the new issues being given prominence is violence against women
(Blackburn 1999b). It has emerged as a major concern for the international
women's movement; for instance it featured at the Beijing Women's Conference. In the early 1990s Indonesian women's organisations took up the cause
of domestic violence and rape but made little headway against government
and media indifference. As in most other countries, under-reporting of both
phenomena made it impossible to ascertain their real incidence in Indonesia
or whether they were increasing. However, the violence that accompanied the
fall of the Soeharto regime, particularly the rapes of women of Chinese
descent, brought the issue into much higher public profile and caused the

Habibie government to set up the National Commission against Violence against Women, which will keep the matter on the public agenda. Rape by the military in areas such as Aceh has galvanised many women, and the economic and social instability associated with the Asian monetary crisis has made it acceptable and necessary to talk about violence against women as a life-threatening, traumatic and inhibiting factor in daily life.[8]

WOMEN AND WORK

During the 20th century problems faced by women in the workplace received relatively little attention in Indonesia and few women's organisations campaigned on these issues. Under colonial rule it was extremely difficult to do so, since the regime watched vigilantly for signs of labour unrest. Circumstances were more promising after independence, and the government moved quickly to pass legislation that favoured equality of the sexes, including at work, but in practice great obstacles confronted working women. Gerwani and a few other women's organisations took up the issue in a small way but made little progress. Unions took little interest and in any case only a tiny minority of working women were unionised. Any attempts to organise workers were suppressed by the New Order regime and it is only now that women's organisations have some freedom to publicise this issue. The rights of women working in factories, a growing contingent in the last couple of decades, have been raised, and industrial disputes waged on their behalf. More recently, women's organisations have campaigned actively on behalf of female migrant workers, especially those employed in the Middle East.[9]

Why, one might ask, should this be considered a gender issue rather than an industrial or class matter? Women's organisations point to the fact that certain categories of workers are predominantly female and that this negatively affects their employment situation. Women industrial workers are treated differently from men, as are female domestic workers among the migrant workers in the Middle East. Isolated and unorganised, the latter are particularly vulnerable and susceptible to lower pay, sexual harassment and intimidation. Domestic workers suffer exploitation in part because it is assumed that their work is something 'natural' for women and therefore they should not be paid as skilled workers. While factory hands and migrant workers constitute only a minority of the female workforce, it seems likely that if there is success in fighting for these particular groups, the principles behind these campaigns may well be transferred to struggles on behalf of other downtrodden women workers, notably domestic servants in Indonesia itself. Such campaigns would be hindered by divisions among women themselves: middle-class working women often depend on cheap home help from poorer women.

WOMEN'S POLITICAL ROLE

Another issue gaining momentum among women's organisations relates to their political representation, a matter of relatively little public importance in the past. During the colonial period there were few opportunities for any Indonesians to have political representation. In the 1930s a small, low-key campaign was fought by some women's organisations for the right to vote, and in 1945 universal suffrage was gained. Politically speaking, most of women's efforts were absorbed by the male-led nationalist movement. During the period of liberal democracy in the 1950s, women's organisations worked to ensure that women understood their political rights and participated in the 1955 general elections. A small minority of women were elected to parliament and regional assemblies but very few took leadership positions: the barriers of unfamiliarity, of prevailing attitudes against women in politics and of male dominance of political parties kept women largely out of the public political arena. From the late 1950s until the end of the New Order, authoritarian governments excluded women from leadership positions. Although they were represented in public assemblies, their role was strictly circumscribed within the limits of state definitions of depoliticised femininity. There were no women in New Order cabinets until 1978 and less than a handful in any of Soeharto's governments, always in stereotypically feminine roles.

Preoccupied with what they considered to be more pressing concerns and inhibited by political considerations, women's organisations have been reactive rather than proactive on the issue of their lack of political power. Women's role as public leaders became controversial because of the elevation to leadership of the Indonesian Democratic Party of Struggle (PDI-P) of Megawati Sukarnoputri in 1996, against the strong opposition of the regime. Clothed in the charisma of her father, the late President Sukarno, and symbolising resistance to New Order authoritarianism, Megawati attracted an enormous following – the first woman to do so in Indonesian politics. In some Islamic circles doubts began to be raised about the appropriateness of women holding positions of national leadership. These concerns were magnified after the fall of Soeharto in May 1998 as possible contenders for the presidency could now be canvassed freely and Megawati's support increased. By the time of the lead-up to the general elections of June 1999, controversy raged as to whether Islam had any reason to deny the legitimacy of a woman becoming president. Despite plenty of evidence of women leading other Islamic nations, Muslim leaders were divided on the issue and women's organisations were slow to come to Megawati's defence because they feared being seen to support her personally and politically.

Most women's organisations are not overtly political, at least in the sense of aligning with parties, and apart from that Megawati had never shown any sign of defending women's rights. Rather late in the day, women's organisations rallied to defend the right of women to become president when it became clear that the PDI-P had won the most votes (although not a majority) in the election. However, the opposition to her from the other (male-led) parties, particularly those associated with Islam, was too strong and at the October 1999 meeting of the People's Consultative Assembly (MPR), which constitutionally selects the president, Megawati lost out to the respected Islamic leader Abdurrahman Wahid, who gave her the position of his deputy. The issue of a woman's right to the top job remains on the table as Wahid's future as president continues to be questioned.

To many observers, including myself, the strength of the opposition to Megawati's ascendancy came as something of a surprise and aroused concerns that the revival of Islam in Indonesia in recent decades has taken a stronger sexist turn than expected. It is, however, hard to unravel to what extent Islamic leaders were using arguments against women leaders merely as ammunition in their battle to thwart her party, the PDI-P, which they regarded as insufficiently pro-Islamic.

Megawati's personal strengths and weaknesses will long be debated but the principle of gender equality in Indonesian politics has been brought into sharp public focus by her remarkable popularity. Even more insidious is the lack of women in Indonesian representative bodies: in the parliament (DPR) the percentage of women actually declined from 16% at the end of the New Order to a little over half that level in the year 2000. Once democracy conferred real power on the parliament, seats became prizes that men were reluctant to forego, and women's lack of experience in political parties meant they were easily excluded. Women's organisations are only now beginning to absorb this fact and to recognise that the lack of women at the top means that in practice, at least temporarily until more women can be elected, democracy is as biased against the representation of women's concerns as were the previous authoritarian regimes. During the election campaign the effort to educate women in politics began (Blackburn 1999c), and women's organisations are now talking about quotas for parliamentary seats,[10] but judging by our own experience in Australia it will take many years for women to make their mark on Indonesian politics.

THE REGIONS ASSERT THEMSELVES

Finally, in the 21st century we can expect to see women outside Java making known the special needs of their regions. Thus far, Jakarta-based organisations have tended to dominate agenda setting, due to poor communications, the lower levels of education and awareness of women in more remote areas, and their relative lack of access to foreign aid funding. Women from the provinces have resented articulate Jakarta women taking the limelight and assuming that women from far-flung parts of the archipelago shared their analysis of what Indonesian women wanted. In 1995 a survey by Solidaritas Perempuan revealed that most members of women's organisations located outside Jakarta 'believed that women's organisations in Jakarta had a great deal of access to information but did not share it, had more access to international funding agencies ... and felt free to label their interests as "national" in order to gain overseas funding' (Muchtar 1999, p. 142). At a national conference of Indonesian women's organisations, called in December 1998 to demonstrate the new independence of women from state control, the resentment of regionally based women's groups against the 'Jakarta clique' was palpable (Krishna Sen 1999). These groups are now able to argue for the importance of their own local concerns, which often differ radically from the 'national' priorities. Communal conflict in Maluku, to give only a most obvious example, has very urgent impact on women in that region, overshadowing other concerns. Women's organisations in eastern Indonesia have for some time been arguing that levels of violence against women are disturbingly high there, more akin to Melanesian than to Javanese custom.[11] We can expect to see a much more diverse range of wants advanced within the Indonesian women's movement, reflecting the diversity of the situations in which Indonesian women live. In Aceh, for example, women have courageously tried to take a mediating role for peace in the bloody conflict between the military and the secessionist movement (Bianpoen 2000).

Also, with increased provincial autonomy, local governments are likely to take varying approaches to gender issues, intensifying the regionalisation of gender concerns. For instance, the prospect of the introduction of shari'ah (Islamic law) in Aceh makes gender discrimination likely: already extremist elements have attempted to enforce the wearing of the jilbab (Tapol 2000).

CONCLUSION

Organised women have always identified areas where there is gender inequality in Indonesia. The desired changes and the levels of dissatisfaction have varied not just with objective conditions but also with the characteristics of women's organisations and the nature of the state at any time. My analysis suggests that women were in agreement during most of the 20th century that education and marriage were areas where women had unequal status, and much was done to redress these concerns. Whereas for a long time it was difficult for women to press for change on other matters, towards the end of the century new organisations led by younger women were raising a number of

new areas of discrimination, including work, violence and political representation. The rise of regional assertiveness has also complicated the picture by
highlighting the diversity among women.

An interesting aspect of these demands is that they do not always relate to
what an outside observer might consider the most urgent needs of women. For
instance, the continuing high rate of maternal mortality in Indonesia would
seem to be a grave matter for women, yet until very recently it has had little
attention. This appears to be a case of a campaign driven by statistics: only
relatively recently have official data on maternal mortality been made available.[12] It also highlights how most perceptions of status relate to comparisons
of men and women, whereas certain aspects of women's lives, such as child-
birth, are obviously not comparable. More generally, although I have focused
in this chapter on the demands of women *qua* women, I am struck by the
reluctance of Indonesian women to express wants on their own behalf: in the
past they have tended to defend improvements in their own status as necessary for their children or families, or for the nation. Whether or not you
choose to say this is because Indonesian women have a satisfactory position
in Indonesian society is a matter for judgment. I would be more inclined to
conclude that because Indonesian women have been socialised to care for others rather than for themselves, they have been unaccustomed to identify and
defend their own rights. The fact that the prevailing Indonesian political culture has rarely encouraged anyone to adopt a rights discourse only makes it
more difficult for women (Blackburn 1999a). Now that Indonesian society is
opening up to new possibilities, we can expect to hear more about the gaps in
gender equality in that country.

NOTES

1   For discussion of the views of early travellers in Southeast Asia on women there,
    see Reid (1988, pp. 146–58, 162–72). For positive 20th century views by foreign
    observers, see Blackburn (1997), Geertz (1961), Winzeler (1996) and Dube
    (1997).
2   The statistics used relate to the percentage of seats held by women in parliament
    (12.2% in 1994 for Indonesia), the percentage of administrators and managers
    (6.6% in 1992) and of professional and technical workers (40.8% in 1992) that are
    women, and the share of earned income that goes to women (25.3%).
3   I am highly dubious about the gender-disaggregated GDP per capita used by the
    UNDP in its GDI, cited in Table 22.1.
4   Raden Ajeng Kartini (1879–1904) was a Western-educated Javanese woman
    famous for her letters to Dutch friends in which she advanced modern feminist
    ideas.
5   In 1997, 98.6 % of girls of primary school age were enrolled at school, which was
    99% of the male ratio. In the same year the figures for secondary schooling were

53.4% and 91% respectively; and in 1994–97 there were 812 female tertiary students per 100,000 women, which represented 53% of the male ratio. All these statistics represented a considerable improvement over figures for 1985 (UNDP 2000, p. 257).

6   Examples of the new organisations include Solidaritas Perempuan, Kalyanamitra, Mitra Perempuan, Yayasan Annisa Swasti (Yasanti), Lembaga Studi dan Pengembanan Perempuan dan Anak (LSPPA) and Asosiasi Perempuan Indonesia untuk Keadilan (APIK). A ready means of identification of the 'new wave' of independent women's organisations is their use of the word *perempuan* for women instead of the more genteel *wanita*.

7   These organisations include, for example, the Centre for the Development of Islamic Boarding Schools and Society (P3M), and its newspaper *Sehat*.

8   I refer here, for example, to frequent reports of assaults on women by unlicensed taxi drivers.

9   Examples of these campaigns have been increasing rapidly over recent years. In 2000 the State Minister for the Empowerment of Women, responding to the calls of women's organisations, requested that female labour exports to the Middle East be stopped temporarily after an increasing number of sexual harassment cases. The protests were rejected by the Minister for Manpower and Transmigration ('"Export" of Female Labour to Continue', *Jakarta Post*, 30 August 2000). The waters of this debate have been muddied by the issuing of a ruling (*fatwa*) by the Indonesian Council of Islamic Scholars (MUI) proclaiming that women should not work overseas without being accompanied by their husbands ('Fatwa MUI Soal TKW Harus Diperjuangkan', *Surabaya Post*, 24 August 2000).

10   This call has been taken up even by Islamic women leaders; see, for instance, the interview with Hj Aisyah Hamid Baidlowi, president of Muslimat NU ('Dekonstruksi Peran untuk dan Oleh Perempuan', *Kompas*, 31 March 2000).

11   This was confirmed by interviews with women activists in Kupang when I visited in October 1998.

12   In 1990–98 Indonesia reported a maternal mortality ratio of 450 per 100,000 live births, compared with 160 and 170 respectively for its poorer neighbours Vietnam and the Philippines and 39 for Malaysia (UNDP 2000, pp. 187–8). The reliability of these statistics has been questioned (Iskandar et al. 1996). Health statistics as a source of feminist campaigns are an interesting subject: one thinks of campaigns for more government attention to breast cancer in Australia and the outrage in India after the release of statistics about the declining sex ratio in the 20th century.

23

THE CRIMINAL STATE: *PREMANISME* AND THE NEW INDONESIA

Tim Lindsey

Vigilante Justice/Mob Rules
… Vigilante justice in Indonesia has reached new extremes with the storming of a courtroom by an angry crowd who lynched a defendant on trial for murder. A distressed district court judge in the remote provincial town of Putussibau on the island of Borneo today recounted details of the attack in his courtroom by up to 400 angry villagers intent on revenging the murder of a local. Judge Aini Basrah said about 50 police had been guarding the courthouse yesterday for the trial of 31-year-old Usnata, accused of killing money changer James Sandak. The police had earlier increased their guard when they heard rumours that a mob was on its way to revenge the killing of Sandak. But they were outnumbered when truckloads of men armed with traditional machetes and home-made rifles arrived in search of the defendant. 'They broke in through the court windows', Judge Basrah told AAP by telephone from his office today. 'I was terrified and hid in my office with a guard.' He said Usnata was mobbed and killed inside the very courtroom, and was being buried today. 'This is the first time and I hope this is also the last time such a thing has happened in my court', said the judge, who has been posted to the remote town in the province of West Kalimantan near the border with Malaysia for five years. (*Jakarta Post*, 14 December 2000)

This recent news item is typical of a rising tide of reporting in Indonesia not only of widespread vigilantism, but also of the proliferation of violent standover rackets; a linking of religion and ethnicity to gang warfare and the systematic killing of minority groups; terrorist bombings; and the failure, or even complicity, of law enforcement officials in such events. They are in part a consequence of the power vacuum created by the resignation of President Soeharto. As McLeod (2000b) has demonstrated, his departure left the corrupt political and business 'franchise' that he had built without its lynchpin, its 'godfather'. This led to a fragmentation of systems of political control and the rise of intense rivalry for power between the political groups Soeharto once dominated. Inevitably, this has resulted in a gradual pushing out or reconfiguring of the elites through which he ruled. It has also led to a loss of certainty and confidence in the security forces – his 'enforcers' – who have always sought a monopoly on the use of public violence. In this environment of uncertainty, political flux, confusion about lines of authority and a reduced capacity for prompt, coordinated and consistent state responses, longstanding community tensions exacerbated by economic crisis have easily mutated into violence, creating cycles of revenge.

Stepping back, these events can be seen more broadly than as simply a response to the tumultuous political and economic events that have wreaked havoc in Indonesia since 1997. They are the latest in a long sequence of violent acts by Indonesians against Indonesians. Since Soeharto's fall these include the destruction of East Timor by military-backed militias; the communal wars in Ambon, Maluku and elsewhere in eastern Indonesia; the war with the Independent Aceh Movement (GAM); and the emerging battle with separatists in Irian. These events can be seen as part of a continuing pattern, one that Siegel (1999, p. 214) has described as 'an intermittent civil war in which, by definition, members of the same nation kill each other'.[1] This 'war' is, however, one that has historically involved the state to some extent. In recent incidents, and those historical events discussed below, the state either has been a protagonist or, at the very least, has been implicated by providing the political circumstances that have led to the acts of violence and criminality. In fact, under Soeharto, the state came to be a fundamentally violent and criminal player in public life.

THE *PREMAN* AS PARADIGM

This chapter will argue that the real structures and systems by which the New Order operated were illegal. This argument builds on, but goes beyond, the readings of the state authority in Indonesia suggested by critiques based on authoritarian state capitalism (Jayasuriya 1999) or patrimonialism. I argue that the New Order state's methods of operation – violence, extortion and secrecy – were, in fact, most closely analogous to those of criminal gangs. The key to my analysis is the idea of the *preman*. Derived from the Dutch for 'free man' and originally used to refer to irregular or demobilised soldiers (Ryter 2000), the term came to mean bandit and then gangster or, more commonly, standover man. At times the term has overlapped with the *jago* (literally, 'fighting cock'), the village 'tough' of ancient tradition who in an urban context became a gang boss; the *rampok* bandits; and the *laskyar* (militias or irregular forces,[2] particularly during the revolutionary period) (Cribb 1991a, 1991b, pp. 18–19, notes 26–7).

Today, the *preman* or, in their own slang, *jawara*, are the toughs found throughout Indonesia who extort illegal rents, or *japrem*, from people living or carrying on a business in territory they have 'won' by fighting and defeating other *preman* (Barker 1999, pp. 119–22).

> In owning an area, the *jawara* establishes the right to collect on the debt that people have simply by virtue of living or doing business there. This debt is resolved by paying to the *jawara* a percentage of any commercial activity that takes place in his territory. ... Even pickpockets who successfully extract a wallet from passersby through the area feel obliged to pay the *jawara* a tenth of their take, even though the *jawara* is not their boss. The money that is collected is called tribute (*upeti*) or *japrem* ... and is generally collected not by the *jawara* himself, but by his underlings (*anak buah* or '*kronco*'). Indeed tribute is the right name for it: it is the fee paid under duress for the right to live or do business in the *jawara's* domain (Barker 1999, p. 120).

Under Soeharto, the territorialised system of the *preman* as urban standover criminal was writ large as the state used violence, systematic terror and intimidation to extract the *japrem* that funded the crony capitalism of the New Order. This led also to a proliferation of *dekking* or *bekking* ('backing'), the mechanism by which state officials protected street-level *preman*. Rival criminal 'gang' structures linked political and business elites through the military to *preman*, who sometimes mutated into private armies or militias linked to political and business leaders (Gunawan and Patria 2000). This system permeated virtually every aspect of public life under the New Order, from contracting to law enforcement to narcotics and even the operation of public transport. The *dekking* system operated outside the law but (as seen below) often overlapped official, formal structures of state. Invariably, it subverted any state structures with which it came into contact.

Post-Soeharto *reformasi* succeeded in publicly identifying the essential criminality of many state systems and in some cases forced the state to close down such 'rackets' (Tommy Soeharto's clove monopoly, for example). It has, however, failed to effect any real systemic change. In many cases, the rackets or gangs pushed out of the state's systems have simply gone 'private', operating now as covert enemies of the government. An ironic consequence of this is that it is now much more difficult for the state to control this form of criminality: it is harder to manage *preman* if you are no longer the 'boss'. This is demonstrated by aspects of militia activity in eastern Indonesia and the rise of vigilantism, both responses to state loss of control.

It is necessary to consider the origins of state criminality in order to understand the nature of New Order state *premanisme,* the state's relationships with *preman* groups and the implications of the *dekking* system. The state's attitude to and use of criminal violence can be tracked to the revolutionary period and, in particular, to the political ideas that formed the 1945 Constitution.

THE DISPLACEMENT OF LAW AND THE NECESSITY FOR TREASON

The chief drafter of the 1945 Constitution was Professor Dr Raden Soepomo, who was an impassioned advocate of the rejection of Western socialist and liberal ideas (Bourchier 1990). He set out to create a constitution that could 'give the greatest accent to the government', while being itself 'also account-able to the government and primarily the head of state' (Indra 1990, p. 44). This was predicated on the notion that the integralist state – because it was 'integrated' – could never be at odds with the individuals comprising it, 'because the state is not a powerful body or political giant standing outside the sphere of individual freedom' (Yamin 1959, p. 114). On this basis, there was no need for a civil (private) legal sphere independent of the state – and thus able to place checks on it – because the state *was* all citizens and their inter-ests were therefore identical (Nasution 1992).

The failure of Soepomo's romantic union of a state and its people (Bourchier 1999) has been consistently clear from soon after the institution of the 1945 Constitution with Indonesian independence in the same year, because governments and citizens do not, of course, think and act as one (Inoue 1998, p. 59). Indeed, Indonesia's 'imagined community' (Anderson 1991, pp. 6–7) has been a fragile one, historically marked by constant violent objection to its existence. Awareness of the 'dis-integrated' nature of Indone-sia's integralist state has not diminished the legitimacy of the 1945 Constitu-tion for those who have governed by it or for those who have accepted the government's legitimacy – in fact it has sometimes strengthened it. This is because Soepomo's integralist model was implicitly founded upon the notion of the state and the people being one, and of the people being under threat. On this reading, a failure of the state or the law is a result not of its flaws but of sabotage and betrayal by traitors; the state has constructed a greater evil to justify its extra-legality.

The violent realisation in state action of this notion of the integralist state dependent on betrayal for legitimacy can be dated back to the killings of pro-Dutch Indonesians and personal or political enemies during the Indonesian revolution; the massacre of communists after Madiun in 1947 (Siegel 1999, p. 211); the guerilla war with Darul Islam in West Java from the 1940s through to the early 1960s; and the brutality that accompanied the crushing of the PRRI–Permesta rebellions in the late 1950s.

Under Soeharto the pattern continued with the renewed slaughter of tens of thousands of communists and 'leftists' – and the gaoling of more – from the mid-1960s (Cribb 1991b); countless smaller-scale military attacks on civilians, such as the Tanjung Priok shootings and the Petrus killings (*penem-bak misterius*, or 'mysterious killings') of 1983–85; the Dili massacre; the murder, apparently by government and military figures, of 'enemies' such as the labour activist Marsinah (Fehring 1999), the journalist Udin or even the troublesome mistresses of soldiers (Sunindyo 1999a, 1999b); the ethnic and religious violence in Kalimantan (Parry 1998); the 'ninja' killings of *dukun santet* (traditional mystics or shamans) that appeared to involve military or government support (Darmawan et al. 2000); and the rapes of ethnic Chinese in Jakarta and elsewhere in May 1998. Of course, it also includes the events described in the first part of this chapter.

The state's brutality, though not always fully acknowledged, was thus widely evident to its citizens. It was so pervasive that only a widespread acceptance of imminent crisis could make it acceptable. It did not matter that this acceptance often took place only in official rhetoric, because rhetoric was the fundamental formal mode of political communication and legitimacy under Soeharto (Hooker 1995).

This is part of the explanation for the New Order's potent reimagining of Indonesian history since 1945 – but more so since 1965 – to justify the trope of the embattled republic, powerful, but perpetually vulnerable from within. The New Order was ultimately predicated on the fear of nameless subversives on the verge of toppling the republic, even if they did so in a way that was incapable of detection and produced no evidence. The quintessence of this genre was the notion of *organisasi tanpa bentuk*, the 'organisations without form' that had to be destroyed by aggressive force in order to maintain the union between state and people. So Siegel saw the New Order as characterised by its fetishing of invisible enemies. He gives the example of Attorney-General Ali Said banning a book by Pramoedya Ananta Toer on the grounds that it 'was an example of the "infiltration of society that went unfelt by it"' and that communists had now decided that 'organisations without form are best' (Siegel 1999, p. 215). The power of this tradition is demonstrated by its continued use by former New Order figures such as Amien Rais, who – incredibly – recently described East Javanese protests against the government as organised 'by communists and the long arm of the PKI [Indonesian Communist Party]' (AFP 2001).

THE LAW-LESS STATE

It is easy to find examples of this sort of statement from senior New Order politicians and security and enforcement officials, and even from communal leaders like Rais, because they were such an essential part of the state's public dialogue. They were common – however absurd they seemed at times – because they justified state violence. From time to time, war was thought necessary against particular Indonesians to prevent the putative descent into chaos and the national slaughter of many more Indonesians. It was actually *necessary* that state violence occurred from time to time, to give some weight, however feather-like, to the state's constant polemic of brinkmanship. Richard Tanter (1990b) has memorably described the New Order as an intelligence or security state, but perhaps a more appropriate title would have been 'insecurity state', because the New Order relied on a constant and official state of precariousness to justify it acting in an essentially extra-legal or lawless way.

Siegel (1999, p. 218) takes this further, describing the New Order state and its president as 'the new criminal type of Jakarta'. Examining the Petrus killings of 1983–85, Siegel focuses on Soeharto's justifications for ordering the murder of tattooed *gali* gangsters, who, the president claimed, were 'inhuman'.[3] The inhumanity or *sadis* (sadism) that Soeharto attributed to the *gali* was matched by the state's own brutality and lack of regard for the law. Disguised members of the military were sent to abduct and murder selected *gali*, usually leaving the corpses, with multiple bullet shots or stab wounds, in streets and rivers. Soeharto claimed this was done 'for *shock therapy*' (Siegel 1999, pp. 227–30; Pemberton 1994).

Siegel (1999, p. 228) argues that the Petrus killings were an attempt to appropriate the power of the *gali* by asserting that the state was the only institution that could go beyond the limits of the law. In my view, this appropriation was unnecessary, because the integralist state has rarely experienced real limits on its authority. It does not need more power. This is a quibble, however, as it is clear that the state emerged from these events as the unchallenged possessor of law-less power, as the mediator of violence – as Soeharto had clearly intended and, as a good integralist, he clearly believed was its right.

LINKING STATE VIOLENCE AND STATE CORRUPTION

Under the New Order, power was equivalent to wealth. It was secured through violence and centred around an elite that was equivalent to the state itself. To secure this equivalence the New Order consciously created a parallel 'secret' state to ensure elite access to illegal or extra-legal rents; and it was through this system that business and administration were really carried out (Lindsey 2000b, 2000c). The key to the creation of this 'secret' or 'black' state was state violence in order to force compliance. So pervasive was this violence that for most, there was little real alternative but complicity for financial survival. For those who chose to operate in competition, as criminals or as dissenters, violence was the sanction.

Perhaps the most startling evidence of this formalised, unofficial but bureaucratic system of 'secret' corruption and state-managed violence was the extraordinary evidence given at the murder trial of labour activist Marsinah by a local Ministry of Manpower official. He testifed that, despite the existence of a formal industrial relations system, labour disputes in the Sidoarjo region (where Marsinah had worked) were in fact conducted though a secret network of government, military and employer representatives known as the Sidoarjo Intelligence System and run by the local Ministry of Manpower office – and that identical networks existed all across Indonesia (Fehring and Lindsey 1995, p. 9).

The New Order state was thus a standover operation offering protection (against *gali* or communists, for example) and meting out punishment in the form of brutality (as with Marsinah and Udin). In this sense, the state was an enterprise that operated on the same basis as the street *preman*, with whom it sometimes competed and whom it at times coopted, as is seen below. The *preman* occupy an ambiguous position, accepted but feared:

> On the one hand, the *jawara* is resented for the extra economic burden he places on people, but on the other hand, there is always the attempt to keep up good relations with him ... 'If we are good to them, they don't hassle us' (Barker 1999, p. 121, n. 49).

Of course, these words apply equally well to the New Order blend of violence and corruption typified by the Sidoarjo Intelligence System and the Petrus killings: state *premanisme*. This is a model of state oppression and intervention that goes far beyond models proposed of East Asian authoritarian state capitalism or economic constitutionalism (Jayasuriya 1999), of the powerful, patrimonial centralist state committed to economic development. In fact, in some ways Indonesia's state *premanisme* is the opposite of authoritarian state capitalism, because the quest for illegal rents for the elite took place *even if* it impeded development. The Timor national car fiasco and the Busang/Bre-X goldmine scandal of the late 1990s are excellent examples of this. Development occurred not principally for ideological reasons or in response to the market but rather at elite direction to fund Soeharto's 'franchise' system. *Premanisme* has thus historically been more, rather than less, prevalent when the economy is booming, as there are more *japrem* available for criminals (Barker 1999, p. 123) – and, I would add, the criminal state.

The tradition of the state as the ultimate illicit rent-seeker can be traced back to the revolution. The anti-colonial forces – whether the republican government, its armed forces or the *laskyar* militias and bandit forces – required funds to continue their opposition to the Dutch. Singapore, for example, became a key transit point in the early years of the revolution for imports of Indonesian government opium and Dutch guilders and exports of arms and materiel (Lindsey 1997, pp. 190–95; NEFIS 1947). The armed forces' need to operate as guerillas and live off the land without reliable financial support from the government led to personalised links with traders and suppliers, and was funded by raising rents on trading within areas under Indonesian control. This inevitably led to a blurring of identity between *jago*, *preman*, soldiers and the state (Cribb 19991b; Lindsey 1997, pp. 147–61).

The roots of the New Order business–military alliance thus lay in the revolutionary period – through military commander Soeharto's financial arrangements with the Chinese trader, Liem Sioe Liong (Soedomo Salim), for example (Robison 1986; Schwarz 1994). Likewise, the interlinking of the political elite with business and military forces – and thus *jago* and *preman* – that marked the New Order began not with the rise of Soeharto in the mid-1960s but during the revolution in which he fought 20 years earlier. These origins created a 'state style' that from the start blended power, violence and commerce. Although muffled during the parliamentary period from 1950 to 1957, and developing during the Guided Democracy period, this style of government came into its own after the military-backed killings of 1965–66 removed any substantial political opposition to the military. It also shifted official ideology to the right and power into the hands of Soeharto, a long-standing exponent of this style who had previously been disciplined by the army for involvement in corrupt business practices within his command (Schwarz 1994).

Nonetheless, state *premanisme* is a product of the fundamental inseverability of state, individual and economy that underpinned Soepomo's 1945 Constitution and the practical manifestations of that unity that characterised the emergence of the republic during the revolution. All that was required for the shift from Soepomo's romantic integralist state to the *preman* state was for Soepomo's imagined 'benevolent father' to be substituted by a wicked criminal stepfather: Soeharto.

DEKKING: THE *PREMAN* IN THE *PREMAN* STATE

The relationship between the *preman* state and the *preman* themselves is not straightforward. Barker (1999), who describes the overlap between state-sanctioned security officials and *preman* in Bandung's Local Security System (Siskamling),[4] makes the point that *preman* are often coopted by the state as enforcers, 'a necessary component in the maintenance of state power and the collection of taxes', and that a *preman*'s control of territory for rent extraction is negotiated with the state (p. 122). The key here is the concept of *dekking* (backing) by an arm of the state. Put simply, this is a system by which *preman*, having extracted dues from citizens, in turn pay *setoran* (rents) to government representatives, usually members of the military or police, in return for the right to operate.

In a sense, the New Order system – predicated on a deliberately low-wage economy and repressive control of the labour market by brutal bureaucratic–military 'intelligence systems' (Fehring 1999) – made *premanisme* necessary by restricting access to wealth, particularly for the urban poor. As the economy boomed on the back of low-wage industries, *premanisme* became a rational way to get access to the wealth that trickled down from above, hence the increase in *premanisme* in boom times identified by Barker.

A typical approach to creating *dekking* mechanisms was for government or military associates to create formal youth groups or work-related associations as bases for criminal gangs. Ryter (2000) traces the inheritance of *premanisme* in Medan to the army-created anti-communist youth gang, Pemuda Pancasila (PP), still notorious for its violent support of military ideological causes. In the 1980s, the PP splintered and a rival group, Ikatan Pemuda Karya (IPK), was formed. The two groups have contested access to standover rents in Medan markets. Despite PP's *dekking* by the Police Mobile Brigade, Brimob (NE and Ade Nursa'adah, 2000a, 2000b), the IPK now seems to have gained control of DPR/MPR seats and regional political posts – including, most notably, the position of mayor (Ryter 2000). Recently, tensions led to the kidnapping and assault of political candidates and the killing of Brimob supporters at a roadblock (NE and Ade Nursa'adah 2000a). The incident demonstrates typical *preman* procedures for extracting *japrem* – *sweeping*, for instance, involves establishing roadblocks and demanding payment to pass or, similarly, systematically searching buildings to demand payment from tribute-payers, usually at gun or knife-point.

Another example of the *dekking* system, and the cracks appearing in it since Soeharto's fall, revolves around the creation of the ironically named Ikatan Keluarga Besar Tanah Abang (IKBT, or Big Family of Tanah Abang Association) in 1997. An initiative of the mayor of Central Jakarta, the role of the IKBT was to collect the daily fees from *mikrolet* (public minivan) drivers serving the busy Tanah Abang routes around Jakarta, as a solution to the collection of unauthorised fees. The aim was to prevent the establishment of *sweeping* operations by paying 'local youths so they would not create trouble, such as asking for money from drivers entering the area' ('Unauthorised Fee Approved by Mayor: Tanah Abang Union', *Jakarta Post*, 28 June 2000). However, by 2000 drivers were protesting and staging demonstrations about additional unauthorised fees, such as those imposed by *pak ogah* (illegal traffic wardens), which the IKBT had promised to curb once they applied the permitted Rp 2,000 levy. Central Jakarta Police Deputy-Chief Major Iza Fadri acknowledged, 'The police have arrested the illegal traffic wardens, but they will start asking the drivers for money again, once they are released'. The reality of the threat of violence that underlies such events was illustrated the next day when five men were 'mobbed to death' and then set alight at a nearby bus terminal, another natural collection point ('Alleged Shaman Mobbed to Death', *Jakarta Post*, 29 June 2000).

The breakdown of the *preman* state is also spreading to other areas of Indonesian society:

> Nightspot owners pledged on Monday to get tough, saying they would hire 1,000 private guards to combat the spate of attacks by radical religious groups. The Secretary-General of the Association of Nightspot Operators, Adiran Maelite, said the civilian guards would consist of security guards already employed at nightspots and residents living near the entertainment spots ... He contended the nightspot owners were forced to take this measure because the police had done little to ensure the safety of their establishments from repeated mob attacks. ... Inside sources told *The Jakarta Post* these religious groups often blackmailed nightspot owners. 'They once asked me, through a messenger, for Rp 40 million (US$4,300) to keep them from raiding my place. ... They often come to my office for money', the source added. Another source confirmed this, saying some nightclub owners who were willing to pay usually were able to keep their businesses open during the holidays. 'They pay around Rp 50 million each time the group comes and asks for money, so these places never receive any threats from them', the source said (*Jakarta Post*, 14 December 2000).

The restricted access to wealth caused by the economic crisis has brought with it a backlash against *premanisme* and a growth in anti-*preman* vigilantism. The weakening of state control and the loss of direction among the military since Soeharto's fall have both diminished control over the 'masses' and weakened *dekking* protection for *preman*. Popular protests against *jawara*, as well as attacks on *preman*, have increased markedly over the last year in Jakarta. There are no official figures on vigilante killings but Indonesian newspapers are full of reports every day. The problem appears to be growing as *dekking* breaks down and *preman* start losing their state protection. In the six months to June 2000, Jakarta's Cipto Mangunkusomo hospital reported 100 victims of mob vigilante killings, 'more than one every two days – and has now set up a special unit to handle the cases' (*Jakarta Post*, 29 June 2000; Djalal 2000, p. 68).

A SENSIBLY PARANOID SOCIETY

One consequence of the symbiosis between state *premanisme* and private *preman* in the operation of the corrupt *aspal* (original but false) state legal system (Lindsey 2000b, 2000c) has been the creation of an atmosphere of intimidation in most political, administrative and commercial contexts. The prevalence of acts of private or state-sanctioned brutality, as reminders or enforcement of the *aspal* system, leads to a common and understandable perception that every aspect of the entire state system is unremittingly criminal. In other words, state *premanisme* inevitably creates a loss of faith in the state and an attitude of almost abject fear among citizens who are not 'players' in the *aspal* system.

These qualities are manifest in the common attitude of absolute cynicism towards any form of authority; an assumption of the worst in any assessment of government actions; the proliferation of widely accepted conspiracy theories; and an expectation of violence as the state's response to any crisis. Barker (1999, p. 103) gives a compelling anecdotal account of this when he describes the public reaction of Indonesians to broadcasts showing the destruction of contraband goods by police.

> [A]lmost without exception, they note cynically that the goods destroyed are only a small part of what was confiscated, or that the crates being burned are empty and that the remainder – those things not destroyed – are being sold by the police for profit. Thus, although the police may see the spectacle only as a demonstration of the power of surveillance, what viewers see is the generation and appropriation of a surplus. They see a performance in which the state's power (of surveillance) is converted into personal wealth.

A more recent example comes from Magelang, Central Java, where in late November 2000 Musaheri and Abdul Kowi were convicted of murdering Tri Warsono, an *ojek* (motorcycle taxi) driver in the course of a bungled attempt to steal his motorcycle. When they were sentenced to death:

> [t]he audience cheered, but not for long. Suddenly pandemonium broke out. The hundreds of fellow *ojek* drivers apparently weren't satisfied with the sentence. They demanded that the murderers be executed then and there. 'We want to see them executed now. We want to see their dead bodies', they shouted. Some started to hurl stones at the courthouse. ... To try and cool the atmosphere the panel of judges invited the crowd to dialogue. The crowd agreed. The dialogue proceeded in the judges' room and was also attended by the General Crimes Section Chief of the Magelang Public Prosecutor's Office, Hidayat, and the Chief of the Undercover Unit of the Magelang Police ... It was agreed that five *ojek* drivers would be allowed to witness the execution. ...[W]hen the agreement was announced, the crowd who had packed the courthouse yard since early morning insisted upon being told exactly when the execution would take place. They demanded that some judicial agency be prepared to shoulder the blame should the execution be put off.
> Trouble returned. Suddenly stones were hurled at the courthouse windows. This prompted the police to evict all drivers from the courthouse. Adamant, the crowd continued to attack with bottles, rocks and even nutmeg fruit, smashing roof tiles, ornamental lamps, and window panes.
> The frenzied mob even pulled out the iron fences. When the police charged them again, a violent clash was inevitable. Casualties fell. Two trial spectators were rushed to Tidar hospital, where one of them, Sugeng Riyanto, died (Wicaksono and Idayanie 2000, p. 53).

Public mistrust of the state and, in particular, utter cynicism regarding the judicial process lead the public to assume that sentences will not be carried out. They expect state officials will simply 'convert' sentences into personal surplus (to use Barker's term), by accepting a bribe either to secure the defendant's appeal or to turn a blind eye to his escape. This is what is popularly believed to have occurred when Tommy Soeharto (Hutomo Mandala Putra) disappeared after his petition for clemency was refused by President Abdurrahman Wahid. Recent reports that the president improperly met twice with Tommy and his sister Tutut (Siti Hardiyanti Rukmana) at Jakarta hotels to discuss the transfer of Tommy Soeharto's assets in return for clemency created the widespread perception of corrupt dealings to circumvent an already tarnished legal process (Budi 2000, pp. 16–17).

Allegations of Tommy Soeharto's involvement in terrorist bombings link violent intimidation to judicial incompetence and presidential corruption, in the public perception at least. It is not hard to understand why.

> Following a series of bomb blasts and threats in the capital recently, the Attorney General's office initiated on Tuesday a routine bomb sweep within the office compound, an official said ... As of Tuesday evening, a police bomb squad and the office's security guards were still checking the compound ... in South Jakarta. A strong explosive device severely damaged a lavatory on the ground floor of the office building of the Deputy Attorney General for special crimes on July 4, an hour after former President Soeharto's youngest son Hutomo Mandala Putra left. He had appeared for questioning as a witness in his father's alleged graft case. Another bomb, which did not explode, was found in a lavatory on the second floor of the building. The bomb bore a military code (*Jakarta Post*, 9 August 2000).

This expectation of corruption and violence feeds on itself; it becomes a self-fulfilling prophecy. If the police know that everyone believes they routinely steal confiscated goods or take protection money from *jawara*, then there is little incentive for them not to do so. Likewise, if the Indonesian people believe that the state is always lying and implicated in violence and crime, then they themselves adopt a similar means of response – hence the rise of brutal vigilantism across Indonesia, particularly evident in increased courthouse rioting and lynch attempts. In this way corruption and violence become self-perpetuating and 'normal', with horrific consequences for ordinary people.

> Husein could do nothing when the mob set his son Dian on fire. 'If I had protested, they would have killed me too', he says simply. 'I held in my emotions.' Dian, 24, and three of his friends had been caught trying to steal a motorbike in the town of Jati Murni, West Java. Within minutes of their being discovered by the bike's owner a small crowd had gathered and began beating the men. Soon the crowd numbered in the hundreds, pounding on the men as they pleaded for mercy. Kerosene was eventually found and poured over the four victims, two of whom

were still alive. Three hours after their ordeal began, the men were left as charred corpses (Djalal 2000, p. 68).

Another consequence of the common expectation of violence, corruption and conspiracy is the assumption that any unwanted event must be the product of these forces, that is, that behind-the-scenes players are manipulating everything for their own benefit. This is one reason why Indonesian gossip so frequently focuses on conspiracy theories involving a supposedly covert political *dalang* (puppeteer or mastermind), or his provocateurs and saboteurs. As one Indonesian official remarked sarcastically to me in late 1998: 'When it rains, the little people say Prabowo must be behind it. When it floods, it is Soeharto'.

This is, of course, the flipside of the New Order's preoccupation with 'formless organisations' and 'shadowy figures'. Only now, instead of being communists or ideological enemies, these dark forces are presumed to be controlled and directed by members or former members of the state elite; the accusers are now the accused. Common bogeymen include members of the Soeharto family, especially Tommy, Prabowo and Tutut, and the ageing and supposedly ill former president himself. Other candidates include Akbar Tanjung, Susilo Bambang Yudhoyono, Wiranto, Feisal Tanjung – supposedly once a market *preman* in Medan (Ryter 2000) – Hartono, Syarwan Hamid, Zacky Makarim and Ginandjar Kartasasmita, and even figures from the more distant past such as Benny Murdani. State intelligence and security agencies such as Intel, BAIS and Bakorstanas are equally shadowy threats. There is, of course, justification for some of these fears of conspiracy. However, the almost paranoid fear of illegal semi-secret activities against citizens by the state has moved beyond reason to become a pervasive expectation that dominates public attitudes to Soepomo's state.

CONCLUSION

Despite the end of the New Order, the limited statutory reforms of the last two years and the rise of President Abdurrahman Wahid (who has an undoubted and longstanding personal opposition to the use of violence), the Indonesian constitution's emphasis on obligations, not rights, and its statement that 'all citizens have a duty to uphold the state' still inform political and legal culture in Indonesia. This means that the president heads a government that must deal with the infiltration of exponents of state *premanisme* who survive from the New Order era, whether as members of the bureaucracy, armed forces or even ministries, or simply as de facto power-holders outside of government.

The protests and demands of *reformasi* initially forced the state apparatus to act against some of the *preman*, but this appears to have been short-lived. The *preman* are back again. Unravelling the New Order system of violence and corruption – which dates back not to 1966 but to 1957, when Sukarno suspended democratic processes – is not something that can be done in the first years of the presidency of Abdurrahman Wahid. It has become clear that his government has limited authority to control the state apparatus, that it offers little guarantee of the proper functioning of the legal system, and that it has almost no ability to effectively prevent or punish violence or corruption through legal or political measures. To date, there has not been a single corruption trial resulting in the gaoling of a senior member of the former Soeharto elite, whether civilian or military.[5] Whatever the wishes of the president, the government is an amalgam of competing interests, many of them committed to the old model. If the best legal response to violence it can deliver is a show trial of selected scapegoats, with a dead or disappeared defendant as in the Aceh human rights trials, then little has changed since military court 'trials' of communists in the mid to late 1960s.

There are alternative models for the legal relationship between the Indonesian state and its citizens, most notably the constitutions of 1949 and 1950 with their strongly stated 'Bill of Rights', and the unfinished debates of the Constituent Assembly (Konstituante). But President Abdurrahman Wahid is increasingly a prisoner of state politics as he struggles to deal with the *aspal* system of state corruption and violence – particularly since the advent of impeachment threats by the parliament from mid-2000. To suggest a new Konstituante now would probably hand a weapon to those survivors of the New Order who see the current government and the emerging democratic system as their enemy. There is therefore unlikely to be a real shift in the legal treatment of violence until the *preman* state is significantly rethought – and that will require much more than Abdurrahman's government has so far shown itself able to deliver.

NOTES

1   It should be noted, however, that many of those killing or being killed, in Aceh, Irian and East Timor, for example, do not acknowledge the authority of the Indonesian nation state.
2   In Cribb's definition, 'those armed groups which excluded themselves, or were excluded, from the official armed forces of the Republic' (Cribb 1991b, p. 72).
3   The *gali* (*gabungan anak liar*) were groups of wild youths, an official euphemism for criminal gangs.
4   The Siskamling is a combination of any of the SATPAM (united security), HANSIP (civil defence) and much older *ronda* or night guard. The SATPAM patrols commercial and public buildings while the other two patrol residential areas.

Employees of SATPAM and HANSIP are paid low wages; the *ronda* are usually volunteers. See, generally, Barker (1999), especially page 95 and note 3.

5 Some officials – including one regent – have been convicted of corruption and gaoled, *and* have exhausted their rights of appeal, but none could be said to be a 'big fish'. At the time of writing, Tommy Soeharto had failed in his attempt to obtain a presidential pardon for his land fraud conviction but remained at large as a fugitive (Djalal 2001). Mohamad (Bob) Hasan (timber tycoon, intimate of the Soeharto family and briefly Minister for Trade in the last cabinet of his business partner, Soeharto) was convicted of stealing US$75 million of Ministry of Forestry funds. He was fined Rp 15 million and sentenced to two years imprisonment of which he had already served 14 months while on remand. He is behind bars but his appeal process has yet to begin and it remains to be seen whether his sentence will stand. In a sense these two are 'soft' targets. Tommy has long been enormously unpopular, while Hasan's Chinese ethnicity makes him vulnerable. The real test is whether a *pribumi* crony who retains political power can be convicted. So far this has not occurred.

24

INDEPENDENCE FOR JAVA? NEW NATIONAL PROJECTS FOR AN OLD EMPIRE

Robert Cribb

East Timor is no longer a part of Indonesia. Aceh and Papua are seething with secessionist tension. The resource-rich provinces of Riau and East Kaliman-tan have put in ambit claims for independence, and talk has even been heard of independence demands from Bali and Sulawesi. The Indonesian experi-ment, a multi-ethnic state stretching more than 5,000 kilometres from east to west, is under challenge today as never before, and all over the Asia-Pacific region defence analysts are pondering the question of whether the early 21st century will see the disintegration of Indonesia in the way that the late 20th century saw the disintegration of the Soviet Union and Yugoslavia. For the first time since the Second World War, there is a serious possibility that the extended archipelago to Australia's north could be divided not into five or six states as at present, but into a dozen or more. Within this fluid environment this chapter examines the historical nature of the Indonesian empire and its future status, with particular emphasis on the island of Java.

Discussion of the possibility that Indonesia will disintegrate has focused on centrifugal forces in the outlying regions of Indonesia. Observers have accepted that the provinces outside Java felt exploited and dominated by the centre during the three decades of the New Order and that there is an appetite for autonomy across the whole archipelago (see, for example, Booth 1992a). Except in relation to Aceh and Papua, however, most observers have shied away from regarding this restiveness as embodying true local nationalist aspi-rations. There seems to be a general consensus that the current drawn-out attempt at decentralisation of power in Indonesia is primarily an administra-tive recognition that some functions of government can best be carried out by local and regional government, rather than by the central authorities. The unsuccessful efforts of the Dutch in the late 1940s to establish federal borders based on ethnic distinctions seems to show that Indonesia cannot simply be pulled apart into a number of ethnically coherent states (Cribb 1999). There is concern that a failure of the decentralisation program might create a political crisis and a sense of despair which could drive prosperous provinces to seize their own independence. This possibility has to be set against the fact that there are few significant international forces with an interest in Indonesia's disintegration and against the continuing power of the idea of Indonesia. The Indonesian state may have been created by the force of Dutch arms, but the idea that a single large state is the best possible institution to deliver modernity to the people of the archipelago and to protect them from the depredations of the outside word is still persuasive and has deep emotional roots among Indonesians.

In this discussion, the general assumption has been that Indonesia's survival will be determined by the interplay between centrifugal forces in the outlying provinces and the capacity of the centre to accentuate the positive features of a single Indonesian state. If we set the Indonesian state in a comparative analytical context, it becomes clear that a third key element in the events of the future is likely to be the island of Java. Independence for East Timor does not destroy Indonesia or even transform it significantly; even the loss of Aceh and Papua would leave Indonesia as the fourth most populous country in the world. If Java wanted to go it alone, however, then the Indonesian experiment would truly be over.

EMPIRES

The idea that Java might wish to leave Indonesia is, at first sight, bizarre. The island is the centre of political power in the archipelago; Javanese have held a majority of the powerful positions in the state; and Javanese culture appears to have deeply penetrated the state and political cultures of the archipelago. Not all observers have been willing to regard Indonesia as a Javanese empire, ruthlessly exploited by the resource-poor main island and held together by force of arms, but most agree that Java has appropriated more than its share of the natural resources of the other islands, that Javanese have been unduly prominent in the affairs of state, and that Javanese officials outside Java are often condescending and brutal in a style reminiscent of their colonial predecessors. In fact, however, Java's relationship to Indonesia is a good deal more complex, and we can appreciate that complexity best, perhaps, by setting Java and Indonesia in the broader, comparative context of empires as a political form.

Empires can be defined simply as polities that cover a large territory and rule a large, ethnically varied population. This definition excludes one or two polities traditionally called empires – Vietnam and pre-1895 Japan, for instance – but it highlights the two factors that make empires vulnerable. It is not just because of Gibbon that empires are assumed to 'decline and fall': the difficulties of communication and the strength of ethnically based resistance together make empires much more fragile than smaller, more homogeneous units. Historically, most empires have been created when a particular society develops a technological (generally military) innovation or a particularly effective form of social organisation (often including a gifted leader) which enables them to sweep across a vast territory and to topple enemies one after another. The Roman empire was built on the military prowess of the legions; the Mongols conquered half the world thanks to superior horsemanship, superlative communications and great generalship. The European empires were made possible by a combination of firearm and military technology, along with generally superior logistical backing. The advantages that allow a society to create an empire, however, tend to be short-lived. Technology can be transferred and forms of organisation can be learnt. Even if the imperial power remains superior to its subordinate peoples, it may not remain so superior that it can retain control. Successful empires, therefore, require a political format.

In a few cases, this format involves the absorption or extermination of the subject peoples, as was done in much of the Americas, in Australia and by China. More common, however, is the construction of an imperial ruling elite and an imperial ruling idea. The successful empires of world history have generally engaged their subject peoples in the imperial enterprise by creating a multi-ethnic administrative and military elite which was accessible to the best and the brightest from among at least some of those subject peoples. The Mongol, Ottoman and Austro-Hungarian empires were all ruled by administrative corps that included many peoples other than Mongols, Turks or Austrians, and these administrative elites meant that each empire took on a character different from that of the supposedly dominant ethnic group. The Soviet Union, too, was an empire in precisely this way. Even though it was dominated by Russians and held together by force, there was always the opportunity in the Soviet Union for capable figures of other nationalities – Georgians, Ukrainians, Kalmyks and so on – to achieve power and influence. Even the United States is an empire in some respects. Its traditional centre of power may have been the northeast, but its great regional diversity is held together by an imperial idea that can deliver presidential power to a Georgian or a Texan. The words 'empire' and 'imperial' today resonate with connotations of repression and inequality, but the successful empires of world history have been rather meritocratic, the imperial bureaucracies, civil and military, typically providing avenues of social mobility for ambitious men who might never have been able to make much of themselves in a smaller, more rigid society.

The history of the colonial empires of the West has also reflected this dynamic. Established by force of arms and the strength of capitalism, these empires could survive only by recruiting subject peoples into the ranks of the colonial army and the colonial bureaucracy. One of the clearest examples of this process is the way in which England's dominance over Scotland from the 17th century was made palatable by the expanding range of opportunities that Scots began to enjoy in the empire, but to a lesser extent individuals from other ethnic groups, especially Indians, also participated in the imperial venture.

The paradox of empire is that the more successful the construction of a broad imperial identity is, the less palatable it may become to the supposedly dominant group. Rather than being 'their' empire, it becomes an empire that rules them, often through people of other nationalities. Thus the Turks became a subject people under the Ottoman Empire, the Russians a subject people in the Soviet Empire and so on. This condition of subordination, or the threat of it, tends to produce an unpleasant chauvinist reaction within the ethnic group which imagines that it should be dominant. This chauvinism may be expressed in an attempt to discard imperial identity in favour of imposing the national identity of the dominant group; Turkish nationalists took powerful positions in the Ottoman empire in the late 19th century and sought to impose Turkish culture on the Arabs of the empire. It may be expressed in the imposition of ethnic discrimination; in the Dutch and British colonies, the rise of formal racial discrimination coincided with the emergence of educated Indonesian and Indian elites who were every bit as capable as their European rulers and who would have risen to positions of great authority if the colonial powers had been willing to allow the principle of meritocracy to continue (Fasseur 1994; Ballhatchet 1980).

In the worst of circumstances, this chauvinism may lead to expulsion or extermination, as in the Turkish treatment of Greeks and Armenians in the early 20th century. No parallel to the Turkish example has occurred in Indonesia, although there was perhaps an element of such chauvinism in the 1740 massacres of the Chinese in Batavia. Facing pressure from the Chinese and Eurasian communities for a greater say in public affairs in the Dutch East India Company colony, the company authorities responded to rumours of an impending Chinese rebellion by launching a massacre of Chinese in the city, despite the importance of the Chinese to the colonial economy. More often, however, chauvinism leads to a withdrawal from empire. The withdrawal of the United States from the Philippines is perhaps one of the clearest examples of an imperialist power that was not prepared to pay the social and ideological price of empire by treating the Philippines in a way that would make it content to be a permanent part of the American empire. Nor was Australia, for that matter, prepared to pay the social and ideological price of retaining control of Papua New Guinea. The fact that armed struggle, or the threat of it, contributed to the end of many empires obscures the common decision on the

part of one imperial power after another that the measures necessary to inte-
grate their colonies into an effective empire were not worth the benefits. The
Mongol Yuan dynasty in China made precisely this decision in the 14th century. Faced with the political and administrative challenges of famine and the
Ming uprising, the Mongols preferred to give up power in China and to return
to the purity of their steppe-based nomadism (Christian 1998). In the disintegration of the Soviet Union and Yugoslavia, too, we can see not only centrifugal tendencies among subordinate peoples but also a decision by Russians
and Serbs that the price of empire was greater than they wished to pay.

JAVA AND INDONESIA

What, then, of Java and Indonesia? Whether or not it is a nation, Indonesia is
also an empire, a vast, ethnically diverse territory under a single central government. As an empire, Indonesia is unprecedented in the history of Southeast
Asia. For most of the last 2,000 years there have been two major power centres in maritime Southeast Asia: Java, because of its fertile soil and abundant
rainfall, which in turn allowed it to sustain a dense population and sophisticated political forms; and the Melaka Strait zone, less fertile and with a
smaller population but prosperous by virtue of its strategic commercial location on Asia's main maritime trade route. Each of these centres exercised a
wide cultural influence in the archipelago and even beyond, but neither of
them created a substantial or lasting overseas empire beyond their immediate
heartland in the Javanese and Malay-speaking regions.

European colonialism altered this persistent pattern in two important
ways. First, it greatly weakened the power of the Melaka Strait region. The
Portuguese captured Melaka in 1511, and thereafter the European presence
prevented the emergence of any true successor to Melaka and its Sumatran
predecessor Srivijaya. The partition of the Melaka Strait region between
British and Dutch zones in the Anglo-Dutch treaty of 1824 perpetuated this
weakness. Second, during the 19th and early 20th centuries the military power
of the Dutch lashed to Java a vast archipelagic empire. Not only did the
Netherlands Indies include Java's 'natural' hinterland in eastern Indonesia,
but it also incorporated the whole of Sumatra. Never before had an empire
based in Java come anywhere near to controlling the western shoreline of the
Melaka Strait.

Even before the outlines of this empire were fully in place, it began to take
on characteristics of the classic empires of world history, drawing into its
administrative structures capable and ambitious young men from among its
subordinate peoples. The Dutch reserved for themselves a greater proportion
of the positions of power in colonial society than did their Western counter-

parts in the Philippines, Indochina and India. Even so, Javanese, Bataks, Malays, Minangkabau, Timorese and Manadonese began to congregate in the lower rungs of the colonial administration and to learn the ways of the West. During the 19th century, the Dutch attempted to limit access to even junior administrative positions in the Western sector to the sons of aristocrats, that is, to individuals who were assured of position and authority in their own societies. Quickly, however, the demands of the colonial state outstripped the capacity of these gilded youth and avenues of education had to be opened to capable people from more modest backgrounds. The Dutch empire became a tool for social mobility in Indonesian societies. Indeed, to men, and a tiny handful of women, who might otherwise have been trapped by low or mediocre status in small societies, the Netherlands Indies offered a vast stage on which to present new and previously unimaginable dramas.

Many scholars have capably told the story of how this new Indonesian elite found its path to power blocked by colonial racism and intransigence. We know how educated Indonesians, finding themselves second or third class subjects in their own country, paid less, excluded from social clubs and key administrative positions, bonded together against the Dutch as the single clearest obstacle to prosperity and modernity in their society. But we tend to forget that the Indonesian nationalist movement was also profoundly anti-Javanese. Of course it was not at all hostile to individuals of Javanese ethnicity, but it was strongly hostile to what were seen as the hierarchical assumptions of Javanese society. Nationalists spurned Javanese aristocratic titles, spurned even the Javanese language. We tend to see the rise of the nationalist movement in Indonesia in the early 20th century as simply the rise of an *Indonesian* nationalist movement, that is, a movement aiming at independence for the entire Netherlands Indies. Nonetheless, this national awakening includes not only such Java-based organisations as Budi Utomo and Jong-Java whose inclusion as Indonesian movements is debatable, but even a Committee for Javanese Nationalism which was unabashed in its preference for basing the future on a Javanese identity, rather than a broader archipelagic one. This committee argued explicitly for Javanese nationalism precisely because of the deep cultural strengths of Java (Shiraishi 1981). The idea of Javanese nationalism, however, was driven out of the political arena rather quickly by the idea of an Indonesia that was to be dedicated to prosperity, modernity and opportunity in a way that old Java had never been (or at least was imagined never to have been).[1] The idea of Indonesia came into the hands not of Javanese nationalism but into those of the 'metropolitan super-culture' described by Hildred Geertz (1967, p. 35).

Incorporation into Indonesia brought many advantages for Javanese. Not least was the social mobility that enabled a village boy like former Sergeant Soeharto to rise to power in the army and ultimately to the presidency, carrying with him others whose careers in a traditional Javanese society would almost certainly have been modest. But the Javanese shared Indonesia with other ethnic groups; Minangkabau, Bataks, Bugis and others all achieved real power in the Indonesian state, which was governed, after all, not from the Javanese heartland but from Jakarta on the relatively remote northwestern coast of the island. The Javanese language was treated, like all of Indonesia's regional languages, as a picturesque remnant, a language for the home and the fields, a repository of ancient wisdom but not a language for administration, politics, science or intellectual debate. Javanese children learnt their native language in schools for only three years, exactly as long as children elsewhere in the archipelago studied their own local vernacular, and generations of young Javanese became less certain of the nuances of their complicated hierarchical language.

This process was masked by what appeared to be the clear influence of Java on political practice in Indonesia (Dahm 1969; Resink 1975; Anderson 1972a; McDonald 1980). Javanese terminology crept into the Indonesian language and the Indonesian state made heavy use of Javanese imagery. Javanese were numerous among officials posted in other parts of the country, and of course comprised the majority of transmigrants. It has become a truism in recent years that Soeharto behaved as a kind of latter-day Javanese sultan (Loveard 1999). Indonesians from other ethnic groups could easily come to feel that Javanese culture was being imposed on them. To the Javanese, however, the official culture of the Soeharto era was a bowdlerised, sanitised and manipulated version of Java's rich culture, with complicated philosophical positions reduced to simple, often banal, aphorisms supporting the existing order (Pemberton 1994).

Along with the rest of Indonesia, moreover, Java suffered from the negative features of the bold Indonesian experiment. Despite the inspiring power of the idea of Indonesia as a big state delivering modernity and prosperity to all its people, and despite Sukarno's efforts to give Indonesia's identity a noble ideological framework in the form of the Pancasila, Indonesia remained an enormously diverse country in terms of ethnicity, religion and socioeconomic development. An exceptional charismatic leader such as Sukarno could bind the country together with oratory, but for most leaders, and certainly for uncharismatic military figures such as Soeharto, there were few nationally accepted political cues available for generating political support. Soeharto was left with trying to create his own national ideology in the form of the re-shaped Pancasila of 1975–98, and with military force.[2] All states are held in place ultimately by some recourse to coercion, but Indonesia's diversity means that the recourse to violence was closer to the surface than in many countries. This is not to say that violence was required to hold Indonesia together in its early years – though military force was indeed needed to end the separatist Republic of the South Moluccas in the early 1950s – but rather that a whole host of dissident movements, from Andi Aziz in South Sulawesi and the unappealing Army of the Just Prince (APRA) of 'Turk' Westerling in West Java to the major challenges presented by Darul Islam[3] and the PRRI–Permesta[4] movements, took up arms to promote their political views and were suppressed by armed force. Indonesia's size and diversity, in other words, helped to create a military to whom the practice of violence became increasingly routine. The Army Paracommando Regiment (RPKAD) units that slaughtered hundreds of thousands of people in Java in 1965–66 had learnt their craft in a decade and a half of intermittent warfare elsewhere in the archipelago before they turned on the Javanese.

Second, Indonesia's access to natural resource wealth in the outlying provinces had a profoundly distorting effect on national politics. Even though resource revenue had an undoubtedly positive effect in paying for infrastructure and public capital investment, the income from the sale of natural resources was effectively 'free' money to the ruling elite, money which it could employ independently of the political responsibility that is generally attached to tax revenues. In other words, even if the distribution of resource revenues unfairly took capital away from the other islands, it had its most profoundly distorting social effect in Java, where the rentiers who gained those revenues were unreasonably advantaged over agricultural and industrial entrepreneurs.

The disadvantages for Java of being part of Indonesia have been hard to see, partly because the promise of Indonesia as a prosperous and modern society remains beguilingly attractive, and partly because of the conventional wisdom that resource-poor Java depends on the Outer Islands. The continuing power of the idea of Indonesia should not be underestimated, but the argument that Java needs to control outer Indonesia politically in order to extract its resources is seriously outdated. Natural resources of all kinds are abundantly available on the open market in today's global economy. Political control of resources may suit the interests of particular individuals in Jakarta, but for Java as a whole there is little point in controlling what can easily be bought in any case. It needs hardly be said that the examples of Japan, South Korea and Taiwan all point to the relative unimportance of natural resources as a basis for economic take-off. People, along with their productive and intellectual capacities, are the truly valuable resource of the new century.

In fact, Java's potential was beginning to become clear during the 1990s. For the generations of Indonesia specialists who grew up regarding Java as the basket-case of the archipelago, poverty-stricken, overcrowded and underdeveloped, it is worth pointing out that this condition is anomalous in the history of the region. For most of the last two millennia Java was prosperous, except when it was wracked by warfare. A catastrophic decline in Java's welfare took place in the 19th century, evidently as a direct and indirect consequence of aspects of colonialism. Recovery began in the early 20th century, but it was slow and fitful. Only under Soeharto's New Order did Java make dramatic progress in the form of educational expansion, industrialisation, and declining birth rates. Under the New Order, most of Indonesia's industrial capacity was located in Java and most foreign investment ended up there, not because of government fiat but because Java offered the best infrastructure and the most abundant educated workforce. By the time the Asian economic crisis hit Indonesia in 1997, Java was more than earning its keep, and it had begun to attract economic migrants from other parts of Indonesia (Manning 1998).

Not far from Java are two countries where a compact geography, dense population and relative cultural homogeneity have helped to deliver rapid economic progress. Thailand had the enormous political advantage that European colonial powers stripped away most of its outlying subject territories in the late 19th and early 20th century, leaving it under the overwhelming cultural domination of the Siamese culture of the Chao Phraya valley. Taiwan, of course, was separated from China by the communist victory on the mainland in 1949. Both countries started from a base of underdevelopment and authoritarian rule, but they have managed to emerge as relatively prosperous and relatively democratic. Java, of course, remains ethnically divided between Javanese, Sundanese and Madurese, but the existence of an Isan (Lao) minority in Thailand and the mainlander–Taiwanese divide in Taiwan suggests that the Javanese–Sundanese–Madurese division in Java need not prevent the emergence of a functioning democracy.

PROSPECTS FOR AN INDEPENDENT JAVA

At the moment there are few signs of Javanese restiveness or political assertiveness and no indication of that direct discrimination against other indigenous ethnic groups that was a harbinger of the disintegration of the Western colonial empires and the empires of the Ottomans and the Mongols. On the other hand, President Habibie's actions in permitting East Timor to escape from Indonesia showed precisely the rational argument which can lead a country to shed the burden of empire. President Abdurrahman Wahid's abortive offer of a referendum to Aceh was made in the same spirit, but was foiled by the continuing emotional power of the 'idea of Indonesia' in ruling circles, especially among the military.

Nonetheless, this emotional power is under pressure. Serious shortcomings in the functioning of democracy at the national level and the failure of the political elite to deal with the moral legacies of the Soeharto era (both of them, it must be said, enormously difficult problems) have led to an unprecedented disillusionment with the idea of Indonesia. At the moment, many Indonesians appear to have placed their hopes of bringing government closer to the people in the decentralisation process. That process, however, is moving slowly and there are strong indications that the structures being put in place will lead to greater inefficiency and will strengthen the power of local elites, many of them with strong criminal ties. If the decentralisation exercise ends unsatisfactorily, then Indonesians will be all the more ready to try radical solutions, and Java's moment for seeking independence may yet come.

NOTES

1   For a refutation of romantic ideas of traditional Javanese hierarchy and harmony, see Kumar (1980). Henley (1995) is a stimulating discussion of the contingency of the emergence of Indonesia as a nation.

2   The Pancasila was formulated by Sukarno in 1945 to show that the Indonesian people, for all their diversity, were united by a set of noble and profound principles. Apart from implying unity, it had no significant political implications and indeed was rarely referred to during the revolution against the Dutch (1945–49). During the 1950s and early 1960s, the Pancasila gradually took on an anti-communist character, because it was widely believed that communists could not accept the principle of belief in God (though communists themselves argued that they accepted that other people believed in God). During the early New Order, the Pancasila still stood for the unity of all non-communist Indonesians and little more, but after the Malari affair of 1974 Soeharto appears to have decided to shape it into a much more prescriptive corporatist ideology, drawing on powerful corporatist traditions in Indonesian politics. This reshaping began to influence politics from about 1975 and the result was a Pancasila ideology whose political meaning was obedience and discipline, rather than unity in the pre-1975 sense. The corporatist Pancasila ideology in fact had begun to show signs of weakness by the early 1990s and it largely disappeared from Indonesian political discourse with the fall of Soeharto in 1998.

3   The Darul Islam (House of Islam) movement was founded in 1948 and aimed to turn Indonesia into an Islamic state. Its greatest strength was in West Java and South Sulawesi, but it had a presence in several other regions. It was suppressed by the army in a long series of military campaigns ending in 1962.

4   Permesta denoted the unilateral declaration of martial law by local commanders in eastern Indonesia in March 1957. The movement was strongest in North Sulawesi and had largely been defeated by June 1958. The PRRI was formed in February 1958 by regional and anti-communist politicians opposed to Sukarno's abrogation of parliamentary rule, Nasution's centralism in the army and the growing power of the Indonesian Communist Party (PKI) in politics. It was based in West Sumatra and was largely defeated by June 1958.

PART V

LOOKING FORWARD

25

INDONESIA'S HISTORY UNFOLDING

Grayson J. Lloyd and Shannon L. Smith

> It is almost impossible in our concern for the modern study of Indonesian history not to feel the impact of the ahistorical attitude of Indonesian traditional culture on its students ... This can be seen in the strong disposition to mythologize, the precipitous inclination to see relationships of a moral significance between events that are not necessarily related at all.
> (Soedjatmoko 1965, p. 411)

There is much truth in the words of Soedjatmoko: studying Indonesian political, economic and social history is a process fraught with difficulty, possibility and, occasionally, disappointment. Discerning myth from reality and form from content is a constant challenge not just for historians (in their various forms), but for those other disciplinarians such as political scientists, anthropologists, demographers and sociologists. To paraphrase John Legge (1980), Indonesia is still a picture being painted. This is particularly the case at the present time when nothing – and no one – is beyond scrutiny or reproach.

One of the greatest challenges for anyone attempting to interpret patterns or structures, illuminate basic identities and define fundamental contiguities and polarities in Indonesian history is to recognise connections between different episodes and to avoid drawing parallels – where on first inspection they appear to exist – between events that are sometimes totally unrelated. In studying a society as heterogeneous and complex as Indonesia, it is imperative to be cognisant of the perpetual likelihood of change, contradiction and paradox, and prepared to constantly rethink supposedly 'fixed' principles or positions.

One should always be mindful of the need to study the present with reference to the past, rather than the past with reference to the present. Indonesia's diversity – ethnic, linguistic, geographic and so forth – is a further complication because it includes multi-faceted and separate yet parallel (and sometimes shared) histories and experiences. The unfolding of Indonesia's history has, as Legge notes, 'been a triumph of co-existence' (Legge 1980, p. 193). Indeed, it is perhaps less amazing that the issue of the potential disintegration of the nation has arisen again than that the Indonesian nation has survived until now, albeit tenuously at times.

The 20th century was a period of significant challenge, achievement and evolution in Indonesia across a variety of spheres. It was also a period of distinct contrasts. Among other things it contrasted unitarism and nationalism (and its multiple interpretations) with separatism and regional inequality; the solipsistic tendency of presidential leadership with consultation (*musjawarah*); and the incompatibility of authoritarianism and democratic ideals. It juxtaposed ideological homogeneity with pluralism; secularism with nonsecularism; militarism with the notion of a civil society; economic development with economic democracy; social welfare and laissez faire; and conservatism with radicalism. The latter demonstrated a propensity to latch onto social, ethnic and religious violence in times of economic downturn and transmogrify the inherently moderate nature of Islam in Indonesia, creating friction between Muslims and Christians and other religious groups. The question is whether these are themes or, rather, episodes, unrelated yet similar and recurring.

Because of its huge and ethnically diverse population and the problems of communicating across an elongated archipelago, Indonesia's leaders have often dealt ineffectively with such issues, sometimes resulting in the occurrence of violence, popular protest or the revival of religious movements. While violence is rarely an appropriate response to problems arising from the size and diversity of Indonesia, it is at least an understandable method of expressing social dissatisfaction. However, the widespread and endemic socio-religious and ethnic violence in Indonesia today, and the accompanying increase in vigilantism in the socio-political sphere, constitutes an additional significant threat to the maintenance of the nation's unity and harmony. Popular protest and mass mobilisation have been a part of the relationship between the elite and the masses at least since the declaration of independence if not earlier. Mass political movements played a role in the fall of the Dutch colonial, Sukarno, Soeharto and Habibie regimes, but the masses have also been manipulated by elites to serve political, social and economic objectives. Indeed, political parties – particularly in the modern context – use their mass supporter bases and paramilitary wings to maintain positions of power and challenge rival factions. Indonesia's history also contains a strong current of millenarian-like radicalism and illustrates a capacity for radical religious appeal to mobilise mass support. As M.C. Ricklefs notes in this volume, volatility goes hand in hand with Indonesia's search for a better future.

Periods of development and transition in any society can easily produce vertical and horizontal cleavages and discrimination against the marginalised, disadvantaged or ethnically 'other'. In Indonesia's case, such divisions were pre-existing and often exacerbated by times of economic or social hardship. Consequently the imagined community of Indonesia, to borrow Anderson's famous term, has been beset by constant violent opposition to its existence. Nonetheless, despite the fragility of ethnic and social harmony and a raft of other factors, the sense of community of the Indonesian people has survived, underpinned by a utopian conception of nationalism – set against a background of colonial (and thus shared) oppression. It has instilled confidence in the survival of the nation and engendered an optimistic belief in a better future propelled by change and renewal. This attitude is reflected in an address given in 1956 by Mohammad Hatta to Gadjah Mada University: 'Confronting realities – particularly very bitter ones – people often conceive of ideals as a cure for their wounded spirit, ideals that give them hope for the future and inspire them to do everything in their power to determine their own destiny' (Hatta 1956, p. 1).

It is beholden on those individuals and institutions involved in the study of Indonesian history – both Western and indigenous – as well as on the Indonesian politicians and bureaucrats charged with the fashioning of economic, political and social policies in Indonesia, to investigate the past carefully. There are dangers inherent in change in any society, especially one undergoing a transition from an authoritarian to a democratic system within a period of profound economic, legal and social dislocation. Change is perceived differently from one generation to the next, and its importance varies according to the individual or group and the economic and political conditions pertaining at a given time. What one generation may view as an insupportable cost may be considered a sacrifice essential for progress by another. A danger is that ephemeral views of the present, couched in the here and now and designed to redress immediate problems, will prevail over a more balanced historical review, and will, moreover, distort realistic and pragmatic appraisals of the future. Indonesia's history will not provide a crystal ball view of the future.

History can function as a guide to the future – but only as an indicator and not as a predictor of events. One key is to learn from what we do know of the past. There is still much that we do not know or fully understand and much that remains the subject of considerable conjecture – the events of September–October 1965 and May 1998 spring readily to mind. We do not necessarily endorse the underlying pessimism of the Hegelian view that: 'What experience and history teach is this – that people and governments never have learned anything from history, or acted on principles deduced from it' (Hegel 1944, p. 6). In order to deal more effectively with the challenges of the present – to say nothing of coming to terms with the troubles of the past – then history must fulfil a basic requirement: that it should be relevant to society at all times. A more complete understanding of patterns where they appear, or of re-emerging themes, ideas, policies and actions employed in different eras and in evolving economic, social and political circumstances, can assist in the navigation of some potentially treacherous waters in Indonesia in the time ahead.

It would seem to be an appropriate time in Indonesia today for historians to come to the fore, focusing in particular on Indonesia's experience with a range of social and cultural experiments, economic programs, and political systems, ideologies and leaders. While Indonesia has met a number of the challenges delivered by history, it has not always absorbed (or adequately applied) the lessons emerging from them. This means confronting problems and issues in different eras, and coming to terms with key questions in social and political history such as national identity and difference – with the episodes and decisions that cause shame, and which some prefer to forget, as well as with those that provide cause for celebration. It does not mean forgetting or sublimating events that have been, and in some cases continue to be, deemed un-Indonesian or anathema to Indonesian culture or society. Certainly Indonesia needs to deal with the conjectural occurrences of the past, particularly of the New Order. Two glaring but by no means isolated examples are the May 1998 attacks against the ethnic Chinese (Lloyd 2001) and the massacres of members of the Indonesian Communist Party (PKI) and suspected associates in 1965–66. But confronting the past also means coming to terms with unresolved difficulties of the present: the violence in Maluku province and the tensions between Dyaks and Madurese in West Kalimantan are two examples. A dangerous legacy of such events is their tendency to live in the memory for years (and sometimes generations), and consolidate hatred and mutual distrust to be crystallised in the future.

In this respect the struggle continues in the writing of social history and in dealing with Indonesia's 'moral' history (or historical memory) and the search for truth, reconciliation and forgiveness – a variation on the fight for freedom against the colonial Dutch over half a century ago. Indonesia attained its sovereignty through a combination of *diplomasi* and *perjuangan* (struggle). The diplomats and *pejuang* (freedom fighters) of today are those who are attempting to define the parameters and consolidate the structures of a civil society and implement wide-ranging reform against the wishes of those who adhere to past elitist and regressive ideals. Concomitant with this struggle is a process of social and historical inclusion. This involves bringing the voices of the marginalised – for instance, non-middle-class women living outside Jakarta – and dispossessed nearer to the historical stage so that their words may be recorded and their ideas listened to, while simultaneously examining the mistakes of the past and not absolving the guilty.

When writing of the 'administrators' and the 'solidarity-makers' nearly 40 years ago, Herb Feith (1962) noted that whereas the former were concerned with the immediate future, the latter were preoccupied with images of a distant utopia – the Indonesia of the future overflowing with prosperity, justice, harmony and strength – to which the Indonesian revolution was a bridge. In Feith's words, the problem was essentially this: 'Virtually none of the leaders of 1949 were attempting to link long-term ends with short-term administrative programs, ideological appeals with the solution of practical problems' (Feith 1962, p. 34). The imposition of the flamboyant 'solidarity-maker' period of Guided Democracy under President Sukarno did little to remedy this deficiency, especially in the economic sphere.

While Soeharto's New Order was more administrator-like in its approach to the future – in that its focus was on economic development and security (often at any cost) – its political conservatism, or ultra-conservatism, and moribund ideological, cultural and social policies excluded the overwhelming majority of people from any meaningful role in the political process or equitable share of the benefits of economic development. In retrospect this regime arguably did more to threaten Indonesia's future than it did to safeguard it. Scholarly work since the 1950s has gradually reflected an awareness of the need to focus on the cultural context of political activities – an understanding of how society and politics interact – and not merely on the Byzantine world of intra-elite conflict in Jakarta and elsewhere. One wonders, however, whether the Indonesian leaders of today will be more successful than their predecessors in addressing the concerns raised by Feith's analysis of the landmark social and political transition of the 1950s, some of which are probably as relevant today as they were then.

There is a real and increasing need in Indonesia to provide social justice and equality and to develop a discourse on human rights. Moreover, it is the obligation of all historians working on Indonesia to investigate the manifestation of these concepts and their interaction with broader political and economic goals. All Indonesians – irrespective of gender, origin or ethnicity – must be incorporated in conceptions of the economic, social or political future. The comparatively recent burgeoning of the study of Indonesian economic history can assist in this endeavour. As a result of this we are learning more about the nature and origins of poverty and employment, labour practices, and some of the means of attaining more sustainable and equitable distribution of economic resources.

Furthermore, there is a need to foster and safeguard a form of representative democracy in a civil society that is strengthened by a commitment to the rule of law, freedom of the press and freedom of expression. The current reform program has at best been half-hearted, and complicated by the troubling issue of the competency of leadership – not just of President Abdurrahman Wahid, but of other prominent leaders such as Amien Rais, Megawati

Sukarnoputri and Akbar Tanjung. Underlying them is a multitude of less well-known but equally (or more) capable and ambitious individuals ready to take charge. The rise of the new leadership may not bring about the reforms and changes desired by all, but it will constitute a break with the lingering vestiges of the past.

At the moment the search for a solution to Indonesia's woes appears to be mired in the Machiavellian political schisms within and between the major political parties, the armed forces and their leaders, and between the president and the parliament. The absence of a political compact and collective political will is the result of a lack of trust, common purpose and ethics – a hangover of the pervasive corruption of the Soeharto era – and of the struggle by parties to maintain their share of revenue and power. One consequence of this process is Indonesia's 'semi-parliamentary' system. Writing on the Indonesian political system and Pancasila several years before the collapse of the Soeharto regime, Doug Ramage noted that 'Indonesia illustrates ongoing contention over ideological differences' (Ramage 1995, p. 201). These ideological differences (and differences based on ideology) have persisted in the post-Soeharto era, as many predicted they would, and there is every reason to suggest that they will be evident in the unfolding of Indonesian history in the future in one form or another. This is, however, the crux of a democracy, whether single party, dual party or multi-party.

Those who believe Indonesia is experiencing an historical 'enlightenment' – involving a transition from a tyrannical and suffocating regime to a democratic government underpinned by political, economic and social rights and freedoms – are frustrated by the magnitude of the reform task at hand and the continuation in power of individuals and institutions beholden to and reliant upon New Order ideas, concepts and processes. Now is not the time to look to the past for legitimation of self-interest or the propagation of narrow sectarianism, which many Indonesians of all persuasions view as destructive of social cohesion. It is clearly unrealistic to expect that such a transformation will occur in the short term. But the need to effect a change of mind-set in the government and bureaucracy is a necessary medium to long-term goal. A resolution of the current political stasis is crucial to the facilitation of legal, constitutional, social and military reform and the gradual permeation of the ethos of democratisation throughout society.

On the economic front, recovery from the downturn created by *krismon* poses a substantial but not insurmountable challenge. The government must focus on increasing Indonesia's attractiveness to foreign investors and the competitiveness of its exports in world markets (Smith, 2001). Similarly, the implementation of decentralisation and other administrative and bureaucratic reforms is crucial to Indonesia's economic and social cohesion. As, indeed, will be future consideration of the status of Papua and Aceh – two distinct areas with unique histories and problems. History has demonstrated that unity emanated from the centre in Indonesia and was usually propelled by force. One wonders whether the future will witness the emergence of new patterns and identities or the manifestation of old practices clothed in new garb.

The brief consideration given in this book to the unfolding of Indonesia's history may be viewed in some quarters as somewhat unhistorical. The idea that history can point to the future as well as illuminate the past, while popular among some, understandably does not sit comfortably with historians who have been trained to deal with the known and analyse how and why things happened – or did not happen, as Namier would have it (Namier 1957, p. 375). But the study of Indonesian history should not be restricted to specific periods or events; it should also be about the study of problems and not (simply) periods, to paraphrase Acton (quoted in Collingwood 1973, p. 281). Examined in this context, one should recognise that many issues confronting Indonesia now and in the future have been evident for many decades and are likely to remain so, presuming a status quo. In scholarly terms, more needs to be done to address the sparsity of autobiographies, credible biographies and accurate representations of the New Order. Furthermore, additional and diverse work needs to be undertaken on women's roles in Indonesian history – and on aspects of public and private violence against women – as well as on the nature of interaction between different ethnic groups, aspects of social mobility and representations of difference. To analyse future possibilities based on established precedents seems a less egregious abuse of history than to disregard past events altogether.

Comprehensive change of the sort proposed in Indonesia today is seldom easy to implement, particularly when many of the structures required for its implementation are newly created, conceptual or even non-existent. The search for a clean slate (*tabula rasa*) – the opportunity to start anew – is a recurring theme in Indonesian history, and an impossible dream. It is the product, as the transition from Soeharto to Habibie attests, of a natural current of optimism engendered by political change and the collapse of an authoritarian regime. However, what it neglects are the thematic continuities in Indonesian history: while periods differ, leaders (and their policies) are always framed by the successes and failures of the past, whether or not they choose to recognise this. It therefore remains to be seen whether (or for how much longer) in this current period of social and political atrophy it can still be said of Indonesia – as Wertheim did some four decades ago – that: 'For the moment, the forces making for unity still seem far to surpass the disrupting tendencies' (Wertheim 1956, p. 343). It would seem that the scales are now rather evenly balanced. The dynamic and ever-changing history of Indonesia will continue to unfold in what is an increasingly globalised world.

REFERENCES

BOOKS AND JOURNAL ARTICLES

Abeyasekere, S. (1976), 'One Hand Clapping: Indonesian Nationalists and the Dutch, 1939–1941', *Monash Papers on Southeast Asia No. 5*, Clayton, VIC: Centre of Southeast Asian Studies, Monash University.

Abrams, M.H. (1962), *A Glossary of Literary Terms*, New York: Holt, Rinehart and Winston.

Acciaioli, Greg (1997), 'What's in a Name? Appropriating Idioms in the South Sulawesi Rice Intensification Program', in Jim Schiller and Barbara Martin-Schiller (eds), *Imagining Indonesia: Cultural Politics and Political Culture*, Monographs in International Studies, Southeast Asian Series, No. 97, Athens, OH: Ohio University Center for International Studies, pp. 288–320.

Adams, Cindy (1966), *Sukarno: An Autobiography as Told to Cindy Adams*, Hong Kong: Gunung Agung.

Aditjondro, George (2000), Notes on the Jihad Forces in Maluku, Unfinished research notes posted on Joyo news service, aditjondro@psychology. newcastle.edu.au, 4 October.

AFP (2000), 'Jakarta Threatens to Get Tough against Separatism', Jakarta, 22 November, www.kabar-irian.com.

AFP (2001), *Indonesia Opposition Accused of Trying to Stir up Anti-left Sentiment*, press release, Jakarta, 12 February.

Ahluwalia, S. Montek and Hollis Chenery (1974), 'The Economic Framework', in Hollis Chenery et al., *Redistribution with Growth*, London: Oxford University Press, pp. 38–51.

AJI (Aliansi Jurnalis Independen) [Alliance of Independent Journalists] (1995), *Wartawan Independen: Sebuah Pertanggungjawaban AJI*, Jakarta: AJI.

Akita, T. and R.A. Lukman (1995), 'Interregional Inequalities in Indonesia: A Sectoral Decomposition Analysis for 1975–92', *Bulletin of Indonesian Economic Studies*, 31 (2), pp. 61–81.

Alfian (1979), Rural Indonesia before Television: A Benchmark Survey, Unpublished report prepared for East-West Workshop on Evaluation and Planning for Satellite Communication Research, Honolulu, 15–28 July.

Alfian and Godwin C. Chu (eds) (1981), *Satellite Television in Indonesia*, Hawaii: East-West Center.

Ali, Abdulla (1999), 'Aceh Dahulu, Sekarang dan Masa Depan', in Tulus Widjanarko and Asep S. Sambodja (eds), *Aceh Merdeka dalam Perdabatan*, Jakarta: PY Cita Putra Bangsa, pp. 3–14.

Anderson, Benedict R. O'G. (1972a), 'The Idea of Power in Javanese Culture', in Claire Holt, Benedict R. O'G. Anderson and James Siegel (eds), *Culture and Politics in Indonesia*, Ithaca, NY: Cornell University Press, pp. 1–69.

Anderson, Benedict R. O'G (1972b), *Java in a Time of Revolution: Occupation and Resistance, 1944–1946*, Ithaca, NY: Cornell University Press.

Anderson, Benedict R. O'G. (1982), 'Perspective and Method in American Research on Indonesia', in Benedict Anderson and Audrey Kahin (eds), *Interpreting Indonesian Politics: Thirteen Contributions to the Debate*, Ithaca, NY: Cornell Modern Indonesia Project, pp. 69–83.

Anderson, Benedict R. O'G. (1983), 'Old State, New Society: Indonesia's New Order in Comparative Historical Perspective', *Journal of Asian Studies*, 42 (3), pp. 477–96.

Anderson, Benedict R.O'G. (1990), 'Old State, New Society: Indonesia's New Order in Comparative Historical Perspective', in Benedict R.O'G. Anderson, *Language and Power: Exploring Political Cultures in Indonesia*, Ithaca and London: Cornell University Press, pp. 94–120.

Anderson, Benedict R. O'G. (1991), *Imagined Communities: Reflections on the Rise and Spread of Nationalism*, London: Verso, revised 1991.

Anderson, Benedict R. O'G. (1999), 'Indonesian Nationalism Today and in the Future', *Indonesia*, 67, April, pp. 1–11.

Arndt, H.W. (1971), 'Indonesia – Five Years of "New Order"', *Current Affairs Bulletin*, 47 (5), pp. 67–78.

Article 19 (1996), *Muted Voices: Censorship and the Broadcast Media in Indonesia*, London: Article 19, International Centre against Censorship.

Asher, Mukul G. and Anne Booth (1992), 'Fiscal Policy', in Anne Booth (ed.), *The Oil Boom and After: Indonesian Economic Policy and Performance in the Soeharto Era*, Singapore: Oxford University Press, pp. 41–76.

Ballhatchet, Kenneth (1980), *Race, Sex, and Class under the Raj: Imperial Attitudes and Policies and Their Critics, 1793–1905*, London: Weidenfeld and Nicolson.

Bangkit Online (2000), 'Papua, Aceh and Riau reject the 17th', Edisi 47, http://www.bangkit-tabloid.com.

Bappenas (1999), *Looking at the Future of the Indonesian Economy*, Jakarta: Bappenas.

Barker, Joshua (1999), 'Surveillance and Territoriality in Bandung', in

Vicente L. Rafael (ed.), *Figures of Criminality in Indonesia, the Philippines, and Colonial Vietnam*, Ithaca, NY: Southeast Asia Program Publications, Cornell University, pp. 95–127.

Barton, Greg (1994), 'The Impact of Islamic Neo-modernism on Indonesian Islamic Thought: The Emergence of a New Pluralism', in David Bourchier and John Legge (eds), *Indonesian Democracy: 1950s and 1990s*, Clayton, VIC: Centre of Southeast Asian Studies, Monash University, pp. 143–59.

Barton, Greg (1995), 'Neo-modernism: A Vital Synthesis of Traditionalism and Modernism in Indonesian Islam', *Studia Islamika*, 2 (3), pp. 1–75.

Barton, Greg (1996), 'The Liberal, Progressive Roots of Abdurrahman Wahid's Thought', in Greg Barton and Greg Fealy (eds), *Nahdlatul Ulama, Traditional Islam and Modernity in Indonesia*, Melbourne: Monash Asia Institute, pp. 190–226.

Barton, Greg (1997a), 'Indonesia's Nurcholish Madjid and Abdurrahman Wahid as Intellectual *Ulama*: The Meeting of Islamic Traditionalism and Modernism in Neo-modernist Thought', *Islam and Christian–Muslim Relations*, 8 (3), October, pp. 323–50.

Barton, Greg (1997b), 'The Origins of Islamic Liberalism in Indonesia and Its Contribution to Democratisation', in Michele Schmiegelow (ed.), *Democracy in Asia*, New York, NY: St Martins Press, pp. 427–51.

Benda, H.J. (1962), 'The Structure of Southeast Asian History: Some Preliminary Observations', *Journal of Southeast Asian History*, 3.

Benda, H.J. (1966), 'The Pattern of Administrative Reforms in the Closing Years of Dutch Rule in Indonesia', *Journal of Asian Studies*, 25 (4), pp. 590–605.

Berg, C.C. (1961), 'The Work of Professor Krom', in D.G.E. Hall (ed.), *Historians of Southeast Asia*, London: Oxford University Press.

BHKPU (Biro Humas Komisi Pemilihan Umum) (2000), *Pemilu Indonesia Dalam Angka dan Fakta Tahun 1955–1999*, Jakarta: KPU.

Bianpoen, Carla (2000), 'Aceh's Women Show the Road to Peace', *Indonesian Observer*, 12 March, p. 4.

Bird, Kelly (2000), The Waiting Game: Corporate Debt Restructuring in Indonesia, unpublished paper, Partnership for Economic Growth Project, Jakarta.

Blackburn, Susan (1997), 'Western Feminists Observe Asian Women: An Example from the Dutch East Indies', in Jean Gelman Taylor (ed.), *Women Creating Indonesia: The First Fifty Years*, Clayton, VIC: Monash Asia Institute, Monash University.

Blackburn, Susan (1999a), 'Women and Citizenship in Indonesia', *Australian Journal of Political Science*, 34 (2), July, pp. 189–204.

Blackburn, Susan (1999b), 'Gender Violence and the Indonesian Political Transition', *Asian Studies Review*, 23 (4), December, pp. 431–46.

Blackburn, Susan (1999c), 'The Indonesian Elections of 1999: Where Were the Women?', in Susan Blackburn (ed.), *Pemilu: The 1999 Indonesian Election*, Clayton, VIC: Monash Asia Institute, pp. 87–98.

Blackburn, Susan and Sharon Bessell (1997), 'Marriageable Age: Political Debates on Early Marriage in Twentieth Century Indonesia', *Indonesia*, 63, April, pp. 107–41.

Booth, A. (1992a), 'Can Indonesia Survive as a Unitary State?', *Indonesia Circle*, 58, June, pp. 32–47.

Booth, A. (1992b), 'Review Article: The World Bank and Rural Poverty', *Journal of International Development*, 4 (6), pp. 633–42.

Booth, Anne (1998a), *The Indonesian Economy in the Nineteenth and Twentieth Centuries: A History of Missed Opportunities*, London: Macmillan.

Booth, Anne (1998b), 'Rural Development, Income Distribution and Poverty Decline in Southeast Asia', *AERC Working Paper Series No. CR 1-4*, African Economic Research Consortium, Nairobi, February (revised draft).

Booth, A. (1999), 'Survey of Recent Developments', *Bulletin of Indonesian Economic Studies*, 35 (3), pp. 3–39.

Booth, A. (2000), 'Poverty and Inequality in the Soeharto Era: An Assessment', *Bulletin of Indonesian Economic Studies*, 36 (1), April, pp. 73–104.

Booth, A. and R.M. Sundrum (1981), 'Income Distribution', in Anne Booth and Peter McCawley (eds), *The Indonesian Economy during the Soeharto Era*, Kuala Lumpur: Oxford University Press, pp. 181–217.

Booth, A., W. O'Malley and A. Weidemann (eds) (1990), *Indonesian Economic History in the Dutch Colonial Era*, Monograph Series No. 35, New Haven, CT: Yale University, pp. 296–321.

Bourchier, David (1990), 'Law, Crime and State Authority in Indonesia', in Arief Budiman (ed.), *State and Civil Society in Indonesia*, Clayton, VIC: Centre of Southeast Asian Studies, Monash University.

Bourchier, David (1996a), 'Totalitarianism and the "National Personality": Recent Controversy about the Philosophical Basis of the Indonesian State', in Jim Schiller and Barbara Martin-Schiller (eds), *Imagining Indonesia: Cultural Politics and Political Culture*, Monographs in International Studies, Southeast Asian Series, No. 97, Athens, OH: Ohio University Center for International Studies, pp. 157–85.

Bourchier, David (1996b), Lineages of Organicist Political Thought in Indonesia, PhD thesis, Politics Department, Monash University, Melbourne.

Bourchier, David (1999), 'Positivism and Romanticism in Indonesian Legal Thought', in Tim Lindsey (ed.), *Law and Society in Indonesia*, Sydney: Federation Press, pp. 186–96.

Bourchier, David and John Legge (eds) (1994), 'Democracy in Indonesia,

1950s and 1990s', *Monash Papers on Southeast Asia*, Monash University, Clayton, VIC.

BPS (1999), *Statistical Yearbook of Indonesia, 1998*, BPS: Jakarta, June.

BPS (2000), *Statistik Keuangan Pemerintah Daerah Tingkat II, 1997/98–1998/99*, Jakarta: BPS.

Brodjonegoro, B. and S. Asanuma (2000), 'Regional Autonomy and Fiscal Decentralization in Democratic Indonesia', Paper presented to the International Symposium on Decentralisation and Economic Development in Asian Countries, Hitotsubashi University, Tokyo.

Budi SP, Johan (2000), 'Tommy's Last Shot', *Tempo* (English edition), 4 December, pp. 16–18.

Budianta, Melani (2000), 'Discourse of Cultural Identity in Indonesia during the 1997–1998 Monetary Crisis', *Inter-Asia Cultural Studies*, 1 (1), pp. 109–28.

Budiardjo, Miriam S. (1956), 'The Provisional Parliament of Indonesia', *Far Eastern Survey*, 15 (2), February, pp. 17–23.

Budiardjo, Miriam S. (1994), *Demokrasi di Indonesia: Demokrasi Parlementer dan Demokrasi Pancasila*, Jakarta: P.T. Gramedia Pustaka Utama.

Budiman, Arief (2000), 'Imagining Gus Dur', in Harry Bhaskara (ed.), *Questioning Gus Dur*, Jakarta: *Jakarta Post*, pp. 165–9.

Cameron, L. (2000), 'Poverty and Inequality in Java: Examining the Impact of the Changing Age, Educational and Industrial Structure', *Journal of Development Economics*, 62, pp. 149–80.

Castles, Lance (1974), 'Economic Recovery under the New Order: Miracle or Illusion', in Oey Hong Lee (ed.), *Indonesia after the 1971 Elections*, London: Oxford University Press/University of Hull, pp. 97–111.

Chauvel, Richard (1990), *Nationalists, Soldiers and Separatists: The Ambonese Islands from Colonialism to Revolt 1880–1950*, Leiden: KITLV Press.

Christian, David (1998), *A History of Russia, Central Asia, and Mongolia*, Oxford: Blackwell.

Chu, Godwin C., Alfian and Wilbur Schramm (1991), *Social Impact of Satellite Television in Indonesia*, Singapore: Asian Mass Communication Research and Information Centre.

Coedès, Georges (1948), *Les États Hindouisés d'Indochine et d'Indonesie*, Paris: E. de Boccard.

Collingwood, R.G. (1973), *The Idea of History*, Oxford: Oxford University Press.

Crafts, N.F.R. (1997), 'The Human Development Index and Changes in Standards of Living: Some Historical Comparisons', *European Review of Economic History*, 1, pp. 299–322.

Cribb, Robert (1991a), *Gangsters and Revolutionaries: The Jakarta People's Militia and the Indonesian Revolution 1945–1949*, Honolulu: University of Hawaii Press.

Cribb, Robert (ed.) (1991b), *The Indonesian Killings 1965–1966: Stories from Java and Bali*, Monash Papers on Southeast Asia No. 21, Clayton, VIC: Centre of Southeast Asian Studies, Monash University, second edition.

Cribb, Robert (1992), *Historical Dictionary of Indonesia*, Metuchen, NJ, and London: Scarecrow Press.

Cribb, Robert (ed.) (1994), *The Late Colonial State in Indonesia: Political and Economic Foundations of the Netherlands Indies 1880–1942*, Leiden: KITLV.

Cribb, Robert (1999), 'Not the Next Yugoslavia: Prospects for the Disintegration of Indonesia', *Australian Journal of International Affairs*, 53 (2), pp. 169–78.

Cribb, R. and C. Brown (1995), *Modern Indonesia: A History since 1945*, London: Longman.

Crouch, Harold (1988), *The Army and Politics in Indonesia*, Ithaca, NY: Cornell University Press, revised edition.

Dahm, Bernhard (1969), *Sukarno and the Struggle for Indonesian Independence*, trans. Mary Somers Heidhues, Ithaca, NY: Cornell University Press.

Darmawan Sepriyosa et al. (2000), 'News Capsule', *Tempo* (English edition), 4 December, p. 32.

Davey, K.J. (1989), 'Central–Local Financial Relations', in N. Devas (ed.), *Financing Local Government in Indonesia*, Athens, OH: Ohio University Press.

Day, Anthony (1982), 'Ranggawarsita's Prophecy of Mystery', in David Wyatt and Alexander Woodside (eds), *Moral Order and the Question of Change: Essays on Southeast Asian Thought*, New Haven, CT: Yale University Press.

de Certeau, Michel (1998), 'The Practice of Everday Life', in John Storey (ed.), *Cultural Theory and Popular Culture: A Reader*, London: Prentice Hall, pp. 483–94.

Dick, H.W. (2001), 'Survey of Recent Developments', *Bulletin of Indonesian Economic Studies*, 37 (1), forthcoming.

Dick, H., J. Fox and J. Mackie (eds) (1993), *Balanced Development: East Java in the New Order*, Kuala Lumpur: Oxford University Press.

Dick, H., V. Houben, T. Lindblad and Thee Kian Wie (2001), *The Emergence of a National Economy: An Economic History of Indonesia, 1800–2000*, Sydney and Leiden: Allen & Unwin and KITLV, forthcoming.

Diehl, F.W. (1993), 'Revenue Farming and Colonial Finances in the Netherlands East Indies, 1816–1925', in J. Butcher and H.W. Dick (eds), *The Rise and Fall of Revenue Farming: Business Elites and the Emergence of the Modern State in Southeast Asia*, London: Macmillan, pp. 196–232.

Direktorat Televisi (1972), *Televisi di Indonesia: TVRI 1962–1972* [Television in Indonesia: TVRI 1962–1972], Jakarta: Department of Information.

Djalal, Dini (2000), 'A Bloody Truce', *Far Eastern Economic Review*, 5 October.

Djalal, Dini (2001), 'On the Run in Indonesia: Tommy's Case Has More Turns than a Twister', *Bangkok Post*, 24 January.

Djopari, John R.G. (1993), *Pemberontakan Organisasi Papua Merdeka*, Jakarta: Gramedia.

Dobbin, Christine (1983), *Islamic Revivalism in a Changing Peasant Economy: Central Sumatra, 1784–1847*, London & Malmö: Curzon Press.

Drakard, Jane (1999), *A Kingdom of Words*, Kuala Lumpur: Oxford University Press.

Dube, Leela (1997), *Women and Kinship: Comparative Perspectives on Gender in South and South-east Asia*, Tokyo: United Nations University Press.

Eickelman, Dale F. and Jon W. Anderson (eds) (1999), *New Media in the Muslim World: The Emerging Public Sphere*, Bloomington and Indianapolis, IN: Indiana University Press.

Fane, George (2000), 'Survey of Recent Developments', *Bulletin of Indonesian Economic Studies*, 36 (1), pp. 3–44.

Fasseur, C. (1993), *De Indologen: Ambtenaren voor de Oost 1825–1950*, Amsterdam: Bakker.

Fasseur, C. (1994), 'Cornerstone and Stumbling Block: Racial Classification and the Late Colonial State in Indonesia', in Robert Cribb (ed.), *The Late Colonial State in Indonesia: Political and Economic Foundations of the Netherlands Indies 1880–1942*, Leiden: KITLV Press.

Fealy, Greg (1998), Ulama and Politics in Indonesia: A History of Nahdlatul Ulama, 1952–1967, PhD Thesis, Monash University.

Fealy, Greg (2001a), 'Islamic Politics: A Rising or Declining Force?', in *Rethinking Indonesia*, Bathurst, NSW: Crawford House Publishing, forthcoming. (A version of this paper was presented at the 'Rethinking Indonesia' conference, Melbourne, 4–5 March 2000.)

Fealy, Greg (2001b), 'Inside the Laskar Jihad', *Inside Indonesia*, forthcoming.

Fehring, Ian (1999), 'Unionism and Workers' Rights in Indonesia – the Future', in Tim Lindsey (ed.), *Law and Society in Indonesia*, Sydney: Federation Press, pp. 367–80.

Fehring, Ian and Tim Lindsey (1995), 'Indonesian Labour Law under the New Order: The Military and Prospects for Change', *Working Paper*, Centre for Employment and Labour Relations, University of Melbourne, Melbourne.

Feith, Herbert (1962), *The Decline of Constitutional Democracy in Indonesia*, Ithaca, NY: Cornell University Press.

Fisher, H.A.L. (1936), *A History of Europe*, London: Edward Arnold & Co.

Forum Keadilan (2000), 'Wawancara dengan Ja'far Umar Thalid', *Forum Keadilan*, 3, 23 April, pp. 26–30.

Frye, Northrop (1990), *Anatomy of Criticism: Four Essays*, first published 1957, London: Penguin Books.

Furnivall, J.S. (1944), *Netherlands India: A Study of Plural Economy*, Cambridge, UK: Cambridge University Press.

Geertz, Clifford (1960), *The Religion of Java*, Glencoe, IL: Free Press.

Geertz, Clifford (1963) *Agricultural Involution: The Process of Ecological Change in Indonesia*, Berkeley and Los Angeles, CA: University of California Press.

Geertz, Clifford (1965), *The Social History of an Indonesian Town*, Cambridge, MA: Massachusetts Institute of Technology.

Geertz, Clifford (1968), *Islam Observed*, New Haven, CN: Yale University Press.

Geertz, Clifford (1980), *Negara: The Theatre State in Nineteenth Century Bali*, Princeton, NJ: Princeton University Press.

Geertz, Hildred (1961), *The Javanese Family*, New York, NY: Free Press of Glencoe.

Geertz, Hildred (1967), 'Indonesian Cultures and Communities', in Ruth T. McVey (ed.), *Indonesia*, New Haven, CT: HRAF, pp. 24–96.

Gerschenkron, A. (1962), *Economic Backwardness in Historical Perspective*, Cambridge, MA: Belknap.

Giay, Benny (2000), *Menuju Papua Baru: Beberapa pokok pikiran sekitar Emansipasi Orang Papua*, Jayapura/Port Numbay: Deiyai/Elsham Papua.

GKI (Gereja Kristen Injil di Tanah Papua) (2000a), *Keputusan dan Ketetapan: Sidang Sinode XIV GKI di Tanah Papua Tahun 2000*, Sorong: GKI.

GKI (Gereja Kristen Injil di Tanah Papua) (2000b), *Notulen: Sidang Sinode XIV GKI di Tanah Papua Tahun 2000*, Sorong: GKI.

Glassburner, Bruce (1983), Oil, Public Policy, and Economic Performance in the 1980s, Canberra, Australian National University, mimeo.

Greene, Graham (1966), *The Comedians*, New York, NY: Viking Press.

Gunawan, F. Rudi and Nezar Patria (2000), *Premanisme Politik*, Jakarta: Institut Studi Arus Informasi.

Hall, D.G.E. (ed.) (1961), *Historians of Southeast Asia*, London: Oxford University Press.

Hardjono, Joan (1994), 'Resource Utilisation and the Environment', in Hal Hill (ed.), *Indonesia's New Order: The Dynamics of Socio-economic Transformation*, Sydney: Allen & Unwin, pp. 179–215.

Hartley, John (1999), *The Uses of Television*, London: Routledge.

Hatta, Mohammad (1956), *Past and Future, An Address Delivered by Mohammad Hatta upon Receiving the Degree of Doctor, Honoris Causa, from Gadjah Mada University at Jogjakarta on 27 November 1956*, Ithaca, NY: Cornell University Press.

Hefner, Robert W. (1997a), 'Introduction: Islam in an Era of Nation States: Politics and Religious Renewal in Muslim Southeast Asia', in Robert W. Hefner and Patricia Horvatich (eds), *Islam in an Era of Nation States: Politics and Religious Revival in Muslim Southeast Asia*, Honolulu: University of Hawaii Press, pp. 3–40.

Hefner, Robert W. (1997b), 'Islamization and Democratization in Indonesia', in Robert W. Hefner and Patricia Horvatich (eds), *Islam in an Era of Nation States: Politics and Religious Revival in Muslim Southeast Asia*, Honolulu: University of Hawaii Press, pp. 75–127.

Hefner, Robert W. (2000), 'Soeharto's Maluku Legacy', *Wall Street Journal Interactive Edition*, 16 August.

Hegel, G.W.F. (1944), *The Philosophy of History*, New York, NY: Willey Book Co.

Heine-Geldern, Robert (1942), 'Conceptions of State and Kingship in Southeast Asia', *Far Eastern Quarterly*, 2 (1), November, pp. 15–30.

Henley, David E.F. (1995), 'Ethnogeographic Integration and Exclusion in Anticolonial Nationalism; Indonesia and Indochina', *Comparative Studies in Society and History*, 37, pp. 286–324.

Hidayat, S. (1999), Decentralised Politics in a Centralised Political System, PhD thesis, Department of Asian Studies and Languages, Flinders University of South Australia, Adelaide.

Higgins, Benjamin (1957), *Indonesia's Economic Stabilisation and Development*, New York, NY: Institute of Pacific Relations.

Hill, David T. (1994), *The Press in New Order Indonesia*, Nedlands, Perth: University of Western Australia.

Hill, Hal (1996), *The Indonesian Economy since 1966: Southeast Asia's Emerging Giant*, Hong Kong: Cambridge University Press.

Hill, Hal (1998), 'The Challenge of Regional Development in Indonesia', *Australian Journal of International Affairs*, 25 (1), pp. 19–34.

Hooker, Virginia Matheson (1995), 'New Order Language in Context', in Virginia Hooker (ed.), *Culture and Society in New Order Indonesia*, Kuala Lumpur: Oxford University Press.

Hugo, G.J. et al. (1987), *The Demographic Dimension in Indonesian Development*, Oxford: Oxford University Press.

Hull, Terence H. (1999), Striking a Most Delicate Balance: The Implications of Otonomi Daerah for the Planning and Implementation of Development Cooperation Projects, Research paper, a collaboration the Center for Population and Manpower Studies, Indonesian Institute of Sciences (PPT-LIPI), Jakarta, and the Demography Program, Research School of Social Sciences, Australian National University, Canberra.

Human Rights Watch (1996), *Human Rights Watch/Asia*, 8(C), August, Robert F. Kennedy Memorial Center for Human Rights, Human Rights Watch, New York.

Huntington, Samuel P. (1996), *The Clash of Civilizations and the Remaking of World Order*, New York, NY: Simon & Schuster.

ICG (International Crisis Group) (2000a), 'Indonesia: Keeping the Military under Control', *International Crisis Group Asia Report No. 9*, Jakarta/Brussels: ICG, 5 December.

ICG (International Crisis Group) (2000b), 'Indonesia's Maluku Crisis: The Issues', *ICG Indonesia Briefing*, 19 July, Jakarta/Brussels: ICG.

Indra, Dr Muhammad Ridhwan (1990), *The 1945 Constitution: A Human Creation* (details not available; copy on file with Tim Lindsey).

Ingleson, J. (1986), *In Search of Justice: Workers and Unions in Colonial Java, 1908–1926*, Singapore: Oxford University Press.

Inoue, Tatsuo (1998), 'Liberal Democracy and "Asian" Values', in Morigiwa Yasutomo (ed.), *Law in Changing World: Asian Alternatives*, Stuttgart: Frans Steiner Verlag.

Iqbal, Farrukh (1995), Deregulation and Development in Indonesia, Paper presented at the conference, 'Building on Success: Maximising the Gains from Deregulation', Jakarta, 20–28 April.

Iskandar, Meiwita B. et al. (1996), *Unravelling the Mysteries of Maternal Death in West Java*, Depok: Center for Health Research, Research Institute, University of Indonesia.

Jaya, W.K., Mardiasmo and Matfatih (2000), *Standard Spending Assessment on the Central Java Budget*, Jakarta: PAU FE UGM and Ministry of Regional Autonomy.

Jayasuriya, Kanishka (1999), 'The Rule of Law and Governance in the East Asian State', *Australian Journal of Asian Law*, 1 (2).

Jones, Gavin W. (1994), 'Labour Force and Education', in Hal Hill (ed.), *Indonesia's New Order: The Dynamics of Socio-economic Transformation*, Sydney: Allen & Unwin, pp. 120–78.

Kahin, Audrey K. and George McT. Kahin (1995), *Subversion as Foreign Policy: The Secret Eisenhower and Dulles Debacle in Indonesia* New York, NY: New Press.

Kahin, George McT. (1952), *Nationalism and Revolution in Indonesia*, Ithaca, NY: Cornell University Press.

Kantoor voor de Volkstelling (1938), *Volkstelling 1930, Vol. 8*, Batavia: Landsdrukkerij.

Kartohadikoesoemo, Soetardjo (1965), *Desa*, Bandung: Sumur Bandung, first published 1953.

Keane, John (1998), *Civil Society: Old Images, New Visions*, Stanford: Stanford University Press.

Kell, Tim (1995), *The Roots of Acehenese Rebellion, 1989–1992*, Ithaca, NY: Cornell Modern Indonesia Project.

Kerchman, F.W.M. (ed.) (1930), *25-Jaren Decentralisatie in Nederlandsch-Indië* [25 Years of Decentralisation in the Netherlands Indies], Semarang: Vereeniging voor Locale Belangen.

Kitley, Philip (1999), 'Above the Law? The Political Economy of Regulating Broadcasting in Indonesia', *Indonesian Law and Administration Review*, 5 (1), pp. 51–72.

Kitley, Philip (2000), *Television, Nation and Culture in Indonesia*, Athens, OH: Ohio University Press.

Kompas (2000), *Wajah Dewan Perwakilan Rakyat Republik Indonesia Pemilihan Umum 1999*, Jakarta: Kompas.

Krom, N.J. (1926), *Hindoe-Javaansche Geschiedenis*, M. Nijhoff: The Hague.

Krueger, A. and A. Tornell (1999), 'The Role of Bank Restructuring in Recovering from Crises: Mexico 1995–98', *NBER Working Paper No. 7042*, Washington, DC: NBER.

Kumar, Ann (1980), 'The Peasantry and the State on Java: Changes of Relationship, Seventeenth to Nineteenth Centuries', in James J. Fox et al. (eds), *Indonesia: Australian Perspectives*, Canberra: Australian National University, pp. 577–99.

Legge, J.D. (1961), *Central Authority and Regional Autonomy in Indonesia: A Study in Local Administration 1950–60*, Ithaca, NY: Cornell University Press.

Legge, J.D. (1980), *Indonesia*, Sydney: Prentice-Hall, third edition.

Lindblad, J. Th. (1993), N*ew Challenges in the Modern Economic History of Indonesia*, Leiden: PRIS.

Lindblad, J. Th. (ed.) (1996), *Historical Foundations of a National Economy in Indonesia, 1890s–1990s*, Amsterdam: Royal Netherlands Academy of Arts and Sciences/North Holland.

Lindert, P. (2000), 'Three Centuries of Inequality in Britain and America', in A.B. Atkinson and F. Bourguignon (eds), *Handbook of Income Distribution*, Amsterdam: Elsevier, pp. 167–216.

Lindsey, Tim (1997), *The Romance of K'tut Tantri and Indonesia*, Kuala Lumpur: Oxford University Press, pp. 107–23.

Lindsey, Tim (ed.) (2000a), *Indonesia: The Commercial Court and Law Reform in Indonesia*, Sydney: Desert Pea Press.

Lindsey, Tim (2000b), 'Black Letter, Black Market and Bad Faith: Corruption and the Failure of Law Reform', in Chris Manning and Peter van Dierman (eds), *Indonesia in Transition: Social Aspects of Reformasi and Crisis*, Singapore: ISEAS, pp. 278–92.

Lindsey, Tim (2000c), 'Abdurrahman, the Supreme Court and Corruption:,

Viruses, Transplants and the Body Politic in Indonesia', in Damien Kingsbury and Arief Budiman (eds), *Rethinking Indonesia*, London: Routledge.

Lipton, Michael (1978), *Why Poor People Stay Poor: Urban Bias in Development*, London: Temple Smith.

Little, Graham (1983a), 'What FDR and RJH Have in Common', *The Age*, 30 July.

Little, Graham (1983b), 'Hawke in Place: Evaluating Narcissism', *Meanjin*, 4, 431–44.

Little, Graham (1985), *Political Ensembles: A Psychosocial Approach to Politics and Leadership*, Melbourne: Oxford University Press.

Little, Graham (1988), *Strong Leadership: Thatcher, Reagan and an Eminent Person*, Melbourne: Oxford University Press.

Little, Graham (1999a), 'Middle Way Leaders', paper presented to the Annual Conference of the International Society of Political Psychology, Amsterdam, 17–21 July.

Little, Graham (1999b), John Alderdice: In-between Man: An Essay in Political Psychology, unpublished paper.

Litvack, J. and J. Seddon (eds) (1999), *Decentralisation Briefing Notes*, Washington, DC: World Bank.

Lloyd, Grayson J. (2001), 'Chinese Indonesians: Unsettled Past, Uncertain Future', in Michael R. Godley and Grayson J. Lloyd (eds), *Perspectives on the Chinese Indonesians*, Adelaide: Crawford House Publishing, forthcoming.

Logemann, J.H.A. (1953), 'The Indonesian Parliament', *Parliamentary Affairs, Journal of the Hansard Society*, 6, August, pp. 346–52.

Loveard, Keith (1999), *Suharto: Indonesia's Last Sultan*, Singapore: Horizon Books.

Loveman, B. and T.M. Davies (1978), *The Politics of Antipolitics: The Military in Latin America*, Lincoln: University of Nebraska Press.

LSPP (Lembaga Studi Pers dan Pembangunan) (1999), *Pemilihan Umum 1999: Demokrasi atau Rebutan Kursi?* Jakarta: LSPP.

Mabbett, I.W. (1977), 'The "Indianisation" of Southeast Asia', *Journal of Southeast Asian History*, 8 (1 and 2).

MacAndrews, C., A. Sibero and H. Fisher (1982), 'Regional Development Planning and Implementation in Indonesia: The Evolution of a National Policy', in R.P. Misra (ed.), *Regional Development: Essays in Honour of Masahiko Honjo*, Tokyo: Maruzen Asia.

Mackie, J.A.C. (1967), *Problems of the Indonesian Inflation*, Ithaca, NY: Cornell University Press.

Mackie, J.A.C. (1999), 'National Integration, The State and Market Forces in the Transition Era, 1945–1965', *Crisis and Continuity: Indonesian Economy in the Twentieth Century*, Yogyakarta: Gadjah Mada University, pp. 1–13.

Maddison, A. (1999a), 'Poor until 1820', *Wall Street Journal (Europe)*, 11 January 1999.

Maddison, A. (1999b), Economic Progress: The Last Half Century in Historical Perspective, Unpublished paper presented at the 'Academy of the Social Sciences in Australia Symposium: Facts and Fancies of Human Development', Australian National University, Canberra, 8 November.

Maddison, A. (2000), Asian Historical Statistics Database, Unpublished paper presented at Hitotsubashi University, Tokyo, January.

Maddison, A. and G. Prince (eds) (1989), *Economic Growth in Indonesia, 1820–1940*, Dordrecht: Foris.

Mahi (2000), 'Prospek Desentralisasi di Indonesia ditinjau dari Segi Pemerataan Antar Daerah dan Peningkatan Efisiensi', *Analisis CSIS*, (29) 1, pp. 54–75.

Makarim, Nono Anwar (1978), 'The Indonesian Press: An Editor's Perspective', in Karl D. Jackson and Lucian W. Pye (eds), *Political Power and Communications in Indonesia*, Berkeley, CA: University of California Press, pp. 259–81.

Manning, Chris (1995), 'Approaching the Turning Point? Labor Market Change under Indonesia's New Order', *The Developing Economies*, 33 (1), March, pp. 52–81.

Manning, Chris (1998), *Indonesian Labour in Transition: An East Asian Success Story?* Cambridge: Cambridge University Press.

Mardiasmo (1999), The Impact of Central and Provincial Government Intervention on Local Government Budgetary Management: The Case of Indonesia, Unpublished PhD thesis, International Development Department, School of Public Policy, University of Birmingham, Birmingham.

Marianto, M. Dwi (1994), Yogyakarta Surrealism. PhD dissertation, Wollongong: University of Wollongong.

Marx, Karl (1926), *The Eighteenth Brumaire of Louis Bonaparte*, London: George Allen & Unwin Ltd.

Masindo (2000), *Indonesian Media Guide*, Jakarta: Citra Buana Masindo/Gold Group Asia/Pacific, first edition.

McBeth, John (2000), 'Wahid's Coming Clash', *Far Eastern Economic Review*, 3 February.

McCarthy, J.F. (2000), Implications of Regional Autonomy for Forest Management, Paper presented to the Asian Studies Association of Australian Biennial Conference, Melbourne, July.

McDaniel, Drew O. (1994), *Broadcasting in the Malay World*, Norwood, NJ: Ablex.

McDonald, Hamish (1980), *Suharto's Indonesia*, Melbourne: Fontana.

McIntyre, Angus (1988), 'The Aging Narcissistic Leader: The Case of Sir

Oswald Mosley at Mid-life', in Angus McIntyre (ed.), *Aging and Political Leadership*, Melbourne: Oxford University Press, pp. 44–58. First published in 1983 in *Political Psychology*, 4, pp. 483–99.

McLeod, Ross H. (2000a), 'Survey of Recent Developments', *Bulletin of Indonesian Economic Studies*, 36 (2), pp. 3–38.

McLeod, Ross H. (2000b), 'Soeharto's Indonesia: A Better Class of Corruption', *Agenda*, 7 (2), pp. 99–112.

McQuail, Denis (1994), *Mass Communication Theory: An Introduction*, London: Sage Publications, third edition.

McVey, Ruth (ed.) (1963), *Indonesia*, New Haven, CT: HRAF Press.

McVey, Ruth (1965), *The Rise of Indonesian Communism*, Ithaca, NY: Cornell University Press.

Mehmet, O. (1994), Rent-seeking and Gate-keeping in Indonesia: A Cultural and Economic Analysis, Seminar paper at the Institute of Southeast Asian Studies, Singapore.

Mietzner, Marcus (2000), 'The 1999 General Session: Wahid, Megawati and the Fight for the Presidency', in Chris Manning and Peter van Diermen (eds), *Indonesia in Transition: Social Aspects of Reformasi and Crisis*, Singapore: Institute of Southeast Asian Studies, pp. 39–57.

Mietzner, Marcus (2001), 'The First 100 Days of the Abdurrahman Presidency: An Evaluation', in Damien Kingsbury (ed.), *Re-thinking Indonesia*, forthcoming.

Minister for Information (1965), Decree No. 29 Concerning 'Basic Norms for Press Enterprises within the Context of the Promotion of the Indonesian Press', Jakarta: Government of Indonesia.

Moertopo, Ali (1982), *Strategi Pembangunan Nasional*, Jakarta: Centre for Strategic and International Studies. (Collection of writings including 'Dasar-dasar Pemikiran tentang Akselerisasi Modernisasi Pembangunan', 1972, pp. 1–125, and 'Strategi Politik Nasional', 1974, pp. 127–277).

Moertopo, Ali (1983), 'Membina Ketahanan Ideologi Pancasila, Ceramah pada Penataran P4 Tingkat Instansi Pusat Departemen Penerangan RI, 24 May 1980', *Peningkatan Penerangan yang Berwibawa: Himpunan Pidato Menteri Penerangan RI 1978–82*, Jakarta: Departemen Penerangan Republik Indonesia (Indonesian Information Department), pp.197–215.

Muchtar, Darmiyanti (1999), The Rise of the Indonesian Women's Movement in the New Order State, MPhil thesis, Murdoch University, Perth.

Mufson, Steven (2000), 'World Bank Chief Warns Indonesia on Militias', *Washington Post*, 12 September.

Mulyana, Deddy (1997), 'Peluang dan Tantangan TVRI' [Opportunities and Challenges for TVRI], in Deddy Mulyana and Idi Subandy Ibrahim (eds), *Bercinta Dengan Televisi* [In Love with Television], Bandung: Remaja Rosdakarya.

Nakamura, Mitsuo (1983), *The Crescent Arises over the Banyan Tree: A Study of the Muhammadiyah Movement in a Central Javanese Town*, Yogyakarta: Gadjah Mada University Press.

Namier, L.B. (1957), 'History and Political Culture', in Fritz Stern (ed.), *The Varieties of History, from Voltaire to the Present*, New York, NY: Meridian Books, pp. 371–87.

Nasution, Adnan Buyung (1992), *The Aspiration for Constitutional Government in Indonesia: A Socio-legal Study of the Indonesian Konstituante, 1956–1959*, Den Haag and Jakarta: CIP-Gegevens Koninklijke Bibliotheek and Pustaka Sinar Harapan.

Nasution, A.H. (1985), *Memenuhi Panggilan Tugas, Jilid 5: Kenangan Masa Orde Lama*, Jakarta: CV Haji Masagung.

Nasution, A.H. (1989), *Kenangan Masa Orde Lama*, Vol. 5 of *Memenuhi Panggilan Tugas*, Jakarta: CV Haji Masagung.

Nasution, Anwar (1995), 'Survey of Recent Developments', *Bulletin of Indonesian Economic Studies*, 31 (2), pp. 3–40.

NDIIA (National Democratic Institute for International Affairs) (2000), *Indonesia's Bumpy Road to Constitutional Reform: The 2000 MPR Session*, Jakarta: NDIIA.

NEFIS (Netherlands Forces Intelligence Services) (1947), Service Dossier on K'tut Tantri; Mevrouw vannine Walker, Doorkiesnummer 070-3486811, Netherlands Ministerie van Buitenlandse Zaken, Notitie, 24 March, 21 April.

Nursa'adah, NE and Ade (2000a), 'Berebut Rezeki di 'Medan Perang'', *Forum*, 20 August, pp. 80–83.

Nursa'adah, NE and Ade (2000b), 'Senior Superintendent Sedaryanto: 'Polisi Tidak Menjual Harga Diri', *Forum*, 20 August, pp. 80–81.

Nursyahbani Katjasungkana (1993), 'Kedudukan Wanita dalam Perspektif Islam', in Lies M. Marcoes-Natsir and Johan Hendrik Meuleman (eds), *Wanita Islam Indonesia dalam Kajian Tekstual dan Kontekstual*, Jakarta: INAI.

Oates, W.E. (1999), 'An Essay on Fiscal Federalism', *Journal of Economic Literature*, 37, pp. 1,120–49.

Onghokham (1978), 'The Inscrutable and the Paranoid: An Investigation into the Sources of the Brotodiningrat Affair', in Ruth T. McVey (ed.), *Southeast Asian Transitions: Approaches through Social History*, New Haven, CT: Yale University Press, pp. 112–57.

Parry, Richard (1998), 'What Young Men Do', *Granta*, 62, pp. 83–124.

PDAT (Pusat Data dan Analisa Tempo) (1997), *Panduan Memilih Perguruan Tinggi 1997*, Jakarta: Grafiti Pers.

Pemberton, John (1994), *On the Subject of 'Java'*, Ithaca, NY: Cornell University Press.

Penders, C.L.M. and Ulf Sundhaussen (1985), *Abdul Haris Nasution: A Political Biography*, St.Lucia, QLD: University of Queensland Press.

Penerbit Sinar Grafika (1999), *Tiga Undang-Undang Politik 1999*, Jakarta: Penerbit Sinar Grafika.

Pigeaud, T.G.Th. (trans.) (1960), *Java in the Fourteenth Century*, 4, The Hague: M. Nijhoff.

Poeze, Harry (1994), 'Political Intelligence in the Netherlands Indies', in Robert Cribb (ed.), *The Late Colonial State in Indonesia: Political and Economic Foundations of the Netherlands Indies 1880–1942*, Leiden: KITLV, pp. 229–46.

Polak, J.J. (1943), 'The National Income of the Netherlands Indies, 1921–1939', in P. Creutzberg (ed.), *Changing Economy in Indonesia, Volume 5: National Income*, reprinted 1975, The Hague: Nijhoff, , pp. 26–94.

PPPI (Persatuan Perusahaan Periklanan Indonesia) [Indonesian Association of Advertising Agencies] (1997/98), *Media Scene*, Jakarta: PPPI.

Presiden Republik Indonesia (1963), *Keputusan #215 Tentang Pembentukan Jajasan Televisi Republik Indonesia* [Decree No. 215 concerning the Establishment of the Indonesian Television Foundation], Jakarta: Sekretariat Negara.

PSHK (Pusat Studi Hukum dan Kebijakan Indonesia) (2000), *Semua Harus Terwakili*, PSHK, Jakarta.

Quinn, George (1996), 'Kelompencapir: Indonesia's Rural Mass Media Discussion Groups', Conference paper presented at the Asian Studies Association of Australia Conference, La Trobe University, Melbourne.

Ramage, Douglas E. (1995), *Politics in Indonesia: Democracy, Islam and the Ideology of Tolerance*, London: Routledge.

Reeve, David (1985), *Golkar of Indonesia: An Alternative to the Party System*, Singapore: Oxford University Press.

Reid, Anthony (1974), *Indonesian National Revolution: 1945–1950*, Melbourne: Longman.

Reid, Anthony (1988), *Southeast Asia in the Age of Commerce 1450–1680, Vol. 1: The Lands below the Winds*, New Haven, CT: Yale University Press.

Republik Indonesia (1974/75), *Rencana Pembangunan Lima Tahun Kedua 1974/75–1978/79* [Second Five-year Development Plan 1974/75–1978/79], Jakarta: Government of Indonesia.

Resink, G.J. (1975), 'From the Old Mahabharata to the New Ramayana-Order', *Bijdragen tot de Taal-, Land- en Volkenkunde*, 131 (2/3), pp. 214–35.

Ricklefs, M.C. (1974), *Jogjakarta under Sultan Mangkubumi, 1749–1792: A History of the Division of Java*, London: Oxford University Press.

Ricklefs, M.C. (1998), *The Seen and Unseen Worlds in Java, 1726–1749: History, Literature and Islam in the Court of Pakubuwana II*, Honolulu:

Asian Studies Association of Australia in association with Allen & Unwin and University of Hawaii Press.

Ridwan, Saiful B. (1997), From Tempo to Tempo Interaktif: An Indonesian Media Case Study, Conference paper presented at the Third Australian World Wide Web Conference, 5–9 July, Southern Cross University, Lismore, NSW, http//ausweb.scu.au/proceedings/ridwan/paper.html.

Risseeuw, Clara (1988), *The Fish Don't Talk about the Water: Gender Transformation, Power and Resistance among Women in Sri Lanka*, Leiden: Brill.

Robinson, Geoffrey (1998), 'Rawan Is as Rawan Does: The Origins of Disorder in New Order Aceh', *Indonesia*, 66, October, pp. 127–56.

Robison, Richard (1986), *Indonesia: The Rise of Capital*, Sydney: Allen & Unwin.

Rohdewohld, R. (1995) *Public Administration in Indonesia*, Melbourne: Montech.

Romano, Angela (1999), Journalistic Identity and Practices in Late New Order Indonesia, PhD dissertation, Queensland University of Technology, Brisbane.

Rondinnelli, D. (1999), 'What Is Decentralization?', in J. Litvack and J. Seddon (eds), *Decentralization Briefing Notes*, Washington: World Bank.

Rose, Mavis (1987), *Indonesia Free: A Political Biography of Mohammad Hatta*, Ithaca, NY: Cornell Modern Indonesia Project.

Rosner, P. (2000), 'Export Performance during the Crisis: Distinguishing between the Quantity and Price Effects', *Bulletin of Indonesian Economic Studies*, 36 (2), pp. 61–96.

Ruckert, J.J.G.E. (1930), 'De Ontwikkeling van de Financiën der Autonome Gemeenschappen' [The Development of the Autonomous Local Governments], in F.W.M. Kerchman (ed.), *25-Jaren Decentralisatie in Nederlandsch-Indië* [25 Years of Decentralisation in the Netherlands Indies], Semarang: Vereeniging voor Locale Belangen, pp. 97–124.

Ryter, Loren (2000), 'A Tale of Two Cities', *Inside Indonesia*, 63, www.insideindonesia.org, September.

Sadli, Mohammad (1999), 'The Indonesian Crisis', in H.W. Arndt and Hal Hill (eds), *Southeast Asia's Economic Crisis: Origins, Lessons, and the Way Forward*, Singapore: Institute of Southeast Asian Studies, pp. 16–27.

Salim, Emil (1997), 'Recollections of My Career', *Bulletin of Indonesian Economic Studies*, 33 (1), pp. 45–74.

Sartono Kartodirdjo (1973), *Protest Movements in Rural Java*, Kuala Lumpur: Oxford University Press.

Sato, Shigeru (1994), *War, Nationalism and Peasants: Java under the Japanese Occupation, 1942–1945*, ASAA Southeast Asia Publications No. 26, Sydney: Allen & Unwin.

Schulte Nordholt, Henk (1991), 'The Jago in the Shadow: Crime and "Order" in the Colonial State in Java', *RIMA*, 25 (1), pp. 74–91.

Schwarz, Adam (1994, revised 1999), *A Nation in Waiting: Indonesia in the 1990s*, Sydney: Allen & Unwin.

Sekretariat DPR-GR (1970), *Seperempat Abad Dewan Perwakilan Rakjat Republik Indonesia*, Jakarta: Sekretariat DPR-GR.

Sekretariat Jenderal DPR (2000a), 'Rekapitulasi Rancangan Undang-Undang yang Dibahas DPR-RI Periode 1987–1992 dan 1992–1997', http://www.dpr.go.id/hukum/2000.htm, accessed October and November.

Sekretariat Jenderal DPR (2000b), 'Rancangan Undang-Undang yang Dibahas Periode 1999–2004', http://www.dpr.go.id/hukum/2000.htm, accessed October and November.

Sen, Amartya (1999), *Development as Freedom*, New York: Oxford University Press.

Sen, Krishna (1999), 'Women on the Move', *Inside Indonesia*, 58, April–June, pp. 14–15.

Sen, Krishna and David Hill (2000), *Media, Culture and Politics in Indonesia*, Melbourne: Oxford University Press.

Shah, A. et al. (1994), *Inter-governmental Fiscal Relations in Indonesia*, Washington, DC: World Bank.

Shannon, C. and W. Weaver (eds) (1949), *The Mathematical Theory of Communication*, Urbana, IL: University of Illinois Press.

Shiraishi, Takashi (1981), 'The Disputes between Tjipto Mangoenkoesoemo and Soetatmo Soeriokoesoemo: Satria vs. Pandita', *Indonesia*, 32, pp. 93–108.

Shiraishi, Takashi (1990), *An Age in Motion: Popular Radicalism in Java, 1912–1926*, Ithaca, NY: Cornell University Press.

Siegel, James (1979), *Shadow and Sound*, Chicago, IL: Chicago University Press.

Siegel, James T. (1998), *A New Criminal Type in Jakarta: Counter Revolution Today*, Durham and London: Duke University Press.

Siegel, James T. (1999), ' A New Criminal Type in Jakarta: The Nationalisation of Death', in Vicente L. Rafael (ed.), *Figures of Criminality in Indonesia, the Philippines, and Colonial Vietnam*, Ithaca, NY: Southeast Asia Program Publications, Cornell University, pp. 210–30.

Siregar, Ashadi (1995), *Sketsa Sketsa Media* Massa [Sketches of the Mass Media], Yogyakarta: Bentang Budaya.

Sjahrir, Sutan (1968), *Our Struggle,* Ithaca, NY: Modern Indonesia Project, Cornell University (translated from Dutch by Benedict Anderson).

Sjamsuddin, Nazaruddin (1985), *The Republican Revolt: A Study of the Acehenese Rebellion*, Singapore: Institute of Southeast Asian Studies.

Smail, John (1961), 'On the Possibility of an Autonomous History of Modern Southeast Asia', *Journal of Southeast Asian History*, 2 (2), pp. 72–102.

Smith, Shannon L. (2001), *Batam: Politics and Economic Development in Indonesia*, Sydney: Allen & Unwin, forthcoming.

Soediman Kartohadiprodjo (1970), *Beberapa Pikiran Sekitar Pantja Sila*, Bandung: Alumni.

Soedjatmoko (1965), 'The Indonesian Historian and His Time', in Soedjatmoko, Mohammad Ali, G.J. Resink and G.McT. Kahin (eds), *An Introduction to Indonesian Histroriography*, Ithaca, NY: Cornell University Press, pp. 405–15.

Soedjatmoko (1967), 'Indonesia: Problems and Opportunities', *Australian Outlook*, 21 (3), December, pp. 263–86.

Soeharto (1989), 'Role of the Press in National Development', in Achal Mehra (ed.), *Press Systems in ASEAN States*, Singapore: AMIC, pp. 131–4.

Soemarsaid Moertono (1963), *State and Statecraft in Old Java: A Study of the Later Mataram Period*, Ithaca, NY: Cornell University Press.

Spyer, Patricia (2000), *The Memory of Trade: Modernity's Entanglements on an Eastern Indonesian Island*, Durham & London: Duke University Press.

Stephenson, Neal (1999), *Cryptonomicon*, London: Arrow.

Stoler, Ann Laura (1985), *Capitalism and Confrontation in Sumatra's Plantation Belt 1870–1979*, New Haven, CT: Yale University Press.

Stone, M. (1998), 'Corporate Debt Restructuring in East Asia: Some Lessons from International Experience', *IMF Working Paper 13/1998*, IMF.

Suh, Sangwon Suh and Tom McCawley (2000), 'Archipelago in Flames', *Asiaweek*, 14 January.

Sukarno (1945, reprinted 1965), *Lahirnja Pantja-Sila: Pidato Pertama tentang Pantja Sila jang Diutjapkan pada tg. 1 Djuni 1945 oleh Bung Karno, sekarang Presiden Negara Republik Indonesia*, Jakarta: P.N. Penerbit Pradnjaparamita.

Sukarno (1956), *Pidato President Sukarno pada Hari Sumpah Pemuda tgl. 28 Oktober 1956 di Djakarta*, Jakarta: Kementrian Penerangan R.I.

Sukarno (1957), *Menjelamatkan Republik Proklamasi: Tjatatan Stenografis dari Pidato Presiden Soekarno tgl. 21 Pebr. 1957 Djam 20.05 di Istana Merdeka*, Jakarta: Kementerian Penerangan R.I.

Sukarno (1958), 'Pidato P.J.M. Presiden [Sukarno] pada Rapat Umum di Saparua pada Tanggal 8 Nopember 1958', Jakarta, mimeo.

Sukarno (1965a), *Tenaga Gadungan lebih Berbahaja daripada Imperialis!: Amanat Presiden Sukarno pada Rapat Raksasa peringatan Ulang-Tahun ke-45 PKI, tanggal 23 Mei 1965 di Stadion Utama Gelora 'Bung Karno', Senajan, Djakarta*, Jakarta: Departemen Penerangan R.I.

Sukarno (1965b), 'Amanat PJM Presiden Sukarno pada Rapat CGMI di

Istora, Senajan, Djakarta, 29 September 1965', Sekretariat Negara Kabinet Presiden Republik Indonesia, Jakarta, mimeo.

Sulistyo, Hermawan (2000), *Palu Arit di Ladang Tebu*, Jakarta: Kepustakaan Populer Gramedia.

Sunindyo, Saraswati (1999a), 'Murder, Gender and the Media: Sexualising Politics and Violence', in Tim Lindsey (ed.), *Law and Society in Indonesia*, Sydney: Federation Press, pp. 145–57.

Sunindyo, Saraswati (1999b), 'En-gendering Democratization', in Tim Lindsey and Drew Duncan (eds), *Prospects for Reform in Post-Soeharto Indonesia*, Victoria, BC: Centre for Asia Pacific Initiatives, University of Victoria, pp. 16–28.

Supomo, S. (1979), 'The Image of Majapahit in Later Javanese and Indonesian Writing', in Anthony Reid and David Marr (eds), *Perceptions of the Past in Southeast Asia*, Singapore: Heinemann, pp. 171–85.

Suranto, Hanif, Hawe Setiawan and Ging Ginanjar (1999), *Pers Indonesia Pasca Soeharto* [The Indonesian Press after Soeharto], Jakarta: Lembaga Studi Pers dan Pembangunan and Aliansi Jurnalis Independen.

Susanto, Astrid (1978), 'The Mass Communications System in Indonesia', in Karl D. Jackson and Lucian W. Pye (eds), *Political Power and Communications in Indonesia*, Berkeley, CA: University of California Press, pp. 229–58.

Sutherland, H.A. (1979), *The Making of a Bureaucratic Elite: The Colonial Transformation of the Javanese Priyayi*, ASAA Southeast Asia Series, Singapore: Heinemann.

Sutjipto (ed.) (1967), *Tumbuhnja Tunas Baru diatas Humus dari Daun Tua-Kering jang Berguguran (Sebuah Capita Selecta)*, Jakarta: Penerbit Fakta.

Tan, T.K. (ed.) (1967), *Sukarno's Guided Indonesia*, Brisbane: Jacaranda Press.

Tanter, Richard (1990a), 'Oil, Iggi and US Hegemony: Global Pre-conditions', in Arief Budiman (ed.), *State and Civil Society in Indonesia*, Clayton, VIC: Centre of Southeast Asian Studies, Monash University, pp. 51–98.

Tanter, Richard (1990b), 'The Totalitarian Ambition: Intelligence and Security Agencies in Indonesia', in Arief Budiman (ed.), *State and Civil Society in Indonesia*, Monash Papers on Southeast Asia No. 22, Clayton, VIC: Centre of Southeast Asian Studies, Monash University, pp. 215–88.

Tanter, Richard (1991), Intelligence Agencies and Third World Militarization: A Case Study of Indonesia, 1966–1989, PhD thesis, Monash University, Melbourne.

Tapol (2000), 'Defending Women's Rights in Aceh', *Tapol Bulletin Online*, 157, April, www.gn.apc.org/tapol/157ndefe.htm.

Thee Kian Wie (1998), 'Determinants of Indonesia's Industrial Technology Development', in Hal Hill and Thee Kian Wie (eds), *Indonesia's Technological Challenge*, Singapore: Institute of Southeast Asian Studies, pp. 117–35.

Thomas, Nicholas (1994), *Colonialism's Culture: Anthropology, Travel and Government*, Cambridge, UK: Polity Press.

Tobing, Sumita (1991), Development Journalism in Indonesia: Content Analysis of Government Television News, PhD Dissertation, Athens, OH: Ohio University.

Törnquist, Olle (1990), 'Rent Capitalism, State, and Democracy', in Arief Budiman (ed.), *State and Civil Society in Indonesia*, Clayton, VIC: Centre of Southeast Asian Studies, Monash University, pp. 29–50.

Tsing, Anna Lowenhaupt (1993), *In the Realm of the Diamond Queen: Marginality in an Out-of-the-way Place*, Princeton, NJ: Princeton University Press.

UNDP (United Nations Development Program) (1993), *Human Development Report*, New York, NY: UNDP.

UNDP (United Nations Development Program) (1995), *Human Development Report 1995*, New York, NY: Oxford University Press.

UNDP (United Nations Development Program) (2000), *Human Development Report 2000*, New York, NY: Oxford University Press.

van Bruinessen, Martin (1996), 'Traditions for the Future: The Reconstruction of Traditionalist Discourse within NU', in Greg Barton and Greg Fealy (eds), *Nahdlatul Ulama, Traditional Islam and Modernity in Indonesia*, Clayton, VIC: Monash Asia Institute, pp. 163–89.

van den Doel, H.W. (1994), 'Military Rule in the Netherlands Indies', in Robert Cribb (ed.), *The Late Colonial State in Indonesia. Political and Economic Foundations of the Netherlands Indies 1880–1942*, Leiden: KITLV, pp. 57–78.

van der Eng, Pierre (1992), 'The Real Domestic Product of Indonesia, 1880–1989', *Explorations in Economic History*, 29, pp. 343–73.

van der Eng, Pierre (1994), 'Food Supply in Java during War and Decolonisation, 1940–1950', *Centre for South-east Asian Studies Occasional Paper No. 25*, Hull: Centre for South-east Asian Studies.

van der Eng, Pierre (1998), 'Exploring Exploitation: The Netherlands and Colonial Indonesia 1870–1940', *Revista de Historia Económica*, 16 (1), pp. 291–321.

van der Eng, Pierre (1999), 'Economic Growth and Political Change in Indonesia: The Late-Colonial and New Order Periods Compared', in R. Minami et al. (eds), *Growth, Distribution and Political Change: Asia and the Wider World*, London: Macmillan, pp. 178–205.

van der Eng, Pierre (2000a), 'Food for Growth: Trends in Indonesia's Food Supply, 1880–1995', *Journal of Interdisciplinary History,* 30 (4), pp. 591–616.

van der Eng, Pierre (2000b), Growth and Inequality: The Case of Indonesia since the 1960s, Unpublished paper, Australian National University, Canberra.

van der Eng, Pierre (2001), 'Indonesia's Growth Performance in the 20th Century', in A. Maddison et al. (eds), *The Asian Economies in the Twentieth Century*, London: Edward Elgar, forthcoming.

van Klinken, Gerry (1997), Minorities, Modernity and the Emerging Nation: Christians in Indonesia, A Biographical Approach, PhD thesis, Griffith University, Queensland, July, p. 82.

van Leur, J.C. (1955), *Indonesian Trade and Society*, The Hague: van Hoeve.

van Niel, R. (1960), *The Emergence of the Modern Indonesian Elite*, The Hague: Van Hoeve.

Wahyudi, J.B. (1985), *Jurnalistik Televisi: Tentang dan Sekitar Siaran Berita TVRI* [Television Journalism: Commentary on TVRI's News Broadcasts], Bandung: Alumni.

Wallace, W. (1999), 'Fiscal Policies for Economic Recovery', paper presented to the LPEM-FUEI/PEG-USAID conference, 'The Economic Issues Facing the New Government', Jakarta, 18–19 August.

Wardhana, Veven Sp (1997), *Kapitalisme Televisi dan Strategi Budaya Massa* [Television Capitalism and Mass Culture Strategies], Yogyakarta: Pustaka Pelajar.

Wertheim, W.F. (1956, 1959), *Indonesian Society in Transition: A Study of Social Change*, The Hague and Bandung: W. van Hoeve Ltd.

Wertheim, W.F. (1965), 'The Sociological Approach', in Soedjatmoko et al. (eds), *An Introduction to Indonesia Historiography*, Ithaca, NY: Cornell University Press.

Wicaksono and L.N. Idayanie (2000), 'Death Is Not Enough!', *Tempo* (English edition), 4 December, p. 53.

Wieringa, Saskia (1995), The Politicization of Gender Relations in Indonesia: The Indonesian Women's Movement and Gerwani until the New Order State, PhD thesis, Amsterdam: University of Amsterdam.

Wild, Colin (1987), 'Indonesia: A Nation and Its Broadcasters', *Indonesia Circle*, 43, pp. 15–40.

Wild, Colin (1991), 'The Radio Midwife: Some Thoughts on the Role of Broadcasting during the Indonesian Struggle for Independence', *Indonesia Circle*, 55, pp. 34–42.

Winters, Jeffrey (1999), 'Re: Gonjang-ganjing Manuver Gus Dur: Mari Berpikir Dialektis', wahana@centrin.net.id, posted 3 January.

Winzeler, Robert (1996), 'Sexual Status in Southeast Asia: Comparative Perspectives on Women, Agriculture and Organization', in Penny Van Esterik (ed.), *Women of Southeast Asia*, DeKalb, IL: Northern Illinois University, revised edition.

Wolters, O.W. (1967), *Early Indonesian Commerce*, Ithaca, NY: Cornell University Press.

Wolters, O.W. (1982, revised 1999), *History, Culture and Region in Southeast Asian Perspectives*, Singapore: ISEAS.

Wonohito, Madikin (1977), *Teknik Jurnalistik: Sistim Pers Pancasila* [Journalistic Technique: The Pancasila Press System], Jakarta: Garda.

World Bank (1990), *World Development Report 1990: Poverty*, New York, NY: Oxford University Press.

World Bank (1993), *The East Asian Miracle: Economic Growth and Public Policy*, New York, NY: Oxford University Press.

World Bank (1995), *Indonesia: Improving Efficiency and Equity – Changes in the Public Sector's Role*, Report No. 14006-IND, Washington DC: World Bank, July 24.

World Bank (1996), *Indonesia: Dimensions of Growth*, Report No. 15383-IND, Washington DC: World Bank, 7 May.

World Bank (1997a), *Indonesia: Sustaining High Growth with Equity*, Report No. 16433-IND, Washington DC: World Bank.

World Bank (1997b), *World Development Indicators 1977*, Washington DC: World Bank.

World Bank (1998), *World Development Indicators 1998*, Washington DC: World Bank.

World Bank (1999), *World Development Indicators 1999*, Washington DC: Development Data Center, World Bank.

World Bank (2000a), *Managing Government Debt and Its Risks*, Report No. 20436-IND, Washington DC: World Bank.

World Bank (2000b), *Accelerating Recovery in Uncertain Times*, Economic Brief to the CGI, Washington DC: World Bank.

Yamin, H. Muhammad (1959), *Naskah Persiapan Undang-Undang Dasar 1945*, Vol. 1, Jakarta: Yayasan Prapanca.

Yong Mun Cheong (1982), *H.J. van Mook and Indonesian Independence: A Study of His Role in Dutch–Indonesian Relations, 1945–48*, The Hague: Martinus Nijhoff.

Zariski, Raphael and Mark O. Rousseau (1987) *Regionalism and Regional Devolution in Comparative Perspective*, New York, NY: Praeger.

NEWSPAPERS, MAGAZINES AND OTHER PERIODICALS

Age
Antara
Asiaweek
Australian
Bangkit Online
Bangkok Post
Detik
Editor
Far Eastern Economic Review
Forum
Forum Keadilan
Gamma
Gatra
Indonesian Observer
Inside Indonesia
Jakarta Post
Kompas
Kompas Online
Kritik
Media Indonesia
Monitor
Observer
Panji Masyarakat
Republika
Suara Merdeka
Suara Pembaruan
Sydney Morning Herald
Tabloid Jurnal Islam
Tajuk
Tapol Bulletin Online
Tempo
Tifa Irian
Tifa Papua
TNI Watch!
Wall Street Journal
Washington Post

INDEX